THE
BEATLES

THE
BEATLES

The Illustrated and Updated Edition of
the Bestselling Authorized Biography

HUNTER DAVIES

 W. W. Norton & Company
New York London

CONTENTS

Introduction   7

PART ONE: LIVERPOOL

1 John   53
2 John and the Quarrymen   61
3 Paul   69
4 Paul and the Quarrymen   77
5 George   83
6 George and the Quarrymen   89
7 John at Art College   95
8 From Quarrymen to Moondogs   101
9 Stu, Scotland and the Silver Beatles   107
10 The Casbah   113
11 Hamburg   121
12 Astrid and Klaus   129
13 Liverpool – Litherland and the Cavern   139
14 Marking time – Liverpool and Hamburg   149
15 Brian Epstein   159
16 Brian signs the Beatles   169
17 Decca and Pete Best   177
18 Ringo   189
19 Ringo with the Beatles   197

PART TWO: LONDON AND THE WORLD

20 George Martin and Dick James 207

21 Touring 215

22 Beatlemania 225

23 USA 235

24 Britain and back to the USA 245

25 The End of Touring 253

26 The Death of Brian Epstein 261

27 The Beatles, from drugs to Maharishi 271

PART THREE: 1968

28 Friends and Parents 283

29 The Beatles' Empire 295

30 The Beatles and their Music 303

31 John 323

32 Paul 337

33 George 347

34 Ringo 359

END BIT

Postscript 1985 373

Appendix A – Discography of Beatles' original records 406

Appendix B – Beatles places to visit 412

Appendix C – Beatles memorabilia 413

Appendix D – Beatles books 414

Picture Credits and Acknowledgements 416

INTRODUCTION

This book, or at least the main bulk of it, first appeared in 1968, when the world was young and the Beatles seemed old. That's how it seemed, back in 1968. Six years at the top, in the news, in our ears, in our senses, had felt like a fairly long time, and there were those waiting for the bubble to burst, for the Beatles to disappear, for a new sensation to come along. As early as 1966, one national newspaper, the *Daily Sketch*, had a headline saying 'Are the Beatles on their way out now?'

In a sense, they were right to ask this, for in 1970 the Beatles unraveled, rather than burst, going into voluntary liquidation. The causes and motives of the split were mixed – bored by Beatledom, inspired by new passions, distracted by new people in their lives, beset by inner strifes and tensions. So that seemed it. Bye-bye Beatles, goodbye.

Unlike the *Daily Sketch*, which not long afterwards was gobbled up by the *Daily Mail* and is now totally forgotten by the great British public, the Beatles are still with us. In fact, they have never been away. Without producing anything new, they have never grown old.

My 1968 book, although I was not to know it at the time, turned out to be their only authorized biography. The four of them, as a group, never helped anyone else again. They gave me access to their homes and to their lives, enabling me to meet their wives, parents, relations, associates and friends, and allowing me to watch them at work and play, composing on their own, as well as recording together at Abbey Road.

That book trundled on, as it was, with nothing changed, a primary rather than a polished source for all Beatles lovers, until 1985, when I added a new Introduction and a Postscript. This is the first new version since then, and the first time it has appeared in a fully illustrated edition – but once again, the original biography has been left as it was, sandwiched in the middle. The 1985 Postscript is also the same. In it I described what happened after the original book came out, how Paul and Linda came to stay with me in Portugal, the death of John and what the others were then doing.

The point of this new Introduction is twofold: firstly, to reflect on some of the changes and developments since 1985, bringing the story roughly up to date, considering the state of the Beatles now; and secondly, to go back to 1968 and explain how I came to do the book in the first place, including observations and information I didn't use in 1968, partly because there wasn't space, partly because there were things I couldn't say, not at the time.

Feel free, of course, to go straight to the good stuff, to the heart of the matter, to the material as it was, to the unvarnished record, fresh from their mouths, rather than any additional thoughts, which, naturally, have the benefit of hindsight – though I like to think that the new and the old will illuminate each other.

Perhaps the most surprising thing about the Beatles during the last few decades is that the further we get from them, the bigger they have become.

There was a period in the mid-1970s when it seemed their stars might fade, their fame and influence recede, that they would be superseded by new and better music and musicians, and, if not better, then more popular music and musicians, and, if not more popular, then definitely different sorts of music and musicians, thus making them appear very 1960s, old hat, rather dated.

But it hasn't happened. Since 1980, and the death of John, their curve has gone ever upwards, not downwards. This is mainly a value judgement, somewhat hard to prove, based on observations rather than statistics, but I can think, immediately, of seven ways, seven areas, in which the Beatles are still growing bigger, every day.

Firstly, in musical influence. In the year 2000, at the end of the 20th century, in those millennium polls that were conducted in most countries, the Beatles were rated the most important, most influential, most loved, most fab, most bla bla group in the entire history of the universe – well, since pop music began. Whether it's a survey of pop fans around the world, of present-day performers, or of music and popular culture experts and commentators, the Beatles are always up there, usually at number one. *Revolver* is the album most named, when it comes to the most named album. Even when it comes to album covers, a Beatles cover, usually *Sergeant Pepper*, seems to be awarded the title of most influential, sometimes even seminal. And quite right too.

Secondly, in political influence. This is a bit more hypothetical, and impossible to prove, but there's a body of opinion today that believes the Beatles helped bring about the collapse of the Soviet Union. This has to be taken slowly, but the theory is that young Russians preferred Lennon to Lenin, liked listening to Beatles music and lyrics rather than to political dogma. Ergo, they refused to consider Western culture as decadent and Westerners as the enemy, and grew cynical about their own Communist propaganda.

'It sounds ridiculous,' so Milos Forman, the eminent film director, was recently quoted, 'but I'm convinced the Beatles are partly responsible for the fall of Communism.' Well then.

Thirdly, commercially. They still sell, in trillions, despite the lack of an obvious marketing point, i.e., a new product. Old stuff repackaged, as in *1*, the compilation album of their number-one hits, released in 2000, topped the charts in 34 different countries. During that year, it was EMI's biggest selling album. They shifted 21.6 million copies. (In second place, as you've asked, came *Lenny Kravitz Greatest Hits*, which sold 6.7 million.) The *Guinness World Records* has now decided it's the bestselling album of all time.

Released in 1995 and 1996, *The Beatles Anthology* CDs in theory contained two 'new' songs – 'Free as a Bird' and 'Real Love'. The latter had been written by John on his own, but had never been released, till the others decided to knock it into shape. 'We took the attitude,' said Paul, 'that John had gone on holiday, saying "I finished all the tracks except this one, but I leave you guys to finish it off." Once we agreed to take that attitude, it gave us a lot of freedom.'

There were three *Anthology* CDs, plus a major TV series, which appeared as six programmes in the UK and three in the USA. The TV series sold in 100 countries. In the USA, 48 million watched Part One. This had dropped to 25 million by Part Three, but, even so, a hell of a lot of people watched and listened, and a hell of a lot of money was made. There was also a radio series and, later on, in 2000, a whopper of a book, also called *The Beatles Anthology*. Huge in size, big in scope, excellent on illustrations, if not all that revelatory when it came to words. About the only thing missing was an ice show.

Fourthly, the Beatles as a source of academic or literary study. In the early 1980s, I was asked to be an outside examiner for a student at London University who was doing a PhD on the Beatles. I thought it was a leg-pull at first. I'd heard that some minor American universities had introduced such studies, but not any British ones, certainly not one as distinguished and rigorous as London University. I can still remember her name, Melody Ziff. She was, in fact, American, but London University had accepted her to study for a PhD. Her thesis, as I remember, was called 'The Beatles' lyrics as poetry.'

Today, there are universities, colleges and schools all over the globe, eminent and otherwise, offering courses that include a study of the Beatles. They have even made the National Curriculum for children in the UK between the ages of nine and eleven.

Fifthly, as creators of employment. The Beatles industry has a bigger workforce today than it had back in 1970. Regular Beatles conferences get held across the USA, as well as in Britain, Europe and Japan, run by people whose full-time job is organizing Beatles events. In Japan, Beatle fans are so keen that it takes 40 Beatles conferences a year to cater for them. A new and magnificent museum, devoted to John Lennon, was opened in Tokyo in 2000, the first of its kind in the world. There is also a new Beatles museum in Brescia, Italy, which was opened in 2001.

In Liverpool, where the local airport has been renamed John Lennon Airport, a new £8 million, 120-room hotel is being built, to be called The Hard Day's Night Hotel, primarily catering for visiting Beatles fans doing Beatles tours or just coming to gape.

Then there are all the dealers, shops and collectors' fairs throughout the so-called civilized world. When you add in the number of Beatles look-alike groups, performing full time, both here and abroad, I estimate that there are now 5,000 people living on the Beatles. Even Apple in its heyday had no more than 50 staff.

Sixthly, Beatles memorabilia. There is no argument here. The auction sales clearly show increases, year after year, as Beatles tat – sorry, Beatles treasures – once overlooked and considered mere souvenirs, continue to fetch huge prices. When I read the catalogue for the first Sotheby's sale in 1983, and saw that lot 198 was the 'Beatles signatures, obtained at Heathrow Airport, estimate £40–60', I thought, no chance, no one will pay that sort of money. Whoever sold them that day is probably now regretting it. Their autographs are today worth at least ten times as much. Lot 246 that day was John's handwritten lyrics to 'Imagine', estimated to go for £800–1,200. Today, it would be expected to go for 40 times as much. In 1999, John's handwritten lyrics for 'I am the Walrus' went for £80,000.

Seventhly, more and more new books about the Beatles, for the academic, the anorak and the general market, get published every month, all promising new material, which usually means the old cake gets sliced even thinner. There are Beatles Brains, who were never alive when the Beatles played live, who know more about the Beatles than the Beatles themselves. They can tell you what they were doing and where, for every minute of every day of their performing lives.

I have contributed, in a small way, to the recent spate of Beatles books, with the publication, in 2001, of *The Quarrymen*, the first book I've done in over 30 years with any sort of Beatles or related connection. I did try not to intrude, producing over 30 books in the meantime, on a variety of other subjects.

It all began in 1998, when I was in Cuba, working on a travel book about the Caribbean, for which I visited 27 different West Indian islands. I was astonished to arrive in Havana and find that the Third International Beatles Conference was about to take place. I hadn't been aware of the First, or the Second. Or that the Cubans were even interested in the Beatles.

Beatles memorabilia continue to fetch huge prices at auctions. At this Sotheby's sale, in the early 1980s, the street sign of Abbey Road was sold for £320. Other items offered for sale included George Harrison's guitar and John Lennon's moped.

I should have done, because during a visit to Russia in 1986, accompanying my wife as a guest of the Russian Writers' Association, I was asked, everywhere I went, about the Beatles. I learned that underground copies of my original biography had been passed from hand to hand for years. I even met a woman in Moscow, the daughter of a general, who was running an unofficial Beatles fan club.

In Havana, I had a drink with the Cuban who was running the Conference and agreed to give a little chat, being awfully kind, the first time I'd ever been to a Beatles conference, anywhere. I was totally amazed by the knowledge and love for the Beatles expressed by all the Cubans I met. I was told that Fidel Castro was a fan, which turned out to be true. In 2000, he unveiled a sculpture of John Lennon in Havana's 17th Street, watched by 3,000 Cuban dignitaries. (Which leaves me wondering if the Beatles helped finish off Communism in Russia, how come they didn't do the same in Cuba?)

The 1998 Conference in Havana turned out to be highly academic, with many learned papers being read. No signs of any commercial stalls selling Beatles tat or bootlegs. There were old Beatles clips and ancient TV videos being shown, and also some live music – which included 'Los Quarrymen'. So it said in the programme. Some mistake, so I thought at first, surely they can't be here, those five boys from that skiffle group John started at Quarry Bank School in the 1950s (see Chapter Two). But they were there, in Cuba, the original Quarrymen. No longer boys of course.

While John went on into history, they had gone their respective ways, remaining mere footnotes in the Beatles story. Known by name to all Beatles Brains, but lost sight of since 1958, by which time Paul and George had come along and the five original Quarrymen had left the stage. For ever. Or so it seemed.

I had interviewed one of them, Pete Shotton, when working on my original book in 1967, as he had remained one of John's closest friends, and did so until his death. John told me in 1967 that he had given Pete £20,000 to buy a shop. In today's terms, that's about a quarter of a million. Pete was an affable, amusing bloke, but it seemed to me he'd probably waste the money. John said he didn't care. Pete would have done the same for him, he said, if the roles had been reversed.

For the next 30 years, until 1998, I never knew what had happened to Pete. Was he alive or dead, in prison or bankrupt? Nor did I know what had become of the other original Quarrymen.

In Cuba I discovered that Pete had become a multi-millionaire, having built up a chain of restaurants called Fatty Arbuckle, several years after he had finished running his original shop.

Rod Davis, who had played banjo in the original Quarrymen, had gone on to Trinity College, Cambridge, the only one to go to university. He had, for a time, been on the dole, done some teaching and led overland expeditions, before becoming a lecturer in tourism. He's now semi-retired, living in Uxbridge.

Colin Hanton, the Quarrymen's drummer, was still living in Liverpool, still working as an upholsterer, as he had been in the days when he first joined the Quarrymen. Len Garry, formerly on tea chest, had emigrated to New Zealand for a while, then returned to Liverpool, where he is now a care worker.

Eric Griffiths, guitar, went into the merchant navy for eight years after he left the Quarrymen. He then did some odd jobs, before joining the Civil Service, rising to the heights of Head of Planning and Production for the Scottish prison service, based in Edinburgh, where he still lives. He's now retired from the Home Office, but has his own small chain of dry-cleaners.

They'd met up again in 1997, for the first time in 40 years, at a Cavern reunion in Liverpool, where they were persuaded to play a few tunes. Luckily, Rod had put an old tea chest and a washboard in the back of his car, just in case. They were then invited to play their old skiffle stuff at the 1997 Woolton Fête anniversary. After that, they were invited to play in various parts of Europe and in America, from New York to Las Vegas. And in Havana, which was where, by chance, I had met them.

What fun for them, at their age, in their retirement years, travelling round the world, playing the sort of stuff they had played 40 years ago, but not played since. John would have been amused. Naturally, I asked if they attracted groupies. 'Oh yes,' said Pete, 'but the trouble is, they are also approaching 60. At our age, though, we can't be too choosy.'

Their memories of growing up with John, in the same streets, at the same Sunday school and same grammar school, then playing with him in the Quarrymen during those two or three years, was to me utterly fascinating. Pete always kept in touch with John, working at Apple, working as his PA, then visiting him in New York. His memories of John are among the most intimate and revealing of any accounts I have ever read.

Having done Havana and delivered my little speech, I then agreed to go to Liverpool in 2000 for their annual Beatles Week, the first time I had attended such an occasion. For many years, Liverpool was not all that interested in the Beatles. There was a feeling in the city, during the late 1960s and the '70s, that the Beatles had turned their backs on Liverpool. They'd gone off to London, then gone global, and appeared to have forgotten about their home town. Or it might simply have been that prophets don't get raved about as much in their own back yard as they do in far-flung foreign parts.

The first Beatles conference in Liverpool was held in 1981. It was partly as a result of John's death, which had brought about a sudden increase in Beatle fans coming to Liverpool. The Merseyside Tourist Centre was created and Beatles guides were introduced, but in 1986, there was extensive local government reorganization, and the new council was not as keen, or as able, to run Beatles-related tours. It went into private hands, taken over by two local lads, Bill Heckle, a comprehensive schoool teacher, and Dave Jones, both of whom had been Beatles guides. In 1991, they took over the lease of the rebuilt Cavern Club, which was where, in 1997, at the 40th anniversary of the Cavern, the original Quarrymen met each other again.

Cavern City Tours, which is what they still call themselves, has today a staff of 100. Twenty years earlier, there was no such organization, no such industry. Throughout the year they run Beatles tours, events, shops, clubs and publications, as well as the annual Beatles Week. They are the people currently building the new hotel.

During the 2000 Week, 150 foreign journalists turned up, and on one of the days, for a free street festival, the crowd numbered 250,000 people. Over 250 different groups performed live, almost all of them look-alike or play-alike Beatles. They came from all over the world, including the USA, Japan, Argentina, Sweden, Venezuela, Germany and Brazil. Back in their own countries they perform Beatles music full time – and appear to make decent livings.

As I watched them performing, my mind constantly went back to the 1960s, trying to scroll back and wondering if I ever expected such a thing to happen, all these decades later. No, is the answer. Some of the music to survive, certainly, but not this three-dimensional devotion to them as people. Their clothes, style, thoughts and personalities live on, along with the music. Yet it was somehow eerie, watching young Japanese or young Argentinians playing Beatles music, sounding almost as good as the original, and doing it while wearing Beatles wigs, Beatles suits, Beatles boots. One or two of the groups had even forced themselves into rather tight, but authentic, Sergeant Pepper costumes. While singing, their English and even Liverpool accents were excellent. Off stage, few could speak a word of English. A lot of the audiences were also in some form of Beatles or 1960s outfits, if just a Beatles cap or miniskirt.

I wondered if, in the end, after a few more decades, this would be the future of the Beatles? Surely they can't keep on getting bigger, in the various ways I mentioned, for ever? Perhaps they will eventually become museum pieces, seen as historic figures, like Beefeaters or Maypole dancers, known for their funny clothes, which are good fun to dress up in, good sport to mock.

After a gap of 40 years, the original members of John's Quarrymen started playing again as a group, at venues across the globe, from Liverpool to Cuba.

The fans, by the way, were all ages, from children to grandparents. The average age was probably about 35–40. They loved everything. No cynicism, no criticism, all of them friendly, kind, simple, straightforward people, some of whom had spent thousands to get to Liverpool from all over the world, mostly on organized Beatles tours.

I can recommend the annual Beatles Week in Liverpool, for any true Beatles fan, though one day was enough for me. I was exhausted looking round all the stalls, on which I spent too much money, and I soon tired of the massive crowds.

Other, more recent and more subdued Beatles attractions in Liverpool include 20 Forthlin Road, Paul's old house in Liverpool, which has been bought and carefully renovated by the National Trust. Quite surprising, that the National Trust, normally associated with stately homes, should have decided to buy a council house. I was brought up in a 1950s council house, very similar to Paul's, as were millions of others, so I am pleased that such a modest residence will now be preserved for ever. It was where Paul and John used to go, when Paul's dad was out at work, and where they wrote several of their early songs together. Not quite 'the birthplace of the Beatles', as some have suggested, but pretty important in the Beatles legend and well worth visiting. In February 2000, it was voted Merseyside's Visitor Attraction of the Year. The competition was pretty stiff, including such delights as Southport Pleasureland and Chester Zoo.

In 2002, Yoko Ono put up the money for John's old house in Menlove Avenue to be bought, saving it from a developer, who wanted to convert it with a suite for honeymooners. Like 20 Forthlin Road, it is now going to be restored by the National Trust and opened to the public.

In London, the priceless collection of original Beatles handwritten lyrics, which used to be in the British Museum, has now moved to the British Library, that big red new building near St Pancras railway station. There are usually around ten Beatles manuscripts and other bits on view. Not far away is the Magna Carta and manuscripts relating to Shakespeare, Jane Austen, Beethoven, Mozart and Handel. The Beatles display usually attracts the most visitors at any one time. The Queen, when she opened the gallery, made a particular point of admiring the Beatles' manuscripts, being, of course, well versed in modern culture. Which was nice.

Many of these items I picked up from the floor of Abbey Road in the 1960s – had I not, they would have been chucked out by the cleaners. The Beatles, at the time, had no interest in such things and said I could have them. I used some as illustrations in the book, then stashed them in drawers, along with scraps I have collected while working on other books over the years, such as entrance tickets for Hadrian's Wall forts and Tottenham Hotspur laundry lists. All treasures, to me.

When my children got older, I put the Beatles bits on the walls, for amusement, and added to them, whenever I could, at a time when no one seemed to be collecting Beatles material. I woke up one morning, when those Beatles sales at Sotheby's first began, to find that the stuff on my walls had suddenly become more valuable than the house. That's when I decided to offer them to the British Museum. I thought at first they might refuse, considering pop lyrics too trivial, too ephemeral. I like the fact that they are all together, as a collection. I don't think Paul would ever speak to me again if I sold them, but I have no intention of doing so. In my will they go to the nation.

The death of George from cancer in November 2001, at the age of 58, means that half the Beatles are now gone. The news made front-page headlines around the world, and drew tributes from all sectors of society, from Prime Ministers to pop stars. Yet George was meant to be the quiet one, supposedly a semi-recluse for the last few years of his life. It showed how much he was loved by so many, and how his songs were recognized and admired. They will live on, as will his memory.

Between 1982 and 1987 George produced nothing. Then came his album *Cloud Nine*, which was well received. He did some appearances and tours in 1991 and 1992, followed by another public silence. Early in 2001, his classic album *All Things Must Pass* was re-released.

Most of the time, over those years, George was busy with his homes and gardens, living a private, contemplative life, still making music occasionally, but for his own purposes, his own pleasures. In 1999 he was stabbed by an intruder who broke into his house near

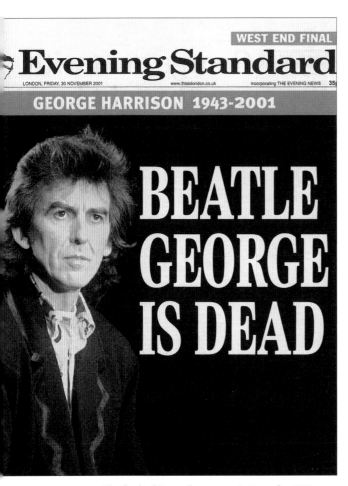

Evening Standard

WEST END FINAL

LONDON, FRIDAY, 30 NOVEMBER 2001   www.thisislondon.co.uk   Incorporating THE EVENING NEWS   35p

GEORGE HARRISON 1943-2001

BEATLE GEORGE IS DEAD

The death of George from cancer in November 2001 made front-page headlines across the world. Presidents, prime ministers and fans mourned. Half the Beatles were now gone.

Henley-on-Thames. It was cruelly ironic that George, the private Beatle, who hardly went out and about and never encouraged publicity, should have been the one to be attacked.

George had a spiritual life, right to the end, retaining his interest in Indian music and religions, and also his sense of humour. The last song he worked on, 'Horse to the Water', was given the copyright credit 'RIP Ltd 2001'.

My memory of George will always be of how he would take things so seriously, like reincarnation, going on and on, but then suddenly stop and mock himself, or break into a funny voice, as he did when I was with him at his Esher home, picking up the phone to say, in broad cockney, 'Esher Wine Store'.

There has also been the tragic death from breast cancer of Linda McCartney, in 1998. She gave Paul so much, and their long marriage was wonderfully successful, but he has now found a new partner in his life, Heather Mills, with whom we all hope he will have many happy years.

Paul is still very active, involved in many projects, from classical creations to rock and roll. In April 2002, he did an American tour, 'Drivin' USA', at which time it was calculated that Paul had now done 1,967 live concerts – 1,630 with the Beatles, 142 with Wings and 195 as a solo artist. A new album of his songs, *Driving Rain*, inspired by his love for Linda and Heather, came out at the end of 2001. Earlier that year, he produced a volume of poetry and lyrics, *Blackbird Singing*, published by the distinguished literary firm Faber & Faber. The previous year he produced a book of his paintings, plus an exhibition. What next? Will he give us all a novel one of these days? I remember when he stayed with us in Portugal in 1968 I caught him banging away at my typewriter, writing what looked like the beginning of a novel. I tried hard, when he wasn't around, to have a sneak look at it, but he'd hidden it away. He did complete a manuscript based on his experiences in prison, when he was busted, which, as far as I know, is still locked away (see page 403).

Ringo has also been very busy in the last decade, though his 'busy-ness' has been mostly abroad, rather than in the UK. He's been playing with his All Starr Band, the line-up for which varies from year to year and also includes occasional one-off appearances by well-known musicians. He released seven albums between 1990 and 1999 and made many TV and radio appearances. In 2000, his All Starr Band, mark six, did a gruelling two-month coast-to-coast tour of the USA, during which they performed Beatles tunes and rock and roll standards, with a bit of personal chat from Ringo between numbers. They've also toured in Canada and Japan. When he reached 60 in July 2000, Ringo said he was hanging up his drums soon and retiring, but it doesn't seem to have happened. In 2001, he toured North America again. He doesn't need the money, of course. He just likes the fun.

Derek Taylor, the Beatles' former press officer and close friend, and a close friend of mine, has also died. The title 'press officer' does little justice to the fact that he was a most original, creative, influential and amusing personality. Alas, the disappearance of vital characters in the Beatles saga will become more common as life moves on.

The two remaining Beatles are now gentlemen in or around their 60s, senior citizens – but then so are we all, we who were around at the time when they were young and vibrant.

It's the classic period of the Beatles I like best, those Beatlemania years, when I used to hang around Abbey Road. I grew quickly tired of the later rows and legal arguments. I also find my eyes going glazed when some of today's Beatles Brains, the real experts, start on the discographies, on the minutiae of the various recordings, the bootlegs and underground versions. But at least they will carry the flag, keep up the passion and enthusiasm, for the generations to come.

Linda McCartney died from breast cancer in 1998. She married Paul in March 1969. It was to be a wonderfully happy and successful marriage that lasted almost 30 years and produced three children.

The music matters most, of course. The Beatles gave us 150 songs, which will remain for ever, as long as the world still has the breath to hum the tunes. This is the book that covers most of that period, written when it was still happening, back in 1968.

* * * *

The Beatle I first met was Paul in September 1966. It was a great year, 1966. In July, England won the World Cup at Wembley, England's first ever world success. I sold the film rights of my first novel, which had come out the previous year, to United Artists, and I was commissioned by BBC TV to write a Wednesday play. In October 1966 there was the world premiere of *Georgy Girl*, a film written by my wife, from her own novel. It was *annus mirabilis* in the Davies household.

My full time job was as a journalist on the *Sunday Times* of London, where I was writing the Atticus column. I had been on the staff since 1960, though for the first three years I had beavered away without once getting my name in the paper. It is hard to believe it now, but in those days, by-lines were infrequent and the *Sunday Times* was a very traditional newspaper. Atticus, the newspaper's gossip column, had always been equally old fashioned, devoting itself to news about bishops, gentlemen's clubs, ambassadors. As a working-class lad from the North, who had grown up in a council house, gone to the local grammar school and then a provincial university, I had neither the background, the accent nor the interests of the accepted Atticus columnists. They had tended to be old Etonians, Oxbridge types, who actually did know bishops and went to the best clubs. Some had also been very distinguished – Ian Fleming had only recently given up Atticus (in 1959) and before him previous incumbents had included writers like Sir Sacheverell Sitwell.

But a funny thing happened to British life in the mid-1960s. Not just on the Atticus column, but out in the world at large, traditional roles and rules were being upset. My interests, when I took over the column, were in novelists from the North, Cockney photographers, jumped-up fashion designers, loud-mouthed young businessmen. I did it partly to annoy, as I knew that the old guard on the paper hated such people, but mainly because I was fascinated by their success.

We all laughed and scoffed when *Time* magazine in New York came out with the idea of Swinging London and sent over battalions of writers and photographers to report and analyse all the exciting things supposedly happening here. Looking back, there *was* a sort of explosion in London in the 1960s. Now that we see how life can be so dire and desperate for so many, what happened in the 1960s was exciting and revolutionary for young people. The Beatles, of course (you thought I'd never get to them), were a vital element in this overthrowing of old values and accepted manners.

I didn't take much notice of 'Love Me Do' when it came out, thinking here was a one-off group, who showed no signs of being able to develop, and when I first heard John copying the Americans and screaming 'Twist and Shout' it gave me a headache. But I loved 'I Want to Hold Your Hand', and from then on could not wait for their next record. I went to one of the concerts – I think it was at Finsbury Park in London – which was fascinating, but the girls' screaming annoyed me. I wanted to hear them properly, not be deafened by adolescent shop girls and hairdressers.

I identified completely with their background and attitudes. My home town is Carlisle, further up the northwest coast from Liverpool, where we consider ourselves real Northerners and Liverpool might as well be on the Mediterranean. Although I was four years older than John, I felt his contemporary, as he, Paul and George had gone to the same type of school.

Until the Beatles, nobody had sung songs for *me*, songs that had a connection with *my* life, from their own experience, about my experience. I had enjoyed but despised the

American-style pap we had all been brought up on, with middle-aged men in shiny suits saying we were a very wonderful audience, and they sure were glad to be here, before singing another sloppy ballad with banal words. All the same, I can still remember all the words of at least three Guy Mitchell songs.

Despite the Beatles' enormous popularity, there were still, in the mid-1960s, many people who said their success was basically a matter of fashion. The clothes, the hair, the accent, the irreverence, the humour, that was what made people like them, not their music. It was all publicity and promotion. A new group would soon displace them.

In August 1966, 'Eleanor Rigby' came out (the B side of 'Yellow Submarine'), and that seemed to me to *prove* that they could write real lyrics. The music, once again, was a development, using classical instruments and harmonies.

I went to see Paul at his house in Cavendish Avenue, St John's Wood. It was pure self-indulgence. I wanted to meet him, but I also wanted to hear the background to 'Eleanor Rigby'. I presumed he had written it, as it was his voice singing, though in those days they were simply Lennon-McCartney songs and no one bothered to separate them. I had never read any interview in which they had been asked seriously about how they composed. The popular newspapers were obsessed by the money and the crowd mania, while the fan mags wanted to know their favourite colour and favourite film stars.

I planned to reproduce all the words of 'Eleanor Rigby', to let the ignorant see how good they were, admire the imagery, feel the quality, but my superiors on the newspaper were against it. They didn't want so much space wasted on humdrum pop songs. So, what I said was that no pop song at present had better words or music.

The interview was revealing, so I thought, though reading it now, Paul does come out a bit self-satisfied, while at the same time appearing to be self-aware and even self-deflating. Has he really changed all that much? In it he used the word 'stoned'. Until then, in normal English usage, it referred to drink, not drugs, which was how I took it at the time.

I think I got on well with him. We talked about the background to many of their other songs, though I had no room to write about them. It struck me afterwards that there was so much I didn't know about them or their work, and that everybody had been asking the same old questions about their fame and success, and wondering when the bubble would burst.

There were only two books I could find on the Beatles, both unsatisfactory. There had been a fan club book, a short paperback, called *The True Story of the Beatles*, which came out in 1964, produced by the people who did *Beatles Monthly*. There was also a book by a young American, Michael Braun, called *Love Me Do*, which was much better, but limited, based on conversations with them on tour. This also had come out in 1964. They had developed so much since, but nobody had looked at their whole career, or spent time talking to them properly, or their friends and relations, or even tried to investigate what had happened in Hamburg, let alone their school days.

It seemed a good idea, but why should the Beatles agree to co-operate on such an enterprise? They were already, in 1966, millionaires, rich and famous and successful enough not to be interested in any more boring old chats about being Beatles. So I forgot about it, and went on with the business of living and working. My second child, Jake, was born in 1966.

I was already in the middle of my third book, a documentary study of universities, a look at students and teachers in Britain, to be called the *Class of '66*. I had so far completed about half of it, including profiles of two young girl students, one at Manchester University called Anna Ford and one at Sussex called Buzz Goodbody, and had written 10,000 words on each.

Then in December 1966 I paused from the book to get started on the screenplay of the novel that had been bought by United Artists, *Here We Go, Round the Mulberry Bush*, a slice-of-life, Northern story, about a boy on a council estate, hoping to pick up a girl from a semi. I was surprised when it was bought by the film people – and even more surprised now that they planned to make it. Far more books get bought than ever get filmed. It was going to be a contemporary, teenage film, and the director, Clive Donner, had the idea that Paul McCartney might do the theme tune for us. He had already done some film music.

On this occasion I went to Cavendish Avenue not as a journalist, looking for good quotes, but as a film writer, hoping he would collaborate on the project. He did seem interested, and we had several meetings and telephone chats, but in the end he said no. (The music was eventually done by Stevie Windwood plus the Spencer Davis Group – and was very good.)

Talking to Paul, this time with a slightly different hat on, I put to him the idea that had originally struck me. How about a *proper* book on the Beatles, a serious attempt to tell the whole story, to get it all down, once and for all, so that for ever more when people ask the same old dopey questions, you can say it's in the book; wouldn't that be a good idea, hmm?

It was always difficult to get any of the Beatles to concentrate on anything for more than a few moments. Even in his home, there was a queue of record people, designers, artists, assistants, sitting around waiting to see him. So I threw it out, not expecting a reaction or a reply there and then, but he said fine, why not, it would be useful. But there was only one problem. I thought for a moment that some other writer had already asked and been granted permission.

'What you'll have to do first of all is talk to Brian,' said Paul. 'He's the one who will decide. But come on, sit down, I'll help you draft a letter.'

So there and then I sat down and did a rough letter. The next day I typed it out and sent it to Brian Epstein. How funny that for all these years I should have kept a copy. I found it only the other day in an old drawer. It was on the lines Paul had suggested, boasting what a big cheese I was, saying I had 'interviewed the Beatles several times'. Did I make that up? Or have I forgotten? No, now it comes back to me, I did interview them, on the set of *A Hard Day's Night*, in 1964. I remember a complicated joke John made that day. They were about to record a song in a studio and a light came on saying 'Sound On'. John started making up doggerel about 'Sounds on, Sound on'. There used to be a phrase 'Sounds on' meaning something seemed possible, or all right. I think I must have made a mess of trying to explain the joke, such as it was, because the article, as far as I can remember, never got into the newspaper.

My appointment with Brian Epstein was made for Wednesday, 25 January 1967. At the last minute, he cancelled, through pressure of work, and made it the next day. Even so, he kept me waiting a long time, so I mooched around his drawing room, admiring his two fine paintings by Lowry. He lived at the time at 24 Chapel Street, Belgravia, a very posh address, right in the middle of the diplomatic area.

```
                                    11 Boscastle Road
                                    London, N.W.5.

                                    31st December, 1966


Brian Epstein, Esq.,
Nems Enterprises Ltd.,
5 Argyll Street,
London, W.1.


Dear Mr. Epstein,

       I've mentioned the idea of doing a big, definitive, serious
book about the Beatles to Paul McCartney. He was very interested
and said he was sure the rest of the group would also help, but of
course I had to approach you.

       So, I wonder if you could spare a few minutes some time to
discuss the idea?

       I am a journalist, writing the atticus column on the Sunday
Times. I've interviewed the Beatles several times, the latest being
the interview with Paul about Eleanor Rigby, which I enclose. I'm
also an author. I've done three books in all, the latest has been
in the London best seeling list for the last few months.

       I've got a commission from Heinemann to do another non-fiction
book and would dearly love to do it on the Beatles. Not a fan book,
but a full study of what happened and why during the last five years.

       I'm sure the boys, and you yourself, might forget in the years
to come exactly what happened. And anybody doing a history of the
sixties in the years to come should also have a proper record. It
would be a very good book, in every sense. As Truman Capote put to-
gether a murder, I'm sure there's need for a full anatomy of the
Beatle phenomenon.

       Anyway, I know the whole thing would have to be properly discussed
and arranged before anything could be done, but I do hope you will be
interested.
                               Yours sincerely,
```

The letter to Brian Epstein, dated 31 December 1966, which began the book...

He eventually appeared, in a suit as always, looking very fresh, chubby-cheeked and healthy, but rather distracted. He played for me the tapes of 'Penny Lane' and 'Strawberry Fields', their new single, about to be released in a few days' time. He sat back with a sort of paternal pride and watched me, not really listening to the music, just watching me listening. I was amazed by 'Strawberry Fields'. It was such a leap forward, an enormous advance on juvenile stuff like 'Yellow Submarine', full of discordant jumps and eerie echoes, almost like Stockhausen. I wondered if Beatle fans would like it. I asked him what the title meant. He didn't seem to know.

He carefully locked the tape away, saying that he could not be too careful. A previous Beatle tape had been stolen and it was very embarrassing. They could fetch a lot of money, if they were leaked to the pirate radio stations before the official launch date. In those days, there were several pirate radio stations around Britain. I didn't actually believe him, that people would steal tapes, just to get a few days ahead of their rivals.

I eventually got the conversation round to my letter, asking what he thought, had he taken the topic further? He appeared not to know much about it at first, though he smiled and was very charming, so I went over the details, and he said yes, it did seem a good idea and he would have to put it to all four Beatles.

I then added what I had not put in the letter, which was that I expected to share the proceeds with them, if they agreed to give me exclusive co-operation. That seemed only fair. He waved his hand, his white shirt showing expansively over his well manicured fingers, as if that was a trifling consideration. I told him that my publisher was Heinemann, a very distinguished imprint, and he said he would like to meet them, and my agent, so we could all agree on the details. He arranged another meeting for the following Wednesday, 31 January. By then, he said, he would know what the Beatles thought.

The boss of the literary agency I was then with, Curtis Brown, the biggest agency of its type in the world, said he would like to come in person, as did Charles Pick, managing director of Heinemann, and I told them just to stand by. I would ring from Epstein's, if it looked as if the deal was going forward. I saw Brian at three, and he said the Beatles had raised no objections, so I rang Spencer Curtis Brown and Charles Pick and told them both to come round, sharpish.

I'm sure they just wanted to get inside Epstein's house, to see how this man of the moment lived, as the deal in prospect was not really a very big one. I had already talked to other people in the publishing firm, about the possibility of this book, and no one had been very impressed. We know all we'll ever want to know about the Beatles, as one person said. And anyway, books about pop stars don't sell. Look at that Cliff Richard book, that didn't do very well. I said, this is practically sociology, about a group that has affected the way we live now. Sociology? Who needs sociology? That doesn't sell either.

Brian explained to the three of us that I could do the book, and that he would give me all facilities, but he couldn't force each Beatle not to talk to other people. This rather worried me. I left it to Spencer to discuss how we should split the proceeds, and he suggested one third to the Beatles and two thirds to me, as I was doing all the work, and would have to go round the world, interviewing former friends and associates. It would be a big job, as we all wanted it to be the definitive book, not a cheap, paperback, fan-mag quickie. Brian agreed.

The contract was eventually drawn up, with Brian organizing it personally, in his capacity as their manager. Heinemann agreed to pay £3,000 for the book, which meant £2,000 to me, less ten per cent, of course, for the agent's fee. Even in those days, it was not a large amount. Now, of course, it looks unbelievably small, when I know that one subsequent writer of a Beatles book in the 1980s managed to earn 100 times that amount.

However I was very pleased. I had secured access to the four people I most wanted to meet. Even if it all collapsed for some reason, I would have been inside their homes and been in the recording studios and seen them at work. One worry was that other people might get to hear about the book, and do a quick version, based on some passing conversations with them, or just newspaper cuttings, so we all agreed to keep the project secret.

I also worried, though I hate to admit it now, that perhaps there was some truth in the feeling, held by many in 1966, that the bubble would very soon burst. I liked their music, but the world at large in two years' time could have moved on to something else. That would explain why nobody had done a proper book about them so far. I didn't want it to be a flop, with poor sales, and I would feel embarrassed about having taken the money. As for the *Class of '66* book, it was agreed I could put that back till I had finished the one on the Beatles. We could always call it the *Class of '67*.

On 7 January 1967, my 31st birthday, I started work on the book by talking to Ringo. I thought he might be the easiest. With all biographical books, at least to do with living people, there is always the fear of falling out, of not getting on before the project is properly under way. Ringo always looked kind. As a fan, that was the image I had picked up.That same day, I got a call at the *Sunday Times*, where I was still writing the Atticus column, planning to do the Beatles book in the evenings and at weekends, which was how I had produced my previous two books. It was from a strange-sounding lady called Yoko Ono. She said I was the most eminent columnist in London, so she had been told, creep

creep, and that she wanted to feature my bare bottom in a film she was making. Don't bugger around, I said, who are you? I thought it must be some drunken journalist from the *Observer*, having me on.

No, no, she said, this is very serious, and she proceeded to list other films she had done, all of them sounding equally dopey. She gave me the address where the filming was taking place and implored me to come along. I said I might, but I wasn't promising; anyway, if it meant revealing my bottom, she would have to contact my agent.

I went along, as it sounded the sort of daft story I might need for the column that week, though still half expecting it to be a hoax. Sure enough, there was a queue of blokes in this very smart apartment in Park Lane, lining up to stand on a revolving stage, like a children's roundabout, while Yoko filmed them as in turn they dropped their trousers. I talked to a rather distracted American called Anthony Cox, who turned out to be her husband, and I gathered he had put up the money as she, apparently, had none. He looked so clean cut, an educated Ivy League American. I found it hard to believe he had fallen for all this nonsense. The more he explained, the more there did seem quite a serious point she was making. I've forgotten now what it was.

Yoko tried to persuade me to strip off. I made an excuse and left, as all the best journalists have done since time immemorial. I could not really write objectively about her film, so I said, if I was in it.

I did a piece in the paper on 12 February 1967. I hoped I hadn't poked too much fun at her, though I worried that the title of the article, 'Oh no, Ono', might offend her, but she had got what she wanted, some prime publicity. She rang me afterwards to thank me.

I never met her again, in the flesh, until I walked into Abbey Road studios one evening in 1968 and there she was, sitting in a transcendental state with John transfixed by her, looking at her adoringly, and the other three Beatles completely bewildered, not knowing what had happened.

Meanwhile, I had a first, quick meeting with Ringo, and then in turn with the other three, but not to interview them, just to say hello, introduce myself, explain the project and get from them the names of school friends, school masters, neighbours and, most of all, an introduction to their parents. I knew I would need that to pave the way.

I had decided I would spend the first six months of my work on the Beatles book by not talking to the Beatles themselves. I sensed, without knowing it, that they must be fed up with the same old questions from people who only knew what they knew by having read it in the newspapers. I wanted to go back in time, and then move slowly, stage by stage, through their careers, so that each time I arrived to see them again, I would bring news and chat and observations about what had happened to all the people and places they had long left behind. That way, I estimated, I might be a welcome visitor. Unless, of course, they were now so fame-drunk and success-sodden that they had ceased to have any interest in *where* they had come from.

So those first chats were brief, hurried conversations, mainly at Abbey Road, before recording sessions. In those early days, I made sure not to outstay my welcome, knowing that they had always refused to have any strangers or outsiders present when they were actually working.

John must have taken in my few words of introduction, saying who I was, where I'd come from and what I was doing. Some time later I received a letter from him, addressed to 'White Hunter Davies, c/o William Heinemann Ltd, 15 Queen Street, London, W1'. Not a bad joke. Inside was a cutting, with no date, which appeared to be from a local Liverpool newspaper, saying a rhythm group called the Beatles had made their debut at Neston Institute.

It is only recently that I have at long last been able to date the cutting, after searches in Liverpool and at the British Museum's newspaper library. It appeared on 11 June 1960 (the day of my wedding) in the Heswall and Neston edition of the *Birkenhead News*. This was the first time that the word 'Beatles' appeared in print. (*Mersey Beat*, the local pop music newspaper, which wrote about them constantly, did not appear till the following year, in June 1961.)

It's interesting that the newspaper should call them 'The Beatles' as only two weeks earlier, on 27 May in the *Hoylake News and Advertiser*, they were still known as the Silver Beetles. They did not permanently call themselves The Beatles till later that year.

The cutting shows that John had stuck to his own name. Paul had become Paul Ramon, giving himself a Hollywood-1920s persona. George was Carl Harrison, after his hero, Carl Perkins. Stu Sutcliffe had become Stuart de Stijl, after the art movement. Thomas Moore, the drummer, an equally false-sounding name, was in fact called Thomas Moore.

Although John always appeared to have no interest in the history of the Beatles, the fact that he had kept this cutting, which obviously must have been a big thrill for him at the time, made me realize that he did have some interest in his past. On the back of the envelope that contained this cutting, John had written the words 'JAKE MY ARSE'.

I must have given him some personal information, during our hurried chat, and told him I had recently had a baby son, though I thought from his short-sighted look, staring blankly through his National Health spectacles, that he hadn't been listening.

I presume he thought that a working-class lad from the North should not be giving his children such poncy names. I didn't know at that time about Julian (as his wife and family were still kept pretty private). Later on, I always made a point of saying what a middle-class name, Julian, really affected, very poncy.

Going to see the parents was one of the strangest parts about researching the book. I wanted to put a good deal about them in the final book, and how they had reacted, and wrote up a hundred pages of notes. In the end, there just wasn't enough space for more than a few paragraphs about what had happened to them (see Chapter 28).

The fact of their sons' fame had taken them completely by surprise, and the recent and sudden transformation, from their working-class homes and environment into luxury homes in the suburbs, was an even bigger shock. In the case of Mimi, John's aunt who had brought him up, she maintained she had always been middle class. Unlike the other three sets of parents, who all lived in council houses, she and her husband owned their home. It was only a modest semi, on a busy road, not at all affluent and certainly not a professional area, though Mimi always had certain aspirations and hated John for getting mixed up with the common crowd. Even for Mimi, there had been some cultural, emotional and social shocks. It wasn't just the fact of the four boys becoming celebrities and millionaires.

The parents had also been turned into celebrities, suddenly living and being treated like millionaires. All of them reacted to this process slightly differently.

Ringo's mother, Elsie, and his stepfather Harry were the most stunned by it, almost frightened, caught like rabbits in the searchlight of fame. They had just moved into a new posh bungalow, and felt completely isolated, knowing nobody, not knowing what to do with themselves all day. I tried, in the book, not to paint it as bleakly as that, but I did feel sorry for them. They had been forced in the end to move from their old terrace house in the Dingle because life there had become unbearable.

I explained to them on the phone what I was doing, and that I had permission. Sitting there, in their new lounge, which still smelled of plastic coverings and paint, I could feel their nervousness, scared of saying the wrong thing, so I rang Ringo, on their phone, and got him to talk to them, before finally they relaxed.

'We began to get really fed up,' said Elsie, 'when they started taking away the letter box, chipping bits off the door, taking stones away from the outside. We came home one night and they'd painted "We Love You Ringo" all over the front door and on every window.

'Most of them were nice kids. They did buy the records, so they deserved something. They'd ask for his old socks, or shirts, or shoes. I'd give them some, till there was none left.

'If Ritchie was at home, he had to sneak in and out in the dark. He'd be crouching inside sometimes, and I'd have to say he wasn't in. So, we just had to move here in the end.'

On the other hand, Louise Harrison, George's mother, was sitting proudly in her new gleaming home, loving it all. She welcomed the fans and the interruptions from the very beginning, enjoying talking to them, opening fêtes, signing autographs, making little speeches. She turned being a Beatle mum into a full time occupation.

When I first went to see her, in early 1967, there were rumours, yet again, about the Beatles splitting up. (It was either that, or one of them, usually Paul, was dead.) To cope with all the mail she was personally getting about this momentous topic, Mrs Harrison had prepared typewritten replies ready to send to fans.

Through the fact of being George's mother, she had opened a new shop in Liverpool and met some Liverpool TV stars, such as Ken Dodd and Jimmy Tarbuck. She and her husband had recently been invited to the funeral of a local pop singer, even though they never knew him. She thought it their duty to turn up, to represent George.

Mrs Harrison was the only one of the parents who actively encouraged their early music, and became something of a groupie herself, going to many of their early concerts. She still loved talking about it. After all, in 1967, it was fresh in her mind.

'I remember when they did "Love Me Do", their first record, and George told us it *might* be going to be on Radio Luxembourg. We all stayed up till two o'clock, glued to the set, and nothing happened. Harold [her husband] went to bed, as he had to be up at five for the early shift on the buses. In the end, I went up to bed as well. I was just in the bedroom, when George came rushing up the stairs with the radio, shouting "We're on, we're on". Harold woke up and said, "Who's brought that noisy gramophone in here?"'

Mrs Harrison had a better memory of their early concerts than the Beatles themselves, which was a great help in getting the sequence of events in order. They were useless, when it came to dates, and even the years.

'I went to 48 of their shows when they became the Beatles. Manchester, Preston, Southport, all over the North. I used to sit in the front rows. In Manchester one night they were doing a show that a TV company was going to record. I got tickets as usual, for the first and for the second house. George said I was daft – I'd never survive because they were going to be really loud for the film people. I managed the first show, but by the beginning of the second, the screams were so loud I almost collapsed. I had to get a policeman to help me out. He didn't believe me when I said I'd been to the first show as well…

'One of the first big things George did for us was in 1963. He said he'd got me a birthday present, but I couldn't see it or hold it. All I had to do was get ready to go to Jamaica on Wednesday. I said I'll need new clothes. He said, all you need is your cossy. That holiday in Montego Bay was the best ever.

'On the beach one day, this bloke sat down and said, hello Mrs Harrison. How do you know I'm Mrs Harrison? He'd got a description of what I was wearing when I left the hotel that morning. He was a reporter. I woke Harold up. I said, there's a reporter taking all your snores down. I was too thirsty to talk to him. I'd need a drink. He sent off this Japanese photographer he had and he came back with eight bottles of beer. He then took us round the clubs at night. We had a great time.

'I think our proudest moment of all was the Civic Reception in Liverpool. Seeing our own townspeople turning out. From Speke airport onwards they were eight deep all the way into town. You should have seen all the poor old people, waving their clean white hankies as we passed. They'd come out specially from their old people's homes, just for once. Oh, Lord, what a day.'

George, at that time, had just started his interest in Indian music, which Mrs Harrison, in a rather convoluted way, thought she might have something to do with.

'I always used to fiddle with our wireless to get Indian music. I'd tuned into Indian stuff once by accident and I thought it was lovely, so after that I was always trying to get it on the wireless. I'm not saying this has affected George. This was all before he was born…'

Jim McCartney, Paul's father, had also taken very easily to the new life, though in a different way, as he tried to keep out of the limelight. Unlike the others, he bought an old Edwardian villa, rather smart and grand, as opposed to a new bungalow, and turned himself into something of a gent, in his smart sports jacket and check trousers, owning a race horse, tending his grapes in his own conservatory. He had of course been a salesman, so he always did look very neat and presentable.

Jim first realized they were doing well when the phone started ringing non-stop. They always had a phone, despite living in a council house, because of his wife being a midwife. 'It seemed to go every second. I answered it in case it was important. Girls would ring up from California and say is Paul there. What a waste of money. If they came to the house from a long distance, I'd say, do you want a cup of tea. Then I'd say, well there's the kitchen. They'd go in and shout and scream because they'd recognize the kitchen from photographs. They knew more about me than I did myself. Fans would make very good detectives.

'I used to think, how far can it go? Every newspaper was full every day of the police having to keep the kids back. All that free publicity. Brian never had to pay for any of it.

'I think their secret was they were attractive to the kids because they represented their frame of mind, they represented freedom and rebellion. And they liked doing it so much, that's why they did it so well.'

I stayed with Jim, and his new wife Angie, several times in their home, and always had a very enjoyable evening. When he came to London, he used to ring me and come round for tea. One night, when I was staying with him in Cheshire, Paul had sent up an advance copy of 'When I'm Sixty Four', which he said he had written with his dad in mind. That evening, they must have played it about 20 times, dancing round and round the drawing room. I was convinced Jim was going to have a heart attack. Angie, a much younger lady, was encouraging him to jump about.

Michael, Paul's younger brother, was also living at home at that stage, and he told a story about Paul's innate sense of diplomacy, which he had always noticed, ever since his young days.

'I was in Paris with them, and George Martin had arranged for them to sing "She Loves You" in German. He waited in this studio for them for two hours, and they didn't turn up. George arrives at the hotel where we all were, the George V, and when they see him come in, they all dive under the tables. "Are you coming to do it or not?" asked George. John said no. Then George and Ringo also said no. Paul said nothing.

'They all went back to their meal. Then a bit later, Paul suddenly turned to John and said, heh, you know that so and so line, what if we did it this way? John listened to what Paul said, thought a bit, and said yeh, that's it.

'That had been the real reason why they hadn't turned up. But without arguing, Paul had cleverly brought the subject round again, sorted it out. Before long, they all got up and went off to the studio.'

Mimi was the only one who had left the Liverpool area, coming down to the South Coast to a new bungalow near Bournemouth. She too had found her life in Liverpool taken over by the fans, though she had always tried to be kind to them, searching round for some old object belonging to John to give them.

'One day I at last couldn't find anything. "Not even a button?" this girl said. Well, I've always had a phobia for cutting buttons off all clothes before throwing them out. So I got out my big button tin I'd had for years and gave her one. She threw her arms round me and kissed me. She said she'd never forget it. She later wrote and said she was wearing it on a gold chain round her neck and all the girls in her factory were jealous.'

This naturally led to all the other girls in the factory writing to Mimi for John's buttons, and then fans everywhere, as the story got round. 'I've sent buttons to every country in the world. America, Czechoslovakia, everywhere.'

In the end she was very upset by two fans who had broken into her house when she was ill in bed upstairs. She'd left the back door open for the doctor and when she heard noises down below, she thought it must be burglars. She crept downstairs, expecting to be attacked, and found two girls, stretched out on her brand new sofa, with a pile of used toffee papers all round them. She told them to go, furious that they had come in without asking, making her house a public property. They did at last leave, but on the way they stole her back door key. Mimi sat down and cried.

'I was like that when the bread man arrived. He very kindly phoned his works and a man came and put a new lock and key on the door. It was the Scott's bread man. One of the kindest things anyone has ever done for me.' It was not long after this that Mimi decided to leave Liverpool completely.

It's interesting to think, all these years later, that many of those Beatle souvenirs are now turning up at Sotheby's in London and being sold for a fortune, before going on to decorate the games room or the bar of some Japanese millionaire.

Mimi was very helpful to me, on my visits to her, though so many of her stories about John as a little boy seemed to clash with his own versions, given by John himself, and by his school friends.

In Mimi's eyes, John had a perfect middle-class upbringing. Yes, he could be naughty now and again, but more on the lines of Just William and his pranks, nothing nasty or horrible and certainly not criminal. She didn't know where such tales came from. Her own stories were mainly about John's early childhood, almost as if she had drawn a veil over most of the rest, determined to keep him young and sweet and innocent for ever, at least in her mind.

Even when she witnessed a triumphal Beatle concert in Liverpool at Christmas 1963, their first return after their number one record success, her mind still went back to John's early days. She was standing at the back, having refused to sit in a front-row seat.

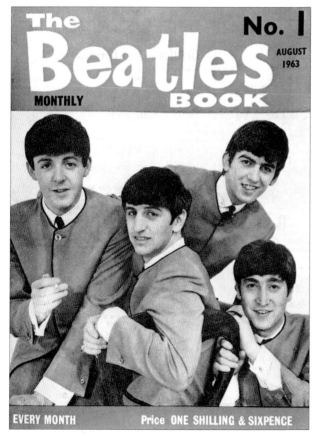

Beatles Monthly: the British fan club magazine was launched in August 1963, and ran for 77 editions, until December 1969. (Since the 1980s it has been appearing again every month.)

'It was at the Liverpool Empire. I was looking at John on the stage, but all I could see was him as a little boy. I always used to take him to the Empire at Christmas for his annual treat. I remember the time we'd seen *Puss in Boots*. It had been snowing and John's Wellingtons were still on in the theatre. When Puss came on in his big boots, John stood up and shouted, "Mimi, he's got his Wellington boots on! So have I." His little voice was heard everywhere and everyone looked at him and smiled.

'I was very proud of course to see him playing on the stage at the Empire. It was the first time I realized what an effect they had. There were mounted police to restrain the crowds. Bessie Braddock was standing with me at the back. It was very exciting.

'But I couldn't help thinking all the time, no, he's not really a Beatle, he's the little fellow who once sat upstairs with me and shouted "Mimi – he's got his Wellington boots on".'

It is true, if you look at the snapshots of John when he was very little – especially the polyphoto strip shown overleaf – he does look a very appealing, innocent little boy.

One of the problems about piecing together the Beatles' early childhood life was the fact that there were two missing parents. Julia, John's mother, was, of course, long dead, and so was Paul's. I knew that Ringo's real father, who had got divorced from his mother Elsie many years ago, was still alive. And I also suspected that Freddie Lennon, or 'that Alfred', as the Mimi side of the family always called him, was still around somewhere. There had at least been no news of Freddie's death. Throughout all of John's school life, Mimi dreaded Alfred turning up one day. I contacted shipping companies and hotels where he was supposed to have worked as a washer-up and failed at first to get any news of him.

I had better luck tracking down Ringo's father, also called Richard or Ritchie. In my first letter, I rather upset him by spelling his name wrong. Tut tut. I was never much good at spelling. I addressed him as Mr Starkie, instead of Mr Starkey. All Beatle fans know that. He reprimanded me in his reply, but said he was willing to talk to me.

He was living in Crewe, working partly as a window cleaner. He did not have a lot to tell me, but I very much admired how he had kept away from Ringo after the divorce, and even now, when his son was famous, he was not cashing in in any way and stoutly refused to contact Ringo or his former wife.

Apart from the parents, I also spent a lot of time in the Liverpool area, tracking down school friends, school masters, people who played with them, at one time, in the Quarrymen.

I went to the Cavern, still going strong in 1967, though as a jazz club again, and saw people such as Bob Wooler and Alan Williams. I bought old copies of *Mersey Beat* and picked up as many old programmes and posters as I could.

Polyphoto strip of John, aged five, looking a very sweet and innocent little boy, as his aunt Mimi always preferred to remember him.

John dug out and gave me an old programme for a bill they had been on, as a supporting group, with Little Richard. On the front of the programme, John had secured Little Richard's autograph, as any ordinary fan might do, plus his address in the USA, in case John might visit America one day. At that time, it seemed a very remote possibility.

The Liverpool interview that stands out in my mind was with Pete Best. He was the drummer sacked by the Beatles on 16 August 1962 (see Chapter 17). By 1967, he had got married and was working in a bakery and he had failed to answer all the letters and messages I had sent him. In the end, I managed to see his mother, Mo Best, who did so much to help the Beatles in their early stages by letting them perform at the little club she had opened, the Casbah.

I saw her in Hayman's Green, in a big overgrown Victorian house, which at one time had the Casbah Club in the cellar. I knocked for 15 minutes, and was beginning to think the house was abandoned before I was let in. The fact that I was working on an 'authorized biography' was in this case not exactly a help. She was still furious about the way her Pete had been treated and I worked hard to convince her that I was simply trying to get at the truth, to hear all sides. She said that she had passed on my messages to Peter, but he didn't want to meet anyone to do with the Beatles. She eventually relaxed and took me through her meetings with the Beatles and the history of the Casbah, all of which I used in the book.

Unbeknown to me, Peter had arrived at the house while we were talking, to visit his mum. He was sitting alone in another room, and refused to come out and talk to me. I asked Mrs Best to send through her younger son Roag, to ask if he would talk to me, just to help me get the dates right of the Hamburg years. In the end, she said come on, I'll take you in to see Pete, it'll be all right. I spent a long time with him, although I used only part of his story in the book.

He stood up and smiled wearily, as if giving in, realizing that, thanks to his mother, he'd been found and trapped. He looked embarrassed and tired. He held his head self-consciously to one side, almost stooping. He seemed sad and a bit pathetic. He talked slowly and quietly. He was tired, having just come off shift work at the bakery. As he talked, there was obviously a great deal of pride left in him.

He went over the Hamburg and earlier days, brightening up as he told funny stories, such as John standing in the street in his Long John underpants.

'I suppose I have got over a lot of it. It took a long time. I had so much press and publicity to live with. I did refuse many offers to sell my stories. I just didn't want to. What good would it have done, apart from the money? It was all over, and that was that.

'Twice I was really at the bottom, really low, and didn't know what to do with life. My wife Kitty said step up, go back and have another go. Mo worked very hard. Mo always wanted me to be a success in show business. She took my side in everything, but it was really my fight.

'When I left show business, it wasn't so bad. I didn't meet other groups who might say I was no good. It was difficult at first starting an ordinary job. Some people said I should have stuck to show business. At work they'd stare at me and say, what's he doing here with us?

'When I'm drinking in a pub, people still come up to me and say, aren't you so and so, you were with the Beatles. They start on me, asking the usual things, labouring into me. They're just sticking their noses in, which I don't like, nobody would. I just try not to say anything.

'I never felt hatred for them, even at the time. At first I did think they'd been a bit sneaky, going behind my back and all the time scheming to get rid of me and never telling me to my face what they had decided. I got over that after a while. I suppose I could see why they'd been sneaky.

'What hurt me was that I knew they were going to be big. I could tell it. We all could. We were getting amazing crowds in Liverpool, everywhere we went. I knew I was going to miss all the fun of that.

'I do try to think of any rows, but I can't. I have recently remembered one little incident.

About two months before it happened, I had heard some sort of rumour that I was going. I asked Brian. He said he hadn't heard anything and he'd find out. He did look into it, but he said there was nothing. I was all right and not to worry.

'I've thought about being too much of a conformist, perhaps that was it. Or not combing my hair down. That sort of thing might have been one of the causes.

'I can't take being thought of as not good enough, that's what hurts. What is a good drummer? It's just a matter of different styles, not a matter of being good. How can you measure someone being good? When we came back from Liverpool my style was in fashion. When they saw how good and successful we were, drummers in the other groups started copying my powerhouse style.

'I know my mother thinks they were jealous of me, but I don't think it was that. We had a group sound. It wasn't just one person. My technique seemed to suit them for long enough, then it didn't. So that was that. I'll never know the real reasons.

'Of course their public image wasn't exactly real. They looked like angels at one stage, in their collarless suits, like choir boys. I knew they were far from angels. But they had to look like that, to conquer the mums and dads.

'I always watch them being interviewed on TV. John seems much the same. They've matured a lot. They're much shrewder. I can't understand their interest in religion, though. That was the last thing I would have expected.'

He hadn't seen or talked to the Beatles since the day he left them, apart from a fleeting few words with John not long after when he was playing with Lee Curtis's group in the Cavern. John had always been closest to him of the Beatles.

'I might accept help from them. If I sort of met them again and we got on and they said, off the cuff, here you are. But if they offered me X amount, just out of charity, then I'd say no.'

After I had interviewed Pete Best, and all the parents and old friends in Liverpool, I went back to see the Beatles in London and told them bits I had picked up on my travels. They were very interested to hear what had happened, except when the subject of Pete Best came up. They seemed to cut off, as if he had never touched their lives. They showed little reaction when I said he was now slicing bread for £18 a week, though Paul did make a face. John asked a few more questions, but then forgot about it, and they all went back to the song they were recording.

I suppose it reminded them that they had been rather sneaky in the handling of Pete Best's sacking, never telling him to his face, knowing that but for the grace of God, or Brian Epstein, circumstances might have been different and they too could have ended up slicing bread for £18 a week.

Later on, at John's home, I did get John to admit that they could have treated Peter rather better. 'We were cowards,' said John.

I was impressed by Pete for never telling his story. He could quite easily have exposed the reality of life in Hamburg, and their rather scandalous behaviour. By that time, he had nothing to lose. The Beatles might well have done so, as in those years Brian Epstein was still trying to make the most of their lovable image. Eventually, of course, John himself told the truth, or even more than the truth, about dressing room life, and so pre-empted any of Pete's revelations.

Later, Pete did write a book. I hope he made a few bob from it. After all, he *was* a Beatle, at a vital time, as opposed to those temporary secretaries and chauffeurs who have rushed into print, despite knowing them only a few weeks, long after the real Beatle days were over.

Hamburg was very hard – I thought I'd never manage to get clear in my mind what had happened there. The Beatles were totally contradictory in their memories of how many times they went there, which order they played the various clubs, and which events had occurred at which time.

I had very long sessions with each of the Beatles and I realized what an important stage Hamburg had been, how it brought them together as a group, developed their personalities, gave them their own sound, and of course their new look. Nobody had tried to write about this vital period in their life, or been back to try and check what happened. I did not quite appreciate, till I got out there, that they were full of pills for so much of the time, trying to keep themselves awake for twelve-hour playing sessions. No wonder they had such hazy ideas about dates and places and people.

I went out to Hamburg in 1967 and visited all the clubs they played at and talked to as many people as I could find who remembered them. I even got a copy of the record contract they made with Bert Kaempfert Production. This was clearly dated 5.12.1961,

The record contract the Beatles signed with Bert Kaempfert in Hamburg. Clause 7 states: 'Mr John W. Lennon is authorized, as the Group's representative, to receive the payments'.

HGR   /   5.12.1961   TRANSLATION

                                    BERT KAEMPFERT PRODUKTION

          A G R E E M E N T

Between

          1) John W. Lennon   )
)
          2) James Paul McCartney)   as Group called
)
          3) George Harrison   )   The Beatles
)
          4) Peter Best   )

domiciled as follows :-

          1) 251, Manlove Ave., Woolton 25, Liverpool

          2) 20 Forthlin Road, Liverpool 18

          3) 25 Upton Green, Speke, Liverpool 24.

          4) 8, Haymans Green, Liverpool 12

hereinafter referred to as the "Group",
                    and
BERT KAEMPFERT PRODUKTION

          Inselstr. 4, Hamburg

hereinafter referred to as "Produktion",

IT IS AGREED AS FOLLOWS :-

                              Cont'd. ./...

advance payments shall in each instance be accounted for at the following accounting date together with the total amount of royalty. The royalty payable on deliveries ex foreign places of manufacture shall be accounted for and paid out at the same dates and this to the amount of the relevant sums received by "Produktion".

The Group has the right of arranging for the books kept in respect of the accounts to be inspected by a chartered accountant.

Mr. John W. Lennon is authorised, as the Group's representative, to receive the payments. With regard to the recordings which have only been made with one member of the Group, the member concerned is authorized to receive the relevant payment. The Group shall not, without the written consent of "Produktion", further assign its claims hereunder nor delegate any third party to collect the royalty. Any payments and notifications intended for the Group shall be effective, as long as "Produktion" is not informed otherwise, if they are sent to the address specified above.

Clause 8 - Outstanding Recordings.

If the contractually agreed recordings are not made in their entirety during the stipulated period of currency the Group shall even after expiration thereof take part in the outstanding recordings in accordance with the terms of this Agreement.

     a)   If the recordings are outstanding for reasons
           connected with the members of the Group this
           Exclusivity Agreement shall be extended,
           without any obligations arising in respect
           of further recordings, until the date when the
           last outstanding recording has been completed.

     b)   If the recordings are outstanding for reasons
           which are the responsibility of "Produktion"
           this Agreement shall continue to hold good
           in respect of the outstanding recordings
           while the Group's personal exclusivity commit-
           ment shall cease to be operative at the same
           time.

                              Cont'd. ./..

which was useful when I started to get the sequence of events straight. It showed, for a start, that Stu Sutcliffe had left the Beatles by then. (He was the Beatle who died in Hamburg in April 1962.)

In the eight-page contract, it gave them, in clause 4, the opportunity of 'listening to their recordings immediately after completion thereof and of raising any possible objections on the spot'. That was a very fair clause, for an unknown foreign backing group, producing a few quick numbers in 1961. It was stated, in clause 7, that 'Mr John W. Lennon is authorized as the Group's representative to receive the payments'.

Armed with documents such as these, and by looking at the record books of the various clubs, I decided that the Beatles had done three Hamburg tours. (John said two – Paul

Astrid Kirchherr with the Beatles. She was one of their most devoted fans and a close friend from the Hamburg years, and also took some of the most memorable photographs of the group.

thought four. George wasn't sure.) I felt all the time that I might have the order wrong and that people would appear with proof that I had put the Beatles in the wrong place at the wrong time.

I am still prepared to admit errors in some of the Hamburg dates. Does it matter? Well, at the time I wasn't *too* worried, thinking that nobody else apart from me would ever be bothered with such apparently minor details. Since then, of course, scores of researchers have been back to Hamburg, digging over the old embers, including a Dr Tony Waine of Lancaster University, who has made a special study of the Beatles in Hamburg, writing about them for academic magazines, in Britain and Germany. Beatle students never cease to amaze me.

The highlight of my Hamburg trip was meeting Astrid Kirchherr. She helped so much with facts and memories of their Hamburg days and was also the first person I had met who had a clear insight into their different personalities and talents.

Astrid, and her little group of Hamburg art school friends, were the Beatles' earliest intellectual fans. Until then, and for many years later, they were mainly appreciated by shop girls and hairdressers, or taken up briefly by low-grade would-be managers, hoping to make some quick money out of getting them a few bookings. Astrid saw something else in them, during 1960–62, which until then no one else had seen, though it was of course Stuart Sutcliffe who she admired most of all and to whom she got engaged.

I was rather shocked by the life she was now leading in 1967. For a start, her room in the house she still shared with her mother was almost a shrine. Like Miss Haversham in *Great Expectations*, she kept it untouched, as it had been in the last few months of Stu's life. Everything was black, the bed, the soft furnishings, the furniture, and the only light came from some candles. It was very eerie and strange, though she herself was calm and controlled, able to talk about Stu and the Beatles without pathos or melodrama.

In 1963, when Beatlemania first began, she gave some interviews to the German press and others. 'I was so happy they were doing well that I wanted to help them. I did my best to see the newspapers got the right facts. The papers at first were full of them being four scruffy blokes who lived in a dirty attic in Liverpool. I wanted them to know how intelligent and talented they were. It never came out the way I told them. Over and over again in all the interviews there were the same questions; did you really invent the Beatle hairstyle?'

Now, she'd stopped giving any interviews. She'd also refused offers to do her life story, although the German magazines have been asking her for years. She'd also turned down a lot of money for a tape recording she has, which Stu gave her, of Stu and John and the others playing in the Art School in Liverpool. (Done on the tape recorder that John persuaded the college to buy, for his own personal use.)

'One record company offered me 30,000 marks for it and I said no. Then they said 50,000. I said no, not for 100,000 or any money. They wanted to put the name Beatles on it and make a lot of money. It wouldn't have done them any good. They were having a laugh, playing around.'

She said she had never made a penny from all the Beatle photographs she took, even the one of the five of them taken in the Hamburg railway station, which went round the world. She gave that and others to them, long before they were famous. In turn, while they were still un-famous, the Beatles gave them to someone who gave them to an agency. Not only did her photographs make a lot of money for others, she set a style in taking their photographs – half in the shadows – which was copied by other photographers and other groups.

'The trouble is I never kept the negatives, so I can't really prove they were mine. Oh, I did get some money once from Brian, for a pile I had given to the boys. He paid me £30.'

She did, of course, get many commissions, on the strength of having taken the Beatle photographs. One famous German magazine commissioned her to take the boys, when they were refusing everyone else, if she could also take along one of their photographers, just to help. 'John said I should agree. I might as well make some money out of it for a change. This other photographer took some nasty pictures of them, when he shouldn't have done. They used all his.'

In 1967, when I met her, she was still in contact with the Beatles and John had come to see her when he was in Germany filming *How I Won the War.*

'John is an original. New ideas just come to him. Paul has great originality, but he's also an arranger. He can get things done, which John can't, or can't be bothered trying.

'They do need, and they don't need, each other. Either is true. Paul is as talented a composer as John. They would easily have done well on their own.

'The most amazing thing about them is that by coming together they haven't become the same, they haven't been influenced by each other. They're each still different, each is still himself. Paul still does sweet music, like "Michelle", that sort of melody. John writes bumpy music. Working so long together hasn't rubbed out the differences, which I think is amazing.

'Now and again at first I did used to wonder if they really cared about people's feelings and people's friendship. They would say awful things in front of people – "I wish that Kraut would go away", that sort of thing. They can still be cruel to people they don't like, tell them to go away, we don't like you. But that isn't too bad. It's worse to pretend you do like someone.

'After Stu died, they were so kind and lovely. I knew then they weren't cruel. It showed me they did know when they went too far and knew when to stop.'

Although Astrid gave so much to the Beatles, which they all acknowledged, in some ways they had wrecked her life. The death of Stu was still obviously very near to her in 1967, though when I met her she had recently got married to another Liverpool exile. The disillusionment with the German press had led her, at the time, to giving up her own career as a photographer.

She was working at the time in a bar, and that evening, after we had talked all day, she took me to it. Hamburg is full of strange clubs and bars, but this was the first lesbian bar I had been into. She got me in, as a friend, and it seemed to be full of prostitutes dancing together, before going off for their evening's work. Astrid was serving behind the bar and was also on call to dance with customers, if required. For this, working all night long, she was getting £40 a week. Yet she was sitting on a small fortune with all her Beatles memorabilia.

I told Paul all about her when I got back to London and it brought back memories of the good times they had in Hamburg. Paul admitted, looking back, that they were rotten to Stu. He had perhaps been jealous of John's admiration for Stu and sometimes felt a little bit excluded.

'I was pretty nasty to him on the last day. We were leaving Hamburg, and he was staying behind with Astrid. I caught his eye on stage, as he was playing with us for the last time. He was crying. It was one of those feelings, when you're suddenly very close to someone.'

It took me a long time to realize that Brian Epstein was homosexual. When I did, I thought at first it didn't matter, either way, but I slowly recognized it was a vital part of his character and of his relationship with the Beatles.

Brian Epstein loved them. When at last I spent some time with him, and managed to get him to sit down and think back to the early days, it was hard to stop him. He gave me copies of his old memos to them, which he had typed himself, telling them how to behave on stage and not to smoke or chew. He also gave me his old typewritten list of their early local engagements, which I had no room for in the book, though they might be of interest to Beatle experts. Whole books have subsequently been written on what the Beatles did each day during their Beatlemania years.

Even more interesting is the note, monogrammed BE, that he sent to George Martin before their first recording session on 6 June 1962, suggesting likely songs they might do. Now I look at that list again, there are some compositions I have never heard of, such as 'Pinwheel Twist'. I wonder what happened to that one?

He also dug out for me the very first press hand-out about the Beatles and the office memos he sent to his staff when NEMS, his company, opened its first office in London. It's full of Brian telling them how to behave and to be courteous to everyone. Very typical.

I collected as many documents as I could during all my interviews, as well as hand-outs and fan club bulletins, both in Britain and in the USA. Brian himself had spare copies of many of them and gave them to me.

He was terribly careful and organized in those early days. It was only as I got to know him better, during 1967, that I learned what a mess his life was now in. He was constantly in the depths of depression, living on pills, having tantrums with his staff and closest friends, over petty things, then collapsing in tears as he apologized to them. He had twice tried to commit suicide, though this had been kept quiet at the time.

In his sexual life, he was not simply a homosexual, but a masochist, deliberately picking up non-homosexual boys, often sailors, bringing them back to the house, treating them, giving them drinks and drugs. It usually ended with him being beaten up and his possessions stolen, very often Beatle material. Then he would be blackmailed, and end up in further depressions.

I spent one weekend with him at his country home in Kingsley Hill, Sussex. On Saturday evening, we had a very enjoyable dinner, at which we were joined by a well-known pop music personality of the time. (Even better known today, but I better not name him.) After the meal, they decided they would like some boys to amuse them, but it was by this time eleven o'clock, and a Saturday evening.

Brian got out a sort of credit card, which was his membership to some homosexual call-boy organization, and dialled a certain number, giving his name and number. There was a lot of discussion on the phone, with the person at the other end saying it was far too late, everyone was booked up, the best boys had gone. When Brian mentioned he was in Sussex, not London, the voice said that was it, no chance. Brian said he would pay for taxis, and

Brian's note for the Beatles, dated June 1962, instructing them that white shirts are essential, and not to be late, as they could get some future dates...

pay double the rates, just send down whatever could be found, then he hung up.

I sat up with them, drinking, until midnight, but then I went to bed. I think it was four in the morning before anyone arrived from London. Next morning, I had breakfast on my own, and left for home about midday. The others were still in bed.

Brian agreed I could mention his homosexuality in the book, though, naturally, I was not going to go into any of the details.

The Beatles did not know the full story of this side of his life either. By the time I got to know him, he had become less of an influence on their lives anyway. Paul was busy taking over the organizational reins, setting up Apple, taking control of things like the cover for *Sergeant Pepper*.

They knew he was homosexual, but that was all. John was the only one I discussed it with, as he was quite interested, but Paul I think was upset by it. Brian realized this and was always especially concerned about pleasing Paul, giving him the biggest presents. Brian's staff told me that he worried most about keeping in with Paul and always answered his calls first.

John told me he had had a one-night stand with Brian, on a holiday with him in Spain, when Brian had invited him out, a few days after the birth of Julian in 1963, leaving Cyn alone. I mentioned this brief holiday in the book, but not what John had alleged had taken place. Partly, I didn't really believe it, though John was daft enough to try almost anything once. John was certainly not homosexual, and this boast, or lie, would have given the wrong impression. It was also not fair on Cynthia, his then wife.

But by 1967, even John did not seem to have much connection with Brian. When I began to realize the extent of Brian's tragic private life, I assumed it was partly the Beatles' fault, edging him out of their lives, discarding him, leaving him without much purpose in life, perhaps helping to cause his terrible depressions. I probably hinted as much in the book. Now, with hindsight, I think the fault was in Brian. I underplayed the fact that he had been discharged from the army on medical and emotional grounds, after being referred to a psychiatrist. He had presented it to me rather as a joke, almost as if he had done it to get out of the army, which was how I reported it (see Chapter 15). It seems clear to me now that he should have had proper psychiatric help from a very early stage. In Liverpool, I did hear stories of certain incidents, but I could never get details.

It could be argued that the Beatles *saved* him from himself, prolonging his life, at least for those six years or so in which he threw himself into their career, using up all his energies and talents and emotions for their good. By 1967, he was back on his own again, and finding himself very difficult to live with.

The official report of his death in September 1967 said it was an accidental overdose, which I believe, though others have tried to prove since it was suicide, and some irresponsible writers have even hinted at murder, as there are still some missing facts about the days before his death. Emotionally, it was suicide, even though I do not think he meant to do it at that time in that way. But I feel it would have happened, sooner rather than later.

I was with the Beatles in Bangor, North Wales, when they heard about Brian's death. The whole weekend had been rather bizarre. Michael McCartney, Paul's brother, had rung me the night before to tell me that they planned to go to somewhere in Wales to meet someone called the Maharishi. It had all begun with George, and his interest in Indian things, and he had persuaded the others to join him. Michael told me to be on the platform at Euston at a certain time for the Bangor train. It was bound to be a happening. Remember Happenings? Very 1960s. I realized it would be the first time they had all gone anywhere as a group, since their touring days. So that at least would be interesting to observe.

I travelled with them in their carriage, on Friday, 25 August 1967 – the four Beatles, plus Mick Jagger, Marianne Faithfull, all in their flower-power clothes. It was very revealing to see Jagger and Lennon together. They seemed wary of each other, careful and respectful, with very little contact.

I knew, from having discussed it previously with John, that John felt jealous of Jagger. Certainly not of his music, or his success, or his fame, but of the fact that Jagger always had a rebel image, right from the beginning, which John felt he should have had as well. I argued that it was the Beatles, breaking so many rules, that allowed the Stones to come along later and build on what the Beatles had done. John at that stage still resented the cleaning up operation Brian had performed on them, ashamed in a way that he had gone along with it, which was why later, I suppose, he overcompensated by dishing out the dirt about himself, making himself worse, if anything, than he had been.

On the train, there was very little conversation between them all, though after they had been ushered into the Maharishi's compartment, further along the train, they all laughed and joked about what he had said to each of them, but at the same time obviously taking it very seriously.

The trip had been meant to be secret, and was arranged at the last moment, but the news leaked out and at various stations along the line crowds of fans gathered. It was almost like Beatlemania days again. Fans rushed to the train when we stopped and shoved autograph books through the windows and doors; quite a killing for the fans, getting such a batch of heroes, all in the same spot at the same time. Most of them dutifully signed, except John, who soon said he was fed up. So now and again I signed his name in their little books, if they looked particularly disappointed. I do hope Sotheby's have found a way of checking the real signatures from the false.

That evening, in Bangor, we all went into the town for something to eat. It was late at night, in a very small provincial town, and we could find only a Chinese restaurant open.

When the bill finally came, I realized I had not enough money, nor had anyone else. The Beatles never carried money, just like the Royal Family, and this time they were without their normal aides and assistants who carried the purse for them.

The Chinese waiter was becoming very upset, thinking we were all going to walk out without paying, when George suddenly put his bare foot on the table. He had taken off his sandals and was examining the sole of the shoes. There was a slit at the front and from it he withdrew £20, more than enough to settle the bill. He had put the money there for such emergencies, months if not years previously, and forgotten about it until that evening.

The news of Brian's death came through on the Sunday, after they had a long session with the Maharishi. They appeared at the time to be rather callous in their reaction, which hurt Brian's family, but it was partly the result of being with the Maharishi, who told them that death meant very little. It was typical of their reaction to such things. Years ago, Paul had once made a silly joke about his mother's death, out of fear rather than cruelty. John had appeared to be uncaring after his own mother had been killed.

The death of Brian Epstein was a watershed, the end of an era, the final chapter of those Beatlemania years, although we did not realize at the time how near it was to the end of the Beatles as an active group. Everyone wondered, though, what the next era would bring. I remember George Martin telling me that he thought they would not manage in the future without some sort of organizer, some figure to lean on. They would always need some sort of help.

As for interviewing the Beatles themselves, I described in great detail in Part Three of the book (see chapters 28–34) what exactly they were doing and thinking in 1967, so there is not much need to add to that. I knew at the time that the minute I wrote anything down it was out of date. They moved on so quickly, changing their minds, changing their clothes, their interests, always into something new.

John was the hardest to talk to. I spent hours at his home in Weybridge in silence, swimming round his pool with him, eating a meal, sitting in his little living room, often without a sound, except for the rotten television set flickering away in the corner. In the end, if conversation seemed impossible, I would pack up and come again another day, when I hoped he would be more forthcoming. With Cyn, he could go on like that for weeks. He seemed to be in a permanent state of mental abstraction. I don't think it was the effect of drugs, though he was smoking a lot, or even Maharishi's meditations. For long spells, he just chose to cut off. Looking back, he was waiting for Yoko to come along, and spark him into life again.

John could still be the strongest personality in the group, if he wanted to, though not as dominant as in the past. He let Paul take control of most things and allowed him to steer the Beatles into new projects, such as *Magical Mystery Tour*, or George to steer them into Indian mysticism.

Even at the private party to celebrate *Magical Mystery Tour*, which was a very jolly affair, with their friends and relations and personal staff, John seemed so subdued. We all came in fancy clothes. I went as a Boy Scout, and my wife as a Girl Guide, which was a bit pathetic and showed little imagination. John looked magnificent as a greasy Rocker, just as he had been, ten years previously. He talked for a while to my wife about books, then sat in a daze.

At his home, and in his head, he had so many half songs, uncompleted bits of verse, which he would play with, before quickly tiring of them. For months I seem to remember he was mucking around with 'Across the Universe', or variations on it. He would play or sing me the same old bits every few weeks, having failed to make any progress with it since I'd last seen him.

Paul was the easiest to talk to. He had such energy and such keenness and, unlike John, enjoyed being liked, at least most of the time. I don't see this as a criticism. John himself could be very cruel about Paul's puppy dog eagerness to please. The irony was, and still is, that John's awfulness to people, his rudeness and cruelty, made people like him more, whereas Paul's genuine niceness made many people suspicious, accusing him of being calculating. Paul does look ahead, seeing what might happen, working out the effect of certain actions, but he often ends up tying himself in knots, not necessarily getting what he thought he wanted. I think there is some insecurity in Paul's nature, which makes him try so hard, work so hard. It also means he can be easily hurt by criticism, which was something that just washed over John.

George, at the time I was doing the book, was an obsessive, which could make it very hard to talk to him. He hated, even then, the Beatle days, and wanted to forget them completely and move on. They all felt that, but George felt it most of all. His development, during those years as a Beatle, was by far the most dramatic. It's easy to forget just how young he was, a callow 17-year-old, when he joined them. For so many years, most people tended to dismiss him as a mere child. John was so dominant and, at that stage in their career, being three years older, it made an enormous difference and he completely over-shadowed George. Presumably John and Paul did see hidden things in George, right from the beginning, apart from his excellent guitar playing. They were proud of him, in a big brotherly way, for being so good on the guitar, and by 1967 their pride had turned to admiration, not just for the excellent songs he had now composed, but for being so knowledgeable about Indian music and culture, going to such trouble to teach himself the sitar. For the first time in his life, he had become a leader, doing it by example, not in any bossy, domineering way.

Going to see Ringo was rather strange. He prowled around his own domain, restless and worried-looking. At home, he was very much an Andy Capp figure, as was John, whereas Paul had picked up more middle-class habits thanks to his friendship with Jane Asher.

I think Ringo worried about the future. The touring days were over and he knew that in the studio, especially with all the new synthesizer equipment then coming in, his drumming was not really as vital as it used to be. Many times Paul would take over the drums in the recording studio, to explain what was wanted. While George and John were fed up with being Beatles, and Paul wanted it to go on a bit longer because he could see there were things they had still not done, Ringo's future seemed blank. Apart from a bit of acting, he couldn't see what else there was for him to do.

Neil Aspinall and Mal Evans, their two road managers from the early days, and still then their constant companions and aides, were always being asked which Beatle they liked best. It was an impossible, but natural question. There were so many facets to each of them. Paul and Ringo, as far as the general public were concerned, were the 'nicest', yet I often met people who worked with them closely who moaned about them all the time. Unlike

John and George, they could turn nasty in private, suddenly deciding they were being taken advantage of, by some assistant or tradesman, especially over money matters. When it came to money, John and George hardly seemed to care.

John was the most original, so I always thought, but Paul was the most naturally gifted. Music flows through him all the time, and he is also gifted with the aptitudes to make the most of his talents. George was a combination, both original and talented, yet in ways different from the other two. Ringo had no pretence, and was totally without intellectual aspirations, unlike the other three, nor did he have any illusions about his work or worth. He had a common sense approach to everything, and could be very quick-witted and sharp.

I looked forward equally to my conversations with each of them, but perhaps enjoyed Paul's and John's company most. They were also interested in my world, life at large, discussing topics of the day, that's if it wasn't one of John's days for not talking to anyone. They were both, surprisingly, starved of good chat, which is why, I suppose, some strange people with odd ideas did come into their life from time to time.

Their lives in the last ten years had been so extraordinary that I was interested in all their observations, however naive. They had so little idea of how the real world worked, having been sealed off from reality for so long. John, for example, could not use the telephone. People had made his calls for so long that he had forgotten how to do it.

They were like specimens, people from another planet, who saw things differently from the rest of us, uneducated, unformed minds, yet they had seen things and experienced events and emotions the rest of us can only imagine. They had no conceit, which I found surprising, neither about their music nor their fame. They honestly believed that everyone, if they put their mind to it, could achieve what they wanted to in life. They had done it, so they did not see why others could not. The whole philosophy of Apple, idiotic and crazy though it was, was based on helping others to help themselves. They believed that education and training of any sort was a waste of time. They had broken all the rules, when people had told them they would never do it, coming from Liverpool, singing like that, so they believed others could do the same.

They were all seeking something, especially John and George, without knowing what it was, feeling a certain vacuum in their lives, an emptiness after all those hectic Beatle years. Every superstar since has felt much the same, and probably every pools winner or bingo millionaire or lottery winner, at least those with the slightest element of sensibility.

I too used to be asked which Beatle I liked most. And I used to reply by saying my favourite Beatle was the one I was last with. That was how Neil and Mal always used to reply, which was why I wanted to carry on observing them for ever, rather than getting on with the more mundane task of putting it all down on paper.

By the beginning of 1968, I was still interviewing away and had amassed about 150,000 words of notes. That book about British universities had almost gone from my mind. I thought about changing the title yet again, to the *Class of '68*, then decided now to scrap the whole thing. There had been student revolutions and demonstrations, and the whole nature of university life had changed.

I was concentrating completely on the Beatles, though I was putting off actually starting to write the book. *Sergeant Pepper* had come out, to enormous acclaim, and that really changed the image of the Beatles in the eyes of those people who still tended to regard them as a passing fancy. Things were still changing and I didn't want to miss any new stages, yet I knew I must soon call a halt and knock it all into shape. Every Beatle record, from 1963 to 1969, contained something new and different. Would I miss a dramatic new musical development by stopping now?

The most enjoyable part of doing the whole book was being present at Abbey Road. John's doziness at home left him when he came into the studio. Working with Paul seemed to make him more alive. If he couldn't finish a song, then Paul would help him out. They remained themselves, producing their own sort of music, but each other's presence seemed to bring out the best in each of them. And if they did get completely stuck, ending up with two bits of tunes that did not appear to gel, as in 'A Day in the Life', then George Martin was there to solve the problem of melding them together.

Outside, inside: the Beatles in June 1967, holding up the photograph from the inside of their *Sergeant Pepper* album, possibly the greatest album cover, ever.

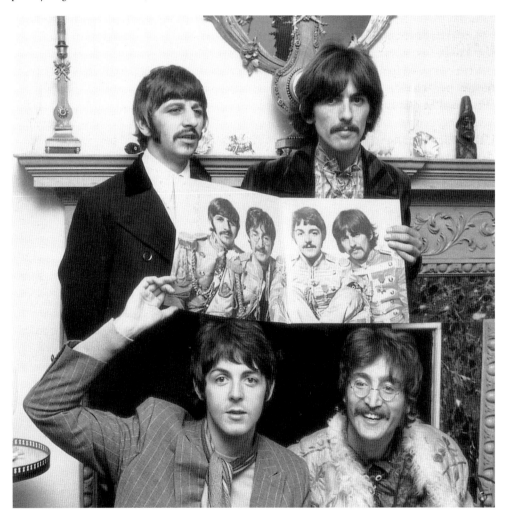

They usually assembled at Paul's house in Cavendish Avenue, St John's Wood, in the afternoon, going up to the top floor where John and Paul would try out any new little ideas they had had on their own. It was all fairly informal, with close friends and relations coming in, hanging about, and they would all break for fried eggs and toast and tea. By the time they got into the studio in the evening, just round the corner in Abbey Road, and George and Ringo had then turned up, it would become more serious. Outsiders would not be allowed in the studio when they were working.

John and Paul would write out on the backs of envelopes or scraps of paper the latest words or versions of the songs they were working on, then give them to Ringo on the drums, so he would know what was happening. Bits would be altered as they went along, and new parts added.

At the end of the sessions, in the small hours of the mornings, I would often pick up scraps lying around, asking first if I could have them, as they obviously didn't want them any more. They always said yes. A great deal of stuff was simply chucked out, or left for the cleaners to get rid of. They themselves never kept any memorabilia or cuttings or scraps about themselves. For years, life had moved on so quickly, that they had no interest in collecting or keeping that sort of clutter.

I know that Paul and George later regretted this and made an attempt to collect their own past, once they started getting into their middle age. I gave George back the original of 'Blue Jay Way', written on the back of someone else's letter when he was in California. He thought it had been lost for ever. And I gave Paul his master plan for *Magical Mystery Tour*, which he had written out for me in 1968 for the purpose of this book, to explain what his idea had been, but which I never had space for in the end. My own collection, bits they had given me as presents, was severely depleted some years ago when our house was burgled and I lost my Beatle records, copies they had personally signed to me. I'm sure their value was not realized. I often wonder where they are now, which is why I watch the Sotheby's sales so carefully. I only wish now I had collected more of their songs from the floor of Abbey Road.

I also wish I had kept better notes, especially during *Sergeant Pepper*. When I was interviewing them alone, in their homes, I would sit with a note book and write down everything, there and then. But in the studios, or when they were all together, or when we were having meals, I tried to be more of a fly on the wall, quietly observing, hoping I would be accepted as someone who just happened always to be around, rather than a writer, prying on them. Afterwards, I would rush straight home (which was, luckily, only ten minutes from Abbey Road) and quickly type out in note form everything that had happened that evening. I still have piles of these notes and, looking at them now, all badly typed and misspelled, there are bits I can't understand.

Memories do play tricks. I was lunching with Neil Aspinall one day (still the boss of Apple) and reminiscing about the night of the *Sergeant Pepper* photo session. I remembered the costumes arriving at Paul's house, as I still had a clear picture of the Beatles trying them on. Neil said no, the costumes were delivered direct to the photographer's in Flood Street. I rushed to my notes, but they didn't include this minor piece of information.

The discussions about the Pepper cover had gone on for weeks. George wanted lots of the figures to be gurus. Paul wanted arty people like Stockhausen. John wanted rebels and baddies, such as Hitler, but, as my notes show, he was talked out of Hitler at the last moment. Hitler's cardboard cut-out figure stood to attention during the whole of the photographic session.

I had suggested to them that their list of heroes should include some footballers. Most boys, especially those coming from Liverpool, are aware of footballing stars. I had always been slightly disappointed that none of the Beatles was interested in sport at all, least of all football. In the end, John stuck in Albert Stubbins, a folk name from his childhood in Liverpool, but I think simply because he thought the name was funny, rather than for his footballing prowess.

I do remember that we left Paul's house in a rush, and he told me to collect up any ornaments lying around his house, just to fill up the tableau. That ornament in the foreground of the *Sergeant Pepper* cover picture, a sort of statuette of what looks like a bullet on a little plinth, was placed there by me, to fill up the gap. I've told my children this, several times, but they are not at all interested.

Who thought of *Sergeant Pepper*? I had always assumed the basic idea came from Paul, as he was the first of them I heard talking about it, though I didn't go into this in the book. I should have paid more attention, as it was a milestone for them, the pinnacle of their recording career. It was also a minor historic moment in popular music, as it has become known as the first 'concept album'. Artistically, it was an enormous achievement, thanks partly to the creative work of Peter Blake. Whole studies have been produced since on what was in that famous cover and what it all meant.

Mal used to say that the word 'Sergeant Pepper' came from him, his overheard mistake for 'Salt and Pepper'. Neil tells me he was the first to suggest to Paul that the whole album should be in the form of Sergeant Pepper's actual show, and that Paul jumped at the idea. Who can tell now? It's like the origin of the name Beatles. George thought it came from Marlon Brando's film, *The Wild One*. There is a group of motorcyclists in the film, all in black leather, called the Beetles, though they are only referred to as such in passing. Stu Sutcliffe saw this film, heard the remark, and came back and suggested it to John as the new name for their group. John said yeh, but we'll spell it Beatles, as we're a beat group. Well, that's one theory. No doubt, in the years to come, there will be new suggestions.

In my book, I was trying to keep off the theories. I still like to think it was all true, though there were things I could not tell at the time. It was simply the truth about what had happened to them up to that time, based on their own memories, and those closest to them, as well as my own investigations and observations.

By early 1968, I eventually decided it was time to stop talking, quit researching, and settle down and get all the material into some sort of shape. I had so much that I did not really know where to begin, or what was important and what would turn out to be utterly trivial.

The first version came to two volumes, then I hacked it down by about 50 per cent to get it to a reasonable size, leaving out lots of interesting material, photographs and documents. My next job, as I had lumbered myself with the title of 'authorized' biographer, was to get agreement from all the main characters in the story. That was when my problems really began.

Firstly, I had to let the Beatles read what I had written. I had carefully worded the contract with them so that they could change any 'factual' mistakes. This always causes great trouble for any writer working with the co-operation of living people. You can never tell which bits might upset people. Usually, it is something minor, a remark in passing which hurts for some reason, not the bits you most expect to have problems with. At first, they don't usually tell you what has caused offence, going on generally about the 'tone' not being right, or it being not as 'deep' as they had expected. Then when you get out of them precisely what they don't like, it is usually fairly easy to put right.

I had naturally not given full details of what precisely had happened in the dressing rooms on tours, about the girls queuing up, begging for their favours. I think any reader over the age of 15, even in 1968, must have been well aware of what really happened, but no one spelled it out in those days. Groupies are a cliché today, and we know all about their excesses. The Beatles were no different from any other group. They just had more to pick from. It was the job of the road managers to say you, you and you, and you five minutes later. In 1968, three of the four Beatles were happily married, as far as the outside world was aware, and the other had a regular girlfriend. The wives, naturally, did not want such things mentioned, nor did the Beatles.

However, I had included quite a few references to drugs, including them taking LSD, which was rather daring, for 1968, though I always referred to it in the past, sometimes saying that of course they did not take pot *now*, which was a lie, though I'm sure I made the truth fairly obvious.

It took me quite some time to get any reaction, as they all found reading books rather hard. Then to my delight each in turn said they had no complaints, no objections, and they agreed to everything going in. I think Paul had some minor factual mistakes, people's names I had spelled wrongly, though I now can't remember what they were.

George was the only one who rang me with any serious comments. He wanted *more* about the Indian stuff and thought I had not taken him seriously enough, or his philosophies, and wanted some bits explained better. I did what he asked, although trying not to add to the length of the book.

I was very relieved by their reactions, and my agent started getting copies made for America, then suddenly I got a letter from John. He had had second thoughts on some bits. He sent me a letter by hand in which he asked me to take out some of his remarks about the man his mother Julia later married, a Welsh man, by whom she had two daughters, Jackie and Julia, John's stepsisters. He was worried about 'the nasty-minded world' they might be faced with in the future.

Most of all, he asked me to make sure Mimi read the book. She was worried SICK, so he said. That was what really bothered me. I could easily have coped with John's second thoughts, all of them minor and I suspected someone had pointed them out to him. I didn't want to have to go round all the families or that could take years.

I sent it to Mimi and she had hysterics. The manuscript came back with almost every paragraph concerning John's childhood heavily crossed out or amended. In the margins she had written beside John's own quotes such things as 'Rubbish', 'Never!'

She denied so many of John's own memories of his childhood, especially if they contradicted her memories of the same people or events. She was against his use of bad

Dear Hunter,

I sorry for a last minute change — but I'd like the bit about the 'Welshman' and my mother left out. I left it this late to see if it still bugged me — but the more I think of the nasty minded world poor Jackie and Julia are faced with (I don't know them well enough to know how they'd take it as well) made me decide to leave it out — I hope you don't mind. Dad's heard from Margaret something about her — I don't remember anything odd about her — maybe its because she don't care out as much a part of the household as she reserves — anyway she'd like to see the bits on her — so do yer duty Hunt lad.

love — John.

I just rang Mimi
— she's worried

Sick — she MUST

See the book before publication
don't let me down.

John's letter to me, 1968, asking me to make changes to the manuscript of the book. Mimi, he wrote, is worried SICK.

language, as she maintained John had never sworn when he was little, and didn't want stories about him stealing.

Some of her comments, in the margins, were quite witty. I had quoted John as saying that he had to practise his guitar behind Mimi's back at home and that she made him stand in the glass porch to play. Above this line Mimi had written 'This wicked woman'. Another time, she added a story about Julia and the new husband, and how they really regarded John, writing it out in the margin, then asking me not to print it, as John had never been told.

She also added some useful comments about the day that John first met Paul, at the Woolton Parish Fête, when John had dressed up as a real Teddy Boy for the first time.

'It was the first time I saw him with others playing,' so Mimi wrote. 'It was a bombshell and a shock. Had no idea he would be there. It was forced home to me that day that I had been fighting a losing battle. Even then I would not give in. What a waste of my life and, more important, my health.'

I could understand the desire to protect Julia's two daughters, as they were only teenagers in 1968, and John had been rather bitchy about their father, so I agreed to all that. It was her determination to censor John's account of himself that seemed very unfair.

Most memories of childhood are suspect. It's what different people choose to remember that is interesting. Who had the better memory anyway, Mimi or John? John, by this time, was fed up with the whole subject and insisted I kept her happy at all cost, so I travelled to Bournemouth and went through the offending paragraphs line by line. A lot of the bad language was removed and some wilder parts of his stories, and she was eventually pacified.

You will notice in the book that Chapter 1 ends rather limply and abruptly with the phrase 'John was as happy as the day was long'. This was at Mimi's insistence. I gave in, a compromise, in order to keep in most of John's other stories. She thought this would soften them. That was the truth about John's childhood, as she saw it. I was relatively happy, as the other truths were still there as well, so readers could decide for themselves.

The book, when it was published, was greeted as a 'candid' biography by all the critics, on both sides of the Atlantic, and in Europe and Japan, and was even described as 'the frankest authorized biography ever written'. I'll spare you the details. It was, of course, a long time ago and lots of things have happened since then. I was upset, several years later, when John, in an interview, said that my book had been 'bullshit'. This was at the time when he had got into his head that the whole Beatle image was a whitewash. As far as my book was concerned, as you can now see in his letter, it was at John's insistence that I had to do some whitewashing on his behalf.

I then had a lot of trouble with some of their side-kicks at Apple, who took it upon themselves to try to alter things elsewhere in the book, on subjects such as drugs. The Beatles by this time had gone off to India, having read and approved the book. Their assistants, left behind in charge of the office, wanted several changes.

I managed, in the main, to fight them off, though I had many agonizing weeks, getting all the necessary approvals, trying to keep track of all the copies, and then the corrected copies, which were flying around. The Beatles themselves, having read their own individual copy, left it lying around at home, or at Abbey Road, or in the Apple office, so everyone was dying to find out if they figured in the book. John, in that letter asking me to make changes, also mentions that 'Dot's heard from Margaret something about her'. Dot was John's housekeeper at the time, and was only mentioned once. As for Margaret, I can't even remember who she was.

I would not like to go through all those weeks again, but the worst was to come. I had forgotten that Brian Epstein had been the one responsible for the main contract, on their behalf. As he was now dead, the Epstein family demanded to see the manuscript. Legally, his mother had inherited his estate. I was therefore technically beholden to Mrs Queenie Epstein, an old lady, who knew nothing about the pop world, and, even worse, nothing about Brian's secret life, for the final clearance on the book.

You can imagine what she thought when she saw references to Brian being homosexual. She denied it. As far as she was concerned, it wasn't true. I was therefore rather stuck, as I needed her agreement. We had by this time sold the American and several other rights, and they naturally wanted to see the legal clearances.

Clive Epstein, Brian's brother, was helpful, though of course he wanted to keep his mother happy. As her beloved son had died only recently, it was thought unseemly to go into all the sordid details of his last couple of years. I hadn't really written much about that and in the end I was persuaded to steer completely clear of his sex life. I thought I did manage to make it fairly clear at the end of Chapter 15, where I said he had only one girlfriend in his life – and then continued to talk about his unhappy love affairs. I also described him as a 'gay bachelor'. The word was not in such common use in England in those days, but it was enough to let many people know the truth.

Did it matter, Brian's homosexuality? I did regret having to disguise it, as he himself had given me permission to mention it and it has been publicly stated since. With most people, their sex life is not relevant, either way, to their work, although these days many people in public life, at least in the arts and show business, make no effort to hide what sort of people they are. With Brian, I think it did matter and it was a vital clue to his personality, to his death, and also to the birth of his interest in the Beatles.

One of the strangest episodes in all the Beatle sagas is how such a person as Brian Epstein came to be interested in them in the first place. What attracted a public-school, well brought-up, middle-class Jewish boy, a rising businessman who loved Sibelius and had shown not the slightest personal interest in any sort of pop culture? What made him go along to see four scruffy, working-class yobbos in a smelly underground coffee bar? He fancied them. That was one explanation, though I was never able to spell it out. Most of all, he fancied John, jumping around in his leather gear and big cowboy boots. (The gossip, years later, was that he fancied Paul, as Paul was always supposed to be the prettiest Beatle, which couldn't have been further from the truth. He liked them butch and aggressive, even when they didn't like him – often *because* they didn't like him sexually.)

Brian Epstein gave the Beatles to the world when others more worldly had already passed them by. They created themselves, their music and their performances, but in the wrong hands – nasty, grasping, short-term hands – their national launching would have been very different. According to popular theory, Brian was simply a very smart Jewish businessman. He'd seen the money in them. In truth, he wasn't a great businessman, as was shown later when many of his deals had to be rearranged. He wasn't materialistic. Brian Epstein loved the Beatles, in every sense of the word. That's all there was to it.

I had one good bit of luck, just as the book was going to press. I suddenly made contact with Freddie Lennon. He first reappeared in about 1964, when the news about John being a Beatle was pointed out to him by a washer-up in a hotel where he was working. As everyone in the Lennon family then refused to see or help him, he disappeared again, after having given a few interviews to various magazines.

John was quite amused by his reappearance, especially when he produced a record, though he knew that Mimi and the rest of the family would never forgive him, if he helped Freddie in any way. Freddie, after all, had deserted his wife and child.

In early 1968, I finally tracked Freddie down to a hotel near Hampton Court, not very far from John's home in Weybridge, where he was working as a dish washer.

'I just live my own little life. Happy go lucky, that's me. I like moving on. I don't like the press finding out where I am, you know.'

He was still very upset that a couple of years earlier he arrived, unannounced, at John's house and the door was slammed in his face. I met him several times, and rather warmed to him, and got him to take me through his early life, which made the basis for the first part of Chapter 1 in the book.

I asked him why he had deserted John and his wife. Freddie himself didn't seem to know. He said he had been very unhappy to lose John, oh yes, it really upset him, especially after the time he spent with him at Blackpool.

'That evening, after John was taken away,' so Freddie told me, 'I was singing at the Cherry Tree pub in Blackpool. I sang the Al Jolson song "Little Pal". I sang the words "Little John", with tears in my eyes.'

I never knew whether to believe half the things Freddie told me, so I didn't put everything in. I had of course no means of checking his own account of his early life, although I think in the book his exaggerations about his own brilliance are pretty clear, especially when he boasted about being 'their best waiter', and Julia's mother loving 'the bones of his body'. Or was this all true?

I told John the stories Freddie had come out with, and how he was living a hand to mouth existence once again, going from hotel to hotel, usually in the kitchen, always willing to give any bar audience a few songs, in the hope of enough money to buy a drink.

Some of his stories sparked off other memories in John's mind, bringing back vague recollections of things Julia had told him about her early married days to Freddie. 'I think they did have some good times together,' said John. 'I don't really hate him now, the way I used to. It was probably Julia's fault as much as his that they parted.

'If it hadn't been for the Beatles, I would probably have ended up like Freddie.'

I remember laughing at this at the time, though there is some truth in it. It is hard to imagine John fitting in with a proper job, or office hierarchy, or even managing to make a living as an artist or designer, not of course that he had passed any of his Art College exams. He would have become bored far too quickly. So he might well have ended up as a bum.

One night, John rang me and asked for Freddie's home number. All I could give him was the hotel, as Fred was sleeping on somebody's floor and didn't have a phone. John didn't want to ring the hotel, so I contacted it, and then went to see Freddie again. I told him John would now like to see him, but it had to be kept a complete secret. If it got out to the press, and worst of all, if Mimi heard, that would be it.

A meeting was fixed up between them and they got on very well. John found Freddie hilarious, which encouraged Freddie to tell even wilder stories about his life and hard times. John started giving Freddie money, shoving wads of it in his hand, and when he discovered he had nowhere to live, he said that Freddie could move in with him for a while.

In the end, John set him up with a flat of his own. Freddie, now he was in the money again, was delighted, and moved into this flat with a 19-year-old girlfriend, who he was going to marry, so he told me. Fred died in 1977, but by that time he had got married to the 19-year-old and they had had a son together.

As a thank-you for bringing them together, Freddie sent me a nice letter and a present of an early photograph of himself (see above). I had been desperate for a photograph of a young Freddie to use in the book, but it arrived too late.

It shows him in a prisoner's uniform, on board ship, holding up his number. Freddie must have been about 40 at the time, the same age as John was when he died. The resemblance is striking.

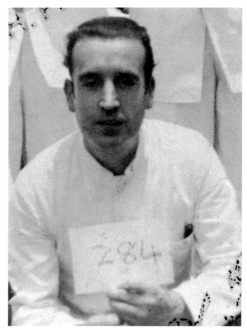

Fred Lennon, holding up his number as a prisoner aboard a liberty ship. He was about 40 at the time, the same age as John was when he was killed. The resemblance is striking.

The book was already at the typist by the time I made contact with Freddie, which was why that first chapter is so staccato and jumpy. I simply poured in as much as I could about Freddie in the quickest possible time.

The book, as a whole, is a rather bumpy read. If I were writing it again now, I would try to improve the style, smooth out the wrinkles, polish the prose, stand back more and try to put things and people and events in perspective. Or would I? Perhaps its virtue is that it is of its time, a first-hand account of an unusual period, an eye witness report on the rise of a phenomenon, then at its height, soon to fall apart, although none of us knew it at the time. Just as well. Hindsight can make us all far too clever. This is the simple story of the Beatles, exactly as it appeared then. With a lot more illustrations this time. I hope you will enjoy the show...

HUNTER DAVIES
London, 2002

PART ONE
LIVERPOOL

1

JOHN

Fred Lennon, John's father, was brought up as an orphan. He went to the Bluecoat School in Liverpool, which at that time took in orphan boys. Fred was put into a top hat and tails and when he came out, so he says, he had received a very good education.

He was orphaned in 1921 at the age of nine when his father, Jack Lennon, died. Jack Lennon had been born in Dublin but had spent most of his life in America as a professional singer. He had been a member of an early group of Kentucky Minstrels. After he retired, he returned to Liverpool where Fred was born.

Fred left the orphanage at the age of 15, with his good education and two new suits to get him through life, and became an office boy. 'You might think I'm bigheaded, but I'd only been there a week when the boss sent to the orphanage for three more boys. He said if they had only half the vitality I had, then they'd be all right. They thought I was terrific.'

Terrific or not, by the age of 16 Fred had left office work for the sea. He became a bell boy and eventually a waiter. He says he was their best waiter, but he had no ambition. He was so good that ships wouldn't leave Liverpool unless they had Freddy Lennon on board, so he says.

It was just before he set out for his great career at sea that Fred Lennon started going out with Julia Stanley. The first meeting was just a week after he had left the orphanage.

'It was a beautiful meeting. I was wearing one of my two new suits. I was sitting in Sefton Park with a mate who was showing me how to pick up girls. I'd bought myself a cigarette holder and a bowler hat. I felt that really would impress them.

'There was this little girl we had our eye on. As I walked past her, she said, "You look silly." I said, "You look lovely," and I sat down beside her. It was all innocent. I didn't know anything.

'She said if I was going to sit beside her, I had to take that silly hat off. So I did. I threw it in the lake. I haven't worn a hat from that day to this.'

Opposite: **John, photographed while filming** *A Hard Day's Night* **in 1964.**

Fred and Julia went out together, during Fred's spells ashore, for about ten years. He says her mother 'loved the bones of his body' but that her father didn't care for him very much. But he had taught Julia to play the banjo.

'Me and Julia used to play and sing together. We'd have been the tops today. One day she said to me, "Let's go and get married." I said we had to put the banns up and do it properly. She said, "I bet you won't." So I did, just for a joke. It was all a big laugh, getting married.'

The Stanley family didn't think it much of a laugh. 'We knew that Julia was going out with Alfred Lennon,' says Mimi, one of Julia's four sisters. 'He was quite good looking, I'll admit. But we knew he would be no use to anyone, certainly not Julia.'

The marriage had taken place at Mount Pleasant Register Office on 3 December 1938. No parents were present. Fred turned up first, outside the Adelphi Hotel, at ten in the morning. There was no sign of Julia so he went off and tried to borrow a pound from his brother. When he got back, Julia still hadn't turned up so he rang the Trocadero cinema. Julia spent a lot of time at the Trocadero, as she'd always been stage struck. She never actually worked there, though she put 'cinema usherette' on her marriage certificate, as a joke. 'I spoke to one of her mates at the Troc,' says Fred. 'They all loved me at the Troc. They used to say to me if you ever fall out of love with Julia, I'll be waiting.'

Julia did turn up and they spent their honeymoon at the cinema. Afterwards, Julia went back to her home and Fred went back to his. The next day Fred got on a ship and went off to the West Indies for three months.

Julia stayed at home with her parents, which was where Fred also lived on his trips back home over the next year. After one trip, Julia found that she was pregnant. It was the summer of 1940. Liverpool was under heavy bombing. No one knew where Fred Lennon was.

Julia was admitted to the Maternity Hospital in Oxford Street to have her baby. He was born during a heavy air raid on 9 October 1940, at 6.30 in the evening and he was called John Winston Lennon. Winston was the result of a momentary fit of patriotism. Mimi, who saw the baby 20 minutes after he was born, chose the name John.

'The minute I saw John,' says Mimi, 'that was it. I was lost for ever. A boy! I couldn't get over it. I went on and on about him, almost forgetting Julia. She said, "All I've done is have him."'

When John was 18 months old, Julia went down to the shipping office one day to pick up her money from Fred, which somehow had been coming through. She was told the money had stopped. 'Alfred had deserted ship,' says Mimi. 'No one knew what had happened to him.' He did reappear, but Mimi says that was really the end of the marriage, though they didn't separate until a year or so later.

'Julia eventually met another man who she wanted to marry,' says Mimi. 'It would have been difficult to take John along as well, so I took John. I wanted him, of course, but it did seem the best thing to do. All he needed was a firm anchor and a happy home life. He already looked upon my house as a second home anyway. Both Julia and Fred wanted me to adopt him. I've got letters from them saying so. But I could never get them both down to the office together to sign the forms.'

Fred Lennon's version of his 'desertion' and what happened to his marriage is naturally a bit different. He was in New York when the war broke out and heard he was to be transferred to a liberty ship as an assistant steward instead of a head waiter. 'It meant I would lose my rating. I didn't mind getting involved in the war, but I couldn't put up with losing my rating, could I? The captain of the passenger ship I'd been working on advised me what to do. He said, "Freddy, go and get drunk and miss your boat."'

This is what Fred did, and he ended locked up on Ellis Island. He was told again to join a liberty ship. Fred said he wanted to be head waiter on the *Queen Mary*. He was at last marched on to a liberty ship, heading for North Africa. When they arrived there, Fred was put in jail.

'One of the cooks on board had said to me one day, go and get a bottle from his room. I was drinking it when the police arrived. I was supposed to have broached the cargo. I hadn't. It had all happened before I got on board, but the whole crew got off, except me. Stealing by finding, that was what it was. I defended myself, but it didn't do no good.'

Fred spent three months in jail. Naturally, he says, his money to Julia stopped. He hadn't any to send her, but he did send her some letters. 'She loved my letters. I said to her, there's a war on, go out and enjoy yourself, pet. That was the biggest mistake of my life. She

John, aged eight, with his mother Julia – a family snap taken in 1949. I have the original copy, which was given to me by John, but until recently I had never known who took it. It was John's cousin, Stanley Parkes. Thank you, Stanley.

started enjoying herself and met someone else. And I'd told her to.'

John has vague memories of his days living with the Stanleys, being looked after by his mother while Fred was at sea, although he could not have been more than four years old at the time. 'One day my grandad took me for a walk to the Pier Head. I had a new pair of shoes on and they hurt me all the way. My grandad slit the heels with a penknife so they would be comfortable.'

He did get the impression from his mother that she and Fred had had some happy times. 'She told me about them always larking around and laughing. I think Fred must have been popular. He used to send us ship's concert lists with his name on singing "Begin the Beguine".'

Julia, according to her sisters, was always singing as well. 'She was gay, witty and full of fun,' says Mimi. 'She never took life or anything seriously. Everything was funny, but she couldn't see into people until it was too late. She was more sinned against than sinning.'

A family snap of John, aged nine. Photographer unknown.

Fred went back to sea again, after Julia had gone to live permanently with the new man, and John went with Mimi. During one leave Fred decided to go and visit John at Mimi's house. 'I rang up from Southampton and spoke to John on the phone. He must have been getting on for five by then. I asked him what he was going to be when he grew up, that sort of thing. He spoke lovely English. When I heard his scouse accent years later, I was sure it must be a gimmick.'

Fred arrived in Liverpool, worried sick, so he says, about John, and went to visit Mimi. 'I asked John how he'd like to go to Blackpool and go on the fair and play in the sea and the sand. He said he'd love it. I asked Mimi if I could. She said she couldn't refuse. So I set off with John for Blackpool – intending never to come back.'

Fred and the five-year-old John spent some weeks in Blackpool, staying with a friend of Fred's. 'I had bags of money at the time. You couldn't go wrong in those days, just after the war. I was on lots of rackets, mainly bringing back black market stockings. They're probably still selling the stuff in Blackpool I brought over.'

The friend he was staying with in Blackpool was planning to emigrate to New Zealand. Fred decided to go with him. All the preparations were made, when one day Julia arrived at the door.

'She said she wanted John back. She'd now got a nice little home and decided she wanted him. I said I was now so used to John I was going to take him to New Zealand with me. I could tell she still really loved me. I said why didn't she come with me? We could start again? She said no. All she wanted was John. So we argued and I said, well, let John decide.

'I shouted to John. He runs out and jumps on my knee. He clings to me, asking if she's coming back. That's obviously what he really wanted. I said no, he had to decide whether to stay with me or go with her. He said me. Julia asked again, but John still said me.

'Julia went out of the door and was about to go up the street when John ran after her. That was the last I saw of him or heard of him till I was told he'd become a Beatle.'

John went back to Liverpool with Julia but not to stay with her. It was his Aunt Mimi who wanted him back. He moved in, for good this time, with Mimi and her husband George at their semi-detached house in Menlove Avenue, Woolton, Liverpool.

'I never told John about his father and mother,' says Mimi. 'I just wanted to protect him from all that. Perhaps I was overanxious. I don't know. I just wanted him to be happy.'

John is very grateful to Mimi for what she did. 'She was obviously very good to me. She must have been worried about the conditions I was brought up in and must have been always on at them to think about me, telling them to make sure the kid's safe. As they trusted her, they let her have me in the end, I suppose.'

John soon settled down with Mimi. She brought him up as her son. She was a disciplinarian and stood no nonsense, but she never hit him or shouted at him. She considers this a sign of weakness in a parent. Her worst punishment was to ignore him. 'He always hated that. "Don't 'nore me, Mimi", he used to say.'

But Mimi allowed his personality to develop. 'We were always an individual family. Mother never believed in being conventional, and neither do I. She never wore a wedding ring all her life and neither have I. Why should I?'

But Uncle George, who ran the family dairy business, was the weak link, if John wanted to be spoiled. 'I used to find notes John had left under George's pillow. "Dear George, will you wash me tonight and not Mimi." Or "Dear George, will you take me to Woolton Pictures."'

Mimi allowed John only two outings of that sort a year – one to the Christmas Pantomime at the Liverpool Empire and the other to a Walt Disney film in the summer. But there were smaller treats, such as Strawberry Fields, a local Salvation Army children's home which each summer had a big garden party. 'As soon as we could hear the Salvation Army band starting, John would jump up and down shouting, "Mimi, come on. We're going to be late."'

John's first school was Dovedale Primary. 'The headmaster, Mr Evans, told me this boy's as sharp as a needle. He can do anything, as long as he chooses to do it. He won't do anything stereotyped.'

John was reading and writing after only five months at school, with the help of his Uncle George, though his spelling was funny, even then. Chickenpox was always chicken pots. 'He went on holiday to my sister's in Edinburgh once and sent me a postcard saying "Funs are getting low". I've still got it.'

Mimi wanted to take John back and forward to Dovedale School herself, but he wouldn't allow it. After only his third day, he said she was making a show of him and she hadn't to come any more. So she had to content herself by walking secretly behind him out of school, keeping about 20 yards behind, shadowing him to see that he was all right.

'His favourite songs were "Let Him Go, Let Him Tarry" and "Wee Willy Winkie". He had a good voice. He used to sing in the choir at St Peter's, Woolton. He always went to Sunday School and was later confirmed when he was 15 of his own free will. Religion was never forced on him but the inclination was there until he was a teenager.'

Until the age of 14, Mimi gave him only five shillings a week pocket money. 'I tried to teach him the value of money, but it never worked.' To get any extra money, John had to work for it by helping in the garden. 'He always refused to, until he was really desperate. We'd hear the shed door being furiously opened, then he'd get the lawn mower out and race across a few feet of the lawn at about 60 miles an hour, then storm in for his money. But money didn't really mean anything to him. He didn't care about it. He was always generous beyond belief when he had any.'

John started writing his own little books when he was about seven. Mimi still has bundles of them. His first series was called 'Sport Speed and Illustrated. Edited and Illustrated by J. W. Lennon.' It contained jokes, cartoons, drawings, pasted-in photographs of film stars and footballers. It had a serial story which ended each week with 'If you liked this, come again next week, it'll be even better.'

'I was passionate about *Alice in Wonderland* and drew all the characters. I did poems in the style of the Jabberwocky. I used to *live* Alice, and *Just William*. I wrote my own William stories, with me doing all the things.

'When I did any serious poems, like emotional stuff later on, I did it in secret hand-writing, all scribbles, so that Mimi couldn't read it. Yes, there must have been a soft soul under the hard exterior.

'*Wind in the Willows*, I loved that. After I'd read a book, I'd relive it all again. That was one reason why I wanted to be the gang leader at school. I'd want them all to play the games that I wanted them to play, the ones I'd just been reading.'

As a little boy, he had golden hair and looked very like his mother's side of the family. People always mistook him for Mimi's real son, which she liked. If they were strangers, she never contradicted them.

Mimi was very protective, looking after him all the time, trying not to let him mix with what she called common boys.

'I was coming down Penny Lane one day and saw this crowd of boys in a ring, watching two boys fighting. "Just like those common scruffs," I said. They were from another school, not John's. Then they parted and out came this awful boy with his coat hanging off. To my horror, it was Lennon.

'John always liked me telling him that story. "Just like you, Mimi. Everybody else is always common," he used to say.'

In his playing, with kids around the neighbourhood, Mimi says he always had to be the boss. But at school it was much more serious. He had his own gang, which led to brawls and physical fights with everyone, just to prove he was the best. Ivan Vaughan and Pete Shotton, his two closest friends at school, say he seemed to be perpetually fighting.

Mimi quite approved of these two friends, as they both lived locally, in the same sort of semis, but not of some of the others.

'I did fight all the way through Dovedale, winning by psychological means if ever anyone looked bigger than me. I threatened them in a strong enough way that I would beat them, so they thought I could.

'I used to go thieving with this kid, pinching apples. We used to ride on the bumpers of tram cars in Penny Lane and ride miles without paying. I'd be shitting myself all the time, I was so scared.

'I was the King Pin of my age group. I learned lots of dirty jokes very young, there was this girl who lived near who told me them.

'The sort of gang I led went in for things like shoplifting and pulling girls' knickers down. When the bomb fell and everyone got caught, I was always the one they missed. I was scared at the time, but Mimi was the only parent who never found out.

'Other boys' parents hated me. They were always warning their kids not to play with me. I'd always have smart-alec answers if I met them. Most of the masters hated me like shit.

'As I got older, we'd go on from just stuffing rubbish like sweets in our pockets from shops, and progressed to getting enough to sell to others, like ciggies.'

On the surface, his environment at home with the loving, kind, but firm Mimi, seemed good enough. But although she never told him about himself, there were the vague memories of the past in his mind and also, as he grew older, more and more unanswered questions which worried him.

'On Julia's visits, he did once or twice ask me things,' says Mimi. 'But I didn't want to tell him any details. How could I? He was happy. It would have been wrong to say your father's no good and your mother's found someone else. John was so happy, singing all the time.'

John, aged eight, at his aunt Mimi's house. On the reverse it says, 'myself in garden at "Mendips", 251'.

John remembers beginning to ask Mimi and being always given the same sort of answers. 'Mimi told me my parents had fallen out of love. She never said anything directly against my father and mother.

'I soon forgot my father. It was like he was dead. But I did see my mother now and again and my feeling never died off for her. I often thought about her, though I never realized for a long time that she was living no more than five or ten miles away.

'My mother came to see us one day in a black coat with her face all bleeding. She'd had some sort of accident. I couldn't face it. I thought, that's my mother in there, bleeding. I went out into the garden. I loved her, but I didn't want to get involved. I supose I was a moral coward. I wanted to hide all feelings.'

John might have thought that he was stifling all his worries and feelings, but Mimi and his other three aunts – Anne, Elizabeth and Harriet – say that to them John was completely open and sunny-natured. They say that John was as happy as the day was long.

2

JOHN AND THE QUARRYMEN

Quarry Bank High School, when John started there in 1952, was a small suburban grammar school in Allerton, Liverpool, not far from Mimi's house. It was founded in 1922. It's not as big or as well known as the Liverpool Institute in the middle of the city, but it still has a good reputation. Two of its old boys went on to become Labour Government Ministers – Peter Shore and William Rodgers.

Mimi was pleased that he was at a local grammar school, rather than one in the city. She thought she would be able to keep an eye on him. Pete Shotton went with him to Quarry but his other close friend, Ivan Vaughan, went instead to the Institute, much to his relief. He was the only academic one of John's gang. He knew that going with John would make all school work impossible. But he was still accepted as a member of John's gang after school hours. Ivan began to bring boys back from his school to join John's gang. 'The first one I brought was Len Garry. But I didn't bring many. I was always very selective about people I brought to meet John.'

John has a clear image of his first day at Quarry. 'I looked at all the hundreds of new kids and thought, Christ, I'll have to fight all my way through this lot, having just made it at Dovedale.

'There was some real heavies there. The first fight I got in I lost. I lost me nerve when I got really hurt. Not that there was much real fighting. I did a lot of swearing and shouting, then got a quick punch. If there was a bit of blood, then you packed in. After that, if I thought someone could punch harder than me, I said OK, we'll have wrestling instead.

'I was aggressive because I wanted to be popular. I wanted to be the leader. It seemed more attractive than just being one of the toffees. I wanted everybody to do what I told them to do, to laugh at my jokes and let me be the boss.'

He was caught with an obscene drawing in his first year. 'That really set me up with the

Opposite: John, in his white jacket, leading the Quarrymen in 1957. On the right is Eric Griffiths, one of the original members, who later became a very important civil servant and dry-cleaning mogul.

masters.' Then Mimi found an obscene poem he'd written. 'She found it under my pillow. I said I'd just been made to write it out for another lad who couldn't write very well. I'd written it myself, of course. I'd seen these poems around, the sort you read to give you a hard on. I'd wondered who wrote them, and thought I'd try one myself.

'I suppose I did try to do a bit of school work at first, as I often did at Dovedale. I'd been honest at Dovedale, if nothing else, always owning up. But I began to realize that was foolish. They just got you. So I started lying about everything.'

From then on, after the first year, it was Lennon and Shotton versus the rest of the school, refusing all discipline or imposed ideas. Pete thinks that without John as his permanent ally he might have gone under and been forced to follow the school line, though John probably wouldn't have done. 'But with two of you,' says Pete, 'it's a lot easier to stick to what you believe in. When you've had a bad time, there's someone to laugh with. It was laughs all the time. We never stopped, all the way through school. It was great.'

Pete says most of their escapades don't sound as funny in retrospect, but they still make him laugh when he thinks about them.

'We must have been very young this first time when we had to go to a senior master for having done something bad. He was sitting at his desk writing when we came in and made me and John stand either side of him. As he was sitting down there, telling us off, John started tickling the hairs on his head. He was almost bald, but with a few wisps across the top. He couldn't understand what was tickling him and kept on putting his hand up to rub his bald head as he was telling us off. It was terrible. I was doubled up. John was literally pissing himself. Really. It started to run down his trousers. He had short trousers on, that's why I know we must have been pretty young at the time. The piss was dripping on to the floor and the master was looking round and saying "What's that? What's that?"'

John had a gift for art which he always managed to do well, despite everything else. Pete in turn was good at maths. John was jealous of Pete's interest in maths, which he could never do, and always tried to spoil it for Pete.

'He tried to ruin my concentration by putting drawings in front of me. Some were obscene, but they were mostly just funny and I'd burst out. "Look at Shotton, sir," the rest of the class would shout as I was in hysterics.

'If I had to stand at the front of the class for some reason, when the master had his back to everyone, John would stand up and hold up a drawing behind the master's back for me to see. I'd no chance. I couldn't stop laughing at him.'

Even when they were up before the head for their very first caning, John was still unoverawed by authority, or appeared to be.

'John had to go in first while I waited outside the head's door. I was in agony, all uptight, worrying what was going to happen to me. I seemed to wait hours, but it was probably only a few minutes. Then the door opened and John came out – crawling on the floor on his hands and knees, giving great exaggerated groans. I burst out at once. I hadn't realized at first that the head had two sets of doors. John was crawling out of the lobby place where no one could see him from inside. I had to go into the head next, still with a smile on my face, which of course they never like.'

John got steadily worse from year to year. By the third year, having started near the top of the first form, he had been demoted to the B stream. His reports contained remarks like:

'Hopeless. Rather a clown in class. A shocking report. He is just wasting other pupils' time.' There was a gap for parents to add their comments. On this one, Mimi wrote: 'Six of the best.'

Mimi kept on at him all the time at home, but she didn't know how badly he was doing or how uncooperative he was at school.

'I only got one beating from Mimi. This was for taking money from her handbag. I was always taking a little, for soft things like Dinkies, but this day I must have taken too much.'

He was becoming closer to his Uncle George all the time. 'We got on fine. He was nice and kind.' But, in June 1953, when John was almost 13, Uncle George had a haemorrhage and died. 'It happened quite suddenly one Sunday,' says Mimi. 'He hadn't had a day's illness in his working life. John had been very close to him. In any little rows John and I had, George had always been John's friend. They went out a lot together. I was often jealous when they had good times. I think John was very shocked by George's death, but he never showed it.'

'I didn't know how to be sad publicly,' says John, 'what you did or said, so I went upstairs. Then my cousin arrived and she came upstairs as well. We both had hysterics. We just laughed and laughed. I felt very guilty afterwards.'

Around the time of Uncle George's death someone else was becoming more and more important in John's life – his mother Julia. She had always kept in touch with Mimi, though Mimi told John very little about her. She was obviously fascinated to see him growing up, developing, becoming a personality. And John, now that he was a teenager, was even more fascinated by her. She had by then two daughters by the man she had gone to live with.

'Julia gave me my first coloured shirt,' says John. 'I started going to visit her at her house. I met her new bloke and didn't think much of him. I called him Twitchy. But he was all right really.

'Julia became a sort of young aunt to me, or a big sister. As I got bigger I had more rows with Mimi. I used to go and live with Julia for a weekend.'

Both Pete Shotton and Ivan Vaughan, John's two constant friends, have very vivid memories of Julia becoming important in John's life and the effect she had on them all.

Pete remembers starting to hear about Julia when they were in about the second or third year at Quarry Bank. By then they were both constantly being warned about the terrible things that lay ahead of them. Pete's parents and John's Aunt Mimi were always warning them. But they laughed at these warnings, on their own. Then Julia came along and laughed with them openly at masters, mothers and everyone.

'She was great,' says Pete. 'A groove. She'd just say forget it, when we'd tell her what was going to happen to us. We loved her. She was the only one who was like us. She told us the things we wanted to hear. She did everything for laughs, just like us.'

Julia was living in Allerton and they often went to visit her after school. Sometimes she came to see them. 'We met her once with a pair of knickers over her head like a headscarf. The knicker legs hung down over the back of her shoulder. She pretended she didn't realize when people stared at her. We just fell over.

'Another time we were walking up the street with her and she was wearing a pair of spectacles with no glass in. She would meet people and they wouldn't realize. As she was talking to them, she'd put her fingers through the glasses to rub her eye. People would stare in amazement.'

Ivan thinks it was Julia who helped to make John a rebel. She encouraged what was there, laughed at everything he did, while Mimi had been strict with him, though no more than most mothers, trying to make sure he didn't smoke or drink. Mimi had to give way a bit, but he naturally preferred Julia which was why he was always going away to stay with her. She had been the black sheep, at least the wild one in her family. She wanted John, who was like her anyway, to be the same.

John was by now in 4C, his first time in a C stream, the bottom stream. 'I was really ashamed this time, being with the thick lads. The B stream wasn't bad, because the A stream had all the drips. I started cheating in exams as well. But it was no good competing with all the mongols and I did as badly as ever.'

Pete Shotton also came down each form with him. 'I wrecked his life as well.'

By the final term of the fourth year he dropped right down to 20th in the class, the bottom of the bottom class. 'Certainly on the road to failure,' wrote one master on his report.

In John's fifth year, a new headmaster arrived, Mr Pobjoy. He soon found that Lennon and Shotton were the school's leading troublemakers. But he genuinely seems to have had some contact with John, which most teachers by this time did not. They knew only too well what he was like.

'But he was a thorough nuisance, full of practical jokes. I didn't really understand him. I did cane him once myself, I'm sorry to say. Sorry because I am against corporal punishment. I inherited the system, but soon did away with it.'

Mr Pobjoy was rather surprised when John failed all his O levels. 'I thought he was capable of passing. He only failed them all by one grade, which was probably one of the reasons I helped to get him into the Art College. I knew he was good at art and felt he deserved the chance.'

Mimi went to see the headmaster when John's future was at stake. 'He asked me what I was going to do with him. I said what are *you* going to do with him. You've had him five years.'

Mimi liked the idea of the Art College, though she probably didn't realize how lucky he was to get in. 'I wanted him to be qualified to earn a living in a proper manner. I wanted him to *be* something.

'At the back of my mind I was thinking of his father and how he had turned out, but of course I could never say that to John.'

Looking back now at his school years John has absolutely no regrets.

'I've been proved right. They were wrong and I was right. They're all still there, aren't they, so *they* must be the failures.

'They were all stupid teachers, except one or two. I never paid attention to them. I just wanted a cheap laugh. There was only one master who liked my cartoons. He used to take them home to his digs with him.

'They should give you time to develop, encourage what you're interested in. I was always interested in art and came top for many years, yet no one took any interest.

'I was disappointed at not getting Art at GCE, but I'd given up. All they were interested in was neatness. I was never neat. I used to mix all the colours together. We had one question which said do a picture of "Travel". I drew a picture of a hunchback, with warts all over him. They obviously didn't dig that.

'But I'd say I had a happy childhood. I came out aggressive, but I was never miserable. I was always having a laugh.

'It was all imagining I was Just William really.'

Towards the end of his days at school, John had become interested in pop music, although pop music was something which Mimi had always discouraged. She never liked him singing pop songs which as a little boy he picked up from the radio.

John had no musical education or training of any sort. But he did teach himself to play the mouth organ, after a fashion. Uncle George had bought him a cheap mouth organ.

'I would have sent him to music lessons,' says Mimi, 'the piano or violin, when he was very young. But he didn't want that. He couldn't be bothered with anything which involved lessons. He wanted to do everything immediately, not take time learning.

'The only musical encouragement he ever got was from a bus conductor on the way from Liverpool to Edinburgh. We packed him off with his cousins in Edinburgh each year to stay with my sister. He'd got a battered old mouth organ from George and played it all the way there, driving everybody mad, no doubt.

'But the conductor was greatly taken by him. When they got to Edinburgh, he said come down to the bus station tomorrow morning and I'll give you a really good mouth organ. John couldn't sleep that night, and he was down there first thing. It was a real good one as well. John must have been about ten at the time. It was the first encouragement he ever had. That conductor didn't know what he started.'

The sort of pop songs John did listen to, when he listened to any, were by Johnnie Ray and Frankie Laine. 'But I didn't take much notice of them.'

Nobody took much serious notice, at least not boys in Britain of John Lennon's age. Pop music, up to the mid-fifties, was all somehow remote and had no connection with real life. It all came from America and was produced by very show businessy professionals in lovely suits with lovely smiles who sang lovely ballads, mainly for shop girls and young mums.

Then three things happened. On 12 April 1954, Bill Haley and his Comets produced 'Rock Around the Clock'. It took a year for it to have any effect on Britain. But when it did, as the theme song in the film *Blackboard Jungle*, rock and roll hit Britain and cinema seats started to be ripped up.

The second event occurred in January 1956 when Lonnie Donegan produced 'Rock Island Line'. This had little connection with the wild rock music, despite the title. What was new and interesting was the fact that it was played on the sort of instruments anyone could play. Lonnie Donegan popularized skiffle. For the first time, anyone could have a go, with no musical knowledge or even musical talent.

Even the guitar, the hardest instrument in a skiffle group, could be played by anyone who mastered a few simple chords. The other instruments, like a washboard, or tea chest bass, could be played by any idiot.

The third and in a way the most exciting event in pop music in the 1950s and the most influential single person in pop at any time, until the Beatles themselves, was Elvis Presley. He also appeared in the early part of 1956. By May his 'Heartbreak Hotel' was top of the charts in 14 different countries.

In a way it was obvious that someone like Elvis should happen. You just had to look at Bill Haley in the flesh, podgy, middle-aged looking and definitely unsexy, to realize that

The Quarrymen performing from the back of a truck in Rosebery Street, Liverpool, 22 June 1957. The band members at this time were Colin Hanton (on drums), Eric Griffiths (in checked shirt), John (at the microphone), Pete Shotton (on washboard), Len Garry and Rod Davis (at back).

this new exciting music, rock'n'roll, eventually had to have an exciting singer to go with it.

Rock was the music that excited all kids. Elvis was the exciting singer singing the exciting songs. 'Nothing really affected me until Elvis,' says John.

All the Beatles, like millions of boys of the same age, were affected. They all have the same sort of memories, of groups springing up in every class at school and in every street at home. There were overnight about a hundred dances in Liverpool with skiffle groups queuing up to perform. It was the first time for generations that music wasn't the property of musicians. Anyone could get up and have a go. It was like giving painting sets to monkeys. Some of them were bound to produce something good sometime.

John Lennon didn't have a guitar or any instrument when the craze first began. He took a guitar off a boy at school one day but found he couldn't play it, so he gave it back. But he knew that his mother, Julia, could play the banjo, so he went to see her. She bought him a second-hand guitar for £10. It had on it 'guaranteed not to split'. He went for a couple of lessons, but never learned. Instead Julia taught him some banjo chords. The first tune he learned was 'That'll Be The Day'.

He had to practise behind Mimi's back at home. She made him stand in the glass porch at the front, playing and singing to himself. 'The guitar's all right, John,' Mimi used to tell him, ten times a day. 'But you'll never make a living with it.'

'We eventually formed ourselves into a group from school. I think the bloke whose idea it was didn't get in the group. We met in his house first time. There was Eric Griffiths on guitar, Pete Shotton on washboard, Len Garry, Colin Hanton on drums and Rod on banjo.

'Our first appearance was in Rose Street – it was their Empire Day celebrations. They all had this party out in the street. We played from the back of a lorry. We didn't get paid or anything.

'We played at blokes' parties after that, or weddings, perhaps got a few bob. But mostly we just played for fun.'

They called themselves the Quarrymen, naturally enough. They all wore Teddy Boy clothes, had their hair piled high and sleeked back like Elvis. John was the biggest Ted of all, which was another reason why mothers warned their sons about him, once they saw him or even when they didn't see him but just heard the stories.

In these first months of the Quarrymen in late 1956, when John was supposedly sticking in hard at school, it was all very half-hearted and irregular. They wouldn't play for weeks. People were always coming and going, depending on who turned up at the party, or who wanted to have a go.

'It was all just a joke,' says Pete Shotton, 'setting up a group. Skiffle was in, so everybody was trying to do something. I was on washboard because I had no idea about music. I was John's friend, so I *had* to be in.'

With John being the leader, there were constant rows, which also led to people leaving. 'I used to row with people because I wanted them out. Once you had a fight, that was the end and you had to leave the group.' One regular was Nigel Whalley, who played now and again but mainly tried to get them dates, acting as a manager.

Over at the Liverpool Institute, the same sort of thing was happening, groups growing up like mushrooms, though Ivan Vaughan had brought Len Garry over from the Institute into John's group. It seemed to go down well.

On 6 July 1957, he took along another friend from his school to meet John.

'I knew this was a great fellow,' says Ivan. 'I only ever brought along great fellows to meet John.'

The occasion for the meeting was the Church Fête at Woolton Parish Church, not far from John's house. He knew the people there and had got them to let his group perform.

Ivan had talked a lot at his school about John and his group. He knew that his friend was interested in that sort of thing, though Ivan himself wasn't.

'Mimi had said to me that day that I'd done it at last,' says John. 'I was now a real Teddy Boy. I seemed to disgust everybody that day, not just Mimi.

'I was looking the other day at the photograph of myself taken at Woolton that day. I look such a youthful young lad.'

What happened that day is a bit cloudy to John. He got drunk, though he was still several years under age. Others remember it very well, especially the friend Ivan brought along – Paul McCartney.

'That was the day,' says John, 'the day that I met Paul, that it started moving.'

3

PAUL

Paul was born James Paul McCartney on 18 June 1942, in a private ward of Walton Hospital, Liverpool, the only Beatle to be born in such luxury. His family were ordinary working class and it was the height of the war. But Paul arrived in state because his mother had at one time been the sister in charge of the maternity ward. She was given the star treatment when she went back to have Paul, her first baby.

His mother, Mary Patricia, had given up hospital work just over a year previously, when she'd married his father, and had become a health visitor. Her maiden name was Mohin and, like her husband, she was of Irish extraction.

Jim McCartney, Paul's father, began his working life at 14 as a sample boy at A. Hannay and Co., cotton brokers and merchants in Chapel Street, Liverpool. Unlike his wife, Jim McCartney was not a Catholic. He has always classed himself as an agnostic. He was born in 1902, one of three boys and four girls.

It was considered very lucky when he left school and got a job in cotton. The cotton industry was at its height and Liverpool was the centre of its importation to the Lancashire mills. Getting into cotton, you were reckoned settled for life.

As a sample boy Jim McCartney got six shillings a week. He had to run round prospective buyers letting them see bits of cotton they were interested in buying. Hannay's imported the cotton, graded it and classified it, then sold it to the mills.

Jim did well at the job and at the age of 28 he was promoted to cotton salesman. This was considered a big success for an ordinary lad. Cotton salesmen usually had more of a middle-class background. Jim was always neat and dapper with a gentle open face.

When he got his big promotion, they put him up to £250 a year. Not a great salary, but reasonable.

Opposite: Paul on the lavatory – an Englishman abroad. The picture is one of five original photographs, still in my collection, of the Beatles messing around in Hamburg, and probably dates from 1960. Photographer unknown.

Jim was too young for the First World War and too old for the Second, although with the use of only one ear – he broke an eardrum falling off a wall when he was ten – he would not have been liable anyway. But he was liable for some sort of war work. When the Cotton Exchange closed for the war, they sent him to Napiers, the engineering works.

In 1941, at the age of 39, he got married. They moved into furnished rooms in Anfield. Jim was working at Napiers during the day and fire-fighting at night when Paul was born. He was able to go in and out of the hospital as he liked, instead of during the normal visiting hours, as his wife had worked there.

'He looked awful, I couldn't get over it. Horrible. He had one eye open and he just squawked all the time. They held him up and he looked like a horrible piece of red meat. When I got home I cried, the first time for years and years.'

Despite his wife's medical work, he'd never been able to suffer illness of any sort. The smell of hospitals made him nervous, a fear he has passed on to Paul.

'But the next day he looked more human. And every day after that he got better and better. He turned out a lovely baby in the end.'

One day when Paul had been out in the garden at home, his mother discovered some specks of dust on his face and said they must move. The work at Napiers on the Sabre engines was counted as working for the Air Force so through that he was able to get a house on the Knowlsely Estate, Wallasey. They were council houses, but some were reserved for Air Ministry workers. 'We used to call them half houses, they were such small, diddy houses, with bare bricks inside. But it was better than furnished rooms with a young baby.'

His work at Napiers came to an end before the war finished and he was moved to a job in Liverpool Corporation Cleansing Department, as a temporary inspector, going round making sure the dustbin men did their job properly.

Jim got little money with the Corporation and his wife went back to health visiting for a while, till the birth of her second child, Michael, in 1944.

But she never really liked health visiting as much as nursing. It was too much nine to five, like an office job. So eventually she went back to midwifery. She took two domiciliary midwife jobs, which meant living on large estates and looking after all the mothers-to-be in that one area. There was a council house thrown in with the job. The first post was in Western Avenue, Speke, and the second in Ardwick Road. She was called out every night.

Jim says she worked far too hard, more than she should have done, but she was always over-conscientious.

Paul's earliest memory, probably from around the age of three or four, is of his mother. He remembers someone coming to the door and giving her a plaster dog. 'It was out of gratitude for some delivery she had done. People were always giving her presents like that.

'I have another memory, of hiding from someone then hitting them over the head with an iron bar. But I think the plaster dog was the earliest.'

One of his other early memories of his mother is when she was trying to correct his accent. 'I talked real broad, like all the other kids round our way. When she told me off, I imitated her accent and she was hurt, which made me feel very uptight.'

Paul started primary school – Stockton Wood Road Primary – when they were living in Speke. His mother decided against a Roman Catholic one as she had seen too many as a health visitor and didn't like them. Michael soon followed at the same one. 'I remember the headmistress saying how good the two boys were with younger children,' says Jim, 'always sticking up for them. She said Michael was going to be a leader of men. I think this was because he was always arguing. Paul did things much quieter. He had much more nous. Mike stuck his neck out. Paul always avoided trouble.'

When the school became overcrowded, they were moved out to another primary school in the country, Joseph Williams Primary School at Gateacre.

Paul perfected his quiet diplomacy even more as he got older, still always doing things quietly – like his mother – instead of noisily like Michael.

'I was once hitting Michael for doing something,' says Jim. 'Paul stood by shouting at Mike, "Tell him you didn't do it and he'll stop." Mike admitted he had done it, whatever it was. But Paul was always able to get out of most things.'

Paul (left), aged seven and chubby-cheeked, with his mother Mary and younger brother Michael.

'I was pretty sneaky,' says Paul. 'If I ever got bashed for being bad, I used to go into their bedroom when they were out and rip the lace curtains at the bottom, just a little bit, then I'd think, that's got them.'

Paul easily passed the Eleven Plus and went to the Liverpool Institute. This is the best known of Liverpool's grammar schools. It was founded in 1825 as a Mechanics' Institute which is how it got its name. Liverpool Art College, which shares the same building, was part of the Institute until the 1890s. The University of Liverpool also shares the same origins. It became an ordinary boys' school, giving up all adult classes, around the turn of the century. Its old boys today include Arthur Askey, James Laver, Lord Justice Morris and the late Sydney Silverman also.

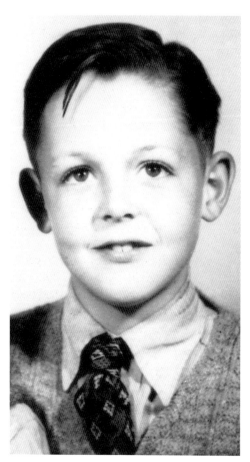

Paul, aged nine.

Michael also passed for the Institute but he eventually ended up in the lowest stream. Paul did very well and was always in the top forms.

'Paul was able to do his homework while watching TV,' says Jim. 'I used to tell him not to, that he couldn't possibly do both. But I once asked him exactly what had been on, and he knew, and he'd also done an essay. He was smart enough easily for a university. That was always my intention for him. Get a BA or a BSc behind his name, then he'd be okay. But when he knew what was in my head, Paul tried to stop himself doing well. He was always good at Latin but when I said he'd need the Latin for a university, he started slacking up.'

At the Institute, Paul became about the most sexually precocious boy of his year, knowing what it was all about, or almost, even from his early years.

'I once did this dirty drawing for the class. I was the lad who did them. It was folded so you just saw the head and the feet of a woman, but when you opened it out, she was all naked. The full schoolboy bit, with pubic hair thrown in, not that I had any idea what that looked like. By mistake I left it in the top pocket of my shirt. This was the pocket I used to keep my dinner tickets in and my mother always searched it before washing as I often left some.

'I came home one day and she held it out to me, did you do this? I said no, no, honest, no. I said it was Kenny Alpin, a boy in our class. He must have put it there. I'd tell you if I'd done it. I kept it up for two days. Then I admitted it. The shame was terrible.'

After the first year, when he got 90 per cent for Latin, he got fed up with school work. 'It was nice and easy that first year. I kept myself clean and eager because it seemed the thing to do. Then it all became woolly. Never once in my school days did anyone ever make it clear to me what I was being educated for, what the point of it was. I know my dad went on about needing certificates and all that, but I never listened to that. You heard it so often. We had masters who just hit you with rulers, or told us a lot of shit about their holiday in Wales or what they did in the Army.

'Homework was a right drag. I just couldn't stand staying in on a summer night when all the other kids were out playing. There was a field opposite our house in Ardwick and I could look out the window and see them all having a good time.

'There weren't many other kids from the Institute living round our way. I was called a college pudding, fucking college puddin' was what they said.

'All I wanted was women, money and clothes. I used to do a bit of stealing, things like ciggies. We'd go into empty shops, when the man was in the house part at the back, and take some before he came in. For years, what I wanted out of life was £100. I thought with that I could have a house, a guitar and a car. So, if money had been the scene, I'd have gone wild.'

However, Paul wasn't all that useless at school. In 1953, he got a school prize for an essay – a special Coronation Prize, a book called *Seven Queens of England* by Geoffrey Trease, published by Heinemann, which he still has. He always got good marks for all his essays. 'I remember a school inspector once asking me how I could write such a technical essay about pot-holing. I'd heard it all on the earphones in bed. They were marvellous, just lying in bed listening to the radio. Did incredible things to your imagination.'

Jim had rigged up a set of microphones for each of them in bed, as an attempt to get them to bed early, keep them there and stop them from fighting. They did fight a lot, but not more than most brothers. Michael used to call Paul 'Fatty' to annoy him. 'He had been beautiful as a baby, with big eyes and long eyelashes,' says Jim. 'People used to say, "Oh, he'll break all the girls' hearts one of these days."' But as an early teenager, he went through a chubby stage.

The McCartneys moved from Ardwick when Paul was about 13. His mother gave up being a domiciled midwife, though she later went back to being a health visitor.

They got a council house at 20 Forthlin Road, Allerton, where Paul spent all his boyhood from then on. It is in the middle of a low terrace row, a bit poky and insignificant, but neat and clean. Menlove Avenue was now just two miles away.

They hadn't been at Forthlin Road very long – Paul was just 14 – when his mother suddenly started to suffer pains in her breast. They went on for about three or four weeks, coming and going, but she put it down to the menopause. She was then 45. 'It must be the change,' she used to say to Jim. She told various doctors but they agreed that was what it was and told her to forget it. But she kept having them, and more and more seriously.

One day Michael came into the house suddenly and found her crying. He thought it was because he and Paul must have been doing something they shouldn't have been doing. 'We could be right bastards.' But he never asked her what it was. She never told them. But she decided this time to see a specialist. He diagnosed cancer. They operated and she died. It had all happened within a month of first having had any serious pains.

'It just knocked me down,' says Jim. 'I couldn't understand it. It was awful for the boys. Michael especially was still only twelve and very close to her. They didn't break down or anything. It just hit them very slowly.'

'I can't remember the details of the day we were told,' says Michael. 'All I can remember is one of us, I don't remember who, making a silly joke. For months we both regretted it.'

Paul remembers what it was. 'It was me. The first thing I said was, "What are we going to do without her money?"'

But they both cried on their own in bed that night. For days afterwards Paul prayed for her to come back. 'Daft prayers, you know, if you bring her back, I'll be very, very good for always. I thought, it just shows how stupid religion is. See, the prayers didn't work, when I really needed them to.'

The two boys moved out for a few days, during the funeral, to stay with their Aunt Jinny. 'I think Dad didn't want us to see him breaking up,' says Paul. 'It was a bit of a drag at Aunt Jinny's. We both had to sleep in the same bed.'

Jim was left with the biggest problem. He'd never done much in the house, as his wife was so organized. He was now left, at 53, to bring up two boys of fourteen and twelve, through perhaps their most difficult years. He had money problems as well. His wife as a midwife had made more than him, as Paul had so cruelly mentioned. By 1956, Jim's salary was only £8 a week. Every other working man was at least feeling the beginnings of affluence, but the cotton trade, in which you were supposed to be secure for life, was having a very tough time.

Two of his sisters helped a great deal – Aunt Milly and Aunt Jinny. One of them would come one day a week to Forthlin Road to clean out the house properly. And when the boys were young, they often popped round in the evening to let them in from school.

'The winters were bad,' says Jim. 'The boys had to light the fires themselves when they came home from school. I did all the cooking.

'The biggest headache was what sort of parent was I going to try to be. When my wife had been alive, I'd been the one who chastised them. I delivered the hard stuff when it was needed. My wife had done the soft stuff. If we sent them to bed without their supper, it would be her who took something up to them in bed later, though it would probably be my idea.

'Now I had to decide whether to be a father or a mother or both, or rely on them and just be friends and all help each other.

'I had to rely on them a lot. I would say, "Don't come in when you come home from school unless one of your aunts is here." Otherwise, they would have their friends in and wreck the place.

'I'd come home and find five eggs gone. They wouldn't let on at first, saying they didn't know what had happened to them. Then they'd say, oh yes, we did give the lads a fried egg each.

'By and large, they were quite good. But I missed my wife. It knocked me for six when she died.'

Michael particularly doesn't know how his father managed it. 'We were terrible and cruel. He was bloody marvellous. And all that time without a woman. I can't imagine it. Paul owes a lot to his Dad. We both do.'

Both of them used to mock his two pet bits of homespun philosophy. 'Here he comes, with his two 'ations,' they used to say. Jim used to tell them that the two most important things in life were toleration and moderation.

'Toleration *is* very important,' says Jim. 'They would laugh at people with infirmities, as kids do. I'd explain to them how *they* wouldn't like it. And moderation, a lot of trouble is caused without that. You're always hearing people say, "I'd string the bugger up", without thinking carefully about what would be the best for someone.'

Jim always did think about what was the best for people. He has a natural charm and courtesy with everyone, but it's not just the salesman's cosy touch, it's much deeper and more genuine than that. In the hands of a less thoughtful or considerate father, they could easily have broken out when their mother died.

From his mother Paul seems to have inherited his capacity for hard work and dedication. He is the sort of person who can always get things done, when he wants to.

In some ways Paul despised school and the whole system of passing on processed rules, as much as John did. But there was a part of him which didn't want to let himself down. He could always turn on the hard work, even in little bursts, enough to get him through. John became completely bolshie and unco-operative. Paul could never be that.

His brother Michael thinks there was one direct result in Paul of their mother's death.

'It was just after mother's death that it started. It became an obsession. It took over his whole life. You lose a mother – and you find a guitar? I don't know. Perhaps it just came along at that time and became an escape. But an escape from what?'

4

PAUL AND THE QUARRYMEN

As a child, Paul showed no particular interest in music. Both he and his brother Michael were sent once for a couple of piano lessons, but nothing happened. 'We made the mistake of starting them in the summer,' says Jim. 'The teacher used to come to the house and all the kids would be knocking at our door all the time, wanting them to come out and play. So I made them go to the teacher's house, but that didn't last long.'

Jim also wanted Paul to join Liverpool Cathedral Choir. 'I made him go, but he deliberately cracked his voice in the audition. Later on he did join St Barnabas Choir, near Penny Lane, for a while.'

Later still Paul was given an old trumpet by an uncle on which he managed to pick out tunes, teaching himself. This talent for picking up music came from his father. As a boy, Jim taught himself to play the piano. Of all the Beatles' parents, Paul's father was the only one with any experience of being a musician.

'I never had any lessons. I just used to pick out chords on an old second-hand piano someone gave us when I was about 14 and living in Everton. It came from North End Music Stores – NEMS – I can remember the name on it. I had good rhythm and could knock out most tunes. I never disgraced myself.'

Not long after he had started work, Jim McCartney began a little ragtime band to play at works dances. This was around 1919, when he was 17.

Their first public performance was a dance in St Catherine's Hall, Vine Street, Liverpool. 'We thought we would have some sort of gimmick so we put black masks on our faces and called ourselves "The Masked Melody Makers". But before half-time, we were sweating so much that the dye was running down our faces. That was the beginning and end of the Masked Melody Makers.'

Instead they called themselves 'Jim Mac's Band'. They all wore dinner-jackets with paper

Opposite: Fifteen-year-old Paul, co-leading the Quarrymen at the New Clubmoor Hall, Liverpool, 23 November, 1957. On drums is Colin Hanton; Len Garry plays the tea chest bass.

shirt fronts and cuffs. 'They were very good. You could buy paper cuffs twelve for a penny. No one could tell the difference.

'I ran that band for about four or five years, just part-time. I was the alleged boss, but there was no distinctions.

'We played once at the first local showing of the film *The Queen of Sheba*. We didn't know what to play. When the chariot race started we played a popular song of the time called "Thanks for the Buggy Ride". And when the Queen of Sheba was dying we played "Horsy Keep Your Tail Up".'

When the Second World War came, and a family, Jim packed in his playing career, although he often played a bit on the piano at home. 'Paul was never interested when I played the piano. But he loved listening to music on his earphones in bed. Then suddenly he wanted a guitar, when he was 14. I didn't know what made him want it.'

His guitar cost £15 and Paul couldn't get anything out of it at first. There seemed to be something wrong with it. Then he realized it was because he was left handed. He took it back and got it altered. 'I'd never been really keen on the trumpet. But I liked the guitar because I could play it after just learning a few chords. I could also sing to it at the same time.'

He'd followed pop music since he was about twelve, like most of his friends. The first concert he went to was Eric Delaney's Band at the Liverpool Empire when he was twelve. At 14 he queued up in his lunch hour from school to see Lonnie Donegan. 'I remember he was late arriving. He wrote out little notes for the factory girls explaining it was his fault they were late back as he'd kept them waiting.

'We used to hang around the stage door waiting for anybody and get their autographs. I once queued up for Wee Willie Harris's autograph.'

He also went to the Pavilion. 'That was where they had the nude shows. They would strip off absolutely starkers. Some of them were all right as well. It was funny, letting us in at that age. But it was just good clean dirty fun.'

Like John and the others, he was influenced by the skiffle phase and Bill Haley's early rock numbers, but, like John again, it wasn't till Elvis Presley that he was really bowled over. 'That was the biggest kick. Every time I felt low I just put on an Elvis and I'd feel great, beautiful. I'd no idea how records were made and it was just magic. "All Shook Up"! Oh, it was beautiful!'

When he got his guitar, he tried to play Elvis numbers or whatever else was popular. His best impersonation was of Little Richard.

'I used to think it was awful,' says his father. 'Absolutely terrible. I couldn't believe anybody was really like that. It wasn't till years later when I saw Little Richard, on the same bill as the Beatles, that I realized how good Paul's impersonation was.'

'The minute he got the guitar, that was the end,' says Michael. 'He was lost. He didn't have time to eat or think about anything else. He played it on the lavatory, in the bath, everywhere.'

There was another friend from his class, Ian James, from the Dingle, who also got a guitar about the same time. He and Paul used to go around together, with their guitars. They played to each other, teaching each other bits they'd learned. 'We used to go round the fairs,' says Paul, 'listening to the latest tunes on the Waltzer and trying to pick them up. We also tried to pick up birds. That never worked. I haven't got the flair for picking them up like that.'

Both Paul and Ian James wore the same sort of white sports jackets – after the pop song 'A White Sports Coat'. 'It had speckles in it and flaps over the pockets. We used to have black drainies as well. We used to go around everywhere together dressed the same and think we were really flash. We both had Tony Curtis hair-cuts. It took us hours to get it right.'

Jim McCartney tried to stop Paul dressing the way he did, but didn't get very far. 'Paul was very clever,' says Michael. 'When he bought a new pair of trousers, he'd bring them home for Dad to see how wide they were and he would say OK. Then he would take them back and get them altered. If Dad noticed afterwards, he'd swear blind they were what he'd agreed.'

'I was very worried he'd turn out a Teddy Boy,' says Jim. 'I had a dread of that. I said over and over again that he wasn't going to have tight trousers. But he just wore me down. His hair was always long as well, even then. He'd come back from the barber's and it would just look the same and I'd say, "Was it closed, then?"'

Paul was just as interested in girls as the guitar. 'I got it for the first time at 15. I suppose that was a bit early to get it. I was about the first in my class. She was older and bigger than

One of the best-known early photographs of John with the Quarrymen, taken by a school friend from Quarry Bank, Geoff Rhind, on 6 July, 1957, at St Peter's Church fête, Woolton. A few hours later, John met Paul for the first time.

me. It was at her house. She was supposed to be baby-sitting while her mum was out. I told everybody at school next day, of course. I was a real squealer.'

Paul remembers vividly that day in the summer of 1957 when Ivan mentioned that he was going to Woolton Parish Church to see this group he sometimes played with, though he wasn't actually playing with them that day. Paul said yes, he'd come along and see them. Might be a few girls to pick up.

'They weren't bad,' says Paul. 'John played the lead guitar. But he played it like a banjo, with banjo chords, as that was all he knew.

'None of the others had even as much idea as John how to play. They were mostly just strumming along.

'They played things like "Maggie May", but with the words a bit different. John had done them up himself as he didn't know them all.

'They were playing outdoors in a big field. John was staring round as he was playing, watching everybody. He told me afterwards that it was the first time he tried sussing an audience, you know, sizing them up, seeing whether it was best to twist a shoulder at them, or best not to move at all.

'I was in my white sports coat and black drainies, as usual. I'd just got them narrowed again during the dinner-hour from school. They were so narrow they knocked everybody out.

'I went round to see them afterwards in the Church Hall place. I talked to them, just chatting and showing off. I showed them how to play "Twenty Flight Rock" and told them all the words. They didn't know it. Then I did "Be Bop A Lula" which they didn't know properly either. Then I did my Little Richard bit, went through me whole repertoire in fact. I remember this beery old man getting nearer and breathing down me neck as I was playing. "What's this old drunk doing?" I thought. Then he said "Twenty Flight Rock" was one of his favourites. So I knew he was a connoisseur.

'It was John. He'd just had a few beers. He was sixteen and I was only fourteen, so he was a big man. I showed him a few more chords he didn't know. Ian James had taught me them really. Then I left. I felt I'd made an impression, shown them how good I was.'

Pete Shotton, however, doesn't recall Paul making any big impression. Pete, being completely unmusical, was a bit harder to impress by 'Twenty Flight Rock', however brilliantly executed.

'I didn't really take in Paul that first meeting,' says Pete. 'He seemed very quiet, but you do when you meet a group of new blokes for the first time. I wasn't really jealous of him, not at first. He was so much younger than us. I didn't think he was going to be a rival. Me and John were still the closest pals. I was always John's friend. I loved him, that's why.'

John remembers mulling over the meeting with Paul in his mind afterwards, before he decided on anything. This was unusual for him, to think things out instead of barging on with whatever he wanted.

'It was with being pissed,' says John. 'It must have slowed me up.'

'I was very impressed by Paul playing "Twenty Flight Rock". He could obviously play the guitar. I half thought to myself – he's as good as me. I'd been king pin up to then. Now, I thought, if I take him on, what will happen? It went through my head that I'd have to keep him in line, if I let him join. But he was good, so he was worth having. He also looked like Elvis. I dug him.'

About a week later Paul went over to Menlove Avenue on his bike to see Ivan. He cycled up through the golf course from Allerton. On his way back he met Pete Shotton. 'Pete said they'd been talking about me. Did I want to join their group? I said OK, right.'

Paul's first public performance, as a member of the Quarrymen, was at a dance at the Conservative Club in Broadway. Paul was going to do his own little solo bit that evening, probably 'Twenty Flight Rock', but something happened and he didn't.

But later on, after the dance, he played a couple of tunes to John he had written himself. Since he'd started playing the guitar, he had tried to make up a few of his own little tunes. The first tune he played to John that evening was called 'I Lost My Little Girl'. Not to be outdone, John immediately started making up his own tunes. He had been elaborating and adapting other people's words and tunes to his own devices for some time, but he hadn't written down proper tunes till Paul appeared with his. Not that Paul's tunes meant much, nor John's. They were very simple and derivative. It was only them coming together, each egging the other on, which suddenly inspired them to write songs for themselves to play. From that day, they never stopped.

'I went off in a completely new direction from then on,' says Paul. 'Once I got to know John it all changed. He was good to know. Even though he was two years older than me and I was just a baby, we thought the same sort of things.'

What happened in the subsequent months was that John and Paul got to know each other. They spent all their time together. They both stayed away from school and went to Paul's house, while his Dad was out at work, and ate fried eggs and practised guitar chords. Paul showed John all the ones he knew. John's banjo chords, taught to him by Julia, were obviously useless. As Paul is left handed, after he had shown John what to do, John had to go home and do it in the mirror on his own, then get it the right way round.

Pete Shotton began to feel a bit out of it. 'My days with the group soon came to an end,' says Pete. 'We were playing at someone's party in Smithdown Lane. It was a right piss-up really. John and I got hilarious, laughing like mad at each other's jokes. Then he broke my washboard over my head. I lay there, in tears, with it framed round my neck. It wasn't the life for me any more, playing in a group. Apart from feeling no good, I didn't like standing up there. I was too embarrassed.'

Ivan Vaughan had long since left the group, though he was still a friend, of John's at home and of Paul's at school.

Paul began to think more and more of the possibility of a great friend of his from his school joining the group. This friend had taken up skiffle and rock and Elvis about the same time, but was coming on even better than most people. Paul thought he would bring him along to see John. He was even younger than Paul, but he didn't think that would matter, as he was so good.

Ivan Vaughan was annoyed when he did. Ivan had taken along first of all Len Garry and then Paul McCartney from the Institute to meet John. He looked upon the procuring as his prerogative. He didn't like the idea of Paul taking someone else along.

This new friend was not just much younger, he didn't even make any pretence at being an intellectual, the way Paul did. George Harrison, as the friend was called, was a real out and out Teddy Boy. Ivan couldn't understand why the Quarrymen should be interested in him.

5

GEORGE

George Harrison is the only Beatle to come from a large family and the only one whose family background is normal and undramatic. He is the youngest of the four Beatles and the youngest of the four children of Harold and Louise Harrison. He was born on 25 February 1943, at 12 Arnold Grove, Wavertree, Liverpool.

Mrs Harrison is stocky, jolly, very friendly and outgoing. Mr Harrison is thin and thoughtful, precise and slowly deliberate. He left school at 14 and worked for a firm that made mangles, the sort once used by housewives on washday. He got 7s. 6d. a week for taking them round on a handcart, then dragging them into people's houses.

He wanted to join the Navy, but his mother wouldn't let him. His father had been killed at Mons during the First World War and he thinks this put her off all Services. But she allowed him to join the Merchant Navy. He was at sea from 1926 to 1936 as a steward with the White Star Line.

He met his wife Louise in 1929. 'No, let me tell this story,' she said. 'It's the funniest thing you ever heard. I'd met him and some other boys in the street one day. One of the other boys had said give us your address, I'm going off to Africa tomorrow and I'll send you a bottle of scent. Well, I thought, it's a bottle of scent, but Harold snatched my address and went off with it.

'What a pandemonium his first letter caused. It had the White Star flag on, so I knew it must be him. There was a deaf and dumb man in the kitchen, the day it came, getting a can of water. My mother was always very kind to everyone.

'Letters were very rare in those days, at least we never got any. This deaf and dumb man bent down and picked up my letter, even though he couldn't read. I could see it said "Miss Louise French" and I tried to grab it from him. But somebody else snatched it. It went round everybody before I got it, with everyone howling at all the kisses. I had to iron it before I could read it.'

Opposite: **An early photo of George with the Beatles, taken in Hamburg around 1960 by Jurgen Vollmer.**

Harold and Louise were married on 20 May 1930. Not in a church, but in Brownlow Hill Register Office. She was a Catholic, but he was not.

Her father had originally come from Wexford in Ireland and had at first spelled his name the Irish way, with a double 'ff'. He was six foot two and he was at one time a commissionaire at New Brighton Tower and then a lamplighter.

'When he was away during the First World War, my mother became a lamplighter herself. She was up a lamppost one day and somebody accidentally took the ladder away. She was left hanging by her hands from the bar and had to fall in the end. She was eight months pregnant as well. But the baby was lovely. Nine pounds.'

Harold and Louise moved into 12 Arnold Grove, Wavertree, when they got married and lived there for 18 years. It was a simple terrace house, two up and two down, and cost ten shillings a week. It is just a few miles away from the areas in which John Lennon and Paul McCartney were living.

Harold was still at sea and Louise was working as an assistant in a greengrocer's shop, a job she kept up until shortly before the birth of their first child Louise in 1931. Their second child, Harold, was born in 1934. Not long after, Harold decided to leave the Merchant Navy. He was fed up anyway, but most of all he wanted to see more of his children.

'I was by then a first-class steward on £7 7s. a month. Twenty-five shillings of that a week was sent home for my wife. I never had enough money, even when we got some "good bloods" on board. I did a lot of cruises and this is what we called people with money who gave us big tips. In my spare time I used to cut people's hair. I was trying to save up in order to come ashore and look for a job.'

'He used to write home and tell me how hard the life was,' says Mrs Harrison. 'He would take his trousers off at night, hang them on the line, but before they'd stop swinging, he was in them again.'

Harold came ashore in 1936. There was a slump on. He was on the dole for 15 months. 'With two kids, I was allowed 23 bob a week. Out of that there was the ten bob rent to pay, plus coal, and food for all of us.'

In 1937 he managed to get a job as a bus conductor and in 1938 became a bus driver. In 1940 their third child Peter was born and in 1944 along came George, the fourth child and third son.

'I went upstairs to see him that first day,' says Mr Harrison. 'I couldn't get over it. There he was, a miniature version of me. Oh no, I thought. We just couldn't be so alike.'

'George was always very independent,' says Mrs Harrison. 'He never wanted any assistance of any kind. When we used to send him to Mrs Quirk's the butcher's we'd give him a note but he'd throw it away the minute he got outside our house. Mrs Quirk used to see his little face coming over the counter and know who it was. "Haven't you got a note?" she would say. "I don't need one," George'd say. "Three-quarters of best pork sausages please." He'd not be much more than two and a half when he did that. All the neighbours knew him.'

They had a great deal of trouble getting George into primary school. The worst of the bulge years were starting. All the schools were full. 'I tried a Roman Catholic school. He'd been baptized a Catholic. But they said I'd have to keep him at home till he was six, then they might be able to take him. He was so intelligent and advanced, so I just sent him to an ordinary state primary school.'

This was Dovedale Primary. The same school that John Lennon was already at. He was two and a half years older and three classes ahead of George. They never met. But Peter Harrison, one of George's brothers, was in the same year as John Lennon and Jimmy Tarbuck, the Liverpool comedian.

'I took him to school that first day, across Penny Lane,' says Mrs Harrison. 'He wanted to stay dinners right from the beginning. The next day, as I was getting my coat off the hanger, he said, "Oh no, I don't want you to take me!" I said, "Why not?" He said, "I don't want you to be one of the nosy mothers, standing round the gate talking." He's always been against nosy mothers. He used to hate all the neighbours who stood around gossiping.'

George's first home memory is of buying live chickens for sixpence, along with his brothers Harold and Peter, and bringing them home. 'Mine and Harold's both died, but Peter's was kept in the back yard and grew and grew. It was massive and wild. People were so scared of it they came round to the front door instead of the back. We ate it for Christmas. A fellow came and strangled it for us. I remember it hanging on the line after he'd done it.'

George was six when they moved from Wavertree to a council house in Speke. 'It was very nice and modern. It seemed fantastic to me, after a two up and two down terrace house. You could go from the hall, to the sitting room then into the kitchen then into the hall again and back into the sitting room. I just ran round and round it all that first day.'

The house was Number 25 Upton Green, Speke. They'd put their name down for a council house 18 years previously in 1930, when Lou was a baby.

'It was a brand new house,' says Mrs Harrison. 'But I hated it from the minute we moved in. We tried to keep the garden nice, but kids just wrecked it. They stole your plants in the middle of the night. It was a sort of slum clearance area, but they'd mixed up the good and bad families together, hoping the good would lift the rest.'

George did fairly well at primary school. 'After we sat the scholarship exam,' says George, 'the teacher asked us who thought they had passed. Only one person put his hand up. He was a little fat lad who smelled. It was very sad, really. He turned out to be about the only one who didn't pass.

'Smelly kids like that were the sort teachers made you sit next to as a punishment. So the poor smelly kids really did get screwed up. All teachers are like that. And the more screwed up *they* are, the more they pass it on to the kids. They're all ignorant. I always thought that. Yet because they were old and withered you were supposed to believe they weren't ignorant.'

George started at the Liverpool Institute in 1954. Paul McCartney was already there, in the year ahead. John Lennon was in his fourth year at Quarry Bank High School.

'I was sad leaving Dovedale. The headmaster, Pop Evans, told us that we may feel smart big boys now, but at the next school we'd be the little boys once again. It seemed such a waste. After all that hustling to be one of the big lads.

'The first day at the Institute Tony Workman leapt on my back from behind a door and said, "Do you want a fight, lad."'

After a short spell of feeling lost and out of it, during which he tried to do a bit of homework and fit in, George gave up being interested in school work. 'I hated being dictated to. Some schizophrenic jerk, just out of training college, would just read out notes to you which you were expected to take down. I couldn't read them afterwards anyway. They never fooled me. Useless, the lot of them.

'That's when things go wrong, when you're quietly growing up and they start trying to force being part of society down your throat. They're all trying to transfigure you from the pure way of thought as a child, forcing their illusions on you. All those things annoyed me. I was just trying to be myself. They were trying to turn everybody into rows of little toffees.'

At the Institute, George was known from the beginning as a way-out dresser. Michael McCartney, Paul's brother, was a year below him. He remembers George always having long hair, years before anybody else did.

John Lennon's rebellion took the form of fighting and causing trouble. George did it by his dress, which annoyed masters just as much.

But one of the reasons George had long hair was that he always hated getting his hair cut. To save money, his father had continued to cut the family's hair, as he had done in the Navy. By this time the shears were old and blunt. 'He used to hurt them,' says Mrs Harrison. 'And they hated it.' 'Yes, perhaps they were a bit rough,' says Mr Harrison. 'Rough? You're joking, boy,' says his wife.

'George used to go to school with his school cap sitting high on top of his hair,' says Mrs Harrison. 'And very tight trousers. Unknown to me, he'd run them up on my machine to make them even tighter. I bought him a brand new pair once and the first thing he did was tighten them. When his dad found out, he told him to unpick them at once. "I can't, Dad," he said. "I've cut the pieces off." George always had an answer. He once went to school with a canary-yellow waistcoat under his school blazer. It belonged to his brother Harry, but George thought he looked terrific in it.'

'Going in for flash clothes, or at least trying to be a bit different, as I hadn't any money, was part of the rebelling. I never cared for authority. They can't teach you experience, you've got to go through it, by trial and error. You've got to find out for yourself you shouldn't do certain things. I always managed to keep a bit of individuality. I don't know what made me do it, but it worked. They didn't get me. Looking back, I feel pleased they didn't.'

For the first three years he was in continual trouble. '"Harrison, Kelly and Workman, get up and get out," that's all I used to hear. If it wasn't that I was being sent to go and stand in the chewer's corner.'

When winkle pickers came in, George had a monster pair in blue suede. 'One of the masters, Cissy Smith, went on at me about them. We called him Cissy because he was always smoothly dressed. He said, "They're not school shoes, Harrison." I wanted to ask him what *were* school shoes, but didn't.'

Cissy Smith's real name was Alfred Smith, the brother of John Lennon's Uncle George. 'I didn't discover that for years later either. I had hysterics when John told me.'

In his fourth year at the Institute, George began to stay out of trouble. 'I learned it was best to keep cool and shut up. I had this mutual thing with a few masters. They'd let me sleep at the back and I wouldn't cause any trouble. If it was nice and sunny, it was hard to keep awake anyway, with some old fellow chundering on. I often used to wake up at a quarter to five and find they'd all gone home.'

Family snap of George (centre), aged eight, with his parents, Harold and
Louise, and, behind, his brothers, Harold (left) and Peter.

Harry, George's eldest brother, had by this time finished school and had become an apprentice fitter. Lou, his sister, was at training college, and Peter was about to start a job as a panel beater.

Harold, George's father, was still a bus driver but he had also become a successful union official. He started to spend a lot of time at Finch Lane, the Liverpool Corporation social centre for conductors and drivers. By the 1950s, he was the MC for most of their Saturday night socials, introducing the guests.

'One of the earliest comedians we launched was Ken Dodd. We'd seen him at the club, having a drink, and we knew he was very funny, but he was always too nervous to go on stage. But he eventually went on. He did this act, "The Road to Mandalay", with shorts on and one of those pith helmets. It was a riot. I don't think he's half as funny now.'

Harold Harrison was naturally pleased that George was at last appearing to stick in at school. He was the only one of his three sons to have got into a grammar school so he wanted him to do well. As a hard working, meticulous union official, he wished he had had the chances George was getting.

He saw education, the way John's Aunt Mimi did and Paul's dad Jim, as the only way, not just to self advancement but to success and respectability in the world.

A good secure job is what most parents want for their children, but particularly people of Harold Harrison's generation. He had been through the worst of the depression days of the thirties, when he had been out of work for years and forced to bring up a family on meagre dole money.

George's individualism and anti-authority doesn't seem to have come from his father. At least his father's tough early life probably drove into him the need for steadiness. But his mother was always an ally. She wanted all her children to be happy. It didn't matter really what their interests were, as long as they enjoyed doing them.

Even when George became interested in something patently pointless, a hobby that nobody could ever make anything of, which clearly didn't lead to security or respectability, his mother still encouraged him.

Mrs Harrison isn't just jolly and outgoing. In her own little way, unlike all the other Beatle parents, she is one of nature's ravers.

6

GEORGE AND THE QUARRYMEN

Mrs Harrison was always interested in music and dancing. Along with her husband, she ran a learners' dancing class – mainly ballroom dancing – at the Finch Lane bus conductors' and drivers' club for almost ten years.

George showed no interest in music as a child, as far as his parents can remember. 'But he would always give you an entertainment if you asked him,' says Mrs Harrison. 'He would get down behind a chair and do you a puppet show.'

It wasn't until George was about 14 that he suddenly came home and started covering bits of paper with drawings of guitars. 'One day he said to me, "This boy at school's got a guitar he paid £5 for, but he'll let me have it for £3, will you buy it for me?" I said all right, son, if you really want. I had a little job by then. I'd gone back to working at a greengrocer's, the job I'd done before I was married.'

The first person to make any impression on George musically was Lonnie Donegan. 'I'd been aware of pop singers before him, like Frankie Laine and Johnnie Ray, but never really taken much interest in them. I don't think I thought I was old enough for them. But Lonnie Donegan and skiffle just seemed made for me.'

His first guitar, the one his mother bought for him for £3, lay in a cupboard for about three months, forgotten. 'There was a screw holding the neck to the box part,' says George. 'In trying to play it, I took it off and couldn't get it back on again. So I put it away in the cupboard. Then one day I remembered about it again and got Pete to fix it for me.'

'George tried to teach himself,' says Mrs Harrison. 'But he wasn't making much headway. "I'll never learn this," he used to say.'

'I said, "You will, son, you will. Just keep at it." He kept at it till his fingers were bleeding. "You'll do it, son, you'll do it," I said to him.'

'I sat up till two or three in the morning. Every time he said, "I'll never make it," I said, "You will, you will."'

Opposite: **George, aged 14, getting to grips with mastering his guitar.**

'I don't know why, really, I encouraged him so much. He wanted to do it, so that was enough for me. I suppose at the back of my mind I remembered all the things I wanted to do as a girl, but nobody encouraged me.

'So when it came to George, I helped all I could. Eventually, he was way beyond anything I could understand. "You don't understand about guitars, do you, Mum?" he said to me once. I said no, but you stick in, I'm sure you'll make it. Keep at it. He said no, he didn't mean that. He needed a new guitar, a better guitar. He said it was like playing a mouth organ. There are certain notes you just can't get because it's not a good enough mouth organ. Well, he'd soon come to that stage with this £3 guitar.

'So I said sure, I'll help you to buy a new one. He got one, £30 it cost. Electric as well, or something.

'Peter had also taken up the guitar. He had one first, in fact, now I think about it. A broken one which he got for five bob. He glued it and put it together and put strings on and it was great.'

'My mum did encourage me,' says George. 'Perhaps most of all by never discouraging me from anything I wanted to do. That was the good thing about her and my dad. If you tell kids not to, they're going to do it in the end anyway, so they might as well get it over with. They let me stay out all night when I wanted to and have a drink when I wanted to. I'd finished with all that staying out all night drinking bit when everybody else came to it. Probably why I don't like alcohol today. I had it all by the age of ten.'

'One day George came home and said he'd got an audition, at the British Legion Club in Speke,' says Mrs Harrison. 'I told him he must be daft. He hadn't even got a group. He said don't worry, he'd get one.'

George did get a group for his big night at the Speke British Legion. He got his brother Peter on guitar, his friend Arthur Kelly on guitar and two others, one on a tea chest and another on a mouth organ. He himself was on guitar. They all left the house one by one, ducking down behind the hedge. George didn't want all the nosy neighbours to know what they were doing.

They got to the hall and found that the real artists hadn't turned up. They had to go straight on and play all night as there was no one else there.

'They were so excited when they came home, all shouting together,' says Mrs Harrison. 'I couldn't make out at first what happened. Then they showed me the ten bob they'd got each, their first professional engagement. The poor boy on the tea chest looked awful. His fingers were bleeding from playing. The blood was all over the tea chest. They called themselves The Rebels for that night. They had it painted on in red.'

George didn't play in a proper group, although he did odd nights sitting in with other groups, until through Paul he joined the Quarrymen.

He first got talking to Paul shortly after he had started at the Institute. They used to meet on the same bus journey. George remembers the day his mother paid his and Paul's fare. When the skiffle phase arrived and they both had guitars, they became closer friends.

'Paul came round to my house one evening to look at the guitar manual I had, which I could never work out. It was still in the cupboard. We learned a couple of chords from it

Opposite: **George (right), aged 15 and with his hair up, at his first dance.**

and managed to play "Don't You Rock Me Daddy O", with two chords. We just used to play on our own, not in any group, just listening to each other and pinching anything from any other lad who could do better.'

They began to spend most of their spare time together, even during the holidays. This started long before Paul had met John and the Quarrymen.

Paul appears to have been with the Quarrymen for at least a year before George joined them, probably not until early 1958. No one remembers the exact date, but the joining probably didn't happen immediately. George, after all, was very young, even though he was getting better all the time as a guitarist and getting numerous stand-in dates.

'I first saw the Quarrymen when they were playing at the Wilson Hall at Garston. Paul was playing with them and said I should come and see them. I'd probably have gone anyway, just for the night out and to see if I could get in any groups. With knowing Paul, I got introduced to John.

'There was this other guitarist in another group that night, Eddie Clayton. He was great. John said if I could play like that, I could join them. I played "Raunchy" for them and John said I could join. I was always playing "Raunchy" for them. We'd be going somewhere on the top of a bus with our guitars and John would shout out, "Give us 'Raunchy', George.'''

'But George never thought he was any good,' says Mrs Harrison. 'He was always saying that, telling me about all the people who were so much better than he was. I told him he could be, if he stuck in.'

John remembers that it was George's youth that made him take some time before asking him to join.

'It was too much, too much. George was just too young. I didn't want to know at first. He was doing a delivery round and just seemed a kid. He came round once and asked me to go to the pictures with him but I pretended I was busy. I didn't dig him on first sight, till I got to know him.

'Mimi always said he had a low Liverpool voice, a real whacker. She said, "You always seem to like lower-class types, don't you, John?"

'We asked George to join us because he knew more chords, a lot more than we knew. So we got a lot from him. Every time we learned a new chord, we'd write a song round it.

'We used to sag off school and go to George's house for the afternoon. George looked even younger than Paul and Paul looked about ten, with his baby face.'

George says he probably did deliberately hang round John a lot. John was by this time about to start the Art College, but as deliberately aggressive and working-class as ever, despite all Mimi's upbringing.

'I was very impressed by John,' says George. 'Probably more than Paul, or I showed it more. I loved John's blue jeans and lilac shirt and sidies. But I suppose I was impressed by all the Art College crowd. John was very sarcastic, always trying to bring you down, but I either took no notice or gave him the same back, and it worked.'

'Meeting Paul was just like two people meeting,' says John. 'Not falling in love or anything. Just us. It went on. It worked. Now there were three of us who thought the same.'

There were still other members of the Quarrymen who came and went, either because they couldn't put up with John's tongue or got bored. They needed other people, when they got their occasional dates, as three guitars don't make a group, even in those days. They desperately needed a drummer but no one they picked up, however useless, ever seemed to stay.

They were moving out of the skiffle era as a group. Tea chests and washboards were just a bit amateurish. All of them anyway preferred rock'n'roll and Elvis in particular and this was the style they were trying to copy, listening to new records on the radio and trying to reproduce the same chords or sounds at home.

John, as the leader, tried to get bookings from all the little one-man managements who were cashing in on the group craze. But he was finding it very difficult to get regular bookings. There were so many groups, and most of them were far better than the Quarrymen.

But they now had two homes to go to – George's almost any time they liked, and Paul's, especially when his dad was out – where they could practise, write music or just draw and mess around. But Mimi was certainly not going to have any Teddy Boys from a rock group coming to her house.

'Paul used to come to my front door,' says Mimi. 'He'd lean his bike against the fence and look over at me with his sheep eyes and say "Hello, Mimi. Can I come in?" "No you certainly cannot", I'd say.'

Mimi wasn't very keen on George, when she first heard about him.

'John used to go on and on about George, what a nice boy he was and how I'd like him. He went to great lengths to impress me with George. "Give you anything, George," he'd say.

'I eventually said he could come in one day. He arrived with a crew-cut and a pink shirt. Well, it wasn't done. I might have been a bit old-fashioned, but schoolboys dressing like that. Up till John was 16 I always made sure he wore his regulation school blazer and shirt.'

So a lot of the practising was done at George's house in Upton Green. The Harrisons came in one day to find George in the tightest pair of jeans they'd ever seen.

'Harold went spare,' says Mrs Harrison. 'When he saw them, he went over the moon. George said John had just given them to him. Then he jumped up and pranced round the room. "How can I do my ballet without tight jeans?" he said, dancing all over the place. We had to laugh at him in the end. George never gave any cheek, but he always got round us.'

The first time Mrs Harrison met John Lennon she was in the kitchen when George brought him home. '"Here's John," George shouted. "Hello, Mrs Harrison," John said, coming forward to shake my hand. Well, I don't know what happened next. He somehow fell and as he did so, he fell on top of me and we both landed on the settee. Dad came in at that moment. You should have seen his face when he saw John on top of me! "What the devil's going on here?" George said, "It's OK, Dad. It's only John."

'John was always a bit of a fool. He was never miserable, just like me.'

7

JOHN AT ART COLLEGE

John had started at the Art College in the autumn of 1957, turning up in his tightest jeans and longest black jacket. His way of getting them past Mimi was to put on old conventional trousers over his jeans, then take them off at the bus stop when he'd got safely away from the house.

'They all thought I was a Ted at Art College when I arrived. Then I became a bit artier, as they all do, but I still dressed like a Ted, in black with tight drainies. Arthur Ballard, one of the lecturers, said I should change a bit, not wear them as tight. He was good, Arthur Ballard, he helped me, kept me on when others wanted to chuck me out.

'But I wasn't really a Ted, just a Rocker. I was only pretending to be one. If I'd met a proper Ted, with chains and a real gang, I'd have been shit scared.

'I got more confidence and just used to ignore Mimi. I went away for longer spells. Wore what clothes I wanted. I was always on at Paul to ignore his dad and just wear what he wanted.

'I never liked the work. I should have been an illustrator or in the painting school because it seemed groovy. But I found myself in lettering. I didn't turn up for something, so they had just put me in that. They were all neat fuckers in lettering. They might as well have put me in sky-diving for the use I was at lettering. I failed all the exams.

'I stayed on because it was better than working. I was there instead of going to work.

'I always felt I'd make it though. There were some moments of doubt, but I knew something would eventually happen. When Mimi used to throw away things I'd written or drawn, I used to say, "You'll regret that when I'm famous", and meant it.

'I didn't really know what I wanted to be, apart from ending up an eccentric millionaire. I fancied marrying a millionairess, and doing it that way.

'I had to be a millionaire. If I couldn't do it without being crooked, then I'd have to be crooked. I was quite prepared to do that – nobody obviously was going to give me money

Opposite: **John, trying hard to be hard, with his leather jacket and greased back hair. 'I was only pretending...'**

for my paintings. But I was too much of a coward to be a crook. I'd never have made it. I did plan to knock off a shop with another bloke, do it properly for a change, not just shoplifting. We used to look at shops at night, but we never got round to doing it.'

Julia, his mother, with whom he was spending more and more time, still approved of the life he was leading. She had now almost taken over from Mimi in his life. He relied on her, because she spoke the same language, liked the same things, hated the same sort of people.

'I was staying with Julia and Twitchy this weekend,' says John. 'The copper came to the door, to tell us about the accident. It was just like it's supposed to be, the way it is in the films. Asking if I was her son, and all that. Then he told us, and we both went white.

'It was the worst thing that ever happened to me. We'd caught up so much, me and Julia, in just a few years. We could communicate. We got on. She was great.

'I thought, fuck it, fuck it, fuck it. That's really fucked everything. I've no responsibilities to anyone now.

'Twitchy took it worse than me. Then he said, who's going to look after the kids? And I hated him. Bloody selfishness.

'We got a taxi over to Sefton General where she was lying dead. I didn't want to see her. I talked hysterically to the taxi driver all the way, ranted on and on, the way you do. The taxi driver just grunted now and again. I refused to go in and see her. But Twitchy did. He broke down.'

Julia died on 15 July 1958. The accident had happened very near Mimi's house.

'I always went out with her to the bus stop,' says Mimi. 'But this night she left early, at twenty to ten. She went out on her own. A minute later there was a terrible screeching. I flew out and she was dead, knocked down by a car outside my house. I never told the rest of the family the exact spot. They all went past it so often, it would have hurt them too much.

'But Julia isn't dead to me. She's alive as ever. I've never been near her grave, nor mother's. They're both alive to me. I loved them so dearly. Julia was a beautiful person.'

When Julia died it must obviously have been a terrible tragedy for John. 'But he never showed it,' says Pete Shotton. 'It was like when masters beat him up. He never gave anything away. His exterior never showed his feelings.'

All John's friends knew about the road accident as soon as it happened. Another friend, Nigel Whalley, had been the last to speak to her as she came out of Mimi's house to cross the road for the bus to go home.

'John never talked about Julia or how he felt,' says Pete. 'But he took it out of his girls. He gave them hell. I remember one of them shouting at him, "Don't take it out of me just 'cos your mother's dead."'

Mrs Harrison, George's mother, remembers the effect it had on John. They were still practising a lot at George's house, the house where they got endless hospitality and encouragement.

'I'd given them all beans and toast this evening. It was several months before John's mother died and he was just getting really close to her. I overheard him say to Paul, "I don't know how you can sit there and act normal with your mother dead. If anything like that happened to me, I'd go off me head."'

'When John's mother did die, he didn't appear to go off his head, but he wouldn't come out. I forced George to go round and see him, to make sure he still went off playing in their group and just didn't sit at home and brood.

'They all went through a lot together, even in those early days, and they always helped each other. George was terrified that I was going to die next. He'd watch me carefully all the time. I told him not to be so silly. I wasn't going to die.'

The death of John's mother brought him even closer to Paul. It was something else they now shared. But other students at the Art College say Julia's death made him outwardly worse, less interested in other people's feelings, more cruel in his humour.

Thelma Pickles was one of his girlfriends at the time, though nothing serious, just one of the people who were in his crowd. She says most of them were in awe of him, amazed by his attitude to life as they'd never come across such a personality before.

'John never had any money. He was a real burn, borrowing from everybody all the time, getting people to buy him chips, or drinks or cadging ciggies. He must still owe people pounds. But he has a sort of magnetic personality and could always get money out of people. He was outrageous, and said things people would be scared to say. He could be very cruel. Walking down the street he would go "Boo" in front of old people. And if he saw anyone who was crippled or deformed, he'd make loud remarks, like "Some people will do anything to get out of the army."

'He used to do a lot of cruel drawings. I thought they were marvellous. He did one of some women cooing over some babies, saying weren't they lovely. All the babies were deformed, with hideous faces. It was really very cruel. The day the Pope died he did lots of cartoons of him looking really awful. He did one of the Pope standing outside some big pillars outside Heaven, shaking the gates and trying to get in. Underneath it said, "But I'm the Pope, I tell you."

'John had a complete disrespect for everything. But he always had an audience round him. There was one girl who was crazy about him. She used to cry over him.

'He was very self-conscious about his glasses and would never wear them even at the pictures. We went to see *King Creole*, an Elvis film, but he still wouldn't put them on. There was a big sexy advert on for nylons, and he couldn't see that either and I had to tell him what it was.

'I never took his music seriously. He would say he'd written this new tune and I would think that was pretty fantastic, someone writing a tune, but I couldn't see what good it was. I knew it took miracles to get anywhere writing bits of tunes, so what was the point.

'I knew he *could* be famous, at something, but I didn't know what. He was so different and original. But I just couldn't see what he could be famous at. Perhaps a comedian, I thought.'

John agrees with most of Thelma's memories of him at Art College. But he remembers it all flatly, with little nostalgia or amusement. That was just how it was. 'I had to borrow or pinch as I had no money at college,' he says. Mimi says she gave him 30s. a week pocket money and can't understand how he spent it. 'I used to cadge all the time from spaniels like Thelma.

'I suppose I did have a cruel humour. It was at school that it had first started. We were once coming home from a school speech day and we'd had a few bevvies.

'Liverpool is full of deformed people, the way you have them in Glasgow, three-foot high men selling newspapers. I'd never really noticed them before, but all the way home that day they seemed to be everywhere. It got funnier and funnier and we couldn't stop laughing. I suppose it was a way of hiding your emotions, or covering it up. I would never hurt a cripple. It was just part of our jokes, our way of life.'

Two new people came into John's life at Art College. The first was Stuart Sutcliffe. He was in the same year but unlike John showed genuine promise, and keenness, as an artist. He was slight and slender, artistic and highly strung, but very fierce and individualist in his views. He and John became immediate friends. Stu admired John's clothes and his presence, the way he created an atmosphere round him with his strong dominant personality. John in turn admired Stu's talent for art, which was better than his, and also Stu's greater knowledge and artistic feeling.

Stu couldn't play any instrument and knew little about pop music, but he was completely bowled over when he heard John and his group play in the Art College at lunch times. He was always saying how good they were, when nobody else was very impressed.

George and Paul appear to have been slightly jealous of Stu and his influence with John, not that outsiders could see how much John admired Stu. John picked on Stu all the time and hurt him when he could. Paul, following John's lead, also began to pick on Stu, even though he was interested in art and, like John, was getting from Stu a lot of new ideas and fashions.

The other important friend John made at Art College was Cynthia Powell, now his wife.

'Cynthia was so quiet,' says Thelma. 'A completely different type from us. She came from over the water, the posh part, from a middle-class area. She wore a twin set. She was very nice, but I just couldn't see her suiting John. He used to go on about her, telling us how marvellous she was. I just couldn't see it.

'I left college for a year, and when I was away I heard they were going strong. I thought that would settle him, calm him down a bit, but it didn't turn out that way at all.'

Cynthia Powell was in the same year as John from the beginning, and in the same lettering class. But for well over the first year they took no notice of each other and moved in completely different circles, she the rather shy and refined girl from over the water, he the loud-mouthed Liverpool Teddy Boy.

'I just thought he was horrible. My first memory of looking at him properly was in a lecture theatre when I saw Helen Anderson sitting behind him stroking his hair. It awoke something in me. I thought it was dislike at first. Then I realized it was jealousy. But I never had any contact with him, apart from him stealing things from me, like rulers and brushes.

'He looked awful in those days. He had this long tweed overcoat which had belonged to his Uncle George and his hair all greased back. I didn't fancy him at all. He was scruffy. But I didn't get a chance to know him anyway. I wasn't one of his crowd. I was so respectable, or I thought I was.'

'She was a right Hoylake runt,' says John. 'Dead snobby. We used to poke fun at her and mock her, me and my mate Jeff Mohamed. "Quiet please," we'd shout. "No dirty jokes. It's Cynthia."'

They had their first proper conversation in a lettering class one day. 'It came out that we were both shortsighted. We talked a bit about it. John doesn't remember that at all. Very disheartening. But I do. After that I found myself getting into the class early, so that I could sit next to him. I used to hang around outside afterwards, hoping to bump into him.

'I didn't make any advances. It was just something I felt which John didn't know. I wasn't seeming to push. I couldn't do that. I don't think even now he realizes how often I used to hang around, on the off chance of seeing him.'

They met, properly, at Christmas time in their second year, in 1958.

'We had a class dance,' says John. 'I was pissed and asked her to dance. Jeff Mohamed had been having me on, saying "Cynthia likes you, you know."

'As we danced I asked her to come to a party the next day. She said she couldn't. She was engaged.'

'I was,' says Cynthia. 'Well almost. I'd been going out with the same boy for three years and was about to get engaged. John got annoyed when I said no. So he said come and have a drink afterwards at the Crack. I said no at first, then I went. I wanted to really, all the time.'

'I was triumphant,' says John, 'at having picked her up. We had a drink then went back to Stu's flat, buying fish and chips on the way.'

They went out every night after that and usually in the afternoon as well, going to the pictures instead of lectures.

'I was frightened of him. He was so rough. He wouldn't give in. We fought all the time. I thought if I give in now, that'll be it. He was really just testing me out. I don't mean sexually, just to see if I could be trusted, to prove to him that I could be.'

'I was just hysterical,' says John. 'That was the trouble. I was jealous of anyone she had anything to do with. I demanded absolute trust from her, just because I wasn't trustworthy myself. I was neurotic, taking out all my frustrations on her.

'She did leave me once. That was terrible.'

'I'd had enough,' says Cynthia. 'It was getting on my nerves. He just went off and kissed another girl.'

'But I couldn't stand being without her. So I rang her up.'

'I was sitting by the phone, waiting for him.'

Cynthia wasn't in a hurry to introduce John to her mother. She wanted to prepare her for the shock. 'He was never over-polite and he looked so scruffy. My mother played it cool. She was good really, though I'm sure she was hoping for it to peter out. But she never tried to stop it.

'The teachers warned me about going out with him, that my work was beginning to suffer. My work did go to pot and they were always on at me. Molly, the cleaning woman, once caught John hitting me, really clouting me. She said I was a silly girl, to get mixed up with someone like that.'

'I was in a sort of blind rage for two years,' says John. 'I was either drunk or fighting. It had been the same with other girlfriends I'd had. There was something the matter with me.'

'I just kept hoping he'd get over it, but I wondered if I could stick it long enough to find out. I blamed his background, his home, Mimi and the College. College just wasn't the place for him. Institutions aren't made for John.'

8

FROM QUARRYMEN TO MOONDOGS

The name Quarrymen had gone by the end of 1959. Paul and George were at the Institute, and had nothing to do with Quarry Bank High School, and John was now at the Art College. They had a succession of names after that, often made up on the spur of the moment. One night they called themselves The Rainbows because they all turned up in different coloured shirts.

The group had made no real progress for about the year after George had joined it, as far as George himself can remember, though his guitar playing was improving all the time.

'I can't remember even getting paid in the first year I was with them. We played mainly at fellows' parties. We'd go along with our guitars and get invited in. We either got free cokes or plates of beans, that was about all.

'The only times we got anywhere near real money was when we started entering for skiffle competitions. We'd get through the early rounds, keeping going to try and win something. But you never got paid for entering, just winning, and the rounds seemed to go on for ever. It was pretty daft of course, having no proper drummer and about 18 guitarists.'

Mrs Harrison was keen on George and his group, but Mr Harrison was very worried. He'd fought a losing battle over George's clothes and his long hair, mainly because Mrs Harrison sided with George. 'It's his own hair,' I used to say. 'Why should anyone tell you what to do with what's your own?'

'But I wanted him to stick in at school and get a good job,' says Mr Harrison. 'I was very upset when I saw he was so mad on the group. I realized you had to be good in show business to get to the top and even better to stay there. I couldn't see how they were going to get anywhere. My other two boys were well set up, Harry as a fitter and Peter as a panel beater. I wanted George to do as well.

'But George said he wanted to leave school. He didn't want to be any sort of penpusher.

Opposite: Three likely lads: George, John and Paul outside Paul's house, in Forthlin Road, 1960.

He wanted to work with his hands. He decided with his mother he wanted to leave, unknown to me. He never took his school cert. He just left.'

George started work in the summer of 1959 when he was 16.

'It became obvious I wasn't going to get any qualifications. The most I could have got, pushing it, would have been two O levels. But you need two O levels before they even let you dig shit. So what good would that have been.

'I stayed till the end of term, sagging off school most of the time to be with John at the Art College. Paul and I used to hang round there a lot.

'I hadn't a job for a long time when I left school. I hadn't a clue. My dad was all keen on the apprenticeship thing, so I tried the apprentice's exam for the Liverpool Corporation, but failed it. Eventually the Youth Employment Officer came up with a job of being a window-dresser at Blacklers, the big department store. I went along, but it had gone. They offered me an apprenticeship as an electrician instead.

'I enjoyed it. It was better than school. And with winter coming on, it was nice to be in a big warm shop. We used to play darts most of the time.

'But I began to think at the time about emigrating to Australia. At least I tried to get my dad interested in us all going, as I was too young. Then I thought of Malta as I'd seen some travel brochures. Then I thought of Canada. I got the papers to fill in, but when I found my parents had to sign them for me, I didn't bother. I felt something would turn up.'

Over at the McCartney household, Jim was struggling to bring up two teenage boys on the right lines. At least Paul was still at school, much to Jim's pleasure. But with spending all his spare time with John and George, messing around with a beat group, it didn't leave much time for school work.

Paul had still managed to stay in 5B, which was looked upon as the main English and languages stream, but he didn't do very well in O levels. He managed to pass only one, Art.

He then thought about leaving, but couldn't think of what job to do. His father was still keen for him to stay on. It seemed easier *not* to leave. School still gave him lots of time for playing. So he stayed on and went into the Remove Form, as he hadn't enough O levels to get immediately into the Sixth. He sat O levels again and got four more this time and so went into the Sixth Form.

'School was still a complete drag, but there was an English master called Dusty Durband I liked, the only one I did. He was great. He liked modern poetry and used to tell us about *Lady Chatterley*, long before we'd heard of it, and *The Miller's Tale*. He said they were considered dirty books, though they weren't.'

This spark of interest kept him in the Sixth Form, although he did no work. Officially he was preparing two subjects, English and Art, for A level, as he was supposed to be going to go to a training college and become a teacher. Everybody knew he was more than capable of it. It kept Jim happy anyway.

'I never thought much of the music Paul was interested in,' says Jim. 'That Bill Haley, I never liked him. There was no tune to it at all.

'But one day I came home at 5.30 and heard them in the house playing. I realized then

Opposite: **Paul with his father Jim and brother Michael, c. 1960. After the death of his wife Mary, at the age of 45, Jim McCartney was left to bring up his two teenage sons alone.**

that they were getting good, not just bashing about. They were making some nice chords.'

Jim began to want to sit in with them, offering advice and hints about how *he* used to do it in the good old days of Jim Mac's Band. Why didn't they play some really *good* tunes? Like 'Stairway to Paradise'? He'd always thought that was a really lovely number. He told them about how he used to run his band and how they should present their numbers.

They said no thanks, very much, just make some tea, eh, Dad? He said all right. But if they didn't like 'Stairway to Paradise' how about some really jazzy numbers, like 'When the Saints'? He could tell them a good way to do that. They said no, more firmly this time.

In the end, Jim restricted himself to making them food. He'd had to take up cooking, after a fashion, when his wife died. He found to his delight that although his own two, Paul and Michael, were very choosy about their food and were poor eaters – and when Paul was busy, he wouldn't eat at all – John and George turned out to be gluttons who would eat anything at any time. 'I used to work off all the stuff on to them that Paul and Michael had left. In the end, I didn't have to disguise it but just say there was some leftovers here, would they like it. To this day I always have to make George some custard when he comes. He says my custard's the best in the world.'

The group was improving, getting some primitive amps together and creating a louder beat, compared with the soft patterings of skiffle. 'But each year seemed five years,' says Paul.

They were now mainly playing at working men's social clubs or church functions and had given up parties. They played at places like the Wilson Hall and the Finch Lane Bus Depot.

They went in for more and more competitions, like all the embryo groups. 'There was this woman who played the spoons who kept on beating us,' says Paul. 'Then there was the Sunny Siders. This group had a great gimmick. They had a midget.'

The members of the group were still constantly changing. As nobody knew them, they could turn up on dates with anyone they could get. 'We had a bloke called Duff as pianist for some time, but his dad wouldn't let him stay out late. He'd be playing away one minute, and the next he would have disappeared, gone home in the middle of a number.'

For their public performances, they were usually all dressed like Teddy Boy cowboys, with black and white cowboy shirts with white tassels from the top pockets and black bootlace ties.

But they spent more time in George's or Paul's house than on stage. 'We used to come back to our house and smoke tea in me dad's pipe,' says Paul. 'Sometimes we'd bring a girl home or sit and draw each other. But most of the time we were playing guitars and writing songs.'

John and Paul wrote about 50 songs in their first couple of years together. Only one was ever used later – 'Love Me Do'.

The first thing they did when they started a new one was write 'Another original by John Lennon and Paul McCartney'.

They were both getting more adept at playing the guitar, thanks partly to watching the big stars of the day on TV. 'I watched the Shadows backing Cliff Richard one night. I'd heard them play a very clever introduction to "Move It" on the record, but could never work out how they did it. Then I saw them do it on TV. I rushed out of the house straight away, got on me bike and raced up to John's with me guitar. "I've got it," I shouted. And we all got down to learning it right away. It gave us a little bit of flash to start off our numbers. I also got some good chords from listening to "Blue Moon".'

As they were always keen to enter any competition, however crummy, there was great excitement when the biggest competition organizer of the day arrived in Liverpool. The advertisement in the *Liverpool Echo* said that 'Mr Star-Maker, Carroll Levis' was due to pay a visit soon as part of his Carroll Levis Discoveries TV show. The show was going to be recorded in Manchester but he was to hold a local audition in Liverpool, at the Empire Theatre, to see which Liverpudlian talent was fit for the programme itself in Manchester.

John, Paul and George, like half the teenage population of Liverpool, went along for the audition. They got through and were invited to Manchester to do the real show.

Mrs Harrison remembers the excitement of it. 'George was dead thrilled by this letter which had come through the post one day. I couldn't see what all the fuss was about. The letter was addressed to some group called "The Moondogs".'

The Moondogs was what they had become, a name thought up on the spur of the moment for the Carroll Levis Show. They were on the bill as 'Johnny and the Moondogs'. All groups had a leader in those days, like Cliff Richard and the Shadows. So they put John's name first. He was the leader anyway, if anyone was.

They did their bit in Manchester and got a reasonable amount of applause afterwards. The whole basis of the Carroll Levis Show was that at the end each group returns, does a few bars from its piece again, and the audience claps like mad, or otherwise. It is this final clap which is registered and the winners decided.

But Johnny and the Moondogs, being poor Liverpool lads, with no transport of any kind to get them back to Liverpool, couldn't wait. The show was running late and they were about to miss their last train back to Liverpool. They hadn't enough money for a night in a Manchester hotel. So when the time came for the final applause, they had gone.

Naturally, they didn't win. They weren't even spotted, or noticed, or given any encouragement by the talent spotters around.

For John, Paul and George it was a big disappointment. Their first time within touching distance of the big-time professionals had come and gone.

9

STU, SCOTLAND AND THE SILVER BEATLES

At the Art College John and Stuart were becoming even closer friends. Stu spent most of his time following the group round and watching them practise. He and John together managed to persuade a college committee to buy them a tape recorder, ostensibly for use by all students. John took it over for himself, to record his group playing, so that they could hear what they sounded like. They also got a 'public address system' bought for use at college dances. This ended up as part of his group's amplification equipment.

Stu was still as interested in art, despite spending so much time with John and his group. He entered some paintings for the John Moores Exhibition, one of the best exhibitions of its type, not just on Merseyside but throughout Britain. It is named after John Moores, a member of the wealthy Liverpool family that is connected with Littlewoods football pools and the mail order firm. Stuart Sutcliffe, although still a student, won a prize worth £60, a huge sum and a great success for one so young.

John, his best friend and biggest influence, immediately saw a way of using the money in the best possible way. Stu had always been saying that he wished he could play an instrument and really be in their group, instead of just hanging around. John said now was his chance to join. With his £60, he could buy a bass guitar. It didn't matter that he couldn't play. They would teach him.

Paul and George were equally keen on the idea, as they needed another member for the group. From what George remembers, Stu was offered an alternative – he could buy himself a bass or a set of drums. They needed both as they had three stars on guitars and no backing of any sort. 'Stu had no idea how to play it,' says George. 'We all showed him what we could, but he really picked it up by playing on stage.'

In those early days, as can be seen from photographs, Stu usually had his back to the audience, so that no one could see how very few chords he was playing. They were doing more and more engagements, still earning only a few bob, playing at working men's clubs

Opposite: Stu Sutcliffe, John's art college friend, looking very cool and Left Bank, in Hamburg, *c.* 1960.

and socials. But as the beat group boom took over Liverpool, little teenage clubs slowly began to spring up. They were basically coffee clubs, on the lines of the hundreds of coffee bars, serving espresso coffee amidst lots of rubber plants and bamboo, which had arisen all over the country. The Liverpool ones occasionally put on live shows for the teenagers, which gave the hundreds of beat groups somewhere to play.

The beat groups could never get into the traditional sort of clubs, like the Cavern. They were only for jazz fans and jazz bands, which was considered a much higher art form. The beat groups were all scruffy and amateur and Teddy Boyish. It was a working-class art form, full of electricians and labourers. There was a tendency to look down upon all beat groups and the people who played in them.

'We were always anti-jazz,' says John. 'I think it is shit music, even more stupid than rock and roll, followed by students in Marks and Spencer pullovers. Jazz never gets anywhere, never does anything, it's always the same and all they do is drink pints of beer. We hated it because in the early days they wouldn't let us play at those sort of clubs. We'd never get auditions because of the jazz bands.'

The beat groups were by now all trying to get wired up, with electric guitars and amps, which skiffle groups had never done. There were other rock-type singers who had come along in Elvis's wake, like Little Richard and Jerry Lee Lewis, spawning many British imitators.

But it was still in London that everything in Britain happened. Britain's first rock and roll singer who had any national success in Britain on the lines of the American stars was a Cockney, who made it in London through the London coffee bars – Tommy Steele. Then there was Cliff Richard, who modelled himself completely on Elvis. John, George and Paul seem to have been unaware of Tommy Steele, at least they can't remember him making any impression on them. But they actively hated Cliff Richard and the Shadows. John says it was Cliff's sort of Christian image, even then, which offended him. But they also hated the traditional pop ballads Cliff Richard went on to sing.

Paul, as the one who always tried to make things happen, was prepared to play down their likes and dislikes and chat up anyone who looked like helping them. He was always trying hard to get them some publicity in the local newspapers.

He wrote a letter around this time to a journalist called Mr Low they had met in a pub.

'Dear Mr Low,

I am sorry about the time I have taken to write to you, but I hope I have not left it too late. Here are some details about the group.

It consists of four boys: Paul McCartney (guitar), John Lennon (guitar), Stuart Sutcliffe (bass) and George Harrison (another guitar) and is called...

This line-up may at first seem dull but it must be appreciated that as the boys have above average instrumental ability they achieve surprisingly varied effects. Their basis beat is off-beat, but this has recently tended to be accompanied by a faint on-beat; thus the overall sound is rather reminiscent of the four in the bar of traditional jazz. This could possibly be put down to the influence of Mr McCartney, who led one of the top local jazz bands (Jim Mac's Jazz Band) in the 1920s.

Modern music, however, is the group's delight, and, as if to prove the point, John and Paul have written over fifty tunes, ballads and faster numbers, during the last three years. Some of

Paul's early handwritten letter to an unknown journalist called Mr Low, seeking some publicity for the group.

these tunes are purely instrumental (such as "Looking Glass", "Catswalk" and "Winston's Walk") and others were composed with the modern audience in mind (tunes like "Thinking of Linking", "The One After 909", "Years Roll Along" and "Keep Looking That Way").

The group also derive a great deal of pleasure from re-arranging old favourites ("Ain't She Sweet", "You Were Meant For Me". "Home", "Moonglow", "You are My Sunshine" and others).

Now for a few details about the boys themselves. John, who leads the group, attends the College of Art, and, as well as being an accomplished guitarist and banjo player, he is an experienced cartoonist. His many interests include painting, the theatre, poetry, and, of course, singing. He is 19 years old and is a founder member of the group.

Paul is 18 years old and is reading English Literature at Liverpool University. He, like the other boys, plays more than one instrument – his specialities being the piano and drums, plus, of course…'

The rest of Paul's highly colourful mix of fact and fiction is, unfortunately, missing. He wasn't, of course, 18 or at Liverpool University, but it was true, as he indicated by the dots, that the group didn't have a name. Later in 1959 they started seriously trying to think of what to call themselves, just as they'd done for the Carroll Levis audition, as it looked as if they were about to get another important audition.

This is when the idea of calling themselves the Beatles came up. No one is definitely sure how it happened. Paul and George just remember John arriving with it one day. They'd always been fans of Buddy Holly and the Crickets. They liked his music, and the name of his group. It had a nice double meaning, one of them a purely English meaning, which Americans couldn't have appreciated. They wished they'd thought of calling themselves the Crickets.

Thinking of the name Crickets, John thought of other insects with a name that could be played around with. He'd filled books as a child with similar word play. 'The idea of beetles came into my head. I decided to spell it BEAtles to make it look like beat music, just as a joke.'

That was the real and simple origin of their name, though for years afterwards they made up different daft reasons each time anyone asked them. Usually they said a man with a magic carpet appeared at a window and told them. Though they'd at last thought of a name they liked, they weren't permanently called the Beatles for a long time.

They met a friend who who asked them what their new name was. They said Beatles. He said you had to have a long name for a group. Why didn't they call themselves Long John and the Silver Beatles? They didn't think much of his idea either. But when this important audition came up and they were asked what they were calling themselves they said 'Silver Beatles', which was a name they stuck to for the rest of that year, 1959.

The important auditioner was none other than the famous Larry Parnes, then the king of British rock and roll who had in his stable Tommy Steele, Billy Fury, Marty Wilde, Duffy Power and Johnny Gentle. They'd heard about Larry Parnes coming to Liverpool while hanging around the Jackaranda, a club where many beat groups used to play. This was owned by a Liverpool-Welshman called Allan Williams. He also ran the Blue Angel, the club in which the Larry Parnes audition was going to be held.

They arrived at the Larry Parnes audition without a definite name – it was only when one of Larry Parnes's assistants asked them for a name that they came out with Silver Beatles. They also arrived without a drummer. A drummer they'd been using had promised to turn up, but didn't. Once again, they were drummerless.

A drummer who was at the Blue Angel for the audition with another group did them a favour and stood in with them. He was Johnny Hutch, looked upon as one of the top three drummers of the time in Liverpool. There is a photograph of the Silver Beatles taken at that audition (see pages 50–1). Johnny Hutch is sitting at the back looking very bored and superior. As usual, you can't see much of Stu. He has his back to Larry Parnes, trying hard to hide his fingerwork on the bass.

The audition was to find a backing group for Billy Fury. Larry Parnes didn't think any group was good enough, but he offered the Silver Beatles a two-week tour of Scotland, as the backing group to one of Larry Parnes's newest but unknown discoveries, Johnny Gentle. It was in no sense their tour. The Silver Beatles were to be very minor. But it was their first ever proper engagement as professionals, and a real tour at that, however short and however second rate.

George, who was then coming on for 16, took his two weeks' holiday so that he could go. Paul at the time was about to sit his O levels, but he had no intention of missing the chance of a tour for something as trivial as studying for his GCE. Ivan Vaughan, his friend at the Institute, remembers arguing with him and saying he was silly to go off and not do any work for his exams. Paul somehow managed to convince his father that he'd been given two weeks' holiday off school. They'd been told to take things easy. He said he would be back just in time for the exams and the tour would be a good rest for his brain. No wonder he passed only one subject.

They had to get yet another new drummer for this tour of Scotland. He was called Thomas Moore. They can't remember anything else about him, except that they went to his flat to get him and that he'd been living on the dole. Thomas Moore, apparently, was his real name. The Silver Beatles, in this first flush of being pro, all wanted to change their names. That was the fashion.

'It was exciting changing your name,' says Paul. 'It made it seem all real and professional. It sort of proved you did a real act, if you had a stage name.'

Paul turned himself into Paul Ramon. He can't remember where he got the Ramon bit from. 'I must have heard it somewhere. I thought it sounded really glamorous, sort of Valentino-ish.' George became Carl Harrison after one of his heroes Carl Perkins. Stu became Stu de Stijl, after the art movement. John can't remember what he called himself, if anything, but others remember him as Johnny Silver.

The tour of Scotland was to be in the far north, round little ballrooms on the northeast coast. Paul can remember Inverness and Nairn but no other names. He sent back postcards to his father saying: 'It's gear. I've been asked for my autograph.'

They were all a bit jealous of the fact that George was getting on particularly well with the star of the tour, Johnny Gentle. He promised to give George a present after the tour, one of Eddie Cochrane's old shirts, so he said. They argued as usual amongst themselves, but most of all they picked on Stu, the newest member of the group. John, George and Paul had been with each other long enough to know that rows and arguments and criticism didn't mean much. If it did, you just argued back.

'We were terrible,' says John. 'We'd tell Stu he couldn't sit with us, or eat with us. We'd tell him to go away, and he did.' At one hotel they stayed at, a variety show had just left. There had been a dwarf in the show and they found out which bed he had slept in and said that would have to be Stu's. They certainly weren't going to sleep in it. So Stu had to. 'That was how he learned to be with us,' says John. 'It was all stupid, but that was what we were like.'

After the great excitement of Scotland, nothing happened. Larry Parnes didn't offer them any more work. He admits now he missed a great chance, but at the time he had enough successful solo stars not to be interested in groups. The Beatles went back to dances full of drunken Teds, working men on their night out, or sleazy clubs.

They got a few dates, not long after Scotland, at a strip club in Upper Parliament Street. They had to accompany Janice the stripper as she shed her clothes. 'She handed us the music she wanted,' says George. 'It was something like the "Gypsy Fire Dance". As we couldn't read music, it wasn't much use to us. We just played "Ramrod" then "Moonglow", as I'd just learned it.'

They did manage a couple of dates at the Cavern Club in Mathew Street around the same time, though it was still a jazz stronghold. They used to get little notes passed up to them telling them not to play rock and roll, so they would introduce the next number as if it were a genuine jazz piece. 'And now an old favourite by Fats Duke Ellington Leadbelly, called "Long Tall Sally".' And they'd go straight into the beat number. Naturally, this wasn't liked by the management and didn't help them to get many further dates.

But most of the time they didn't do much, except hang around each other's houses or, when they had any money, the clubs. 'Scotland had been a faint hope, our first glimpse of show business,' says George. 'It was a bit of a come down being back in Liverpool. We were lucky to get more than two dates a week. All we were making was about 15 bob a night, plus as much eggs on toast and cokes as we could take.'

10

THE CASBAH

One of the places they started going back to, for want of anything better, was the Casbah Club. They'd played there earlier in the year, before they'd gone to Scotland.

Mrs Best, who founded the Casbah, is small, dark-haired and very volatile. She comes from Delhi, India. She met her husband, Johnny Best, an ex-boxing promoter, in India during the war. She came back to Liverpool with him and eventually they bought a large 14-roomed Victorian house at Number 8 Hayman's Green in the good residential district of West Derby.

Pete Best, her elder son, was born in 1941. He went to Liverpool Collegiate, another of Liverpool's good grammar schools. He passed five subjects at O level and went into the Sixth Form. His plan was to be a teacher.

He was handsome and well built, but somewhat shy, almost sullen looking and uncommunicative, especially in comparison with his dynamic, energetic mother. When he began to bring friends back from school, she went to great lengths to encourage this.

During the summer holidays of 1959, when Pete was about to go into his second year in the Sixth, he and a gang of his friends asked his mother if instead of cluttering up all her rooms playing records they could clear out the huge cellar and use that. 'The original idea was that it would be their den,' she says. 'That developed into the idea of making it into a coffee club, just for teenagers, like the ones in town. We decided to make it a private club, charging a membership fee of a shilling, to keep out the Teds and roughs.'

They decided to have some of the beat groups which were springing up all over Liverpool. They knew there would be many who would jump at the chance. Mrs Best, with her flair for running things, and people, welcomed the idea.

The group they found was the Quarrymen, as they were still called. This came through a girl who knew one of the members of the Quarrymen and said how good they were. It

Opposite: Pete Best, drumming with the Beatles, had many fans, who loved him for his mean, moody looks, as well as for his drumming. The other Beatles, however, turned out not to be such fans.

wasn't John, Paul or George she knew, but someone else who was playing the guitar for them at the time, Ken Brown. He was one of the many members of the Quarrymen who were always coming and going in those days.

When John, Paul and George heard they were looking for a group, they all rushed round at once. They were immediately given paint brushes and helped with the final week or so of cleaning and decorating the cellar. John brought his girlfriend, Cynthia Powell, to help.

'I remember telling John,' says Mrs Best, 'to put some undercoat on a wall. When I came back, he'd finished painting but had done it all in gloss. He was so shortsighted he hadn't been able to tell the difference. I was in a panic that it would never dry in time.'

Even up to the opening day, they hadn't decided on a name. 'I went down one evening to see how they were getting on. It was so bloody mysterious, with little dark corners everywhere. It seemed oriental. I thought of this picture I'd just seen with Hedy Lamarr and Charles Boyer, *Algiers* I think it was called, in which they go to the Casbah. So that was the name I chose, the Casbah Club. As I come from India, it seemed very apt.'

It opened at the end of August 1959. There were almost 300 there that first night. The Quarrymen got a great reception. The Casbah seemed launched for a long time.

'I was very pleased,' says Mrs Best. 'Not for myself of course, but for Peter. He had vague notions about going into show business and I thought this might be some sort of experience for him by helping with the club. I thought it would make him less self-conscious, give him more confidence.'

The club thrived. Coffee and sweets were on sale and there were the Quarrymen to listen to. At weekends, there were crowds in the evening of up to 400. Very soon there was a membership of 3,000. A bouncer was hired, Frank Garner, to look after the door and keep out Teds.

All went well for a couple of months. Then a row developed over the Quarrymen. Their fee for playing was 15s. each a night. One night, only John, Paul and George played. Ken Brown was missing. 'I paid the three of them 15s. each then I paid Ken Brown his 15 bob when I saw him. They said he shouldn't have been paid at all as he hadn't been there. They said the fee for the group was really £3 for the evening. The three who had turned up should have got £3 between them, not 15 bob each.'

This is the basis of the disagreement, as Mrs Best and Pete Best remember it. The others can't. Anyway, after the row over the money, Ken Brown left the Quarrymen and not long after the Quarrymen themselves started to move farther afield.

Pete Best had by this time started banging away at an old snare drum, seeing how well the Quarrymen were doing, but mainly to amuse himself in odd moments at the club. When Ken Brown left, it was decided that he and Pete should form a new group. They got two others, and called themselves the Blackjacks, aided and abetted by Mrs Best.

'They were very good,' says Mrs Best. 'I remember Rory Storm, who was very big in those days, issuing a challenge to see who could get the biggest crowd. Rory got 390 but the Blackjacks got 450, the most we ever had.'

Opposite: Paul with the Quarrymen, playing at the Casbah Club, the venue founded by Pete Best's mother, *c.* 1959. Ken Brown (seated, on guitar) was one of the many members of the group who were always coming and going at that time.

The Quarrymen went to Scotland and became the Silver Beatles but did occasional return engagements at the Casbah, when nothing else turned up. The Blackjacks, with Pete Best on drums, had now become the Casbah's resident group. They got better during the following year and Pete Best decided he did want to go into show business.

'I'd been thinking by then of going to a teachers' training college. My five O levels would have got me in. But I got fed up and left before sitting A levels.'

He left school in the summer term of 1960. The Casbah was still a big success and there was enough for him to do there, but then his group began to disintegrate. Ken Brown moved south and the two others went away on courses connected with their full-time work. Pete had left school for a career in show business, but was now left with nothing to do.

But in August 1960, five weeks after he had left school, Paul McCartney rang him.

'Paul said had I still got my drums,' says Pete. 'I told him I'd just got a complete new kit. I was very proud of that. He said they'd got a job in Hamburg and was I interested in being their drummer? I said yes. I'd always liked them very much. They said I'd get £15 a week, which was a lot. Much better than going to a training college.

'I went down to Allan Williams's club, the Jackaranda. I met Stu for the first time. I had an audition. I blasted off a few numbers and they all said fine, you can come to Hamburg with us.'

As Mrs Best had got in on the beat group scene at the teenage coffee club end, Allan Williams, as an experienced night club man, had got on to it slightly higher up the scale. He was not only putting on the groups in his own nightclubs, but also finding groups for other people and acting as a sort of agent-cum-manager for groups looking for work. It was he who had helped the Beatles to get their Larry Parnes audition. The Beatles' money for their Scottish tour, though paid for by Larry Parnes, had come through Allan Williams who had acted for them in getting the tour.

The reasons why Allan Williams, a small-time Liverpool night club owner, came to be exporting groups to Hamburg are rather complicated. The first contact had been established when a German seaman had heard a West Indian steel band in the Jackaranda Club and had told people in Hamburg how good they were. This had led to them being engaged by a Hamburg night club. Allan Williams had followed them over, hoping to interest Hamburg club owners in other Liverpool groups. He went to the Kaiserkeller, which seemed to be the only rock and roll club, and met Bruno Koschmeider. 'I kidded him on that all the best British rock groups came from Liverpool.'

Koschmeider came to Britain to see for himself but instead went to London where he soon found that nobody had heard of the Liverpool groups. He went to the Two I's in Soho, then the centre for British rock (Tommy Steele had played there), and signed Tony Sheridan and his group. He was a big success in Hamburg and Koschmeider came back to London to look for more groups. By a coincidence, Allan Williams happened to be in the Two I's the same evening Koschmeider was looking for another group. Allan Williams was with a Liverpool group called Derry and the Seniors, trying to get them work. He fixed them up to go to Hamburg, the first Liverpool beat group to go there.

Derry and the Seniors were a success and Allan Williams was asked for another Liverpool group. He thought of Rory Storm, but they were going to Butlins holiday camp. So he asked the Beatles. But the Hamburg contract was for a five-piece group and the

Beatles didn't have a drummer. They'd had an occasional drummer, a middle-aged man with a family, but he turned down the chance of Hamburg as his wife was against it. This was when they thought of asking Pete Best. When he agreed, everything was ready.

In the Harrison household there was no undue excitement – apart of course from George. But his mother at least never tried to stop him going. She was worried about him being only 17 and going abroad for the first time, especially Hamburg. She'd heard things about Hamburg. 'But it was what he wanted to do. They were going to get properly paid for once. I knew they were good and were bound to do well. All I'd heard up till then was "Heh, Mum, we've got a booking, lend's the bus fare, eh, and I'll pay you back when I'm famous".'

So Mrs Harrison got George ready. She made him promise to write and gave him a tin of home-made scones.

George, despite his great youth, was at least a working man. But Paul and John were still ostensibly studying. Going to Hamburg was going to ruin their great careers once and for all.

Jim McCartney was naturally all against Paul going to Hamburg. Paul had just sat his A levels – Art and English – and they were all waiting to hear if he'd got through them so that they would then definitely know if he'd got a place at a teachers' training college.

Michael McCartney, Paul's brother, says that Paul, as ever, arranged everything very cleverly. 'I remember coming home from school with Paul the day he told me they'd been invited to Hamburg. He let it out, just casually. I said, Wow! But Paul said he didn't know if he should, pretending he was all undecided. I said it was fantastic! He was going to be a big star, wow! He said, do you think Dad will let me? That was very smart. I was then on his side in persuading Dad. He let me get all excited, so that I was desperately *wanting* him to go.'

Paul says that he was of course very excited. 'We hadn't seemed to have done anything for weeks, just hanging around. It was the long summer holidays and I didn't want to go back to school, or college. But there wasn't much alternative, until suddenly Hamburg came up. That meant I definitely didn't need to go back to school. There was now something else to do.'

There was still Jim to persuade. Paul got Allan Williams to come home, to help soften up Jim. 'Allan Williams never got our names right, though,' says Paul. 'He would call me John.' However, Allan Williams managed to tell Jim how well organized it was all going to be and what a lovely respectable place Hamburg was.

'I think, basically, Dad was quite pleased,' says Michael, 'though he said he wasn't at the time.'

'I knew they were well liked at what they were doing,' says Jim. 'It was their first big engagement and they were determined to go. Paul was just 18. He'd just had four weeks of his school holidays. He went on a student passport. I gave him a pep talk, you know, about being a good lad. What else could I do?

'I was worried all the time that he wouldn't get enough to eat in Germany. He did send postcards, saying "I'm eating plenty. We had this that and the other this evening." That satisfied me, I suppose.'

Jim was slightly satisfied when just after Paul had gone, the results of the GCE A levels came through. Paul had failed Art but passed in English, though by that time even Jim realized it didn't matter any more.

John and Paul in a café in Paris, en route to Hamburg. Paul was only 18 and travelled on a student passport. His father and John's aunt Mimi were very unhappy about the boys suddenly interrupting their college careers to go off to Germany.

But John's Aunt Mimi put up more of a fight. She had discouraged Paul and George that time from coming to her house and John from playing his guitar at home. She'd also tried to ban John from playing in a group. Since the Quarrymen had begun, almost five years previously, John had had to lie to her most of the time about what he was doing. She knew he was still messing around writing silly songs and that, but she didn't know the extent of his interest.

She really thought he was sticking in at the Art College, till one day someone told her how he was spending his lunch hours – playing in a group. She decided to go and investigate for herself, to see just what depth of depravity John had sunk to.

The lunch time she decided to investigate turned out to be one of the days they were playing at the Cavern. They weren't the resident group, as it was still basically a jazz club, but they were getting more dates as people at the Cavern became interested in them.

'I'd never heard of this awful place, the Cavern,' says Mimi. 'It took a long time to find. I just had to follow the crowds in the end, I went down some steps with them all and there was this chap, Ray McFall, taking money. "I want John Lennon!"

'I pushed on in, but the noise was deafening. It had this low ceiling which made it worse. The girls were jammed together, with their arms down by their sides. Try as I might, I just couldn't get near the stage. If I could, I would have pulled him off it. In the end, I just went and sat in one of the dressing rooms. Dressing room! Just a scruffy little cubicle. When he came off, with the girls still screaming, he couldn't see me at first. He's blind without his glasses. Then he put them on and saw me, "What are you doing, Mimi?" "Very nice, John," I said, "this is very nice".'

Mimi made sure he went back to College that afternoon. She went on at him all the time to stick in at his studies, not this silly playing, so that he could get some proper qualifications. But she couldn't stop him from playing.

'What do you mean,' John used to say. 'I'm not a working man and never will be. No matter what you do or say, I'll never end up with a nine-to-five job.'

Then Hamburg came up. This was going to mean a proper severance from Mimi, for a long time in a foreign country. Mimi remembers John trying to get her as excited as he was. '"Mimi, isn't it marvellous," he told her. "I'm going to get £100 a week, isn't that marvellous!"'

A slight exaggeration on the money, but still marvellous, for five teenage lads. John, of course, jumped at the chance of having a good excuse to leave the College. He'd survived three years, just. Arthur Ballard, the lecturer who had most to do with him, saved him from being expelled several times. John had failed all exams and was leaving without any qualifications, though he half thought to himself that they might take him back if Hamburg failed. He was also leaving Cyn.

'The group had started to get its own fans,' says Cynthia, 'I knew they had lots of girls hanging round them, but I never worried or got jealous. I seemed so much older than all the girls. I felt very secure.

'But I was much more worried about Hamburg. That seemed so far away and for such a long time. I knew the Liverpool girls, but I didn't know anything about the situation in Hamburg. Anything could happen to them in Hamburg.'

11

HAMBURG

Hamburg is Germany's Liverpool. It's a large northern port. The inhabitants are rough and tough but underneath they can be soft and sentimental. The climate is wet and windy. They have the same sort of nasal accents, easily recognizable in each country. They even have the same latitude, 53 degrees north.

But Hamburg is twice the size of Liverpool and traditionally a much wickeder city. Hamburg crime and Hamburg sex life are known throughout Europe. The Reeperbahn, the main street in Hamburg's Soho, must have more strip clubs than any other street in the world.

When the Beatles arrived there in 1960, with George sweet 17 and never been kissed, well hardly, wicked Hamburg was at its wickedest. Hamburg, being a free port, had become a centre for FLN gun running during the Algerian crisis. This had brought in foreign gangsters and money. When the Berlin wall went up, in August 1960, a lot of East German crooks and illegal immigrants headed for Hamburg rather than Berlin. The gang warfare which ensued centred round the clubs. Waiters were hired for their strength, rather than their waiting, to be ready to fight off the gangs from the next club.

Allan Williams brought the five Beatles himself to Hamburg. He drove them in a mini-van, via Harwich and the Hook of Holland. The only thing John remembers about the journey is that he stopped off in Holland to do some shoplifting.

They were all very pleased with the attempts at stage dress – their very first, after all they were now professionals – which they were bringing with them. It consisted of little velvet jackets which Paul had got the man next door to him to make for him. They were intending to wear them with their usual Teddy Boy rig-out, tight black jeans, white shirt with black ribbon tie and winkle pickers. They all still of course had their high, greased-back Tony Curtis hairstyle.

Opposite: **The Beatles first went to Hamburg in 1960 and played there, for varying spells, during the next three years. Among their earliest fans in the city was Jurgen Vollmer, who took this photograph of John in a doorway in 1960.**

'Bruno Koschmeider met us when we arrived,' says Pete Best. 'He took us round to the Kaiserkeller where we expected we'd be playing. We met Howie Casey, from the Liverpool group, who were already there.

'We liked the look of the place. We said when do we move in? He said we didn't. Then we were taken round to this other club, the Indra, that was much smaller. It was 11.30 at night and there were just two people in the place.

'We were shown our dressing room which turned out to be the gents' toilet. We expected we'd be living in an hotel, but instead we were taken round to this cinema, the Bambi, where he showed us our sleeping quarters. It was like the black hole of Calcutta. But being young and foolish, we didn't complain. We just went straight to sleep.'

Allan Williams, who stayed on for a few weeks after he'd taken them, says that some members of the Seniors group were annoyed to see the Beatles. 'I was told I was spoiling the scene, bringing over such a crummy group.'

The Indra, where the Beatles started playing next evening, was named after the German for India. It had a large elephant sign hung across the street, the Grosse Freiheit, as its symbol. But inside it was small and poky. None of them liked it, least of all sleeping in the Bambi cinema.

'We would go to bed late,' says John, 'and be wakened up next day by the sound of the cinema show. We'd try to get into the ladies' first, which was cleanest of the cinema's lavatories, but fat old German women would push past us.

'At first, we got a pretty cool reception. Then the manager said we should "Mak Show", like the group down the road were doing. So we tried. We were a bit scared by it all at first, being in the middle of the tough club land. But we felt cocky, being from Liverpool, at least believing the myth about Liverpool producing cocky people.

'The first Mak Show I did was to jump around in one number like Gene Vincent. Every number lasted 20 minutes, just to spin it out. We all did mak showing all the time from then.

'We only once ever tried a German number, playing to the crowd. Paul learned "Wooden Heart", which was very popular.

'We got better and got more confidence. We couldn't help it, with all the experience, playing all night long. It was handy them being foreign. We had to try even harder, put our heart and soul into it, to get ourselves over.

'In Liverpool we'd only ever done one-hour sessions and we just used to do our best numbers, the same ones, at every one. In Hamburg we had to play for eight hours, so we really had to find a new way of playing. We played very loud, bang, bang all the time. The Germans loved it.'

'Once the news got about that we were making a show,' says Pete, 'the club started packing them in. We played seven nights a week. At first we played almost non-stop till 12.30, when it closed, but as we got better the crowds stayed till two most mornings.

'We saw lots of fights. Real big ones, with people swinging from lights and jumping off tables, just like in film fights.'

They all used to beat on the stage with their feet, when they weren't jumping in the air, to add to the noise and increase the beat. Pete Best didn't fit exactly into their ways at the beginning, so they all had to pound out the rhythm as well. But Pete soon improved, as they all did.

The 'Making Show', as the Germans called it, was the vital thing. Although they were a rock group, they'd been pretty quiet in Liverpool. Now they were actively encouraged to let themselves go and make as much show on stage as possible, which of course was easy for John. He made a show all the time, jumping in ecstasy or rolling on the floor, much to the delight of the local rockers they were soon getting as their fans. Stories about John are still told in Hamburg, a lot of them improving with age.

'It was hard work,' says Pete, 'but we were just five fellows having a good time. We did daft things all the time. John had a pair of Long John underpants, as it was getting very cold with winter drawing on. George bet him ten marks that he wouldn't go out, wearing them and nothing else. He went out in the street, just in his Long Johns, with sun specs on and read the *Daily Express* for five minutes. We watched him, killing ourselves laughing.'

But after two months, the Indra was closed. There had been complaints from neighbours about noise. The Beatles then moved to the Kaiserkeller. The stage at the Kaiserkeller was very old, more or less planks on orange boxes. They decided to go

The Beatles' tour bus, en-route to Hamburg in 1960. The only thing John remembered about their journey was stopping off in Holland to do some shoplifting.

through it so they'd have to have a new one. They did go through it in the end, by jumping around and making show, but they never got a new one. They just played on the open floor.

'I drank a lot,' says Pete Best. 'You couldn't help it. They'd be sending us drinks up all the time so we naturally drank too much. We had a lot of girls. We soon realized they were easy to get. Girls are girls, fellers are fellers. Everything improved 100 per cent. We'd been meek and mild musicians at first, now we became a powerhouse.'

The Kaiserkeller was making them work even harder than ever. The group which had been there in the first place had now gone back to Liverpool and been replaced by another Liverpool group, Rory Storm and the Hurricanes. They were officially booked to play six hours a night. As there were now two groups in the same club, they did alternate hours through the night. But their time off was too short to do anything or go anywhere, so they

'Their Name Liveth for Evermore.' John, presumably, was well aware of the words when he photographed the Beatles party at the Arnhem war cemetery, on their way to Hamburg in 1960. From left to right are: Alan Williams, Beryl Williams, 'Lord Woodbine', Stu Sutcliffe, Paul, George and Pete Best.

were in effect playing for a period of twelve hours at a time.

'Your voice began to hurt with the pain of singing,' says John. 'We learned from the Germans that you could stay awake by eating slimming pills, so we did that.' The pills at first were pretty harmless, but they moved on to other ones, like Black Bombers and Purple Hearts, though they never appear to have been dependent on them or to have taken them to excess. But it was the beginning of an interest and a liking for drugs, however minor. All of them tried them at some time, except Pete Best who had no wish to be connected in any way with drugs.

They never let the pills get out of control because they were genuinely taking them to keep awake, not for kicks. They wanted to keep awake because they were loving everything, playing the sort of stuff they wanted to, to wild Hamburg teenagers, for as long as they wanted. They didn't mind the long hours at all.

The times they did get fed up, usually with the living accommodation, were very few. If they hadn't been so far from home, of course, and in a foreign country, they might have packed up many times and gone home to Liverpool. But they couldn't, stuck away in Hamburg. They were also spending all the money as quickly as they got it.

It's surprising their health didn't suffer more. They never ate properly and hardly slept. 'What with playing, drinking and birds, how could we find time to sleep?' says John.

George and Paul knew a little bit of German. Pete knew most of all as he had passed German at O level. John and Stu spoke no German and weren't interested in learning. 'We just used to shout in English at the Germans,' says John. 'Call them Nazis and tell them to fuck off.' The audience just cheered even more.

The audiences were entranced by them, devoted to them, and the Beatles became less scared of the club, the waiters and the fights. They saw the waiters taking money out of the pockets of drunks and as they were hard up, John decided one night to try it himself.

'We chose a British sailor to roll. I thought I could chat him up in English, kid him on we could get him some birds. We got him drinking and drinking and he kept on asking, where's the girls? We kept chatting him up, trying to find out where he kept his money. We just hit him twice in the end, then gave up. We never made it. We didn't want to hurt him.'

The Beatles had lots of little arguments amongst themselves, but nothing serious. It was mainly Stu and Pete, the relatively new boys, being picked on by the rest. Stu took it to heart, but Pete didn't seem to notice. It all passed over his head. He can't remember being involved in any rows or anyone criticizing him or mocking him, though the others do.

But Stu and Pete were proving popular with the audience, though not as much as Paul, who was always the most popular everywhere. Stu wore his sun spectacles on stage and looked very defiant. Pete never smiled or jumped around, the way John did, but simply looked sullen and menacing. Both of them were looked upon as James Dean figures by the audience, moody and magnificent. The others, particularly John, were the wild extrovert ones.

'Paul was telling me the other day,' says John, 'that he and I used to have rows about who was the leader. I can't remember them. It had stopped mattering by then. I wasn't so determined to be the leader at all costs. If I did argue, it was just out of pride.

'All the arguments were just trivial, mainly because we were fucked and irritable with working so hard. We were just kids. George threw some food at me once on stage. We

A rare photograph of Paul and John larking about in underpants in Hamburg. 'It was hard work,' said Pete about their first Hamburg trip, 'but we were just five fellows having a good time. We did daft things all the time...'

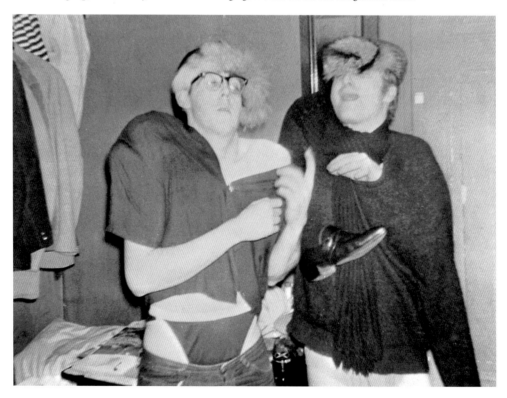

usually ate on stage as we were on so long. The row with George was just over something stupid. I said I would smash his face in for him. We had a shouting match on stage, but that was all. I never did anything.'

They were in the main very friendly with each other and also very friendly with Rory Storm and his group, who were alternating with them at the Kaiserkeller.

They already knew Rory's group very well. He was much better known at the time in Liverpool than they were. Rory had been offered the Hamburg trip before them. Because he turned it down, as he had another engagement, they'd got it instead. Apart from Rory, there were other Liverpool groups doing better than the Beatles in those days, like Cas and the Casanovas. The Beatles, at the time they left Liverpool for Hamburg, were probably about third or fourth in the hierarchy of Liverpool beat groups.

'We all knew Rory,' says George. 'He was the big star of Liverpool, very flash and wild on stage.' George knew the group well because at one stage, before he joined the Beatles, he was thinking of joining them. 'I'd met Rory because I was once trying to knock off his little sister.'

The drummer with Rory Storm's group spent a lot of his sitting-out time watching the Beatles and requesting songs from them.

'I didn't like the look of Rory's drummer myself,' says George. 'He looked the nasty one, with his little grey streak of hair. But the nasty one turned out to be Ringo, the nicest of them all.'

Pete says that he remembered Ringo from the days he had played in the Casbah with Rory Storm, but the others didn't know him. It was a long time before they got to know him really well, but that was their first meeting with Ringo Starr.

Apart from this friendship with Ringo and the rest of Rory's group, they made no other friends. They hardly left the club and made no attempt to make any friends amongst the Germans. 'They were all half-witted,' says John.

They made even less of an attempt to get to know any British people who came into the club. 'When we could smell Senior Service in the audience,' says John, 'we knew there would be trouble before the night was out. After a few drinks, they'd start shouting, "Up Liverpool" or "Up Pompey". Gangs of fucking British servicemen, trying to stir things up. Before the night was over they'd all be lying there half dead, after they'd tried to pick a fight with the waiters over the bill, or just over nothing. The waiters would get their flick knives out, or their truncheons. And that would be it. I've never seen such killers.'

12

ASTRID AND KLAUS

It's not really surprising that they made so few German friends in Hamburg. The majority of respectable Hamburgers rarely go anywhere near the St Pauli district, least of all the Reeperbahn.

But Klaus Voormann and Astrid Kirchherr did. Quite by chance they came across the Beatles. They became fans, the first intellectual fans they'd ever had. They saw qualities in the Beatles which no one had ever seen before.

Klaus was born in Berlin, the son of an eminent doctor. He arrived in Hamburg in 1956 to study at the Art School. He was training to be a commercial artist, but he also took up photography as a special subject, which is how he met Astrid, who became his girlfriend.

Astrid comes from a good solid middle-class Hamburg family. She was specializing in photography. By 1960 they'd both left Art School. Klaus was working for local magazines – Hamburg is a big press centre – doing advertising posters. Astrid was working as an assistant to a photographer.

They'd been going out for about two years and Klaus had moved into a flat on the top of Astrid's house. One evening they had a slight row. Klaus decided to go off to the cinema on his own.

'I came out and was walking around. I was in the Grosse Freiheit when I heard a lot of noise coming from a basement. I went down to see what was going on. I'd never been in a club like it before.

'It was a very rough scene down there. There were some real tough rockers, all in leather. But I was knocked out by the group on stage and the noise they were making. So very carefully I sat down to listen.'

The club was the Kaiserkeller, but it wasn't the Beatles on stage. It was Rory Storm's group, with Ringo on drums. Without realizing it Klaus had sat down beside the other resident group. 'I was staring at them because they looked so funny. They wore check

Opposite: **Astrid Kirchherr, photographer, friend and fashion adviser to the Beatles in Hamburg.**

One of the best-known images of the Beatles, taken at a funfair in Hamburg, in 1960, by Astrid Kirchherr.

jackets, black and white check. The most ridiculous looking of all – Stu as I discovered later – had his hair piled really high and was wearing long pointed shoes and sunglasses. Not really sunglasses, just those sun things you clip over ordinary glasses.

'They went on stage and I realized that they were the other group. They did "Sweet Little Sixteen" with John singing it. They knocked me out even more than Rory did. I couldn't take my eyes off them.

'I wanted to speak to them, to get near them, but I didn't know how to. I was scared with all the rockers. I was embarrassed and felt out of it. But I stayed there all night. I couldn't get over how they played together so well, so powerful and so funny. And all the

time they were jumping around. I gathered they kept it up for eight hours as well.'

He got home in the early hours of the morning and told Astrid where he'd been. She was rather disgusted with him, spending an evening at a club in St Pauli. He told her how marvellous this group was. She wasn't interested. She refused to come back with him the next night. So he went alone.

This time he thought of a way of introducing himself to them, of getting to know them, or at least saying hello. He took with him a pop record cover he had designed for a single called 'Walk Don't Run'. He'd done one or two covers, as a commercial artist, although most of his work had been for magazines. He thought the Beatles would be interested to see it.

He sat around for a long time, trying to get nearer and nearer. When the Beatles at last sat down for their rest turn, he approached John, who seemed to be the leader. In very halting, schoolboy English, Klaus showed him the record.

It made little effect on John. 'I just remember this bloke shoving a cover in my hand, I didn't know why,' says John. John muttered something about Stu being the artist, and he'd better show the cover to him. Klaus started to move towards Stu but something happened and he couldn't get to him. So he had to sit down again, feeling more scared and embarrassed. Instead he just listened to the music all night through again.

The next night, his third visit, Klaus did at last persuade Astrid, against her better wishes, to come with him, along with another friend, Jurgen Vollmer.

'I was frightened when I arrived,' says Astrid. 'But I soon forgot all that, when I saw these five people. I can't explain how I felt. Something got me. I just couldn't believe it.

'I had always been fascinated in a way by Teddy Boys. I'd liked the look of them, in photographs and films. Suddenly there were five of them in front of me, with their hair all high and long sidies. I just sat there open-mouthed and couldn't move.

'The atmosphere around was pretty frightening. They were just the typical Reeperbahn crowd. Broken noses, Teddy Boys, that sort of thing. Schlägers, we would call them in German. Punchers, real toughs.'

More and more of their student friends started to come, when Klaus and Astrid began to rave about the Beatles. They took over their own tables and part of the cellar. The students, with their smoother styles, their more mod clothes, soon began to affect and then dictate the atmosphere of the Kaiserkeller.

The rockers were still there, although not so predominant. 'It became our scene,' says Klaus. 'There was no rivalry between us and the rockers. In fact I became friends with a few, though I'd never known any of them before, and never would have done.

'There were funny little rocker girls I'd never come across before. When they danced they were like little mushrooms. They had short flared skirts with stiffened petticoats to make them stick out.'

The Beatles began to spend most of their spare time sitting talking and drinking with Klaus, Astrid and their friends. They couldn't speak German, but some of the Germans could understand a little English.

'We were suddenly getting a lot of arty types,' says George. 'Existentialists, the lot.' 'They were great,' says Paul. 'A change from the usual Germans. They were knocked out by Stu, doing his James Dean bit.' '"Exis", that's what I called them,' says John. 'They were the first Germans I ever wanted to talk to.'

'I couldn't understand John's accent,' says Klaus. 'But George used to speak very slowly to us and we could understand him. He looked so funny. His big ears stuck out, with his hair being short at the back and piled so high on top.'

After about a week of going there every night, Astrid at last got the courage to ask if she could take their pictures. 'We were getting on so well with them that I felt more protected. I realized that the Reeperbahn rockers all loved them, adored them. They would have killed for them.' She managed to blurt out a couple of words, indicating that she wanted to take their photographs. 'They were made up. I could tell, though John made a few funny remarks. He was always saying terrible things about Krauts in front of people. Not to me. But I felt he wasn't really like that anyway.'

But she wasn't really interested in John's reaction. She wanted to get to know Stu. 'I'd fallen in love with him at first sight. It's true. It wasn't slushy romance and all that. I just had.'

They all made a date to meet in the Reeperbahn next day. She took them to a fairground nearby and photographed them, then she invited them home with her for tea. Pete Best refused. 'Not because I was being antisocial but simply because I had skins to buy for my drums which I'd broken the night before.' But the four others went with her. She gave them tea and they were delighted. It was the first German home they'd been into.

The room Astrid gave them tea in was very dark and mysterious. After the first impression of darkness, all you could see were two colours, black and white. Everything, the walls, furniture and carpets, were either black or white. She had trees growing up the walls and across the ceiling and around the room. The window was obscured and the only light came from candles. There was a black cloth hanging down one wall. One of them drew it aside to see what was behind and found himself looking into a mirror. 'It was my Jean Cocteau phase,' says Astrid.

The tea was a little more prosaic – ham sandwiches. 'Heh, look at these,' said George. 'Ham sarnies! I didn't know the Germans had ham sarnies.' Which shows how much George had seen of German life, stuck for twelve hours at a time at the Kaiserkeller. Then she drove them in her car back to the club for their night's work.

Opposite: **Still at the funfair in Hamburg, this time Stu poses centre-stage, with George and John behind. Astrid's pictures were the first professional photographs taken of the Beatles, and, for many years to come, by far the most artistic.**

Astrid began to bring her camera along all the time and took many photographs of them. They were the first professional photographs taken of them and, for many years to come, by far the most artistic. By clever lighting she managed to take them half in the shadows. This gimmick of a half shadow face, although not original, was used and copied by other photographers for a long time to come. Astrid was the first to see their photogenic potential, a factor which was later invaluable.

She took them out and around other parts of Hamburg to photograph them, lining them up once in the docks, then at a disused railway siding to get unusual photographs. It takes good quality printing and paper to get the best out of Astrid's photographs, to see how excellent they are, but even on cheap newsprint they look dramatic and unusual. 'They were great,' says Paul. 'Nobody could take our picture as well as Astrid.'

The Beatles perform in Hamburg. From left to right are Stu, George and John (both seated). George, who was only 17 at the time, was eventually deported, five months after their arrival in Germany, for working in a club while underage.

She was trying all the time, in those early sessions, to get talking to Stu, trying to say to him she would like to take his photograph on his own. But she couldn't make him understand. He spoke no German. She spoke no English. So she got Klaus to start teaching her English. 'He nearly went out of his mind trying to explain things to me. I just couldn't learn.'

They all came for a meal at her place practically every night after that first tea and she and Stu slowly made more and more progress. Then Stu started to come on his own at other times and they would sit together on her black bed, talking to each other with the help of a German-English dictionary.

'After Stu, I liked John and George. Then I liked Pete Best. I liked him very much, but he was so very very shy. He could be funny, but I didn't have much contact with him. Even in those days one tended to forget him. He was on his own really.

'Paul, I found hard to get close to. He was always friendly. He was by far the most popular with the fans. He always did the talking and announcing and the autograph bit. Most fans looked upon him as the leader. John of course was the leader. He was by far and away the strongest. I don't mean physically, as a personality.

'Stu was the most intelligent one. I think they all agreed on that. John did.

'George, we never thought about George's intelligence one way and another when we were talking about them. We knew he wasn't stupid, but he was just such a young lovely boy. He was so sweet and open about everything, like admiring the ham sarnies. He had a great following. Jurgen used to have a notice which said "I Love George". He was one of the first to do that sort of thing.

'I got on like a house on fire with George. He'd never met anyone like me before and he showed it, so openly and sweetly. After all, he was only 17. There was me, the sort of intelligent girl he'd never come across before, with my own car, working as a photographer, and wearing leather jackets. It was natural he would be very interested in me. I never fancied him or anything like that. It wasn't that sort of thing. I was five years older, so it didn't matter being open. We got on great.'

In November 1960, only two months after their first meeting, Stu and Astrid got engaged. They put their money together and went out and bought the rings – one for each of them, in the German fashion. Then they drove in her car along the Elbe. 'From when we first started being able to communicate with each other we intended to get married.'

Stu was 19, not much older really than George, but much more developed and mature in his thoughts. He was as passionately interested in art as he'd always been, unlike John who had left it all behind, but he was also as passionate about the group. One night he had a fight on stage with Paul. Despite being much smaller and weaker than Paul, Stu's anger was so intense that it gave him extra strength. 'He could become really hysterical when he was angry,' says Astrid. The fight was something to do with Astrid, something Paul had said about her, but no one remembers the details.

The relationship between Paul and Stu, the petty jealousies and rows, is not too difficult to explain. In a way, they were both competing for John's attention. Paul had had it for a couple of years, until Stu came along. Stu was obviously very talented, more mature, more in touch. Even Michael McCartney, Paul's younger brother, remembers how in Liverpool Paul had been a bit jealous of Stu.

The relationship between five Teds from Liverpool and a group of intellectual Hamburg students is harder to explain. They were highly fashionable in their clothes as well as in their thoughts. Klaus and Jurgen had their hair brushed forward in the French style as it was then called. But the Beatles had a rough, natural, undisciplined vitality which they were attracted to.

The exis had nicknames for them all – John was the Sidie Man, George the Beautiful One and Paul the Baby One. The name Beatles, in German, had had everyone amused from the minute they arrived. 'The Peedles', was how they pronounced it. This in German is also a small-boy vulgarity, meaning cock or John Thomas.

The Beatles now had two devoted sets of followers, the rockers and the exis. Their original six-week contract was extended several times by popular demand. Christmas was approaching and they'd been in Hamburg nearly five months. They were scheming to get into an even bigger and better club, the Top Ten. Once they realized they were a success in the Kaiserkeller, they wanted to branch out into a bigger club.

They asked the manager of the Top Ten, Peter Eckhorn, for an audition. 'I liked them and offered them a contract.' Then George was told that he would have to leave the country.

'At all clubs,' says George, 'they used to read out a notice every night saying that all people under 18 had to leave. Someone eventually realized I was only 17, without a work permit or a resident permit. So I had to leave. I had to go home on my own. I felt terrible.'

Astrid and Stu drove him to the station, got him his ticket and a place on the train. 'He was just standing there,' says Astrid. 'Little George, all lost. I gave him a big bag of sweets and some apples. He threw his arms round me and Stu, which was the sort of demonstrative thing they never did.'

The other four had moved to the Top Ten but had done only one night when more trouble struck them.

'Paul and I were clearing out of the Bambi,' says Pete Best. 'John and Stu had already moved their things into the Top Ten. We were getting a light on to see what we were doing and we must have started a fire. It wasn't much, but the police threw us in jail for three hours and then said we were to be deported as well.' Which left John and Stu.

'John appeared a day or so later at my house,' says Astrid. 'He said he was going home as well because his work permit had been taken away. He said he'd sold some of his clothes to buy his ticket.'

'It was terrible,' says John. 'Setting off home on my own. I had my amp on my back, scared stiff I was going to get it pinched. I hadn't paid for it. I was convinced I'd never find England.'

Eventually Stu was told that he too would have to leave. The real reasons for all their deportations, apart from George obviously being under age, were never really clear. Perhaps there was a bit of inter-club rivalry.

Stu was the only one who came home in any style. He flew back to Liverpool. He'd had a touch of tonsillitis. Astrid didn't want him to get worse on a long journey by land and sea, so she'd given him his air fare.

The others dragged themselves back to Liverpool under their own steam. What had been the greatest experience of their careers so far had ended in pathos and squalor.

They got home, in ones and twos, broke and in tatters, dejected and dispirited. They didn't see each other or make any contact for some time. They even wondered if the Beatles would ever get going again.

THE BEATLES
A chronological history of their career highlights

1955	JOHN LENNON (a fifth form student at Liverpool's Quarry Bank High School) acquired a battered old guitar and formed THE QUARRYMEN with a friend. Line-up: Rodney: banjo / Pete Shotton: washboard / Eric Griffiths: guitar / Len Gary: box bass.
June 15	PAUL McCARTNEY introduced to JOHN by a mutual friend; subsequently joined the group which mainly played skiffle and rock 'n' roll.
1955/6	George Harrison, with brother and school friends, were playing as The Rebels.
1958	GEORGE HARRISON (still at school) joined THE QUARRYMEN.
November	THE QUARRYMEN disbanded.
1959	JOHN, PAUL and GEORGE played as trio – JOHNNY and THE MOONDOGS – for a short period and entered a Carroll Levis Talent Contest.
1960	Auditioned for impressario Larry Parnes – went to Scotland as THE SILVER BEATLES backing Johnny Gentle – line-up: PAUL (vocals) JOHN (vocals and rhythm guitar) GEORGE (lead guitar) with Stu Sutcliffe (bass) and a temporary drummer.

RINGO STARR
1959 Received his first drum kit from his parents as a Christmas present – it cost £10. (He was then 18½ yrs).

1960   Joined Eddie Clayton Skiffle Group with Eddie Miles: guitar / Roy Trafford: tea chest bass. Built up to 3 guitars, drums, washboard and bass. Also played with The Darktown Skiffle Group.

1960/62   Played with RORY STORM and THE HURRICANES for 3 yrs. which included 3 seasons at Butlins.

1960	JOHN PAUL and GEORGE went to HAMBURG with Stu Sutcliffe and Pete Best now their regular drummer.

Played THE INDRA CLUB – closed by police.

Moved to THE KAISERKELLAR for 4½ months. (George being under age was playing illegally. Police caught up with him and sent him back to England).

They then went to THE TOP TEN (Kaiserkellar lost all its customers to Top Ten).

During this time RINGO was at the Kaiserkellar with Rory Storm.

Returned to Liverpool at Christmas broke!

13

LIVERPOOL –
LITHERLAND AND THE CAVERN

John arrived back home from Hamburg in the middle of the night. He had to throw stones up at Mimi's bedroom window so that she would get up and let him in.

'He had these awful cowboy boots on, up to his knees they were, all gold and silver. He just pushed past me and said, "Pay that taxi, Mimi." I shouted after him up the stairs, "Where's your £100 a week, John?"'

'Just like you, Mimi,' shouted John, 'to go on about a £100 a week when you know I'm tired.'

'And you can get rid of those boots. You're not going out of this house in boots like that.'

John went to bed and stayed at home for over a week, not because of the awful boots but because there didn't seem much alternative. Cyn was naturally pleased to see him. He'd written to her all the time he was away. 'The sexiest letters this side of Henry Miller,' says John. 'Forty pages long some of them. You haven't destroyed them, have you?'

George, who had got home first, didn't know for some time that the others had eventually followed him. 'I felt ashamed, after all the big talk when we set off for Hamburg. My dad gave me a lift to town one night and I had to borrow ten bob off him.'

Paul was also hanging around at home and soon had his father to contend with. Jim hadn't wanted him to leave school and go to Hamburg in the first place. He said Paul should now get a job and not just mess around doing nothing.

'Satan finds things for idle hands,' so Jim told Paul, with great originality, several times a day. Paul, never a rebel on principle and always willing to please, eventually gave in.

'I went down to the Labour Exchange. That seemed to be the scene. They fixed me up with a job as second man on a lorry. I'd been on the Post Office the Christmas before from school, so I thought I'd try something different.

Opposite: **John in a Hamburg street in his underpants, shortly before the Beatles returned to Liverpool. On the reverse of the photograph he wrote: 'Me sightseeing, Hamburg, November 1960. One Giant Photo Coming Soon.'**

'The firm was called Speedy Prompt Delivery – SPD. They did deliveries round the docks way. I got the early bus down to the docks and bought the *Daily Mirror*, trying to be a real working lad, though I was really just a college pudding.

'I used to sit on the back of the lorry and helped to carry parcels. I was so buggered sometimes. I fell asleep on the lorry when we went to places like Chester. I was with them about two weeks and felt very worldly, having a job and a few quid in me pocket. But I got laid off. The Christmas period was over and there wasn't so much work.

'Dad started moaning again, the usual stuff about the group being all very well but I'd never make a living at it. I half agreed with him, but there was always somebody who said we were promising, some fans liked us and made us feel good.

'I got another job at Massey and Coggins, winding electrical coils. I had to wear a donkey jacket for that. A fellow called me Mantovani, with me long hair. I had to stand astride this winch and wind the coils. I was always breaking it. I did about one and a half coils in a day, some of the others could do eight, even 14. I wasn't much good.

'The tea breaks were great though, with jam butties and all the lads playing football in a sort of prison exercise yard.

'I'd actually gone, now it's all coming back to me, for a job brushing up the yard, which I thought would be all right. When the bloke noticed I had a few GCEs, he became suspicious, as if I might have a criminal record as well. Then he decided I was OK and gave me a better job, which was winding the coils. He said if I stuck in I'd be all right. I imagined myself as working my way up, being an executive one of these days, if I tried hard.

'I was getting £7 a week for winding coils and making the tea. The group had got going again but I didn't know if I wanted to go back full time. I stayed on at work, just going over the wall for lunch-time sessions or being off sick. But I left in the end. I was there about two months all together. I quite enjoyed being a working man. I met this bloke Albert and had some good chats with him.'

'I'll say this for Paul,' says his father Jim. 'He was always a tryer. He wasn't really interested in either job. It was just to oblige me.'

They'd come back from Hamburg in early December 1960. In all they were probably not more than two or three weeks without a date. With a bit of luck, they might have started club work straight away, which would have brightened up their pathetic arrival home. While they'd been away, Allan Williams had decided to build a large beat club on the lines of the Hamburg ones. He'd by now sent so many groups over there, including Gerry and the Pacemakers, that he thought there should be somewhere for them back in Liverpool. Just before the Beatles arrived home, he opened a new Liverpool club called the Top Ten, after the Hamburg one, and put in a manager called Bob Wooler. But six days after it opened, it was burned down. What would have been an ideal place for the Beatles disappeared before they'd even seen it.

Their first post-Hamburg date turned out to be back at the Casbah, Pete Best's mother's club. They got a great welcome there, especially from Pete's friend, Neil Aspinall.

Neil had been a friend of Pete's for a couple of years. He was actually living at the Casbah, at least he'd left home and taken a room in Mrs Best's house. He hadn't gone to school with Pete but had been at the Institute, starting in the same form as Paul. He'd known George as well. They'd both been in trouble for smoking. But he hadn't been affected by the skiffle craze, though he'd supported the local groups. With a gang of his classmates, he'd gone along to cheer the Beatles (or Moondogs) at the Empire in the early audition for the Carroll Levis Show.

Neil had left the Institute with eight O levels and was training to be an accountant. He was getting £2 10s. a week, plus luncheon vouchers, and seemed all set for a professional career. Most of his nights at first were taken up with correspondence courses. 'I hated taking abuse from some fellow 300 miles away. It was like sending it off to the moon, just to get shit on.' When he started hanging around the Casbah, his courses began to slip, especially when he moved in and lived there full time.

'Pete had written to me all the time he was in Hamburg,' says Neil. 'He said it was going great and they'd been asked to stay on another month, then another month, and another.

'Derry and the Seniors had come back from Hamburg first. Pete had sent them round to his mother's and she'd given them an evening at the Casbah. They were very much improved. They said wait till we hear the Beatles.

'When I heard that the Beatles were definitely coming home I wrote out lots of posters saying "Return of the Fabulous Beatles" – I put them up on walls and doors all over the place. I'd never seen them as a group with Pete as a member. I didn't know how they'd changed in Hamburg. They might have been awful.'

But despite Neil's enthusiasm, it wasn't possible to put the Beatles on at the Casbah right away. Nobody seemed to know what the others were doing, or even if they were all back. 'I didn't know for a week after John came back that he had had to leave Hamburg as well,' says Pete Best. 'We didn't know for weeks what had happened to Stu, till well into January.'

But their first post-Hamburg booking was at the Casbah and they did very well.

'They were great,' says Neil. 'They had improved enormously. They began to get other jobs and a big following. Frank Garner, the fellow on the door at the Casbah, started to drive them round in his van. I saw a lot of them from then on as the Casbah was the base for their amps and tackle. Rory Storm also came back from Hamburg and played at the Casbah. It was a big scene.'

But their most important engagement after Hamburg took place on 27 December 1960, at Litherland Town Hall. If it is possible to say that any date was the watershed, this was it. All their development, all their new sounds and new songs, suddenly hit Liverpool that night. Their Casbah fans turned up at Litherland and helped the evening's success. From then on, as far as having a devoted fanatical following was concerned, they never looked back.

They owe that engagement to Bob Wooler, who was about to become DJ at Litherland Town Hall. He'd worked as a clerk for British Railways until the skiffle era began. He wasn't involved in it himself, being by then almost 30, but he was fascinated by its development. 'It was amazing to see teenagers making their own music for the first time and becoming entertainers themselves.'

The idea of a Liverpool Top Ten club had collapsed, which would have been a big chance for him as well as the Beatles. 'They were really sorry for themselves. I knew their capabilities, but they were really down at the time. George was very bitter about the way his Hamburg trip had ended.'

He managed to get them the Litherland Town Hall date. This is a big hall which was used regularly twice a week for teenage dances. It was the biggest hall they'd played in up to then. Their loud, stomping, pounding Hamburg music caused literally a riot, the first they'd ever caused. They also got £6 for the night, again the best they'd had.

'The kids went mad,' says Pete Best. 'Afterwards we found they'd been chalking on our van, the first time it had happened.'

They were billed for that evening as 'The Beatles, Direct from Hamburg'. A lot of the kids who rioted that night, and for many other nights, thought they must be German. When they signed autograph books and were heard to speak they all said with surprise, 'You speak good English.'

'We probably looked German as well,' says George. 'We looked very different from all the other groups, with our leather trousers and cowboy boots. We looked funny and we played differently. We went down a bomb.'

'It was that evening,' says John, 'that we really came out of our shell and let go. We discovered we were quite famous. This was when we began to think for the first time that we were good. Up to Hamburg we'd thought we were OK, but not good enough.'

Not only had the Beatles changed, there had been important changes in Britain while they'd been away. Every group was now trying like mad to be like the Shadows.

Cliff Richard's success had led the Shadows, his backing group of Jet Harris, Tony Meehan, Bruce Welch and Hank Marvin, to go on to become successes in their own right. Their instrumental record, 'Apache', had swept the country. Every group was copying their sober, terribly neat stage dress of grey suits, matching ties and highly polished shoes. They did little dance steps, three one way and three the other. In their appearance as well as in their music, everything was neat, polished and restrained.

The Beatles, on the other hand, played loud and wild, and looked scruffy and disorganized, like some aboriginal throwback. They had continued in the rock and roll style, which had been the fashion when they left Liverpool but was now dying out. If anything, they'd become even more rock and rollish, adding extra pounding, volume and wild 'mak showing' on stage. They had created in effect their own new sound. A sound which was light years away from the discreet Shadows. A sound which you had to run away and hide your ears from, or go as wild and ecstatic as the people producing it.

'It was Hamburg that had done it,' says John. 'That's where we'd really developed. To get the Germans going and keep it up for twelve hours at a time, we'd really had to hammer. We would never have developed as much if we'd stayed at home. We had to try anything that came into our heads in Hamburg. There was nobody to copy from. We played what we liked best. The Germans liked it, as long as it was loud.

'But it was only back in Liverpool that we realized the difference and saw what had happened to us while everyone else was playing Cliff Richard shit.'

Their own passion and personalities, which were contagious and affected the audience, also helped. They had a new sound but it was being made by people who were like the Liverpool audiences, natural, unaffected, unsmooth, untarted up, un-show business.

Bob Wooler, who soon moved on from being the Litherland DJ to the Cavern DJ, was one of the first to rush into print with his analysis of the Beatles. This appeared just six months later in the summer of 1961 in a local Merseyside beat newspaper. He is summing up in this early 1961 period, when they first hit Liverpool after the Litherland Town Hall, long before they had any publicity or promotion of any sort:

> *'Why do you think the Beatles are so popular? They resurrected original rock'n'roll music, the origins of which are to be found in American Negro singers. They hit the scene when it had been emasculated by figures like Cliff Richard. Gone was the drive that inflamed emotions. The Beatles exploded on a jaded scene. The Beatles were the stuff that screams were made of. Here was the excitement, both physical and aural, that symbolized the rebellion of youth.*
>
> *'Essentially a vocal act, hardly ever instrumental, they were independently minded, playing what they liked for kicks, kudos and cash. Privileged in having gained prestige and experience in Hamburg. Musically authoritative and physically magnetic, example the mean, moody magnificence of drummer, Pete Best – a sort of teenage Jeff Chandler. A remarkable variety of talented voices but when speaking, possess the same naivety of tone. Rhythmic revolutionaries. An act which from beginning to end is a succession of climaxes. A personality cult. Seemingly unambitious, yet fluctuating between self-assured and the vulnerable. Truly a phenomenon – and also a predicament to promoters! Such are the fantastic Beatles. I don't think anything like them will happen again.'*

In the New Year of 1961, other large ballroom dates followed their Litherland Town Hall success. In most places it ended in riots, especially when Paul sang 'Long Tall Sally', a standard rock number, but done with tremendous beat and excitement. They were beginning to realize the effect they could have on an audience, and often made the most of it, until things got out of hand. Paul says that some of the early ballrooms were terrifying. 'At the Grosvenor Ballroom in Wallasey, there would be 100 Wallasey lads all ready to fight 100 lads from Seacombe when things got going. They started one night before I realized what was happening and I tried to save my amp. An El Pico amp, it was my pride and joy at the time. One Ted grabbed me and said don't move, son, or you're fucking dead. The Hambledon Hall was another place there was often fights. They used fire extinguishers on each other one night there. When we played "Hully Gully", that used to be one of the tunes which ended in fighting.'

Most of the ballrooms hired large numbers of bouncers to stop that sort of trouble. The bouncers also began to be used for another purpose.

'I remember one hall we were at,' says John. 'There were so many people that we told each other that there must be other managers around and we'd get a lot of work out of it. What we didn't know was that the management had laid on lots of bouncers to stop the other promoters getting near us. So nobody came to us, except this bloke from the management who said he liked us and would give us a long series of dates at £8 a night. It was a couple of quid more than we were getting anyway, so we were pleased.'

They could have made a lot more money from 1961 onwards because they were in demand and very gradually catching up on Rory Storm (Mr Showmaker, as they called him) as Liverpool's leading group. But they didn't have a manager and they didn't really appreciate themselves what was happening to them. 'It took us a while to realize how much better we'd become than the other groups,' says George. 'Then we began to see that we were getting big crowds everywhere. People were following us round, coming to see us personally, not just coming to dance.'

They were still picking on Stu and Pete Best, but there were no serious fights the way there had been in Hamburg. They used to argue instead over the best seat in the van after a show, or fight for food. There was often an argument about who should drive, because it was thought that the driver always had the best seat, instead of being crammed in with all the gear.

'This sort of bickering was usually between me and George,' says Paul, 'as we were about the same age. John was older and the natural leader. George and I were very bitchy, arguing about who would drive. Later on when we had our own van, I'd rush to get the keys and get in the driving seat first. George would get in and say, "Heh, I thought I was driving. You drove last night." I would say, "Well, you're not, are you."'

Their successes at the various ballrooms around Merseyside naturally led to them being offered their own place, where they could be the resident group, where their fans would always know where to expect them. This, thanks to Bob Wooler, was the Cavern Club. They'd outgrown the Casbah coffee club, which was away from the main centre of Liverpool and very much a small local club.

The Cavern had for a long time been the main club for live music in the centre of Liverpool, but it had been purely for jazz. Even at the time of that article by Bob Wooler quoted above, written in the summer of 1961, the Cavern was still being advertised on another page of the same issue as a jazz club, although by then it had become dominated by beat groups, particularly the Beatles.

The Cavern is at Number 8, Mathew Street. This is a narrow lane in the centre of Liverpool, just round the corner from Whitechapel where NEMS, the leading record store is situated. It's a couple of blocks away from the *Liverpool Echo* building and not far from the Pier Head.

Most of the buildings in Mathew Street are fruit warehouses. The street is always littered and untidy and smells of lurking fruit and hidden vegetables. Throughout the day and early morning there are lorries unloading. You go down 17 steps to the Cavern. It's the basement of what was once a wine cellar. It still looks very much like a cellar, dark and poky, with high vaulted pillars. There appears to be no ventilation of any sort, even today when it has all been tarted up into a restaurant-nightclub.

Ray McFall, an ex-accountant, had taken over the Cavern in 1959 and ran it as a jazz club. Johnny Dankworth, Humphrey Lyttleton, Acker Bilk, Chris Barber all played there. But more and more sessions began to be given over to the growing beat groups.

From January 1961, after the Beatles returned from Hamburg, they played regularly at the Cavern, alternating at first with the Swinging Bluejeans, who'd been the resident semi-jazz group before them.

'From January 1961 to February 1962 I introduced the Beatles at the Cavern Club 292 times,' says Bob Wooler. 'For that first lunch-time session they got £5. For the last one they got £300.'

This not only shows how much Bob Wooler must have been impressed by them, to bother to count up the exact times, but also how hard they were working.

'We probably loved the Cavern best of anything,' says George. 'It was fantastic. We never lost our identification with the audience all the time. We never rehearsed anything, not like the other groups, who kept on copying the Shadows. We were playing to our own fans who were just like us. They would come in their lunch-times to hear us and bring their sandwiches to eat. We would do the same, eating our lunch while we played. It was just spontaneous. Everything just happened.'

'It was really a dump,' says Mrs Harrison. 'There was no air at all. The sweat used to drip off them or off the walls and onto the amps and fuse them. But they'd just carry on all the same, singing on their own. John used to shout out things at the audience. They all did.

Paul, John and Pete Best, back from Hamburg, outside the Cavern Club in Liverpool, where they played regularly from January 1961. Between then and February 1962, it is estimated that they appeared at the venue 292 times.

They'd tell them to shuttup. But George never used to say anything or smile. Girls were always asking me why he looked so serious. He used to say, "I'm the lead guitar. If the others make mistakes through larking around, no one notices, but I can't make mistakes." He was always very serious about his music, and the money. He always wanted to know how much they were getting.'

Mrs Harrison, as ever, was one of their most devoted fans. Not just following them, but taking relations and friends along as well. She was at the Cavern that time, before they went to Hamburg, when John's Aunt Mimi had stormed in, determined to pull John out by his ear.

'I saw her on the way out,' says Mrs Harrison. '"Aren't they great," I shouted at her. She turned to me and said she was glad someone thought so.

'I met Mimi a few times after that. She always used to say, we'd all have had lovely peaceful lives but for you encouraging them.'

Everyone who saw them in their Cavern days remembers most of all their impromptu performances. The Shadows had not only influenced how other groups played, but how they got themselves on and off stage and how they introduced their numbers. The Beatles just did what they felt like doing. When anything went wrong, other groups rushed to the wings, doing the big show business bit, till someone mended the fuse. What the Beatles did was get everyone to sing 'Coming Round the Mountains' or some such corny song.

Mrs Harrison approved of it all. Mimi didn't. But Jim McCartney was beginning to learn how to live with it.

He used to spend his lunch hours in the same sort of area as the Cavern, hanging around the Cotton Exchange pubs and cafés, chatting up prospective buyers. This makes his job sound grander than it was. He was still an ordinary cotton salesman, earning under £10 a week and finding it difficult to make ends meet. Michael, Paul's brother, was by this time working, but not doing very well. He'd failed to get into the Art College, and after a series of dead-end jobs was training to be a hairdresser.

'I often used to pop into the Cavern at lunch time,' says Jim. 'They should have paid you danger money to go down there. It reeked of perspiration. When Paul used to come home from the Cavern I would wring his shirt out in the sink and the sweat would pour out.

'The kids would be in a terrible state as well, fighting with each other to get near the front, or fainting with the excitement and the atmosphere. I'd see Paul and the others on the stage, looking like something the cat brought home. I'd try to fight my way through the kids, but never make it. So I used to go to their little dressing room place and wait for them to come off stage.'

He wasn't waiting for their autograph, but because he wanted to see Paul. As Paul and Michael's only parent, cook, cleaner and bottle washer, he had to spend his lunch hour doing the shopping for the evening meal.

'I had to go to the Cavern to give Paul the sausages or chops or whatever it was. I'd be in a terrible rush and I'd just have time to fight off the fans and give Paul the meat.

'"Now don't forget, son," I'd say. "Put this on Regulo 450 on the electric oven when you get home".'

Opposite: **George taking a break from playing at the Cavern Club, *c.* 1961.**

14

MARKING TIME –
LIVERPOOL AND HAMBURG

Their success as a local phenomenon was assured, once the Cavern days arrived. After almost five years of messing around, they had at last built up an individual act and had acquired a devoted following in Liverpool.

But for the next year, throughout most of 1961, nothing really dramatic happened. They improved all the time and their local following grew and became more fanatical. They visited Hamburg again, the first of several return visits, and their success there continued. But they now entered a trough of local success. They seemed destined to play forever in Liverpool or Hamburg. No one else was interested in them.

Their second Hamburg trip began in April 1961, by which time George had become 18. Peter Eckhorn, manager of the Top Ten Club, and Astrid, helped to get all the right work permits. Peter Eckhorn still has the contract. It said they would play every night from seven until two in the morning, except Saturdays when they would play till three. 'After each hour of play there will be no less than a break of 15 minutes.'

The Top Ten was bigger and not as rough as the two other clubs they'd played in. It had better accommodation, décor and audiences. There were even more exis in the audience shouting for them now, many of them photographers who would lie down in front, trying to get unusual angles of the Beatles on stage, and shouting 'more sveat, pleese, more sveat'.

Astrid met them off the train – they were doing it in a bit more style this time – and was wearing a complete leather trouser suit. Previously she'd worn a leather jacket, which they'd all copied, although they'd worn them with their jeans and cowboy boots. Stu was very impressed and got her to make a complete leather suit for him. The others wanted one as well, but they got them done so cheaply that they split almost as soon as they put them on.

Opposite: Astrid Kirchherr and Stu Sutcliffe, *c.* 1961. Stu's brushed-forward hairstyle was worn at Astrid's insistence. Though initially ridiculed by the other band members, the new 'look' was eventually adopted by all the Beatles, except Pete Best.

It was at this time that Astrid got round to telling Stu that she didn't like his greasy, Teddy Boy hairstyle. She said he would suit the sort of style that Klaus and Jurgen had. After a lot of persuading, Stu let her do a special style for him. She brushed it all down, snipped bits off and tidied it up.

Stu turned up at the Top Ten that evening, with his hair in the new style, and the others collapsed on the floor with hysterics. Halfway through, he gave up and combed his hair high. But thanks to Astrid, he tried it again the next night. He was ridiculed again, but the night after, George turned up with the same style. Then Paul had a go, though for a long time he was always changing it back to the old style as John hadn't yet made up his mind. Pete Best ignored the whole craze. But the Beatle hairstyle had been born.

Astrid went on to influence them in other ways, such as collarless suits. She'd made one for herself which Stu had admired so she'd made one for him, despite the jokes from the rest of them. 'What are you doing with Mum's suit then, Stu?'

They all got a bit wilder during this second Hamburg trip, turning to pep pills (all except Pete Best) to keep them going during the all-night sessions. 'But it never got out of control,' says Astrid. 'Neither did their drinking. They hardly drank at all, just now and again.'

John was still doing a little bit of shoplifting, when the urge took him. Astrid says it was great, which is the phrase Pete Shotton, John's school friend, had used.

'It's the way John was,' says Astrid. 'Everyone feels like doing things sometimes, but of course you don't. John would suddenly rub his hands and say, I know, let's go shoplifting now. It was all fun. You couldn't be shocked. The idea had suddenly come into his head, so he acted on it. He wouldn't do it again for weeks. Things don't go round in John's head first, the way they do with Paul.'

John was still turning out his anti-religious cartoons – drawing Christ on the cross with a pair of bedroom slippers at the bottom – and getting involved in other adolescent jokes. He put on a paper dog-collar once, cut himself a paper cross and preached from a window of the club in a Peter Sellers Indian accent to the crowds below.

Snapshot of John from their second Hamburg period. Note that he has combed his hair forward, like Stu.

They made their first record during this trip, though Allan Williams had made them do a demo disc on their first arrival in Hamburg. This had led nowhere, and only five copies were made. This time they were asked to do the backing for Tony Sheridan, the singer from the Top Ten. 'When the offer came,' says John, 'we thought it would be easy. The Germans had such shitty records. Ours was bound to be better. We did five of our own numbers, but they didn't like them. They preferred things like "My Bonnie Lies Over the Ocean".'

Bert Kaempfert, the German orchestra leader and A and R man, did the recording. On the records, backing Tony Sheridan, they were called 'The Beat Boys'. It was thought the name Beatles was too confusing.

Only four of them were involved in this record. Pete Best was still there. He says he thought he was getting on well. He'd had a fight with Tony Sheridan, but that was all.

But Stu Sutcliffe had left. 'We were awful to him sometimes,' says John. 'Especially Paul, always picking on him. I used to explain afterwards to him that we didn't dislike him, really.'

They felt a bit guilty about how they treated Stu, but this wasn't the reason for him leaving. He'd decided to stay in Hamburg, marry Astrid and go back to being an art student. He enrolled at the Art College, thanks to an eminent visiting professor, Eduardo Paolozzi, the Scots-born sculptor. He even managed to get Stu a grant from the Hamburg authorities.

Stu still liked the Beatles' music, but he felt he was better at art than on the bass guitar. Paul could obviously play it much better. It would be best for him to take over, which he did. After he left, Stu became closer friends with all of them than he'd ever been before. They all realized how meaningless their little quarrels had been.

In July 1961 the four Beatles returned to Liverpool leaving Stu in Hamburg. He did well at the Art College. 'He had so much energy and was so very inventive,' says Paolozzi. 'The feeling of potential splashed out from him. He had the right kind of sensibility and arrogance to succeed.'

The Beatles did a special welcome home show when they arrived in Liverpool with another leading group they'd known for a long time, Gerry and the Pacemakers. They played each other's instruments or daft objects, like a paper and comb. They billed themselves as the Beatmakers, which was an in-joke all the fans appreciated.

The Beatles were still lucky to be making £10 a week each, but the Liverpool beat cult had arrived. The most obvious sign of its existence was the birth of a newspaper completely devoted to the doings of beat groups. This was *Mersey Beat*, in which Bob Wooler wrote the article about the Beatles, referred to earlier. Its first edition came out on 6 July 1961. It contained gossip about the leading groups, such as Gerry and the Pacemakers and Rory Storm and the Hurricanes, the group in which Ringo Starr was on drums. These appear to be the two main groups. The Beatles came after them in popularity, judging by the first issues. But the Beatles did provide the only bit of humour in the first edition when John was asked to knock out a bit about their history:

Mersey Beat *July 6 1961*
BEING A SHORT DIVERSION ON THE DUBIOUS ORIGINS OF BEATLES
Translated from the John Lennon

Once upon a time there were three little boys called John, George and Paul, by name christened. They decided to get together because they were the getting together type. When they were together they wondered what for after all, what for? So all of a sudden they all grew guitars and formed a noise. Funnily enough, no one was interested, least of all the three little men. So-o-o-o on discovering a fourth little even littler man called Stuart Sutcliffe running about them they said, quote 'Sonny get a bass guitar and you will be alright' and he did – but he wasn't alright because he couldn't play it. So they sat on him with comfort 'til he could play. Still there was no beat, and a kindly old aged man said, quote 'Thou hast no drums!' We had no drums! they coffed. So a series of drums came and went and came.

Suddenly in Scotland, touring with Johnny Gentle, the group (called the Beatles called) discovered they had not a very nice sound – because they had no amplifiers. They got some. Many people ask what are Beatles? Why Beatles? Uh, Beatles, how did the name arrive? So we will tell you. It came in a vision – a man appeared on a flaming pie and said unto them 'From this day on you are Beatles with an A'. Thank you, Mister Man, they said, thanking him.

And then a man with a beard cut off said – will you go to Germany (Hamburg) and play mighty rock for the peasants for money? And we said we would play mighty anything for money.

But before we could go we had to grow a drummer, so we grew one in West Derby in a club called Some Casbah, and his trouble was Pete Best. We called 'Hello, Pete, come off to Germany!' 'Yes!' Zooooom. After a few months, Peter and Paul (who is called McArtrey, son of Jim McArtrey, his father) lit a Kino (cinema) and the German police said 'Bad Beatles,

Below and opposite: **Paul, John and George in German leather, with cowboy overtones, on a roof in Hamburg, 1961.**

you must go home and light your English cinemas'. Zooooom, half a group. But even before this, the Gestapo had taken my friend little George Harrison (of Speke) away because he was only twelve and too young to vote in Germany; but after two months in England he grew eighteen, and the Gestapoes said 'you can come'. So suddenly all back in Liverpool village were many groups playing in grey suits and Jim said 'Why have you no grey suits?' 'We don't like them, Jim' we said speaking to Jim. After playing in the clubs a bit, everyone said 'Go to Germany!' So we are. Zooooom. Stuart gone. Zoom zoom John (of Woolton) George (of Speke) Peter and Paul zoom zoom. All of them gone.

Thank you club members, from John and George (what are friends).

The jokes, and the deliberate mistakes in John's article, were reproduced many times in the next few years. The whole front page of the second edition of *Mersey Beat* was about their German recording contract. They used one of Astrid's photographs, one of the five of them taken in a railway siding in Hamburg. In the caption Paul is still called 'Paul MacArthy'. In the same issue there were some fashion notes by someone called Priscilla in which she said that 'grey was now the colour for evening wear'. This was Cilla Black, then a typist and part-time cloakroom girl and occasional singer at the Cavern.

The Beatles were by now the main group at the Cavern, but they were still using the Casbah Club, Pete Best's home, as their headquarters. Mrs Best had branched out as a dance promoter, though the Casbah was still her main interest. 'Most people referred to

them as "Pete Best and the Beatles",' so she says. Pete did take the main responsibility for their bookings, helped by his mother, and tried to organize them.

The Casbah became even more their centre when Neil Aspinall, Pete's friend who was still living there, bought himself an old van for £80 and started driving the Beatles round Merseyside. He got five bob from each of them for each session. 'The evenings became a real drag. I'd drive them somewhere, come home and do a bit of studying, then go back for them. I began to think, what am I doing? I was still getting only £2 10s. a week as an accountant, yet I could get £3 for three lunch hours at the Cavern. So in the July I left work for good.'

Neil became their road manager, which he still is, though he hates the term. It was his job to pick up Pete and all their gear from the Casbah then take them all to where they were playing.

'They were beginning to cause riots everywhere,' says Neil. 'The kids would get going, then the Teds would try to wreck the place. John once got his finger broken in a fight in the bogs.'

But despite their large fan following and the fact that some weeks they were earning up to £15, out of which they now had to pay Neil, nothing was really happening. London seemed to be the only place where pop singers came from, or at least the only place where they could make their name.

Mersey Beat was doing them proud, and sellings lots of copies, and Pete Best was trying hard to organize them, but by being on the road so much they missed many bookings. They didn't seem to care about bookings anyway, mocking any promoters who were interested in them. They'd by this time broken with Allan Williams, who had got them their first Hamburg date. He says that during their second Hamburg trip he stopped getting his commission which he should have had. They say that they'd got the Top Ten engagement on their own and didn't think they should therefore pay him a percentage. There was a row, although they later became friends again. 'I felt they'd let me down, after all I'd done for them. I know now what I missed. I suppose I could have held on to them, but I wasn't really a businessman. I was just doing it for kicks.' No other manager or agent was interested. They weren't earning enough to attract the normal manager and anyway, they weren't the sort of clean, neat, well-mannered blokes that managements liked.

They spent most of their time between lunch and evening sessions just walking round Liverpool, sitting in coffee bars or hanging around record shops, listening to records for nothing. They were always hard up. Danny English, who was the manager of the Old Dive, a pub (now knocked down) near the Cavern, remembers them spinning out a glass of brown ale for hours. He told them one day that it was about time they bought the barmaid a drink.

'After a lot of discussion, they asked me what she was drinking. I said stout. They said how much was that. After more discussions they produced 4½d. each and bought her a Guinness.'

Danny English tried to get another of his customers to help them. This was George Harrison, no relation to our George Harrison, who has written a column in the *Liverpool Echo* for what seems like centuries. But he didn't do anything. There were so many groups competing for his attention and the Beatles looked the scruffiest of them all.

They were getting more and more depressed by their lack of progress. All the parents, except Mrs Harrison and Mrs Best, were continually on at their sons once again to give up and get proper jobs.

'I knew John would always be a bohemian,' says Mimi. 'But I wanted him to have some sort of job. Here he was at nearly 21 years old, having thrown away his chance at art college, touting round stupid halls for £3 a night. Where was the point in that?'

When John was coming up for 21, in September 1961, he got some money as a present from his aunt in Edinburgh and decided on the spur of the moment to go off with Paul to Paris. George and Pete Best were naturally very hurt, at being left on their own. 'We got fed up,' says John. 'We did have bookings, but we just broke them and went off.'

In Paris they met Jurgen Vollmer, one of their Hamburg friends. It was during this Paris visit, which was mainly spent hanging around the clubs till their money ran out, that John finally brushed his hair forward.

'Jurgen also had bell-bottom trousers,' says John. 'But we thought that would be considered too queer back in Liverpool. We didn't want to appear feminine or anything like that because our audience in Liverpool still had a lot of fellows. We were playing rock, dressed in leather, though Paul's ballads were bringing in more and more girls.'

John had learned from Stu that Jurgen was in Paris. Even though Stu had left them to study art in Hamburg, he and John sent long letters to each other.

At first the letters were full of jokes and daft stories, the sort John had written as a child, when he did those little scrap books. 'Uncle Norman has just driven up on his moustache.' 'P.S. Mary Queen of Scots was a Nigger.'

He passed on to Stu any good bits of news about the group's progress, such as a Beatle fan club at last being started in Liverpool. (Rory Storm already had one). But the letters soon became full of disappointments and moans. 'It's all a shitty deal. Something is going to happen, but where is it?'

John started including more of his serious poems, the sort he had never shown Mimi. They usually ended in obscenity or self-consciousness. He filled up his letters to Stu with them, when he could think of nothing else.

'I remember a time when
Everyone I loved hated me
Because I hated them.
So what, so what, so
Fucking what.

I remember a time when
Belly buttons were knee high
When only shitting was
Dirty and everything else
Clean and beautiful.

I can't remember anything
without a sadness
So deep that it hardly
becomes known to me.
So deep that its tears
leave me a spectator
of my own stupidity.
And so I go rambling on
With a hey nonny nonny no.'

Stu in Hamburg was filling his letters with the same sort of wailings and anguish, only his began to be much worse than John's. Stu wrote in his letters as if he were Jesus. John, thinking at first it was all a joke, pretended to be John the Baptist.

One day, towards the end of 1961, Stu collapsed at the art college in Hamburg and was brought home. 'He'd been getting a lot of headaches,' says Astrid, 'but we just put it down to working too hard at College.'

Stu went back the next day but in February 1962, it happened again. He collapsed, was

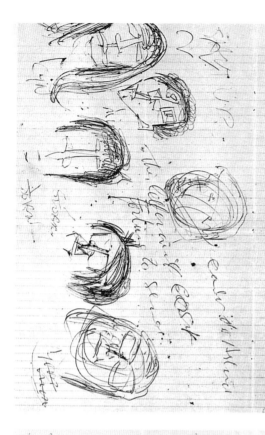

I remember a time when everyone
I loved hated me
because I hated them so what
so what so fucking what
I remember a time when buttons were
knee high
when only shitting was dirty
and everything else clean
+ beautiful
I can't remember anything
with out a sadness
so deep that it hardly
becomes known to me.
so deep that its tears
    leave me a spectator
of my own STUPIDITY
+ so I go rambling
on with a 🎵 hey nonny 🎵
🎵 nonny no. And 🎵

How long can one go on writing
and writing, like you & new dinks
really know who I'm writing to
or why its quiet peculiar I
usually write like this and
forget about it—but if
I post it its a little part
of my almost secret self
in the hands of someone
miles away who will wonder
what the hell is going on or
just pass it off as toilet paper
anyway I dont care really
what happens because when
I think about it its so
bloody unimportant — but what
is important why has she ought
to say that this letter is not
important and means a
something any way — or anyway
+ anyway — yeah!
I wonder what I wanted to write

to be a curtain or something, I
lost it yea.
        Er how are you keeping
Stuart darling are you as
o.k — is life as good — bad shitty
great — wonderful as it was or
is it just 2 thousand years
of nothing, and continue on
a dum a dum.
    I think this is it
Goodbye you dont write
out of 'similarity' its
        well not because you
think you ought to.
write when you feel like
        So Goodbye Brenda
                you...
                the man the glorious
AHAHAH
BYE BYE
    See you soon
        I dont know
    why I said that

brought back to Astrid's and was taken to his room. This time he stayed there. He wrote long 30-page letters to John, did endless drawings and paintings or just walked round and round his room. He had violent headaches and temper tantrums which made it difficult for Astrid and her mother to look after him. He did have medical treatment, but nothing seemed to help. 'He came back from a specialist one day and said he didn't want a black coffin like everyone else. He'd just seen a white coffin in a window and he wanted that.'

Stu died in April 1962 after a brain haemorrhage. 'He lived so much in such a short time,' says Klaus. 'Every second of his short time he was doing something. He saw ten times more than other people. His imagination was fantastic. His death was a tragedy. He would have done so much.'

There is no doubt about Stu's artistic talent. Professor Paolozzi thought he was obviously destined to succeed. He had won prizes in Liverpool at an early age. Since his death, his paintings have appeared in numerous exhibitions in Liverpool and London. He had had a great influence on John and the rest of the Beatles, leading their fashion in hair, clothes and in thoughts.

'I looked up to Stu,' says John. 'I depended on him to tell me the truth, the way I do with Paul today. Stu would tell me if something was good and I'd believe him.'

Even today, they still miss him. It's strange to think that by 1962, the one who was looked upon as the cleverest Beatle had died.

The death of Stu was in a way a macabre climax to their year of apparently getting nowhere and feeling depressed. But back in Liverpool, just before Stu collapsed, the something John was looking for was at last about to happen.

It happened, just to be precise, at three o'clock on the afternoon of 28 October 1961. A youth in a black leather jacket called Raymond Jones walked into the NEMS record store in Whitechapel, Liverpool, and asked for a record called 'My Bonnie' by a group called the Beatles. Brian Epstein, who was behind the counter, said he was terribly sorry. He'd never heard of that record, nor of a group called the Beatles.

Opposite: John's poem and other bits from a letter he wrote to Stu Sutcliffe in Germany. Earlier, Stu had left the Beatles to stay on in Hamburg, study at art college there and marry Astrid.

BRIAN EPSTEIN

The Epstein family fortunes were founded by Brian's grandfather Isaac, a Jewish refugee from Poland, who came to Liverpool at the turn of the century. He opened a furniture store, later called I. Epstein and Sons, in Walton Road, Liverpool. This in turn was taken over by his elder son, Harry, Brian's father.

It is assumed by many people in Liverpool that the Epsteins have always owned NEMS, North End Music Stores, the name which Brian later made famous locally, through the record shop. But NEMS had been going long before the Epsteins. Jim McCartney, Paul's father, remembered having a piano which came from NEMS during the First World War.

The Epsteins didn't take over NEMS till the thirties. It was at the end of the block in Walton Road which contained I. Epstein and Sons and they had always had an eye on it for expansion. Harry saw that its record and music business would fit easily into his furniture firm, but it was the site as much as anything which he wanted when he eventually bought it.

Harry married into another highly successful Jewish furniture family, the Hymans from Sheffield. He married his wife Queenie in 1933 when she was 18 and he was 29.

Brian, their elder son was born on 19 September 1934, in a private nursing home in Rodney Street, the Harley Street of Liverpool. Their second son Clive was born 23 months later.

With two sons, the fortunes of the Epstein furniture firm seemed assured for many decades to come. Harry and Queenie were living in a large five-bedroomed detached house in Childwall, one of Liverpool's most desirable residential areas. The Epsteins lived in this house, 197 Queen's Drive, for the next 30 years, until Clive left to get married. Today it is lived in by the Dean of Liverpool.

The Epsteins lived in some style up to the outbreak of the war. They had two living-in staff – a nanny for the boys and a general help.

Opposite: Brian Epstein, public-school boy and lover of Sibelius, pictured at Liverpool's Cavern Club, where he first met the Beatles in November 1961, before going on to become their manager.

All that Mrs Epstein can remember of Brian as a baby is that he was the most beautiful child she'd ever seen. 'As he began to walk and talk, he developed a very inquiring mind. He always wanted to know everything.' Brian's earliest memories are of the great excitement of being taken through to visit his relations in Sheffield.

His first school of any sort was the Beechanhurst Kindergarten in Liverpool where he hammered wooden shapes into a plywood board. In 1940, when he was six years old, Liverpool was under heavy bombing and the family were evacuated first of all to Prestatyn, in North Wales, and then to Southport, where there was a large Jewish community. Brian was sent to Southport College where he began his formal education, the beginning of a very long and very unhappy process.

'I was one of those out-of-sorts boys who never quite fit,' so he recorded in his 1964 autobiography (*A Cellarful of Noise*, Souvenir Press). 'I was ragged, nagged and bullied by boys and masters. My parents must have despaired of me many times.'

In 1943, the family returned to Liverpool and Brian entered Liverpool College, a private fee-paying school. The following year, at the age of ten, Liverpool College expelled him.

'The official reason was for inattention and for being below standard. I'd been caught in a maths lesson doing drawings of girls. There were other crimes I was supposed to have committed. I'm sure my failings were many.'

He remembered arriving home and sitting on a sofa, with his father saying 'I just don't know what on earth we're going to do with you.'

His mother thinks that in later years he tended to overestimate his own failings at school. She agrees he was hardly happy or successful at any of them, but she thinks it was often as much the fault of the school system as anything. 'It was just after the war. Schools were hard to get into. There was none of the freedom they have today. They just threw you out if they didn't like you.'

Brian himself thought that, apart from his own inability to fit in, there might also have been some anti-semitism. 'I do remember being called Jew or Yid. But it didn't seem to mean much more than the way a red-headed boy gets called Ginger.'

After his expulsion from Liverpool College, his parents found him another local private school, but they kept him there for only a few weeks. They realized it was the sort of pseudo-posh school that took advantage of such parents, caring little for education but a lot for taking money from wealthy parents who couldn't get their kids in anywhere else.

In the end they found him a good Jewish prep school called Beaconsfield near Tunbridge Wells. Here he took up horse-riding, which he loved, and art which he also loved and was encouraged to do for the first time.

At 13 he sat the common entrance exam. This is the examination needed to get into any of the good Headmasters' Conference public schools. He failed this miserably, but it didn't stop his parents trying to get him into one of them. Rugby, Repton and Clifton all turned him down. He went eventually to the sort of establishment that will take anybody. This was a very hearty, outdoor one in the West Country. He was forced to play rugby. He was very unhappy.

But his father didn't give up trying and in the autumn of 1948, just on Brian's 14th birthday, he got him into Wrekin College, a well known and established public school in Shropshire.

He didn't look forward to Wrekin as he'd eventually begun to settle down at the West Country school. He was getting on with his art and at last making a few friends. He wrote in a diary at the time: 'Now for the Wrekin I hate. I am going there only because my parents want me to... it is a pity because it has been a great year for me. The birth of new ideas, a little more popularity.'

He eventually settled down at Wrekin, at least he found ways of putting the time in. His interest in art continued. He became top of the class in art and decided that he was going to be a dress designer.

'I wrote to my father that I wanted to be a dress designer, but he was against it. He said it wasn't the sort of thing for young men to do.'

At the same time, he developed an interest in acting. At home in Liverpool his mother took him to many plays. 'I used to take him first of all to Fol de Rol sort of things. Then later to improve his mind I took him to Peter Glenville. I also took him to hear the Liverpool Phil.'

Brian took a star part in the school's production of *Christopher Columbus*. 'His Daddy and I drove down to see it,' says his mother. 'We sat through it all and the headmaster came up and asked us afterwards if we'd liked Brian. He was just so good we hadn't recognized him.'

He left Wrekin when he was 16, without taking his school certificate. No one thought he could ever have passed it. His father was still against him becoming a dress designer, but Brian decided he wanted to leave school and get a job all the same.

'After seven schools, all of them rotten, I'd had enough. I'd been thwarted in the only thing I wanted to do, so I just accepted anything. On 10 September 1950, very thin, pink-cheeked, curly-haired and half-educated, I reported for duty at the family store in Walton, Liverpool.'

He started as a furniture salesman on £5 a week. The day after he joined he sold a £12 dining table to a woman who had come into the shop to buy a mirror.

He found he was a good salesman. And he enjoyed it. He also started taking an interest in the design and layout of the shop. His father had been naturally pleased that his elder son had at last decided to come into the business. Brian found, to his surprise, that it pleased him as well.

'Brian always had beautiful taste,' says his mother. 'And he always appreciated lovely furniture.'

But Brian didn't think the store's window displays were all that lovely. He started experimenting, doing what was considered at the time very daring things, such as putting chairs with their backs to the window. His father thought perhaps he was doing things a bit quicker than was necessary, but didn't complain as he was so pleased that his son and heir was settling down well in the career he had chosen for him. As further experience he decided to send Brian to another firm, not connected with them, to do a six months' apprenticeship.

Brian spent the six months at The Times furniture store in Lord Street, Liverpool, still on £5 a week. He seems to have done well there too. When he left they presented him with a Parker pen and pencil set. (The pen was the one he loaned to Paul McCartney a few years later, to sign his first contract.)

After the six months, he moved back to Walton. He began to take over the designing of the whole store. 'I enjoyed it, especially trying new things. I enjoyed selling as well, watching people relax and show trust in me. It was pleasant to see the wary look dissolve and people begin to think there were good things ahead for them and I would be the provider.'

He had a few rows over his plans for window dressing. 'They wanted all the windows jam-packed. I preferred very little in the window, perhaps just one chair. I was also crazy about contemporary furniture. It was just coming in and I wanted everybody to know about it. I think if you show the public something lovely, they'll accept it.'

On 9 December 1952, in the midst of his brave new schemes for I. Epstein and Sons, he was called up for national service. If school horrified him, the thought of the army was terrifying. 'I'd been a poor schoolboy. I was sure I was going to make the lousiest soldier ever.'

He applied for the RAF and was made a clerk in the Royal Army Service Corps. He did his basic training at Aldershot.

'It was like prison and I did everything wrong. I turned right instead of left and when I was told to stand still I fell over.'

He managed to get through his square bashing, after a fashion, and even had the notion that he might be chosen to be on parade for the Coronation. The year was then 1953. He thought the Coronation sounded glamorous and exciting and it would be nice to be part of it. But he wasn't chosen. Instead he went round the pubs and clubs and got drunk.

He was about the only ex-public school boy in his intake who didn't become an officer. But in his off-duty hours, dressed as always in impeccable taste and spending his time in smart West End clubs, he could easily have passed for one.

After Aldershot, he managed to get a posting to Regent's Park Barracks in London, one of the most desirable postings for young officers around town. He had lots of relations in London and managed to get out and enjoy himself. He drove himself back one night in a large car, wearing a bowler hat, pin-striped suit and carrying an umbrella over his arm.

As he entered the barracks, the guard saluted him, two soldiers confined to the guard house jerked their heads in Eyes Right and a clerk shouted 'Good night, sir.' But an officer inside wasn't so easily misled. 'Private Epstein. You will report to the company office at 10.00 hours tomorrow morning charged with impersonating an officer.'

He was confined to barracks for some time. It wasn't his first offence. He'd been guilty of other minor insubordinations, or at least inabilities to do the right thing. 'The army was generally getting on my nerves. I really was becoming genuinely upset. It was getting me down so much that I reported to the barracks doctor who referred me to a psychiatrist.'

Other psychiatrists were consulted and all agreed that Private Epstein wasn't one of nature's soldiers. They agreed that he was mentally and emotionally unsuited to military service. After twelve months, his national service only half completed, he was discharged on medical grounds. As is the way of the army, they still gave him most impressive sounding military references. These described him in glowing terms as a 'sober, reliable and utterly trustworthy soldier'.

Brian told the story of his army debacle in very cheerful terms, almost hinting that he might have engineered his discharge. But there seems little doubt that he had been seriously disturbed by it all.

He ran all the way to Euston and caught the first train to Liverpool. He went back to the family store and worked very hard. He began to take an increasing interest in the record side. He'd always been interested in music, classical records mainly, but popular music as well. Edmundo Ros was one of his favourites at the time.

But he began to get even more interested in a new hobby, one he had been very fond of at school – acting. He was beginning to realize that perhaps he was more interested in artistic things than being a furniture salesman. He went to every production at the Liverpool Playhouse and began to spend more and more of his spare time either in amateur productions, or in the company of professional actors from the Playhouse. He became very friendly with two in particular, Brian Bedford and Helen Lindsay.

They suggested that he too could be an actor. He had the interest, the right feelings and

Brian, with Paul and George: he always seemed so smooth, assured and organized, but the Beatles never knew what went on his private life, either before or after he met them.

they were sure the talent. Why didn't he apply for RADA? They would help him. So he applied for the Royal Academy of Dramatic Art. And he got in.

'I read two pieces for the Director, John Fernald. They were from Eliot's *Confidential Clerk* and from *Macbeth*. I got in without a full audition, for some reason. Perhaps the fact that I had no money problems helped.'

His father, naturally enough, wasn't particularly pleased. Acting was second only to dress designing in his list of unmanly jobs. But at 22, his son and heir went off again to interrupt his career. This time willingly, unlike the army. Perhaps even for ever.

He was in the same year at RADA as Susannah York, and Joanna Dunham. Albert Finney and Peter O'Toole had just left. While a student at RADA he took a part-time job in a record shop in Charing Cross Road.

'I was doing reasonably well. John Fernald had great faith in me. But I began to loathe actors and all their social life. I hadn't enjoyed school. And here I was seven years later in another community life. I just didn't like it, or any of the people. I began to think it was too late. I was more a business man after all.'

From the day he'd started RADA his father was always asking him when he was coming back to the business. Each holiday, as he was going back to RADA, he asked him to stay. During the summer vacation of 1957, before he began his fourth term, he asked Brian again over dinner at the Adelphi Hotel. This time he said yes.

His father had decided to open a new branch in Liverpool, this time in the city centre, in Great Charlotte Street. It was hoped it would interest Brian in the firm. Clive, Brian's younger brother, was by this time also working in the firm.

Brian was in charge of the record department with one assistant. Anne Shelton, the singer, opened the new store. On the first morning the record department took £20. In Walton the record department took £70 in a good week.

'Most record shops I'd ever been in were lousy. The minute a record became popular, it went out of stock. I aimed to have everything in stock, even the most way-out records.

'I did this by ordering in triplicate any record that anyone ever wanted. I reckoned that if one person asked for something, there must be others who would want it too. I even ordered three copies of the LP "The Birth of a Baby", just because one person had wanted it.'

Every customer was encouraged to leave an order for a record if by chance it wasn't in. An immediate delivery was always promised. Brian worked out a simple but ingenious stock index whereby it could be seen immediately which record had sold out. This consisted of strings attached inside each folder. When any were dangling down, it could be seen immediately that more records were needed. This was checked constantly throughout the day and replacements put in or re-ordered immediately.

He also worked out his own top twenty bestseller list of the pop records being sold in NEMS. This was checked twice daily. Apart from being a good gimmick, of interest to customers and an encouragement for them to buy certain records, it also showed him exactly which of the up-and-coming records should be ordered in bulk.

'I've never seen anybody work as hard before,' says his mother. 'He seemed to have found something which completely fulfilled him for the first time in his life.'

Brian agreed. 'I did work very hard. I don't think I worked physically harder in my life before or after. I started at eight each day and didn't finish until well into the night. On Sundays I was in the store all day making orders.'

By 1959, two years after opening, NEMS in Great Charlotte Street had an extensive pop and classical department covering two floors of the store. The staff had expanded from two to thirty. Business was going so well that it was decided to open another branch of NEMS in Whitechapel, the heart of Liverpool's shopping centre.

The new shop was opened by Anthony Newley. Brian had got in touch with him through a Decca sales contact. The crowds on the opening day in central Liverpool were compared to the return of a triumphal cup-final team. Nobody in Liverpool had seen such a turnout for a pop singer, up till then.

Both shops thrived and expanded. By the August of 1961 Brian was boasting that the two NEMS records departments in central Liverpool in Whitechapel and Great Charlotte Street contained, 'The finest record selections in the North'. This boast appeared in an advertisement on 31 August 1961, in *Mersey Beat*, that same Merseyside pop music newspaper which had begun the previous month. Brian himself was not personally a fan of pop music. His favourite composer was by then Sibelius. But as a smart businessman, he saw that *Mersey Beat* was thriving and a good advertising market.

In that same issue he started a column called 'Record Releases'. This was by-lined by 'Brian Epstein of NEMS'. In this he reviewed forthcoming records, light, jazz and pop. In that first column he said that 'The Shadows' popularity seems to increase continually'. That must have made the Beatles puke.

The column gave him free publicity for his shops and also helped him to push certain records. But it was also smart of *Mersey Beat* to have got him. In the four years since he'd left RADA, fed up and disillusioned, he'd become about the leading personality in the record retailing business on Merseyside. His name and solid business background gave weight to *Mersey Beat*.

But very soon he was beginning to feel he had expanded as far as he could go. There weren't many fresh fields to conquer in Merseyside, at least in his line. By the autumn of 1961 the feeling of boredom and dissatisfaction was coming on again. His mother remembers sensing it.

'He started taking up teaching himself foreign languages. He became very interested in Spain and Spanish. He also went back to amateur acting again.'

His father was naturally worried that he would want to be off again, having built up two prosperous record stores.

Brian himself remembered this feeling of wanting something new, of being bored and frustrated by business. But his three closest friends at the time don't remember him moaning about that, though they do recall him having other things which bothered him.

Once Whitechapel was established, he had begun to have more of a social life. He used to see a lot of Geoffrey Ellis, a boyhood friend who lived near him. He also went to a public school, Ellesmere College, and then on to Oxford, where he read Law. Geoffrey says Brian was terribly shy and hesitant in his schooldays. But after Oxford, Geoffrey went to New York, to work for an insurance firm, and they lost contact, for a few years.

There was also a friend called Terry Doran, from a completely different background. He was an ex-secondary-modern schoolboy, now a car salesman, with a good line in Liverpool wit and mimicry. 'I met Brian by chance one day in a Liverpool pub in 1959. I just fell in love with him from the beginning.'

Geoffrey and Terry were simply social friends, unconnected with his business, at least in those days. But his third friend, Peter Brown, was a friend in the same business. He eventually became Brian's closest friend of all.

Peter was born in Bebington, went to a Roman Catholic grammar school, worked in Henderson's, the Liverpool store, and then Lewis's where he became manager of their record department.

When Brian came to plan the opening of the new NEMS store, in Whitechapel, he asked Peter to take over as manager of the Charlotte Street record department. Peter was getting £12 a week, managing the record department at Lewis's. Brian offered him £16, plus commission, which he thought was enormous.

'I soon learned all about Brian's highly efficient ordering systems. After closing time at six we had to do all the orders. It could take up from 40 minutes to two hours.'

Terry remembers being kept waiting while they were both doing orders. Brian would tell Terry to meet him after the shop closed. 'I'd go for a drink and end up being there till closing time, still waiting for them.'

There was a slight delay in opening Whitechapel and Peter found that for a few months Brian was still at Charlotte Street with him. 'It was pretty difficult, officially being the manager, but having the boss still there running things. It was one long row. We were still as good social friends, but I think he was disappointed in me as a businessman.

'He was very fond of sending notes to all the staff, even though there were so few of us. His stock control system really was marvellous. It assured that we were never out of stock of any bestselling record. EMI people used to tell us we were the largest sellers in the North.'

Brian always maintained, quite wrongly, that girls didn't find him attractive. But it was about this time that he started going out with a girl from his record store, Rita Harris.

'It took him a long time to realize she had fallen in love with him,' says Peter Brown. 'We all used to go into Cheshire for a meal, Rita and Brian and me and perhaps one or two others.'

This was the most serious romance Brian ever had with a girl, but it eventually came to nothing.

His love life always appears to have ended unhappily. He did have violent affairs with other people, but they rarely lasted long, which worried him a great deal. He never really came to terms with himself sexually. But he decided that was how he was and he never tried to go against his nature. But he sometimes almost had a self-destruction complex.

'He was really very lonely in Liverpool,' says Peter. 'He felt there were few places he could go and really enjoy himself. Our best nights out were in Manchester. Brian, Terry and I used to drive through there most Saturday evenings.

'He had a phobia about his unhappy affairs and also another one just slightly, about being Jewish. I think he imagined anti-semitism sometimes when there wasn't any. Perhaps it wasn't awareness of his Jewishness. Perhaps it was just being part of an environment he didn't really care for – the sort of successful, provincial, furniture-shop Jewishness, when his real nature was towards the artistic and the aesthetic.

'But of course he could be a good businessman when he wanted to, saving pennies and being mean when he suddenly felt he had to. We had lots of rows over money. But it just happened now and again. He was mostly a very lavish spender.'

It's easy to overstate the complexities of Brian's personality and interests at this stage in his career. His parents knew little of his worries. They certainly didn't see any effects of them, although his mother did remember him becoming restless, once both NEMS departments were thriving, and starting to look for something new.

He went off in the autumn of 1961 for a five-week holiday in Spain, the longest he'd had. He took with him a slight feeling of frustration, in his personal life as well as in his business life. Nothing serious, perhaps. Just a feeling of unfulfilment. He'd been too busy really, building up NEMS for the last four years, to ever seriously become worried by it all, the way he had done in the army. One or two did consider him a poor little spoiled rich boy. But as far as most people could see, he was hard working, charming and gay, with a family who loved him.

But he obviously felt he needed something new to fill his life, preferably something in some way artistic. RADA had been an outlet of a sort, the failure of which had stopped his artistic longings for a while. But there is nothing more insidiously frustrating than an artistic leaning, when one's artistic tastes are greater than one's artistic talents, or so it seems.

That was Brian Epstein on 28 October 1961. He was 27. So far he had been a failed schoolboy, a successful furniture salesman, a failed soldier, a successful record salesman, a failed actor, a successful record store executive. When into the shop came a customer asking for the Beatles.

16

BRIAN SIGNS THE BEATLES

The famous Epstein index system was beaten. All these lovely little bits of dangling string couldn't help. Brian Epstein had to admit that he'd neither heard of a record called 'My Bonnie', nor a group called the Beatles.

It's strange, in some ways, that he hadn't heard of the Beatles. After all, he'd been advertising and writing a record column in *Mersey Beat* for several months. His eyes must have passed over their name in articles many times. But then of course his interest in *Mersey Beat* was purely professional, as a retailer taking space in order to sell records.

He was only interested in those groups which had made records, because records were what he sold. None of the Liverpool groups being written about in *Mersey Beat* had made a record. So there was no reason for him to take any notice of them.

He was aware that there were flourishing beat groups and clubs in Liverpool. But he wasn't interested in them personally. At 27, he was well out of the age range for the coffee bars and beat groups. He'd also been, for most of the previous five years, a full-time businessman, with little time for any sort of leisure activities, apart from the theatre.

But he was annoyed by his lack of knowledge of the new record he was being asked for. Surely if this group, wherever they came from, had produced a record, *he* must know about it. So when Raymond Jones made his request he promised to get it for him and wrote down on a pad: 'My Bonnie. The Beatles. Check on Monday.'

Raymond Jones had also mentioned that the Beatles record came from Germany. So that was something to go on. He telephoned a few agents who imported foreign records. But not one of them had the record in stock, or had even imported it.

'I might have stopped there, but for the rigid rule I'd laid down that no customer should ever be turned away.

'I was also intrigued to find out why a completely unknown disc had been asked for

---

Opposite: **Brian Epstein with George at the Royal Variety Performance, 1963. Brian was the Beatles' manager from December 1961 up until his death in October 1967, when they had reached the height of their success and musical genius as a group.**

three times in two days. Because on Monday morning, before I'd started making enquiries, two girls came in and asked for the same record.'

He talked to various contacts around Liverpool and found, to his amazement, that not only were the Beatles a British and not a German group, but that they also came from Liverpool.

He asked the girls in his store about the Beatles. They told him the Beatles were fabulous. Then he found to his surprise that they'd even been in his store. He must have seen them many an afternoon without knowing who they were.

'One of the girls told me they were the boys I'd once been complaining about, hanging around the counters all day listening to records but not buying any. They were a scruffy crowd in leather. But they were supposed to be quite nice really, so all the girls told me, so I'd never actually asked them to leave. Anyway, they filled the shop up in the afternoon.'

Brian decided to go along to the Cavern himself and get some details about the Beatles and their record. If there was such interest in them, especially being a local group, it might be worth his while to import some of their records himself, being a good businessman.

'I wasn't a member of the Cavern and I was very shy about going along to a teenage club. I was frightened they might not let me in. So I asked *Mersey Beat* if they could help me. They rang up the Cavern and said who I was and could I come.'

His first visit was the lunch-time session of 9 November 1961. 'It was dark, damp and smelly and I regretted my decision immediately. The noise was deafening, amplifiers sending out mainly American hits. I remember as I listened to the records they were playing thinking that there might be some tie-up possible between the Cavern and my top twenty selection.

'Then the Beatles came on and I saw them for the first time. They were not very tidy and not very clean. They smoked as they played and they ate and talked and pretended to hit each other. They turned their backs on the audience and shouted at people and laughed at their private jokes.

'But there was quite clearly enormous excitement. They seemed to give off some sort of personal magnetism. I was fascinated by them.'

It was John, the main shouter and jumper-about, who particularly fascinated him. This wasn't apparent at the time, as he didn't know which was which, but he realized it later. He couldn't keep his eyes off John.

But he hadn't come to watch. He'd come simply to do a bit of business. The Cavern DJ, Bob Wooler, announced over the microphone that Mr Epstein of NEMS was in the audience and would everybody give him a big hand.

This helped when he at last managed to get within shouting distance of the Beatles themselves. 'What brings Mr Epstein here?' said George, slightly sarcastically. He explained that he'd had a request for their German disc but didn't know which company produced it. Could they help? George told him the company was called Polydor. George only very vaguely remembers talking to Brian that lunch time. The other Beatles – John, Paul and Pete Best – don't remember him at all this first visit.

Just for company, to hide his shyness amongst all the kids, Brian began to take along one of his assistants from his store on his visits to the Cavern. This was Alistair Taylor who worked on the counter at NEMS but was also Brian's personal assistant. Like sending memos to his staff, when he could have talked to them all in a telephone booth, Brian liked anything which added to the executive image.

It took Brian some time to get his thoughts clear. 'All I was interested in was selling records. But in a few weeks I'd found myself coming to the Cavern more and more often, just to listen and watch. I also found myself asking my record contacts what managing a group meant. How did one do it? What sort of contract one would have with a group, supposing, just supposing, one wanted to become a manager?'

His contacts weren't all that expert on management problems. They were, naturally, mainly on the retail side of records, not the production. But during a trip down to London, purely on retail business, he talked more than usual to people like the general manager of HMV in Oxford Street and the manager at Keith Prowse's shop, picking up any tips he could.

George, Paul and John, with Pete Best, putting on a show at the Cavern Club, hoping to impress. It was at a lunch-time session here, on 9 November 1961, that Brian Epstein first saw the Beatles play and was instantly fascinated by the four musicians. Within just a few weeks, he had signed them.

He also contacted the German record company and ordered 200 copies of 'My Bonnie'. 'I was so fascinated by the Beatles that I thought it was worth taking a chance on selling them all.

'I suppose it was all part of getting bored with simply selling records. I was looking for a new hobby. The Beatles at the same time, though I didn't know it and perhaps they didn't either, were also getting a bit bored with Liverpool. They were wanting to expand and get on to something new.

'I began talking to them at lunch-time sessions. "You should have been here last night," Paul said to me one day. "We were signing autographs. I signed one on a girl's arm." I always seemed to miss their greatest moments.'

He also found out what their present situation was about a manager. He found that Allan Williams had been associated with them at one time and had been the one who had organized their first Hamburg trip. 'I went to see him and he said, "They're nice boys, but they'll let you down all the time".'

On 3 December 1961, he invited them along for a chat at his office at the Whitechapel store. He told them it was just a chat, as he hadn't worked out everything in his mind.

He'd seen a lot of them, prior to that first proper meeting at his office, but the Beatles themselves had still scarcely taken him in. He was just a fringe figure. They have few real memories of him before that meeting.

'He'd looked efficient and rich, that's all I remember,' says John. George says he looked the executive type. Paul was impressed by his Zodiac car. They decided to give him a try.

For that first official meeting the Beatles decided to bring Bob Wooler along with them, just to show they weren't completely alone in the world. John introduced Bob Wooler as his Dad. It was many months before Brian realized that Bob Wooler was not John's Dad. It was even longer before he realized John didn't know who or where his Dad was.

John, with Bob Wooler, arrived at the appointed time of 4.30. And so did George and Pete Best. But there was no sign of Paul. After half an hour, during which Brian was becoming very irritated, he asked George to ring Paul. George returned from the phone to say that Paul was in the bath. 'This is disgraceful,' said Brian. 'He's going to be very late.' 'Late,' said George. 'But very clean.'

Paul arrived at last and they discussed the future of the Beatles – what they all wanted to do, what sort of terms they would like. Nobody knew what contracts were arranged in such circumstances because no one had ever seen one.

They all arranged to meet again the following Wednesday. By that time Brian had been to see a lawyer friend, Rex Makin. Brian was looking for enthusiasm as well as advice. 'Oh, yes,' he was told, 'another Epstein idea. How long before you lose interest in this one?'

They met again on the Wednesday and Brian this time said he definitely wanted to manage them. He said he'd want 25 per cent. They said why couldn't he take 20? He said he needed that extra five per cent as it would entail many expenses in promoting and working for them. He expected to lose money for many months to come.

The contract was signed the following Sunday at the Casbah Club, Pete Best's home and the Beatles' headquarters. Each Beatle signature was signed in the presence of Alistair Taylor. Brian didn't sign.

Brian hard at work, as normal, in his London office. Brian's efficiency and organizational skills immediately transformed the Beatles from a band of scruffy-looking, disorganized lads into a proper professional act. In John's words, he suddenly 'made it all seem real'.

'That was a great boob,' says Alistair. 'I signed my name as a witness to Brian's signature. It made me look a right fool.'

Brian never did sign the contract either. 'I had given my word about what I intended to do, and that was enough. I abided by the terms and no one ever worried about me not signing it.'

He agrees the Beatles liked the idea of him managing them because they liked the look of him. 'I had money, a car, a record shop. I think that helped. But they also liked me.

'I liked them because of this quality they had, a sort of presence. They were incredibly likeable.'

His parents sensed something was happening. They came back from a week in London and found him waiting for them.

'Brian said he wanted us to listen to this record,' says his mother. 'It was "My Bonnie". He said take no notice of the singing, just the backing. He said they are going to be a big hit and I'm going to manage them.'

Before his father could interrupt, Brian added that of course it would just be a part-time interest, but he wouldn't mind if he took a little time off work?

His father wasn't too thrilled. He realized that Brian once again had found something new, but at least this time it was in Liverpool.

Brian decided to start a new company to manage the Beatles and he called it NEMS Enterprises, after the record stores. 'That was a fortunate decision. I might easily have run them simply under the same company as NEMS, without Enterprises. When we sold NEMS, the record shops, years later, that could have been very complicated.'

Clive, his brother, came in with him in setting up NEMS Enterprises. 'This was partly because I needed more money, but partly because I was scheming to get Clive interested in perhaps helping me.'

Their next and third Hamburg trip was as good as fixed long before Brian Epstein came along. Not long after they'd left Hamburg, Peter Eckhorn of the Top Ten and several other club managers came across to Liverpool, scouting for talent.

The Beatles had promised Peter Eckhorn they would come back to his club, but when he arrived in Liverpool, to discuss details with them and see any other likely groups, he found they now had Brian Epstein as manager.

'Brian wanted a lot more money than I was offering,' says Peter Eckhorn. 'I tried Gerry and the Pacemakers, but I couldn't get them either.'

In the end, Peter Eckhorn returned to Hamburg with a drummer, which was all he could get. This drummer, Ringo Starr, was to back Tony Sheridan.

Eventually, other Hamburg club owners came and offered better terms. Brian in the end accepted an offer from Manfred Weislieder, who was opening a brand new club in Hamburg, the Star Club. This was to be bigger and better than any of the others. His offer for the Beatles was 400 marks each a week, about £40. The Top Ten offer had been around 300 marks a week.

These were very good terms, but months before that was settled, Brian was already holding out for better terms wherever they played locally in Liverpool. He made a rule, the minute he took them over, that they would never play for less than £15 a night.

But Brian Epstein did his biggest and most immediate work in generally smartening up the Beatles – in their organization, in their appearance, and in their presentation.

Brian immediately had taken over all the bookings from Pete Best and put them on a properly organized basis. He also made sure that each of them knew exactly where and when they were playing.

'Brian put all our instructions down neatly on paper and it made it all seem real,' says John. 'We were in a daydream till he came along. We'd no idea what we were doing, or where we'd agreed to be. Seeing our marching orders on paper made it all official.'

Brian's instructions were all beautifully typed, usually on paper with his own crest on the top, a clever typographical sign made of his initials, BE. He also added little homilies about looking smart, wearing the right clothes and not smoking, eating or chewing during their performance.

'Brian was trying to clean our image up,' says John. 'He said our look wasn't right. We'd never get past the door at a good place. We just used to dress how we liked, on and off stage. He talked us into the suit scene.'

Brian also smartened up their presentation on stage which up till then had been all ad-libbed. 'He said we must work out a proper programme, playing our best numbers each time, not just the ones we felt like playing,' says Pete Best. 'It was no use just laughing and joking with the kids at the front when there might be 700 or 800 at the back who had no idea what was happening. He made us work out a strict programme, with no messing about.'

Things have changed enormously since then and swung completely the other way. Later John regretted slightly their smartening up, because he knew it wasn't really them, or anyway not really John. But he went along with it. He knew that at the time it was the only way, to join the suit set.

'It was natural we should put on our best show,' says John. 'We had to appear nice for people like the reporters, even the ones who were snooty, letting us know they were doing us a favour. But we would still play them along, agreeing with them, how kind they were to talk to us. We were very two-faced about it all.

'Trying to get publicity was just a game. We used to traipse round the offices of the local papers and the musical papers asking them to write about us, just because that was what you had to do.'

Although they privately laughed at all the people who didn't want to know them, carefully sent them up, or even openly sent them up, they were still very hurt by all the prejudice against them.

'All we ever got in those days,' says Paul, 'was, "Where are you from? Liverpool? You'll never do anything from there. Too far away. You'll have to be in London before you can do it. Nobody's ever done it from Liverpool." That's all we ever heard, for years.'

But Brian was going the right way about making them acceptable to the London sort of mind. 'But I didn't *change* them. I just projected what was there. What was there was this presence. On stage they had this undefinable feeling. But it was being spoiled by smoking and eating and talking to the front few rows.'

Brian had naturally been to see the Beatles' parents, when he decided to become their manager. They were impressed by his manners and obvious wealth, unlike all the previous friends their sons had had.

Only Mimi, John's aunt, seems to have been at all hesitant, though Brian should have impressed her most of all, except that she wasn't impressed by anything to do with beat groups.

'I had misgivings when I first heard of Brian Epstein. Not against him personally. But he was so well off. It seemed just a novelty to him and it didn't really matter whether they sank or swum. He wasn't depending on it, the way they were.

'I found Brian very charming. I always did. But this was the worry I had when he came along. I thought, that'll be it. He'll have finished with them in two months and gone on to something else. While John and the others won't ever have got started.'

MERSEY BEAT EXCLUSIVE STORY

BEATLES CHANGE DRUMMER !

Ringo Starr (former drummer with **Rory Storm and the Hurricanes**) has joined **The Beatles**, replacing **Pete Best** on drums. Ringo has admired The Beatles for years and is delighted with his new engagement. Naturally he is tremendously excited about the future.

The Beatles comment "Pete left the group by mutual agreement. There were no arguments or difficulties, and this has been an entirely amicable decision."

On Tuesday, September 4th. The Beatles will fly to London to make recordings at E.M.I. Studios. They will be recording numbers that have been specially written for the group, which they have received from their recording manager **George Martin** (Parlophone).

THE BEATLES TO PLAY CHESTER

As a result of the phenominal Box Office success of The Beatles during their 4-week season of Monday nights at the Plaza Ballroom, St. Helens, the directors of Whetstone Entertainments, controllers of the ballroom, have engaged The Beatles for a series of four Thursday night sessions at the Riverpark Ballroom, Chester, which commenced on 16th August.

PETE BEST
Photo by Arthur Miller

17

DECCA AND PETE BEST

Almost from the beginning, Brian Epstein started using his record contacts, exerting any pressures he could as the owner of the self-styled 'finest record store in the North'. And almost from the beginning it began to work. Decca said they were interested.

His contacts with Decca had always been the best, though of course they were solely on the retail side. But by getting his credentials passed from department to department, he managed to land a promise that an A and R man – artists and repertoire manager – would come up to Liverpool to see what all the boasting was about.

Mike Smith of Decca duly appeared towards the end of December 1961. Success at his first go. Brian was ecstatic. 'What an occasion it was! An A and R manager at the Cavern.'

Mike Smith was very impressed. He liked the sound of the Beatles and promised to arrange for them to come down to London and have an audition at Decca studios. This sort of audition, just to hear their sound and see how they would react to taping, doesn't mean all that much. But it did to Brian Epstein, to the Beatles and to Liverpool.

The audition was arranged for 1 January 1962. Brian went down to London by train for the appointment. The Beatles – John, Paul, George and Pete Best – were taken down by their road manager, Neil Aspinall, on New Year's Eve.

'I hired a bigger van specially. I'd never been anywhere near London before. It took ten hours and we got lost in the snow somewhere near Wolverhampton.

'We got to London about ten o'clock at night and found our hotel, the Royal, off Russel Square. Then we went for a drink. We tried to get a meal in some place in the Charing Cross Road. We all went in, a right gang of scruffs we were, and sat down. It said six bob for soup and we said, you're kidding. The bloke said we'd have to go. So we had to.

'We went to Trafalgar Square and saw all the New Year's Eve drunks falling in the fountain. Then we met two blokes in Shaftesbury Avenue who were stoned, though we didn't know it. They had some pot, but I'd never seen that either. We were too green.

Opposite: An early copy of *Mersey Beat*, 17 August, 1961, with the story that changed the history of the Beatles.

When they heard we had a van they asked if they could smoke it there. We said, no, no, no! We were dead scared.'

Brian was first at Decca Studios next morning, bang on time. 'The Decca people were late and I was pretty annoyed. Not because we were anxious to tape our songs, but because we felt we were being treated as people who didn't matter.'

At last they were told it was their turn. They got out their old, battered amplifiers and were immediately told to put them away. 'They didn't want our tackle,' says Neil. 'We had to use theirs. We needn't have dragged our amps all the way from Liverpool.'

They got going and George sang, in a very clipped voice, 'The Sheik of Araby'. Paul sang rather nervously, 'Red Sails in the Sunset' and 'Like Dreamers Do'. They didn't try any of their own compositions, although they had scores they could have done. Brian advised them to stick to standards.

'They were pretty frightened,' says Neil. 'Paul couldn't sing one song. He was too nervous and his voice started cracking up. They were all worried about the red light. I asked if it could be put off, but we were told people might come in if it was off. You what? we said. We didn't know what all that meant.'

They finished doing the tapes about two o'clock and everyone seemed very pleased.

'Mike Smith said the tapes were terrific,' says Pete Best. 'We thought we were in. Brian took us all out for dinner that night at some place in Swiss Cottage. He ordered wine, but it never turned up for some reason.'

The weeks passed and nothing happened. They continued playing their local dates on Merseyside, but all the time expecting Decca to whisk them off to the big time. Then in March, after a lot of pestering, Brian heard from Dick Rowe, Mike Smith's boss at Decca, that they had decided not to record the Beatles. 'He told me they didn't like the sound. Groups of guitars were on the way out. I told him I was completely confident that these boys were going to be bigger than Elvis Presley.'

It was suggested to him that as he had a good record business in Liverpool he should stick to it. It was also hinted that there were other ways of having a record made – for a payment of £100, for example, he could hire a studio and an A and R man. He contemplated this for a day or so. But he was still being treated in such an off-hand manner, so he thought, that he decided it was a complete waste of money.

'I think Decca expected us to be all polished,' says John. 'We were just doing a demo. They should have seen our potential.' After that began a long and dispiriting trail round all the other major recording companies. In turn, Pye, Columbia, HMV and EMI turned them down. Other smaller companies also said no.

'I was the last to hear about being turned down by Decca,' says Pete Best. 'John, Paul and George heard long before me. They just let it slip out one day, that they'd known for weeks. Why didn't you tell me? They said they didn't want to dishearten me.'

The others veered between being disheartened and an illogical optimism that something would turn up in the end.

'We did have a few little fights with Brian,' says John. 'We used to say he was doing nothing and we were doing all the work. We were just saying it, really. We knew how hard he was working. It was Us against Them.'

'We used to wait for Brian at Lime Street to hear his news,' says Paul. 'He'd ring us up and we'd think perhaps he'd have something for us. He'd come off the train with his briefcase full of papers and we'd go for a coffee in the Punch and Judy and hear how Pye or Philips or whoever it was had turned us down.'

'But we still used to send up the idea of getting to the top,' says George. 'When things were a real drag and nothing happening, we used to go through this routine: John would shout, "Where are we going fellas?" We'd shout back, "To the Top, Johnny!" Then he would shout, "What Top?" "To the Toppermost of the Poppermost, Johnny!"'

Alistair Taylor, Brian's assistant at NEMS, says that Brian was often near to tears with the trail round the record companies. 'He was bringing all the pressures he could, but there are always 10,000 groups, bringing all the pressures they can. He was getting nowhere.'

In December 1961, *Mersey Beat* announced a popularity poll. John and Paul still have copies of that issue lying around their homes, all with the entry forms cut out. They filled in dozens in assumed names, all putting the Beatles first and Gerry and the Pacemakers last. They were genuinely worried he would win. All the groups were voting for themselves, of course, so any cheating cancelled itself out. In the event, the Beatles were out and out winners.

Brian made the most of the award. For a performance on 24 March 1962, they were billed in big capitals as 'MERSEY BEAT POLL WINNERS! POLYDOR RECORDING ARTISTS! PRIOR TO EUROPEAN TOUR!' The actual concert was held at Barnston Women's Institute, which is rather small beer, after such a build-up.

The 'European Tour', which they were billed as being prior to, was, of course, their third visit to Hamburg. This took place just a week later in April 1962.

They arrived at Hamburg by plane. This was the very first time they'd travelled by plane. 'Brian made us do it,' says Pete Best. 'We were all dead chuffed.'

They were to play this time at the Star Club, the biggest Hamburg club of its type. 'It even had proper curtains on stage,' says George. Astrid, in mourning for Stu, didn't come to their concerts at first, but the Beatles went out of their way to go and get her, give her presents and cheer her up. She says that any slight feelings she might have had that they could be cruel disappeared for ever. 'I'd never realized they could be so kind.'

Meanwhile, back in Britain, Brian was working on a last attempt to get someone interested in the Beatles. He decided he would spend one further outlay of money.

He'd been taking tapes to all the record companies, some of them the ones they'd originally made at the Decca audition back in January. He decided it would be more impressive and much handier for carrying round and letting people hear if he had the tapes made into a record.

His father by this time was becoming more and more annoyed at all the time he was wasting on the Beatles. 'I told my father I wanted to take my tapes to London for an all-out, all-or-failure attack. He agreed, providing it was only for a day or two.'

Brian made for the HMV record-centre in Oxford Street. This is just a normal retail shop, though very large and part of the vast EMI empire. Brian talked to a contact there and asked him how he could get his tapes turned into a disc.

'The technician who recorded the tape told me it wasn't at all bad. He said he'd have a word with a music publisher upstairs, Syd Coleman. Coleman was very excited and said he'd like to publish them and that he would speak to a friend of his at Parlophone, George Martin.'

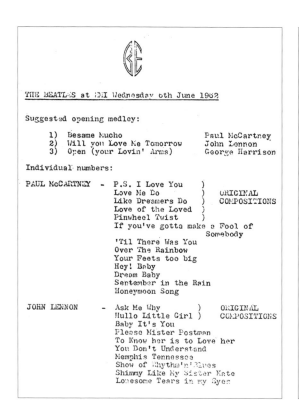

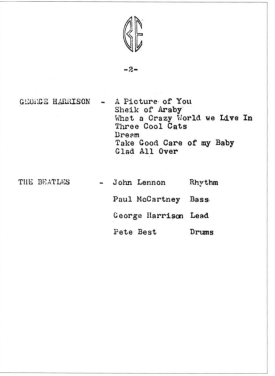

THE BEATLES at EMI Wednesday 6th June 1962

Suggested opening medley:

1) Besame Mucho — Paul McCartney
2) Will you Love Me Tomorrow — John Lennon
3) Open (your Lovin' Arms) — George Harrison

Individual numbers:

PAUL McCARTNEY — P.S. I Love You)
Love Me Do) ORIGINAL
Like Dreamers Do) COMPOSITIONS
Love of the Loved)
Pinwheel Twist)
If you've gotta make a Fool of
Somebody
'Til There Was You
Over The Rainbow
Your Feets too big
Hey! Baby
Dream Baby
September in the Rain
Honeymoon Song

JOHN LENNON — Ask Me Why) ORIGINAL
Hullo Little Girl) COMPOSITIONS
Baby It's You
Please Mister Postman
To Know her is to Love her
You Don't Understand
Memphis Tennessee
Show of Rhythm'n'Blues
Shimmy Like My Sister Kate
Lonesome Tears in my Eyes

-2-

GEORGE HARRISON — A Picture of You
Sheik of Araby
What a Crazy World we Live In
Three Cool Cats
Dream
Take Good Care of my Baby
Glad All Over

THE BEATLES — John Lennon — Rhythm
Paul McCartney — Bass
George Harrison — Lead
Pete Best — Drums

Brian Epstein's monogrammed, two-page note, sent to George Martin before the Beatles' first recording session with him for Parlophone on 6 June 1962, suggesting likely songs they might do. Note Pete Best on drums.

An appointment was made to meet George Martin next day at EMI. Parlophone are part of EMI, the parent company, which had already turned the Beatles down.

'George Martin listened to the record and said he liked Paul's voice and George's guitar playing. Those were the two things he particularly said. John was singing "Hello Little Girl" which he liked very much and Paul sang "Till There Was You".'

George Martin discussed it all with Brian very slowly and calmly and at last said it was very 'interesting'. Yes, and he thought they were interesting enough to give them an audition.

This was May 1962. The Beatles were still in Hamburg. Brian rushed out of EMI and sent them cables with the good news.

'We were all still in bed,' says Pete Best. 'Whoever was first up always went for the post. George was first up this day and got the telegram: 'Congratulations Boys. EMI request recording session. Please rehearse new material.'

'We felt terrific. John and Paul started composing straight away. Brian came out to see us and negotiated a new contract – £85 a week each I think we got then. He thought "Love Me Do" would be a good one for the recording session.'

Klaus says he was disappointed by Brian Epstein when he arrived in Hamburg. 'I didn't like the look of him. He was very shy, not at all powerful, the way I had expected. I was a bit depressed. I had this idea in my head of the manager they were bound to get. He would be the top man in the business, absolutely dynamic, not a shy novice.'

But the Beatles were very pleased with themselves. Klaus remembers their delight at the EMI news, how they went off to show their contracts to the Polydor people, who'd only made them the backing group, not the stars.

'I went to the seaside one day with Paul and George and George was discussing money. He said he felt he was going to make a lot of it. He was going to buy a house and a swimming pool, then he'd buy a bus for his father, as he was a bus driver.'

They came back from Hamburg at the beginning of June 1962. On 6 June, they did their audition before George Martin at the EMI studios in St John's Wood.

Brian, efficient as ever, had sent on in advance to George Martin a neatly typed out list, on his specially crested notepaper, of the suggested numbers they would like to play for Mr Martin, if of course Mr Martin agreed. The list included some original compositions – 'Love Me Do', 'P.S. I Love You', 'Ask Me Why', and 'Hello Little Girl'. But the main suggestions were standard songs like 'Besame Mucho'.

George Martin listened carefully to everything and said very nice. He liked them. It was nice to see the boys in person at last, having heard so much about them from Brian. Very nice. He'd let them know.

That was it. They weren't deflated, or anything as bad as that. But they'd expected a more definite reaction. They travelled back to Liverpool the next day and went into the usual circuit of one-night stands around Liverpool which Brian had fixed up while they'd been in Hamburg. Their first date was a Welcome Home night at the Cavern on the Saturday, 9 June, and then on the Monday a BBC radio show in Manchester which Brian had managed to fix. After that, they were fully booked up as far ahead as July with odd bookings until the end of September.

These bookings included the Cavern, plus the Casbah, New Brighton Tower, the Northwich Memorial Hall, Majestic Ballroom, Birkenhead, Plaza Ballroom, St Helens, Hulme Hall Golf Club, and the Automatic Telephone Company's Royal Iris River Cruise.

Brian as usual sent each of them typed memos with full details of all their dates. He included reminder notes, usually in capital letters, on how they should deport themselves:

Friday 29th June 1962
TOWER BALLROOM, NEW BRIGHTON
Neil will call for you between 6.45 and 7.00 p.m. in order to arrive at the Tower at 7.30 p.m. This is a Leach night for which he has given you excellent publicity as stars of the Bill. With this point in mind and the fact that he has been fairly co-operative over several matters recently, I would like you to give him one of your great performances. And as it's the night before Sam's wedding! It should be a big audience which will be mainly paying to see The Beatles. Programme, continuity, suits, white shirts, ties, etc., etc. One hour spot.

N.B. In the attached copy of 'Mersey Beat' the name 'THE BEATLES' on a rough count has been mentioned 15 times. On the 10 pages of 'Mersey Beat' 'THE BEATLES' appears on 6 pages. There has been a lot of publicity and there will be more and in this connection it will be of vital importance to live up to the publicity. Note that on ALL the above engagements during the performances, smoking, eating, chewing and drinking is STRICTLY PROHIBITED, prohibited.

Brian was trying all this time to get them dates farther afield than Merseyside, but with little luck. During that summer he did manage to get them a date in Peterborough, but it was a complete failure. Nobody knew them and nobody liked them. 'The audience sat on their hands,' says Arthur Howes, the promoter who put them on.

All this time they were waiting anxiously to hear from George Martin. He'd said he'd let them know when they could come down and do a proper recording.

Brian eventually heard from George Martin at the end of July. He wanted them to sign a contract with Parlophone records. He was now trying to think of what songs they might record. Brian, as well as John, Paul and George, were ecstatic.

They didn't tell Pete Best.

'We were playing on the Wednesday evening, 15 August, at the Cavern,' says Pete Best. 'We were due to go the next evening to Chester and I was supposed to be taking John. As we were leaving the Cavern, I asked John what time he wanted me to pick him up for Chester. He said, oh no, he would go on his own. I said, what's up? But he was off. His face looked scared. Then Brian rang, asking to see me and Neil at his office next morning.

'Neil drove me down the next day. Brian looked very shaky, not his usual happy self. He always showed his feelings and it was obvious there was something up. He was fidgeting all the time.

'He said "I've got some bad news for you. The boys want you out and Ringo in." It was a complete bombshell. I was stunned. I couldn't say anything for two minutes.

'I started asking him why and I couldn't get any definite reasons. He said George Martin wasn't too pleased with my playing. He said the boys thought I didn't fit in. But there didn't seem anything definite.

'At last I said if that's the way it is, then that's it. I went out and told Neil who was waiting outside. I must have looked white. I told him I'd been booted out after two years with them. I didn't know why. I said I couldn't get a direct answer.

'Brian came out and spoke to both of us. He asked me if I could stay on till the end of the week, playing on Thursday and Friday, till Ringo could come. I said yeh.

'I just walked around, had a few pints. I didn't tell anyone what had happened. I don't know how the news came out. I didn't tell anyone.'

The news did get out, almost immediately, and there was pandemonium in Liverpool. *Mersey Beat* announced it in their 23 August edition: 'Mersey Beat Exclusive. Beatles Change Drummer.' They didn't give any reasons. They said it was all amicable. But they finished the story by saying that the Beatles were flying to London on 4 September for a recording session at EMI.

Pete Best fans, although they were nowhere as numerous as Paul McCartney fans, were furious. Their idol had been chucked out just at the Beatles' moment of glory. They paraded through the streets, hung around NEMS with placards, picketed outside the Cavern and shouted slogans at all concerts.

John, Paul and George were attacked by Pete Best fans but Brian Epstein became their number one enemy.

'The sacking of Pete Best left me in an appalling position. This was the first real problem I'd had. Overnight I became the most disliked man on the beat scene. For two nights I didn't dare go near the Cavern because of the crowds shouting "Pete for Ever,

Ringo Never", or "Pete is Best". I couldn't stay away for long, so Ray McFall laid on a bodyguard for me.'

Pete Best fans tried to get at the Beatles to hit or scratch them, while John, Paul and George fans tried to keep them off. Ringo fans just kept out of it. In all the fights some girls got hurt, but only George of the Beatles was injured. He got a black eye.

There were scores of rumours round Liverpool. Mal Evans, then a bouncer at the Cavern, says he heard people saying it was because Pete wouldn't smile. Others said it was because he wouldn't change his hairstyle. There seems little doubt that Brian didn't want to do it.

Despite the Beatles topping the *Mersey Beat* poll in January 1962, and becoming a legend in the Cavern lunch hour, Paul was incorrectly named as Paul McArtrey...

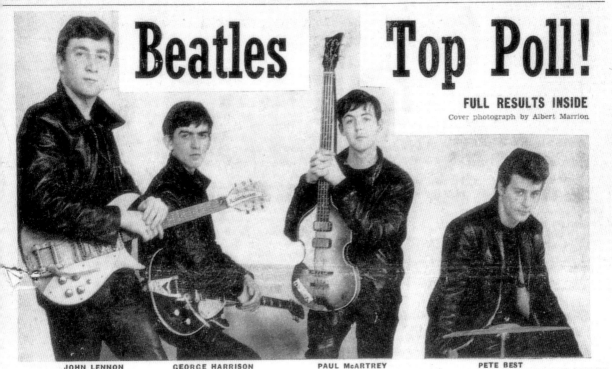

MERSEYSIDE'S OWN ENTERTAINMENTS PAPER

CRANES
The name for Records, Amplifiers Transistor Radios Also Pianos and Organs

HANOVER STREET, LIVERPOOL I
Telephone: ROYal 4714

MERSEY BEAT

N E M S
WHITECHAPEL AND GREAT CHARLOTTE STREET
THE FINEST RECORD SELECTIONS IN THE NORTH
Open until 6-0 p.m. each day
(Thursday and Saturday 6-30 p.m.)

Vol. 1 No. 13   JANUARY 4-18, 1962   Price THREEPENCE

Beatles   Top Poll!

FULL RESULTS INSIDE
Cover photograph by Albert Marrion

JOHN LENNON   GEORGE HARRISON   PAUL McARTREY   PETE BEST

'I knew how popular Pete was. He was incredibly good-looking with a big following. I had got on well with him. In fact, he'd been the first one I'd got to know. I thought the way through was through Pete because he was the easiest to get to know, the simplest.

'So I was very upset when the three of them came to me one night and said they didn't want him. They wanted Ringo. It had been on the cards for a long time, but I'd hoped it wouldn't happen.'

Because Brian was so loath to do it, he dragged in other excuses, like George Martin not liking his drumming, which was half true, but wasn't a main reason for the sacking.

'I did offer to keep Pete on in another group. I was a bit annoyed he didn't turn up at Chester in the evening, when he said he would. I expected him. I hadn't realized he couldn't face meeting the boys again.'

'How could I?' says Pete. 'What was the point, as they didn't want me any more? I just sat at home for two weeks. Not knowing what to do. Birds came to the door all the time. They were camping in the garden and shouting for me.'

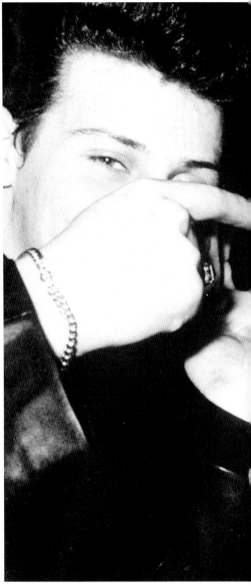

Neil thinks it was George who was most to blame. He thinks John really was fairly close to Pete, and Paul would never have done anything like that on his own. Neil says they all agreed to it, but it was George who gave Brian the final push, as George was the one who was the biggest admirer of Ringo. George's punch in the eye, says Neil, proves that theory.

Mrs Best has the simplest theory of all. 'Pete's beat had made them. They were jealous and they wanted him out. Pete hadn't realized what a following he had till he left. He was always so very shy and quiet, never shot his mouth off, like some people I could mention.

'He'd been their manager before Brian arrived, did the bookings and collected the money. I'd looked upon them as friends. I'd helped them so much, got them bookings, lending them money. I fed them when they were hungry. I was far more interested in them than their own parents.'

There is some justification for a little of Mrs Best's anger. The sacking of Pete Best is one of the few murky incidents in the Beatles' history. There was something sneaky about the way it was done. Admittedly, most people would have done the same and got the manager to do the dirty work. But all of them, especially John, had always been so honest and truthful with everyone.

It's also true what Mrs Best says about Pete having served them well for so long. But it's

Pete Best (left) with John, Paul and George, enjoying happier times during their third trip to Hamburg in April 1962. A few months later Brian broke the news to Pete that his fellow band members wanted him out and Ringo in.

not true, and far from it, that they were simply producing the Pete Best sound, although Pete's drumming played a part in their success.

'When we came back from Germany,' says Pete, 'I was playing using my bass drum very loud and laying down a very solid beat. This was unheard of at the time in Liverpool as all the groups were playing the Shadows style. Even Ringo in Rory Storm's group copied our beat and it wasn't long before most drummers in Liverpool were playing the same style. This way of drumming had a great deal to do with the big sound we were producing.'

The others say that the main reason for keeping Pete so long was not his sound but that their permanent problem for so long had been a drummer. They wanted any good drummer, because the lack of one had hindered their progress. When a reasonable one came along, they stuck to him. Not necessarily because he was great, but because they knew what it was like not having one.

'But if I wasn't that great, why was I kept on for two and a half years? When we first returned to Liverpool, why didn't they get another drummer then? There was plenty of them. Why wasn't Ringo asked then, instead of two years later on the eve of success?'

What makes or doesn't make a good drummer is hard to define, but as a personality there is some evidence to suggest that Pete had not fitted in, as Astrid and Klaus had noticed in Hamburg, although Pete himself seems to have been unaware of it. Stu, unlike Pete, had realized from the beginning when he was being got at. Pete presumed he was a proper part of the group, after so long, and was naturally very surprised when the end came.

But for the sake of Pete's career, whatever happened to the Beatles afterwards, the handling, and especially the announcing, of the sacking might have been done more neatly and cleanly. He could have been fixed up with a job in another group before the news was announced.

It's easy of course to say all this now. Nobody knew how well the Beatles were going to do and what Pete was going to miss. The Beatles themselves did feel a bit guilty, but they say that it was a joint decision, not George's. They'd never felt that Pete was one of them and it was only a matter of time.

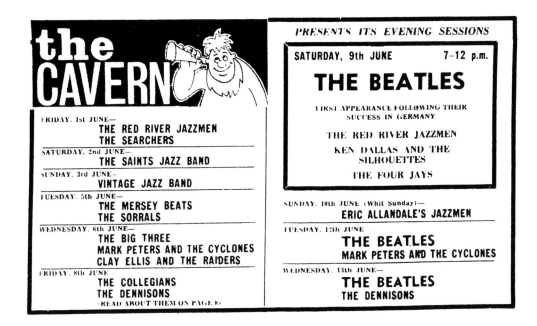

'We were cowards when we sacked him,' says John. 'We made Brian do it. But if we'd told Pete to his face, that would have been much nastier than getting Brian to do it. It would probably have ended in a fight if we'd told him.'

Pete left and lost his chance of show-business fame. But the affair had one happy outcome for the Beatles. Ringo Starr.

18

RINGO

Richard Starkey, or Ringo, is the oldest of the Beatles. He would have been called Parkin today if his grandfather hadn't decided to change his name. When this grandfather's mother remarried and changed her name, from Parkin to Starkey, Ringo's grandfather also changed his name to Starkey. This caused great confusion when at one time Ringo tried to trace his family back. The name Starkey is originally supposed to have come from the Shetland Isles.

Ringo's mother, Elsie Gleave, married his father, Richard Starkey, in 1936. They met when they were both working at the same Liverpool bakery. She is short, stocky and blonde and looks today very much like Mrs Harrison.

When they got married they moved in with the Starkeys, Ringo's father's parents, in the Dingle. After Scotland Road, the Dingle is known as the roughest area of Liverpool. It's in the centre, not far from the docks, far less salubrious than the slightly more airy new suburbs, where John, Paul and George were all brought up.

'There's a lot of tenements in the Dingle,' says Ringo. 'A lot of people in little boxes all trying to get out. You'd say you were from the Dingle and other people in Liverpool would say to you, oh aye, he's bound to be a hard case, which of course wasn't true with most people.'

Elsie and Richard Starkey got themselves a little house of their own just before Ringo was born. This was not in a tenement, but in Madryn Street, a dismal row of low two-storeyed terrace houses. Their house was bigger than most, three up and three down, as opposed to the usual two rooms up and two rooms down. Their rent in 1940 was 14s. 10d. a week.

'We've always been just ordinary, poor working-class on both sides of the family,' says Ringo, 'though there's a rumour in the family that me great-grandmother was fairly well off. She had chromium railings round her house. Well, they were very shiny anyway.

Opposite: Ringo, wearing the rings that gave him his name, backstage at East Ham in 1963.

Perhaps I just made that up. You know what it's like, you dream things, or your mother tells you things so you come to believe you actually saw them.

But me mother's mother really was very poor. She had 14 kids.'

Ringo was born just after midnight on the morning of 7 July 1940, at Number 9 Madryn Street. He was a week late. He was delivered by forceps and weighed ten pounds. He arrived with his eyes open and looking all round the place. His mother told all the neighbours that she was sure he must have been here before.

His mother Elsie was then 26 and his father Richard 28. They christened their first, and only baby, Richard. It is a working-class tradition to always call the first son after the father. They also called him by the pet name of Ritchie, just as his father was called and as they are both called by their families today.

Mrs Starkey, Ringo's mother, remembers lying in bed, still recovering from the birth, when she heard the first sirens of the war. The bombing of Liverpool had begun.

They hadn't yet got round to installing shelters in the Dingle. The first really serious bombing raids occurred a few weeks later. The Starkeys, along with two neighbours who'd been in chatting in the house, all rushed to take shelter in the coal-hole under the stairs. Ritchie started screaming. His mother discovered that in

Ringo, aged eight, with his mother Elsie.

the rush and crush she had put him over her shoulder upside down. She put him the right way up and he slept right through the raid. This was another story which she soon told the neighbours, and still does.

When Ritchie was just over three years old, his parents parted. Except on three occasions later, Ritchie has not seen his father since.

There was none of the drama or hysteria of John's parents when they parted. It appears to have been settled quietly. Elsie took the baby and they were eventually divorced.

Ringo and his mother stayed on alone in Madryn Street for some time, but the rent soon became too expensive and they moved round the corner to Number 10 Admiral Grove. This house has only four rooms, two up and two down. The rent in 1940 was 10s. a week.

Ringo's earliest memory dates from this removal. He thinks he must have been about five at the time. 'I can remember sitting on the back flap of the removal van taking our things round to Admiral Grove.'

He has no memory of his parents' parting. He can only remember meeting his father twice as a very young child, and once later as an early teenager.

'He came once to see me in hospital with a little notebook and asked me what I wanted.

'Then I saw him once later at me Grandma Starkey's. He offered me money, but I wouldn't speak to him. I suppose me mother filled me up with all the things about him. But I suppose if it had been the other way round, if I'd gone with me Dad, I'd have thought the opposite.'

It seems likely that Ringo saw more of his father as a child, after they'd parted, than he remembers, as he spent a lot of time at his Grandma Starkey's. It was some time before his father, still working in a bakehouse, moved away from Liverpool, and remarried.

His mother doesn't remember Ringo being upset in any way by the parting or even later asking any questions about what had happened.

'Sometimes he used to wish there was more than just the two of us. When it was raining he used to look out of the window and say, "I wish I had brothers and sisters. There's nobody to talk to when it's raining."'

Ritchie went to Sunday School at four and primary school at five. This was St Silas's Primary School, just 300 yards' walk from his home. It's a faded red Victorian building, one of the National Schools, erected in 1870.

Elsie got a maintenance allowance from his father of 30 bob a week, but this wasn't enough to live on, so she had to go out to work. She'd done lots of different jobs before her marriage, including working as a barmaid, so she went back to that. She'd always enjoyed it, being jolly and sociable and fond of company, and the hours suited her.

She went back to work again as a barmaid before Ringo started school, doing mornings and lunch times for 18s. a week, leaving Ringo with Grandma Starkey, or with neighbours.

'I never thought of putting Ritchie away in a home. He was my child. With the bar job, I was just able to manage. There was a lot of work to be done in bars, with the war on.'

At six years of age, after hardly a year at school, Ritchie developed appendicitis. The appendix burst and became peritonitis. He was taken to Myrtle Street Children's Hospital and had two operations.

'I remember being taken bad and going out of the house on a stretcher to the ambulance. In hospital this nurse started smashing me stomach. That's how it felt anyway. She probably just touched it.

'I was wheeled in for the operation and I asked for a cup of tea. They said not before the operation, but I'd get one when I came round. I went into a coma and didn't come round for ten weeks.'

He was in hospital in all for just over twelve months. He was on the way to recovering at one stage, but fell out of his cot while showing a present to the boy in the next cot during a birthday party.

Parents were not allowed to visit their children. It was thought it might disturb them too much. But Ritchie was so seriously ill at one time that they let his mother peep at him in his cot, late at night, when she'd finished working in the bar.

He came out when he was seven and went back to St Silas's. He was never very quick at lessons, but with the year in hospital he was completely behind and unable to read or write. Without Marie Maguire he thinks he might never ever have learned. Her mother and Ritchie's mother were lifelong friends. They went out together and left Marie in charge of Ritchie.

'I was very bossy with him,' she says, 'being four years older. He was so much part of our family that people used to come and knock at our door and say "Your Ritchie's doing so and so." When he had meals with us and we were having scouse, I always had to pick the onions out for him. He hates onions. I was always cursing him.

'My very first memory of him was when he must have been about three. There was a terrible thunderstorm and I looked across to his house and I saw him and his mother both huddling in the hall.

'I started teaching him to read and write when he came out of hospital. He wasn't stupid. He'd just missed a lot. We had it properly organized. Twice a week I used to give him lessons, and his mother would give me pocket money for doing it. I bought Chambers's *Primary Readers* and we used to sit up at his kitchen table and read them.

'I would look after him on Saturday nights at our house while our mothers were out. They would leave us bottles of lemonade and sweets. He once took his shirt off and I painted all his back with paints. Sounds very primitive, now I think about it. He once brought his girlfriend to see me. He insisted she was called Jellatine.

'I always liked him. He was just so happy and easy-going, just like his mother. He had lovely big blue eyes. I never ever noticed he had a big nose. It wasn't till the press pointed it out years later that I realized he had.'

Marie was his closest friend for many years, but he also spent a lot of time at his two grandmothers, when his mother was out working.

'My Grandmother Gleave, my mother's mother, lived on her own, but she had this friend called Mr Lester who used to come and play the mouth organ to her. They were both about 60. "Oh aye," we used to say. "We know what you're up to, playing the mouth organ to her in the dark." But she wouldn't marry him. In the end Mr Lester went off and married someone else.

'I used to love going to my Grandad Starkey's when he'd lost a lot of money on the horses. He'd go off his head. They were a great couple. They used to have real fights. He was a boilerman at the docks, a real tough docker, but he used to make me lovely things. He once made me a big train with real fire inside. It caused a riot going down our street. I used to boil apples inside it.'

Ringo has few memories of St Silas's Primary School, except playing truant or holding up kids in the playground and taking pennies off them. 'We used to steal bits and pieces from Woolworths. Just silly plastic things you could slip in your pocket.' Another time his Aunt Nancy found a pearl necklace missing. Ritchie turned up outside a pub in Park Street, offering it for sale for 6s.

At eleven years of age Ringo went to Dingle Vale Secondary Modern School. He didn't sit the Eleven Plus. He failed the Review, which was an exam to see if you were good enough to sit the Eleven Plus.

Opposite: Ringo (right), aged 16, in an early job as a barman on a ferry boat.

'He liked it in spasms,' says his mother. 'Then he'd play truant. He and some others would hang around outside before school till the final bell went and they just wouldn't go in. They'd maintain they'd been locked out. They would go and spend the afternoon playing in Sefton Park.'

When Ritchie was just over eleven years old, his mother started going out with a Liverpool Corporation painter and decorator called Harry Graves. He was a Londoner, from the Romford area. He'd been ill and his doctor had suggested a change of air. For some inexplicable reason, he decided to try the Liverpool air. He still can't remember why. He met Elsie through mutual friends, the Maguires. He got on well with Ritchie from the beginning. They went together to the pictures two or three times a week.

'I told Ritchie that Harry wanted to marry me. If he'd said no, I wouldn't have done. But he said, "You get married, Mam. I won't always be little. You don't want to end up like me grandma."' She was the one who hadn't married Mr Lester and his mouth organ.

Harry Graves and Elsie Starkey were married on 17 April 1953, when Ritchie was coming up for 13. She stopped work soon after. Harry says that he and Ritchie had never had a wrong word between them. Elsie says he was awful. When she used to tell her husband that Ritchie had been giving her cheek he just used to smile and do nothing.

At 13, Ritchie suffered his second major illness. He got a cold, which turned to pleurisy, which in turn affected his lung. He went to Myrtle Street again and then the Heswall Children's Hospital.

Just to cheer him up and give him an interest, Harry put him in the Arsenal Supporters Club. Again, he can't quite remember why. Harry himself didn't think much of Arsenal. He was, and still is, a fanatical supporter of West Ham. 'But Arsenal had a sort of glamour in them days. I thought the boy would like it.'

While Ritchie was in hospital, Tom Whittaker, then manager of Arsenal, happened to be in Liverpool. Harry wrote to him, saying what a nice gesture it would be if he could visit one of his keenest young supporters who was lying ill in hospital. Mr Whittaker couldn't make it, but he did write back a nice letter, which Ritchie treasured very much, so Harry says. Ritchie himself can't remember anything at all about any letter, or ever being in the Arsenal Supporters Club.

But Ritchie had good memories of Harry himself, right from the beginning. 'He used to bring me lots of Yankee comics. He was great. I did used to take his side if he and me Mum had any rows. I thought she was being bossy and felt sorry for Harry. I learned gentleness from Harry. There's never any need for violence.'

Ritchie was in hospital almost two years this time, from the age of 13 to 15. 'I was given lots of things to keep my mind occupied, like knitting. I made a big island out of papier-mâché and a farm full of animals. I had a fight in the hospital with another lad. He went berserk and brought a huge tray down on me, just missed smashing me fingers.'

He came out of hospital at 15 which meant that he'd officially finished his school days, though he'd hardly been at school. He had to go back to Dingle Vale Secondary Modern for a report, so that he could use it as a reference for a job. He says that nobody could remember him, he'd been away so long.

He had to stay at home, recuperating, till he was well enough to start thinking about taking jobs. His mother was very worried about what sort of job he could get. She knew he wasn't strong enough to lift anything heavy and he hadn't had the education to do anything too clever.

Through the Youth Employment Officer, he eventually secured a job as messenger boy for British Railways at 50 bob a week.

'I went for me uniform, but all they gave me was the hat. I thought, what a lousy job. You have to be there 20 years before you get the full uniform. I left after six weeks. It wasn't just not getting the uniform. You have to pass a medical exam and I failed.

'Then I spent six weeks on board a boat, going back and forward to North Wales as a barman. I went to an all-night party and got drunk and went straight on to work. I gave cheek to the boss and he said, get your cards, son.'

After that he got a job at H. Hunt and Son through friends of Harry. 'I went to be a joiner. But all I did for two months was go out on me bike taking orders. I'd by this time turned 17 and was getting fed up with not starting my apprenticeship. So I went to see them and they said there were no vacancies as a joiner, would I like to be a fitter, so I said OK. It was a trade. Everyone always said, if you've got a trade, you'll be OK.'

Nobody else thought he was necessarily going to be OK. He was small, weak-looking and undernourished with very, very little schooling.

'He'd had a difficult childhood,' says Marie Maguire, the girl who'd taught him to read. 'With a broken home and two long illnesses. I just hoped he'd be happy. Not successful or anything. Just happy.'

The two long illnesses must have had a big effect on him, making it very difficult to adjust to school and to work and to ordinary life. Today he can't remember any of his schoolmasters' names, but he does remember two of the nurses who looked after him – Sister Clark and Nurse Edgington.

But he himself never remembers being unhappy. He thinks he had a good childhood.

It was ironic that when he went back to Dingle Vale Secondary Modern that time for a reference, no one could remember him. Just a few years later, on an open day, they brought out a desk which Ringo Starr was supposed to have used. They charged people sixpence a time to sit in it and have their photographs taken.

19

RINGO WITH THE BEATLES

Ringo showed no musical interest and learned no instrument as a boy. 'We did have a ward band in the hospital. There were four kids on cymbals and two on triangles. I would never play unless I had a drum.'

It was when he started to work, as an apprentice fitter, that the skiffle craze arrived. He helped to form a group called the Eddie Clayton Skiffle, which played to the rest of the apprentices in the dinner hour.

His first drums were a second-hand set bought by his stepfather when he was down home in Romford. They cost £10. 'I brought them up from London in the guard's van,' says Harry. 'I was waiting for a taxi home at Lime Street when I saw Joe Loss walking over. I thought, if he asks me if I can play them, I'll have to say no. But he walked right past me.'

His first new set of drums cost £100. He went to his grandad for the £50 deposit.

'If his grandad even refused him a shilling, he'd do a war dance,' says his mother. 'This time his grandad came to see me. "Hey, do you know what that bloody noddler of yours wants?" He always called him the Noddler. But he gave him the money. Ritchie paid it back faithfully, a pound a week out of wages."

His mother was a bit worried about the group taking up too much of his time, as he was supposed to be going to classes at Riverdale Technical College, catching up on some of the schooling he'd missed.

But Harry, his stepfather, was quite interested in the skiffle group. It gave the boy an interest. One night Harry met a bloke in a bar who said he was in a band. The man agreed to give Ritchie a go and Harry made a date for him. Ritchie went along and came back furious. It turned out to be a Prize Silver Band. They wanted to give him a huge drum, strap it on his front, then make him march along the street going bang, bang, in time to a military march.

Opposite: Ringo with the Beatles in 1963, shortly after he was invited to join the band as their new drummer. John told him on the phone that he would have to brush his hair down, but that he could keep his sidies.

Not that he was doing much better in the Eddie Clayton group. Not that there was an Eddie Clayton, come to that. Eddie Miles, who was really the leader of the group, had changed his name – for professional purposes – to Eddie Clayton, the minute the group had begun. Just as Paul, George and John had changed their names when they went to Scotland.

But eventually, after going through the same sort of skiffle competitions and parties and little dance halls that the Beatles had, Ritchie joined Rory Storm's group. When they were offered a season at Butlins, Ringo had to make the decision whether to leave work. He was then 20, with just one more year of his apprenticeship to go. 'Everybody said I shouldn't leave, and I suppose they were right. But I just felt I wanted to. I was getting by then £6 a week at Hunts', and about £8 by playing at nights. Butlins was offering me £20 a week in all, £16 when they took off the money for the chalet.'

Rory's was by then Liverpool's leading group, but the offer of 13 weeks at Butlins was their biggest break. 'We were going to make our names, so we thought we'd better have good ones. Rory Storm had already changed his name twice. He's really Alan Caldwell, then he became Jet Storme then Rory Storm.'

It was at Butlins that Richard Starkey finally became Ringo. Up until then he'd been occasionally called Rings. He'd got his first ring on his 16th birthday from his mother. When his Grandfather Starkey died, he got another, a broad gold ring, which he still wears. By the age of 20 he was wearing up to four rings. His surname was abbreviated to Starr at Butlins so they could announce his solo drumming spot as Star Time. Rings naturally became Ringo, as it sounded better with a one-syllable surname.

Back in Liverpool, Ringo had his 21st birthday party at his home in Admiral Grove. All the leading groups were there, including Gerry and the Pacemakers, the Big Three and Cilla Black. The Beatles didn't come. Ringo didn't know them. They were from another part of Liverpool and just another struggling group.

The living room at Admiral Grove is tiny, just ten feet by twelve feet, but somehow they got 60 people in for the party. They know the number because Ringo lined them up afterwards for a picture on the brick rubble heap opposite the house.

Elsie, Ringo's mum, had known Cilla Black for a long time, as a local lass called Cilla White. For almost a year she'd been coming to Mrs Starkey's, with a friend, every Wednesday after work. Cilla had her tea and then did Elsie's hair for her.

The success of their 13-week season at Butlins led to other engagements. They did a tour of United States air bases in France, but Ringo says this was terrible. 'The French don't like the British, at least I didn't like them.'

Rory's group was doing so well that when the first offer came to go to Hamburg they turned it down. But they went later, joining the Beatles at the Kaiserkeller, which was where they met for the first time. Ringo has a slight memory of catching sight of them once before that in Liverpool. He looked into the Jackaranda Club one day and saw them teaching Stu how to play the bass.

In Hamburg Ringo used to sit around with them between sessions and request numbers when they were playing. He came back to Liverpool with Rory, then returned to Hamburg on his own, accompanying Tony Sheridan. During this spell in Hamburg, he seriously considered staying on for good. He was offered his own flat, a car and £30 a week to stay

Before he joined the Beatles, Ringo (right, with beard) was the drummer with Rory Storm and the Hurricanes at Butlins holiday camp. Rory's group also played at the Kaiserkeller in Hamburg, where Ringo first met John, Paul and George.

for a year. But he decided to come back to Liverpool and Rory Storm again for another season at Butlins. This was when he was asked to join the Beatles. John told him on the phone that he would have to brush his hair down, but he could keep his sidies.

Ringo had to put up with a lot of shouts and threatening letters from Pete Best fans. 'The birds loved Pete. Me, I was just a skinny, bearded scruff. Brian didn't really want me either. He thought I didn't have the personality. And why get a bad-looking cat when you can get a good-looking one.'

It was the money which made Ringo decide. 'I got another offer at the same time, from King Size Taylor and the Dominoes. He offered £20 a week. The Beatles offered £25, so I took them.'

As with all of them, and as with everyone in life, their paths might not have crossed. Much earlier, Ringo was on the point of emigrating to the United States. He and a friend were looking through some records one day and read that 'Lightning Hopkins comes from Houston, Texas'. They went to see the US consul in Liverpool and said they wanted to go to Houston, Texas. He said they had to have a job first. Ringo picked one in a factory. 'Then the really big forms arrived, all about was your grandfather's Great Dane a Commy. I couldn't understand them. If I had done, I would definitely have gone.'

With Ringo fitting in, as a personality and as a drummer, the Beatles were now the indisputable top group in Liverpool. They had a gentleman-manager and had at last made contact with London. But their success, however local, was beginning to split up some of the old loyalties that Ringo, particularly, had been very fond of.

'There were so many groups in Liverpool at one time that we often used to play just for each other. It was a community on its own, made up of groups. All going to the same places, playing for each other. It was all nice. Then when the record companies came up and started signing groups, it wasn't so friendly. Some made it and others didn't.

'You'd meet someone you'd known and he'd say "Fine, man, just crazy. Just did a recording, but they're not releasing it. They said I'm too much like Ray Charles."

'It broke all the community up. People started hating each other. I stopped going to the old places. But it was one of the great times of my life, those early days in Liverpool. Like at my 21st birthday party, they were all there.'

The Beatles, complete with Ringo, were waiting now to hear a definite date from George Martin for their recording debut. In the meantime, other things in Liverpool fell into place. Brian at last decided that running two record stores and a beat group was too much, which is what his father had been saying for a long time. He decided to give up day-to-day work at the Whitechapel record store and moved Peter Brown across from Charlotte Street as manager. He concentrated on NEMS Enterprises, popping down from his upstairs office now and again to see how Peter was getting on. This led to rows, as Brian couldn't bear to see his lovely arrangements being changed. Peter was fired, after a furious row, but was reinstated.

But Brian never had rows with any of the Beatles. The nearest was an incident with Paul. They all came round to pick him up one night, but Paul was in the bath and refused to come out. 'I shouted to them to wait, I'd just be a few minutes. But when I got out, they'd all driven off with Brian. So I said, fuck them, temperamental fool that I was. If they can't be arsed waiting for me, I can't be arsed going after them. So I sat down and watched telly.'

The real reason was that Paul had got it into his head that he should revolt. 'I'd always been the keeny, the one who was always eager, chatting up managements and making announcements. Perhaps I was being bigheaded at first, or perhaps I was better at doing it than the others. Anyway, it always seemed to be me.'

It led to an argument between Paul and Brian, but nothing serious. Paul was soon back to being the keeny. 'I realized that I was being more false by *not* making the effort.'

He and John were as keen as ever on writing songs, turning out 'another Lennon-McCartney original' all the time. But Mimi still thought it wasn't serious. 'I always expected John to come home one day and say he wasn't doing the group any more. "It bores me to death."

'I was the last to realize they were doing well. Little girls started to come to the door and ask if John was in. I'd say, why? They'd say they just wanted to see John. I couldn't understand it. They were such little girls. I knew his only serious girlfriend had been Cyn.'

In the summer of 1962, Cyn found that she was pregnant. 'I didn't know if John would want to get married. I didn't want to tie him down.'

'I was a bit shocked when she told me,' says John. 'But I said yes. We'll have to get married. I didn't fight it.'

They were married on 23 August 1962, at Mount Pleasant Register Office in Liverpool. 'I went in the day before to tell Mimi. I said Cyn was having a baby, we were getting married tomorrow, did she want to come? She just let out a groan.'

No parents were at the wedding. From all accounts, it was conducted in the same spirit as his own parents' wedding, held in the same register office 24 years previously. John, Paul and George all wore black. 'There was a drill going on all the time outside,' says John. I couldn't hear a word the bloke was saying. Then we went across the road and had a chicken dinner. I can't remember any presents. We never went in for them. It was all a laugh.'

They tried to keep the marriage secret from Beatle fans, but one of the tea ladies from the Cavern saw them coming out of the register office and the news leaked out, though they denied it. 'I thought it would be goodbye to the group, getting married, because everybody said it would be. None of us ever took any girls to the Cavern, as we thought we would lose fans, which turned out to be a farce in the end. But I did feel embarrassed being married. Walking about, married. It was like walking about with odd socks on or your flies open."

Cynthia was all for keeping their marriage quiet. 'It was bad enough John being recognized and chased everywhere. I didn't want that to happen to me.'

The girl fans had grown to enormous proportions by this time, fanatically following them everywhere and screaming at the slightest excuse. Yet no one outside Liverpool had heard of the Beatles. They were still waiting for George Martin, the great A and R man in London, to tell them when he was going to record them.

Even in Liverpool, it had all happened with no publicity and promotion. The fans had discovered the Beatles by themselves.

Maureen Cox was one of these fans. She and a friend ran after Ringo in the street one day, just after he'd joined the Beatles. He was getting out of his car. His little grey streak at the front of his hair gave him away. She got his autograph and wrote down his car number

---

LEACH ENTERTAINMENTS (LIVERPOOL)

Present

"The Beatles Show"

RIALTO BALLROOM · LIVERPOOL
THURSDAY, 6th SEPTEMBER, 1962
7.30 p.m. — Midnight
STARRING THE NORTH'S TOP "ROCK" COMBO

"The Beatles"

and the first Merseyside appearance
following his season at Butlins, Skegness

"Rory Storm" and the "Hurricanes"

Supported by The Big 3 — The Merseybeats

Licensed Bar applied for   Buffet

TICKETS 5/- EACH

on her exercise book. She was on her way to night class as a hairdresser at the time, having just left school. 'I can remember his car number to this day – NWM 466.'

Today, Maureen Cox is Ringo's wife. But it was Paul she first kissed, slightly to her embarrassment now.

She was in the Cavern one evening with a friend, and the friend bet her that she wouldn't go and kiss Paul. 'I said to her that it was *she* who was scared to do it. She said I was scared. So just for a bet, I fought my way to the band room and kissed Paul when he came out. My friend was so annoyed and jealous that she started crying. But it was really Ritchie I liked best. I'd just kissed Paul for a dare. So I waited till Ritchie came out and kissed him as well.'

Ringo has no memory of being kissed by Maureen, nor of giving her his autograph. 'That was the scene at the time, getting kissed. It had progressed from getting a Beatle's autograph to touching one, then kissing one. You'd be trying to get to the band room and you'd suddenly have some girl's arms flung round you. I probably thought Maureen was some fly pecking me.'

But three weeks later, at the Cavern, he asked Maureen to dance. He took her home afterwards, but he had to take her friend home as well. This went on for several weeks. Maureen says she didn't like to tell her friend she was in the way. 'I felt a bit scared.'

From then on, Maureen hardly missed a Cavern session, but she soon realized there were fans far more fanatical than even she could be. 'They used to hang round the Cavern all day long, just on the off chance of seeing them. They'd come out of the lunch-time session and just stand outside all afternoon, queuing up for the evening. Ritchie and the boys once went past at midnight and there were fans already queuing up for the next day. They bought them some pies. They were knocked out.

'The object was to get as near the front row as possible, so that they could see the Beatles, and be

---

THE

CAVERN

10 MATHEW ST., LIVERPOOL

✱ ✱ ✱

PRESENTS ITS
LUNCHTIME SESSIONS

FRIDAY, 24th AUG.—
The Beatles.

MONDAY, 27th AUG,—
Mike Berry.

TUESDAY, 28th AUG.—
Gerry and the Pacemakers.

WEDNESDAY, 29th AUG.—
Nero and the Gladiators.

THURSDAY, 30th AUG.—
The Beatles.

FRIDAY, 31st AUG.—
The Big Three.

MONDAY, 3rd SEPT.—
The Beatles.

TUESDAY, 4th SEPT.—
Gerry and the Pacemakers.

WEDNESDAY, 6th SEPT.—
The Big Three.

★ ★ ★

EVENING SESSIONS

FRIDAY, 24th AUG.—
Billy Kramer with the Coasters. Lee Curtis with the All Stars; The Big Three.

SATURDAY, 25th AUG.—
The Red River Jazzmen; The Searchers; The Dakotas

SUNDAY, 26th AUG.—
The Bluegenes; The Red River Jazzmen; The Beatles.

TUESDAY, 28th AUG.—
The Beatles; The Bluegenes; Gerry Levene and the Avengers (Birmingham's No. 1 group).

seen by them. I never joined the queue till about two or three hours before the Cavern opened. It frightened me. There would be fights and rows amongst the girls.

'When the doors opened the first ones would tear in, knocking each other over.

'They'd keep their rollers in and jeans on for the first groups. Then when it got near the time for the Beatles to come on, if there was a gang of four say, they would go off in turns to the ladies with their little cases to get changed and made-up. When the Beatles came on they'd all look smashing, as if they'd just arrived.

'I suppose it was partly sex and partly the music. That was the attraction. They were obviously dying to be noticed and get to know one of them. But no, it was really just everything about being there. It was terrible, the mad screams when they came on. They went potty.'

When Maureen did go out with Ringo, she had to keep completely in the background.

'I might have been killed otherwise. The other girls were not friendly at all. They wanted to stab me in the back. It was part of their image, that they weren't married and so each girl thought she might have a chance. None of them were supposed to have steadies.

'A few eventually found out of course. They used to come into the hairdresser's where I was working. I couldn't do anything about that. I would have to do their hair. Then they would threaten me – "If you see that Ringo Starr again you're for it." When I went outside they'd push me. I used to get threatening phone calls – my brother's going to get you, they used to say.

'They were playing at the Locarno once. Just before they'd finished, Ritchie told me to go outside and sit in the car and wait for him, so no one would see me. I was sitting in the car when this girl came up. She must have followed me.

'She said, "Are you going out with Ringo?" I said no, oh no, not me. He's just a friend of my brother's. "Liar," she said, "I just saw you talking to him." I'd forgotten to wind the window up. Before I could do anything, she had her hand through the window and scratched me down my face. She started screaming and shouting some very select language at me. I thought this is it. I'm going to get stabbed. But I just got the window up in time. If I hadn't, she would have opened the door and killed me.'

PART TWO

LONDON AND THE WORLD

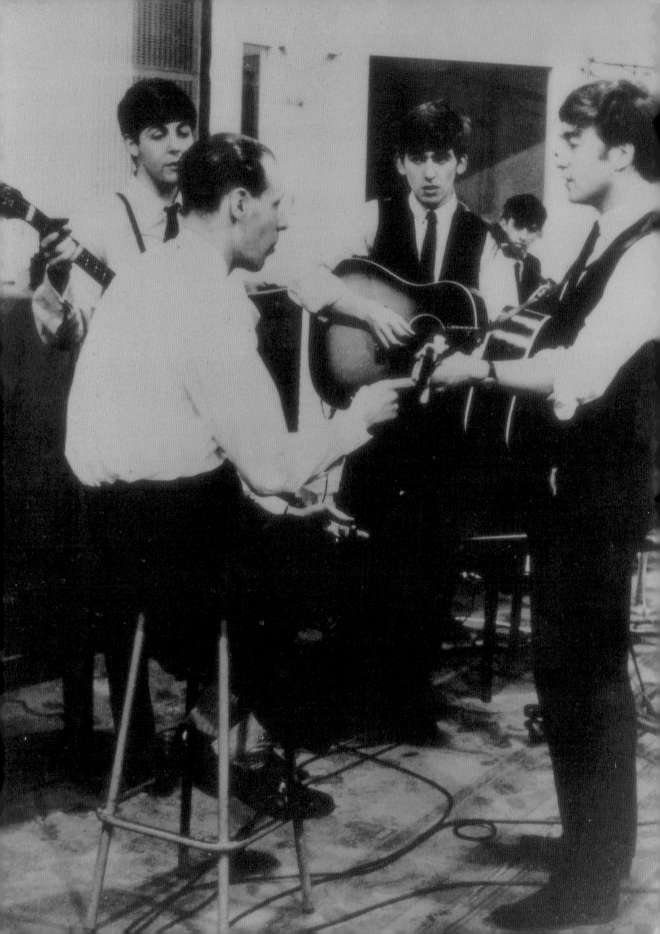

20

GEORGE MARTIN AND DICK JAMES

George Martin always seems light years away from the Beatles in class, tastes and background. He is tall and handsome, in a matinée idol sort of way, with a studied prep schoolmaster manner and a clipped BBC accent. But his early background, at least, was as humble and working-class as the Beatles'.

He was born in 1926, in Holloway, north London, the son of a carpenter. He went first to a Jesuit College in Stamford Hill, then the family moved to Kent and he went to Bromley County School. There was no musical tradition in the family and he had no musical training as a young boy, but he taught himself to play the piano by ear and by the age of 16 he was running his own school dance band.

During the war he served in the Fleet Air Arm, rising to the rank of Lieutenant. He was demobbed in 1947 and found himself with nothing to do. Thanks to someone who'd heard him play the piano in wartime concerts, he tried for the Guildhall School of Music. He spent three years there, taking up the oboe as a second instrument. After graduating, he freelanced for a while as an oboist, but never rose above pit orchestra work or Sunday afternoon playing with bands in London parks. He got the sack from that eventually, for not being good enough.

Late in 1950 a proper job presented itself, as an assistant A and R man at Parlophone, one of EMI's smaller companies. At the time he didn't know what EMI meant. It stands for Electrical Musical Industries, now the world's biggest record organization.

Although it was his Guildhall classical training that had got him the job, he was expected to help with jazz and light music. The range was wide at Parlophone but, in the main, unexciting. 'Parlophone was the poor relation in those days, compared with the EMI big boys, HMV and Columbia. We were still recording on wax when I joined in 1950.'

Parlophone had been bought just before the war from Germany. It had done little since being taken over and a lot of people inside, according to George Martin, expected it not to last very much longer.

Opposite: The Beatles, ever so attentive, listening to George Martin during a recording session for the Parlophone label, 1963.

Its familiar symbol '£', the pound sterling sign, has no connection with the millions of pounds it has made since. It comes from the initial of the founder's surname, Carl Lindberg.

George's salary at EMI was very modest, £7 4s. 9d. a week. To eke it out, he still played occasional Sunday afternoon concerts in the parks, when he could get them, and arranged some school orchestral recitals.

George Martin found himself doing more and more of the popular records. Two of his earliest stars were Bob and Alf Pearson, who used to sing songs about 'My Brother and I'. He also recorded The Five Smith Brothers and the Scottish country dance band, Jimmy Shand and his Band. He recorded their 'Bluebell Polka', still a successfully selling recording. He moved into jazz, recording Johnny Dankworth and Humphrey Lyttleton.

LPs were a great innovation in the early 1950s, though they now seem to have been with us for ever. 'EMI were very late getting on to them, not until 1954. I don't know why it took us so long. Decca had them about 1952. It meant we had a lot of leeway to catch up.'

In the early 1950s, producing records in Britain was a very routine, traditional business. It was like bringing out a regular monthly magazine. Each month, a company like Parlophone brought out around ten new records, all planned about two months ahead, which they called their monthly supplements. They were always very strictly and fairly balanced. Out of the ten new records, two would be classical, two jazz, two dance music – the Victor Silvester sort of dance music – two would be male vocal and two would be female vocal. There was no such category as pop. 'We never talked about pop. All we had was classical, jazz, dance and vocal.'

Out of all these categories, Parlophone had very few of the leading lights. Victor Silvester, for example, was with Columbia, one of EMI's more successful offshoots. The main money-spinning singers came from America. Parlophone had none of them.

But slowly George Martin managed to create a little niche for himself by producing a stream of comedy records, though no one in the record business said they would ever sell.

One of his earliest comedy records was Peter Ustinov's 'Mock Mozart and Phoney Folklore'. He also did Peter Sellers, Flanders and Swann and, later on, 'Beyond the Fringe', recording them in Cambridge, before they came to the West End.

Then skiffle and rock arrived, transforming the teenage pop music scene. British groups at last started to make hit records, though still nothing on the scale of the American stars. But poor old Parlophone was left farther behind, despite George Martin's comedy numbers.

'Everybody seemed to find a group or a singer, except Parlophone. I toured the London coffee bars looking for talent.' He turned down the chance of signing Tommy Hicks, or Tommy Steele as he became, because he thought he was just another Elvis copy.

'I envied so much HMV and Columbia with their American stars or other companies with British stars like Cliff Richard. In a way that is so easy. Once you have a singer or a group that you know the public likes, all you have to do then is find them another song. With comedy, you start each time completely from scratch.'

As rock revealed a huge new teenage market and as record charts and record sales became increasingly important, Parlophone, the company which many people didn't think had much life left anyway, got even farther behind.

By May 1962, unbeknown to Brian Epstein and the Beatles, Parlophone was desperately waiting for something like the Beatles to turn up. The great George Martin, whose every cough and comment they tried to analyse, was far from being great.

Judy Lockhart-Smith, then George Martin's secretary and now his wife, remembers being very impressed by Brian Epstein at their first meeting. 'He had a very nice coat and was well mannered and well spoken, not the usual sort of Charing Cross Road manager.'

George was also favourably impressed. 'But I wasn't particularly knocked out by what he played me. I didn't think a great deal of the songs or the singers. But I did think they produced an interesting sound. I said I'd give them a recording test.'

Brian had gone away ecstatic, but to George it was just another would-be recording group. He was so keen to find a good new group, he was giving tests to a great many.

'I was originally thinking of using them as a backing group with a named lead singer, like Cliff Richard and the Shadows. I desperately wanted my own Cliff. That was how my mind was working at the beginning, looking for the possibilities of one of them being the lead singer. When I met them, I soon realized that would never work.'

George met them for the first time on 6 June 1962, when he gave them their recording test at EMI's Number Three studio in St John's Wood. This was the time Brian sent him the new list of suggested numbers.

'I found them very attractive people. I liked being with them, which was funny I suppose, as they were so insignificant and I was so significant. It shouldn't really have mattered to me, whether they liked me or not, but I was pleased they seemed to. I discovered that John was a fan of Peter Sellers and the Goon records I'd produced.'

George chose only three or four numbers from Brian's list, including 'Love Me Do' and 'PS I Love You'. He thinks it must only have been an early version of 'Love Me Do', because the song itself didn't knock him out. But he again liked their sound and their personalities. 'I thought, I can't lose anything if I sign them up, although I had no idea what to do with them or which songs they could record.'

He was still busy with other records, much more important to him at the time, such as an LP of 'The Establishment', London's first but short-lived, satirical night club. This is when the long wait for the Beatles began, during which time Pete Best was sacked. George Martin was taking his time over fixing a date for the Beatles because he still wasn't sure what he would let them record, whether he could chance them doing something of their own, or whether he should get a song writer to do one for them.

At long last, on 11 September 1962, he brought them down to London to record their first British record, 'Love Me Do', with, on the B side, 'PS I Love You'.

'I chose "Love Me Do" as the best of the bunch in the end. It was John's harmonica that gave it its appeal.'

George Martin had heard that Pete Best had gone and they'd got a new drummer. But he wasn't taking any chances. He decided to hire a really experienced session drummer called Andy White and have him all ready, just in case. He told Brian this, but Ringo wasn't told.

Before they started the session, George Martin explained to them what he was trying to do. 'Let me know if there's anything you don't like,' said George Martin.

'Well for a start,' said George Harrison, 'I don't like your tie.' This was a half-serious joke, and has been recalled many times since, but it didn't go down all that well with George Martin. It was, in fact, a brand new tie, which he was particularly proud of. It was black with red horses on and came from Liberty's. But everyone laughed, and the session proceeded.

It was the first ever recording session for Ringo and he was far from confident. He would have been even more scared, if he'd realized from the beginning, which he didn't, that another drummer was hanging around, waiting.

They went into 'Love Me Do', which took about 17 takes before George Martin was happy. 'I didn't rate Ringo very highly. He couldn't do a roll – and still can't – though he's improved a lot since. Andy was the kind of drummer I needed. Ringo was only used to ballrooms. It was obviously best to use someone with experience.'

'I was nervous and terrified of the studio,' says Ringo. 'When we came back later to do the B side, I found that George Martin had this other drummer sitting in my place. It was terrible. I'd been asked to join the Beatles, but now it looked as if I was only going to be good enough to do ballrooms with them, but not good enough for records.

'They started "PS I Love You". The other bloke played the drums and I was given the maracas. I thought, that's the end. They're doing a Pete Best on me. They then decided to record the other side again, the one on which I'd originally played the drums. I was given the tambourine this time.

'I was shattered. What a drag. How phoney the whole record business was, I thought. Just what I'd heard about. Getting other musicians to make your records for you in the studios. If I was going to be no use for records, I might as well leave.

'But nobody said anything. What could the others say, or me? We were just lads, being pushed around. You know what I mean. They were so big, the London record company and all that. We just did what we were told.

'When the record came out as a single, my name was on "PS I Love You", but I was only playing the maracas, the other bloke was on drums. But luckily for me, they decided to stick to the first version of "Love Me Do", the one in which I'm playing drums, so that was OK.'

'Love Me Do', their first record, was released on 4 October 1962. By that time, they were back in Liverpool, trailing round the local halls and ballrooms again, but waiting for their record to astound the world. Nothing happened.

The Beatles' Liverpool fans very faithfully bought the record in great numbers, but of course sales in a provincial town don't have much effect on the charts. They also wrote in hordes to all the request programmes. The first play of it was on Radio Luxembourg.

Mrs Harrison, George's mother, sat up for hours the night George said they might be on. She got fed up waiting in the end and went to bed, only to be wakened by George screaming that they were on. He also woke Mr Harrison with his shouting, who was very angry as he had to be up early for the first shift on the buses.

'The first time I heard "Love Me Do" on the radio,' says George, 'I went shivery all over. I listened to some of the lead guitar work and couldn't believe it. But the most important thing in our lives was to get into the Top Twenty.'

They eventually crept into the charts at number 49, in the *New Record Mirror*. The next week it started showing up in another pop newspaper, the *New Musical Express*, where it got to 27. It stayed there for some time.

On the strength of having a record, Brian managed to secure them their first TV show, though it was just in the North. This was on Granada's *People and Places* from Manchester.

They were then due to go back to Hamburg for another appearance at the Star Club. They had contracted to do this before their record had been made. They thought that if

Above left: The sheet music for 'Please Please Me', which became the Beatles' first number one, in February 1963.
Above right: Publicity photo released by Parlophone for the band's first record, 'Love Me Do', in October 1962. John and George had been photographed, rather artily, by Astrid in Hamburg. The other two had to be touched up to match.

they were out of the country, unable to get in any live plugs on radio or TV, their record would go straight down. But they went off, on their fourth visit to Hamburg. Their record slowly kept creeping up while they were away, which gave them an excuse each time for wild celebrations. The highest 'Love Me Do' ever got was to number 17.

George Martin, meanwhile, was pleased, but not overexcited, by 'Love Me Do'. 'I didn't think it was all that brilliant, but I was thrilled by the reaction to the Beatles and their sound. The problem now was to get a follow-up record for them.'

He'd found a song he was sure would be a hit. It was called 'How Do You Do It'. He sent it to the Beatles, who didn't like it. George Martin said he did. He was the boss. He wanted them to record it. So they had to. They still said they didn't like it and didn't want it produced.

It was a brave, or perhaps simply naive, show of stubbornness for a group of young, inexperienced provincials, who couldn't even read or write music, to tell the highly knowledgeable and powerful George Martin that they knew better than he did.

'I told them they were turning down a hit. It was their funeral, but if they were going to be so obstinate, then they had better produce something better themselves. They were very self-opinionated in those days. They haven't changed one bit.

'They did produce something better, "Please Please Me", which knocked me out.'

But he was right about 'How Do You Do It'. He eventually gave that instead to another Brian Epstein group, Gerry and the Pacemakers, who made it number one.

The Beatles' second record, 'Please Please Me', was recorded on 26 November 1962, but not released till January of 1963. They came back from Hamburg to do it, then went off again, this time just for a couple of weeks, for their fifth and final session in the Hamburg clubs.

At the end of the year, the *New Musical Express* did their usual popularity poll. The Springfields were voted top of the British Vocal Group Department with 21,843 votes. The Beatles were way down with 3,906 votes, presumably all sent in from Liverpool. But they were in. They existed, though there was still little sign that they might be the group that George Martin and Parlophone so desperately needed.

Dick James is the only traditional show business man who has ever got into the Beatles' circle, either professionally or as a friend. He entered just after George Martin and, like him, he was desperately looking for the Beatles to turn up.

Dick James has always been around in the business. He's from the sort of London Jewish background where you grow up with all the agents and band leaders of the future, the boys who will always help you. Dick James has a lot of schmalz, but it's all genuine. He's a sort of cuddly, boy's own Tin Pan Alley man. They all love Dick James. They tease him about loving ballads. They know that a good corny, 'When I'm Sixty Four' song is going to make Dick James very happy. Dick James is very happy anyway. He's probably the luckiest man in their whole circle. From being a one-man music publisher, when he met them, he now runs a large music publishing corporation. He's a millionaire, not just thanks to them, but to his own hard work.

He was born Richard Leon Vapnick in 1920 in London's East End. His father, a butcher, came from Poland in 1910, around the time that the Epstein family also came from Poland.

At 17 he was a professional singer, appearing with Al Berlin (now an agent) and his band at the Cricklewood Palais. During the war he was in the Medical Corps, not doing anything medical, but playing in the Medical Corps Band. This was when he learned to read music. After the war he joined Geraldo, who immediately changed Dick Vapnick's name to Dick James. For many years, he appeared with most of the big bands of the time, and then went on to become a solo singer.

'I never got to the pinnacle. Nobody ever got hysterical when I came on, the way they did with Donald Peers and David Whitfield.'

But he made a good living. He did a lot of records, though nothing startling. His first was in 1942, during an army leave, when he did a sing-along with Primo Scala's Accordion Band. He was with Decca for a while, but didn't make much money for them. In 1952 he ended up with Parlophone. They had a bright-looking young A and R man called George Martin, who was willing to work hard on any popular singer. In 1955, under George Martin, Dick James did his best-ever record and the only one he is now remembered by. This was 'Robin Hood', the theme song for the TV series. It got to number nine in the charts, the highest either had ever done. It led to Dick James's own 15-minute spot on Radio Luxembourg, produced by another bright young man called Philip Jones.

But despite the success of 'Robin Hood', Dick James knew there wasn't much future for him as a singer, not the way the business was going, with rock and skiffle and all these young lads coming on. 'I felt there was going to be a revolution and I was in the wrong place at the wrong time.' He was still in his early 30s, but he'd been wearing a toupee for some years. 'Just for stage work of course. Not in my private life. That would have been cheating.'

He continued singing until 1959, but by then only part time, and only in the London area, as he wanted to be near his wife and son. As a sideline, he'd taken up music publishing. He became an unpaid assistant to Sid Bron, father of the actress, Eleanor Bron. (She appeared in the Beatles' second film, *Help*.)

In September 1961 he opened his own music publishing firm in two rooms in the Charing Cross Road. He'd got the company going by the summer of 1962, but hadn't discovered any hits.

Through contacts, the son of a friend came to see him one day, with a song he hadn't managed to sell to any other music publisher. This song was called 'How Do You Do It'. He rushed round to George Martin, his old friend at Parlophone. The reason why George Martin was so keen to get the Beatles to record this song now becomes clearer.

'I told George it was brilliant. He said it might do for this new group he'd got, from Liverpool. "Liverpool?" I said. "You're joking. So what's from Liverpool?"'

George Martin knew it was a good commercial song, and persuaded Dick James to let him keep it for a while. Dick was very excited, convinced at last he'd got the hit he was waiting for. But in November 1962, George rang Dick to tell him that the Beatles had written their own follow-up song, 'Please Please Me', which he said was excellent.

That seemed to be it, as far as Dick James was concerned. But George Martin said he had Brian Epstein in his office. He didn't know anyone in London, perhaps Dick could help him. On the phone Dick James said he would. He also asked if he could publish 'Please Please Me', as George had said it was so excellent.

Brian had already arranged to see another music publisher first thing in the morning, but he told Dick James he would come to him afterwards and see what he thought. 'I was in my office at 10.30 next morning, when Brian walked in, half an hour earlier than arranged. He said he'd been to this other music publisher. He'd waited 25 minutes but only an office boy turned up. He said I could have first option instead.

'He played it to me and I said it was the most exciting song I'd heard for years. Could I have it?'

Brian Epstein was fresh out of Liverpool, but he wasn't all that green. He said that if Dick James could get them some promotion, he could have the song. Dick James picked up the phone and rang one of his old contacts. This was Philip Jones, who'd produced his old Radio Luxembourg singsongs. He had just taken over a new TV pop programme, *Thank Your Lucky Stars*.

'Over the phone, there and then, I fixed it up. I played "Please Please Me" to Philip and he said he liked it. He'd fit them into a show.'

In five minutes, Dick James had arranged the Beatles' first London TV appearance – the Granada one in Manchester had been only in the North. Brian Epstein was naturally very impressed. Over lunch, Dick James became the Beatles' music publisher. A music publisher can do pretty well, if he has the right composers writing for him. All copyright fees are shared 50-50 between publisher and composer.

Dick James in many ways had made a wrong choice, way back in the 1950s, when he'd decided to try to be a music publisher rather than a singer. He might have been safer as an agent, which was something else he thought of at the time. Music publishers had for decades existed on the sales of sheet music. Once the record boom started and people stopped playing the piano at home, sheet music had had its day. But by meeting the Beatles, Dick James's day was just about to begin.

21

TOURING

The Beatles began the year 1963 with one record out and another one about to be released. They'd found George Martin and Dick James. They were lined up to appear on their first London TV programme. But they were still completely unknown. Brian Epstein was finding it very hard to get them any publicity, nationally or locally.

He was still trying the *Liverpool Echo*'s George Harrison, but with no success. So he wrote to Disker, the *Liverpool Echo*'s record critic. He'd first written to Disker back in 1962 and been surprised to get a letter from Decca in London signed by someone called Tony Barrow.

Tony Barrow had become Disker in 1953, when he was 17 and still at school in Crosby near Liverpool. He kept it up while he was at Durham University and later when he joined Decca, writing sleeve notes for them. He still is Disker today, though he's also the Beatles' senior press officer.

When Brian wrote to him the first time, it had looked as if Decca had liked the audition and was going to record them. Tony Barrow wrote a little paragraph to this effect, the first time the Beatles were mentioned in print. When it all fell through, Tony Barrow wasn't so keen to write about them again. But when 'Love Me Do', their first record, was out, he wrote about the Beatles again in his Disker column.

Brian came to London more often, once his group had a record out. He met Tony Barrow and asked him for advice on getting publicity.

'Brian didn't know how you promoted a record, so I put him in touch with the trade press. Then he said he hadn't got a press officer. He'd just been sending round duplicated hand-outs on his own. He asked if I could help. So sitting in my office at Decca, I wrote out the very first official press release from the Beatles.'

He hadn't actually met them and he couldn't use his own name or phone number, as he was with Decca. He also hadn't got a mailing list. 'I took out a publicity man I'd met. It was a one and ninepenny lunch at the BBC canteen. He agreed to share his mailing list and

Opposite: George, John, Paul and Ringo get their hair together before taking the stage while on tour in 1963.

addresses.' This publicist was Andrew Oldham, who later worked for a spell with Brian Epstein and later became the manager of the Rolling Stones.

At the same time, October 1962, EMI also did a hand-out to go with their first record, but this was in the main a rewrite of Brian's duplicated letter, which in turn had been based on fan-club literature. It said that John's favourite colour was black, he liked curry and Carl Perkins, hated thickheads and traditional jazz. Under the heading marked 'Type of car' he put 'bus'. All of them, according to this hand-out, had the same ambition – to make a lot of money and retire. This wasn't the correct ambition, judging by the usual hand-outs of the time. Their ambition should have been to be all-round entertainers.

Tony Barrow left Decca and began working for NEMS Enterprises full time on 1 May 1963, from a one-room office in Monmouth Street, Brian Epstein's first London office. For six months he sent out innumerable press releases, most of which were ignored.

The music papers did write about their records when they came out, especially 'Please Please Me', which was eventually released on 12 January. It got to number one on 16 February and they wrote about it well, but the national papers still ignored them as an item of news.

The first, and for six months, the only, general feature in any sort of national paper was in the London *Evening Standard* in February 1963 by Maureen Cleave. 'Please Please Me' still hadn't got to number one and they were still largely unknown, even to the record business. But Miss Cleave had heard about their following in Liverpool. She said in her article how their Liverpool fans had forced Granada TV to film them but were now worried that the Beatles might leave Liverpool. She described how funny and natural they were.

She also drew attention, for the first time in any paper, to their hair. She described it as a 'French hairstyle' with the fringe brushed forwards. This was the correct general term for it at the time, as it had originated on the Continent.

'Although the pop papers did a bit, I could never get any national feature writers or news reporters interested in the Beatles,' says Tony Barrow. 'It wasn't till October 1963 that it all happened.

'I would love to say that it was my brilliant hand-outs that built the Beatles, but they didn't. The national press was very very late catching on. Kids everywhere were starting to go wild about them, not just in Liverpool, yet nobody seemed to notice. They'd got to the top of the hit parade with their second record, but the nationals still couldn't see them as a news or feature story.'

The simple explanation is that, as it had never happened before in Britain, the British press had no way of recognizing it. They had to wait until it jumped out and hit them over the head.

Though they were being ignored nationally, the Beatles were at last getting good coverage in Liverpool. On 5 January 1963, Disker gave a long review of their forthcoming second record, 'Please Please Me' – without mentioning that he also worked part time as the Beatles' PR man.

The famous George Harrison was also lumbering on to the bandwagon. In his 'Over the Mersey Wall' column on 21 February, he gave a plug for the TV appearance they were about to make on *Thank Your Lucky Stars*. He said this had been recorded before 'Please Please Me' had got to number one. He also wondered, in his column, if they were going to be a one-hit group or not.

But a couple of months later there was no holding him. It was his turn to boast that his name was the same as the really famous George Harrison. He said he'd been getting masses of birthday cards addressed to 'George Harrison, Liverpool'. He was even getting requests for locks of his hair, the earliest sign of the fans' craze for getting bits of the Beatles. He only wished he had some hair for himself, never mind to give it away.

People in Liverpool called Lennon, McCartney, Harrison and Starkey were also beginning to be pestered, with strange girls ringing them up all night long.

But the big result of getting into the Top Twenty was not the *Liverpool Echo* writing about them, but getting a national tour. This didn't mean big success, because all packaged tours that go round on one-night stands have big and small stars. But getting on to this circuit was vital to them at this stage. They needed to break out of Merseyside and become exposed nationally, to see if they could have the same sort of effects on strangers as on the Liverpool fans they'd grown up with. Doing a big tour was also the steadiest way of plugging a record, by playing it live all over the country.

The Beatles playing at Birkenhead, early 1963. After months of appearing at venues like this, in and around Liverpool, the band set off on their first UK national tour in February 1963, as the support group to Helen Shapiro.

The first tour the Beatles went on, in February of 1963, was Helen Shapiro's. She was the star of the show. She'd caused a sensation a couple of years previously by becoming the first of the very young teenage girl singing stars.

Arthur Howes, the promoter, was already a success in his field. He'd promoted all the Cliff Richard tours. But by spotting the Beatles very early on, before they'd got to number one, he became the promoter of all their British tours, except one.

Brian had been trying to contact Arthur Howes for a long time, once he'd been given his name as the promoter of the Cliff Richard tours. He was surprised, when he eventually got his home number, to find he lived in Peterborough. This was back in 1962, while he was still trailing round the record companies.

'One Saturday afternoon I got a telephone call at home in Peterborough. Someone saying he was called Brian Epstein was ringing from Liverpool. He said he had a great group, was there anything I could fit them into? He told me their names, Beatles, and I laughed. Oh, God, here we go again, I thought. Another group with a funny name.

'But I've never turned down a group without first hearing them. I said there was a show in Peterborough they could join. Just a two shot at the Embassy Theatre in Frank Ifield's show.' He didn't give them a fee, just their expenses from Liverpool.

Their night at the Embassy, Peterborough, was their first night in a theatre outside Merseyside. It was a complete failure. This was the night the audience 'sat on their hands', as Arthur Howes was quoted as saying earlier. 'It was a Frank Ifield show, so I suppose it wasn't so surprising. They loved him so much that the show was good enough to take ten minutes of a bad group.'

But Arthur Howes liked the look of the Beatles. He put them on at another theatre near Peterborough. Again they were a failure. All the same, Arthur Howes put them under contract. This didn't mean much, but it committed the Beatles to him, if he wanted them. 'I still liked them as people and I saw Brian as a great businessman. I was very impressed by him.'

In January 1963, when they'd at last got a record out, he took up his contract with them and decided to give them a spot on his Helen Shapiro tour. When they set off, in February 1963, their second record was out, but there were few signs that it would get to number one. They were just another group, filling the bill. 'They took six months to happen, as far as I was concerned. My concern is strictly box office. If they don't work, there's no income. There's no romance for a promoter. Just hard work.'

'Touring was a relief,' says John, 'just to get out of Liverpool and break new ground. We were beginning to feel stale and cramped.

'We were always getting the pack-ups. We'd get tired of one stage and be deciding to pack up, when another stage would come along. We'd outlived the Hamburg stage and wanted to pack that up. We hated going back to Hamburg those last two times. We'd had all that scene.'

'It was a big thrill,' says Ringo, 'going with Helen Shapiro and playing in real theatres. We'd done the Empire once in Liverpool, when Brian put on a show, just to get us on somewhere. We were third on the bill. Some Cockney manager of one of the so-called stars had a hassle with us. He didn't want us to be on the show at all.

'But touring properly round theatres was great. We didn't know anything about things like make-up, because we'd never done proper stage shows. It was a long time before we had a go at that. I think it was watching Frank Ifield. His eyes looked amazing. We thought we'd try it ourselves. We pranced on like Red Indians, covered in the stuff.'

They caused no sensation at the beginning of the Helen Shapiro tour. It wasn't till later, when their second record became top, that they started getting a big reaction.

'Helen was the star,' says Ringo. 'She had the telly in her dressing room and we didn't have one. We had to ask her if we could watch hers. We weren't getting packed houses, but we were on the boards, man.'

John remembers there was a bit of screaming in Glasgow. He says they always screamed there. They liked rock and roll, long after everyone else had progressed to liking the Shadows. 'We always got screams in Scotland. I suppose they haven't got much else to do up there.' The Beatles were still basically a rock and roll group. 'Twist and Shout', which they started putting into their act at this stage, was perhaps the most out and out rock and roll style they ever sang.

Although he was on the boards, Ringo, for a long time, was still a bit worried about fitting in with the others. 'When we got to hotels I wondered who I'd be with. They all knew each other so well. What usually happened was that John shared with George and I shared with Paul. It was always OK of course.'

John has general memories of touring, but he can't remember things like the names of towns or places from any tour they ever did. 'We never knew where we were. It was all the same.'

Ringo's only specific memory of that first Helen Shapiro tour was being thrown out of a ball. 'It was in Carlisle I think. There was a ball on in the hotel we were staying in and we thought we'd look in. It was full of soft people, all stoned out of their heads. They chucked us out because we were so scruffy, which we were.'

When 'Please Please Me' got to number one, they became better known to the pop fans. Towards the end, they were getting as much applause as Helen Shapiro, the star of the show.

After the tour, with a number one behind them, Arthur Howes immediately sent them on another one. This started in March 1963. The stars of this show were Chris Montez and Tommy Roe. The Beatles were third on the bill.

Their reception on this tour increased all the time. They were now becoming well known in the pop world. Their appearance on *Thank Your Lucky Stars* helped their record. They were asked to write songs for other people. They did one for Helen Shapiro.

Cliff Richard's new song, 'Summer Holiday', soon toppled 'Please Please Me' from the top. But Gerry and the Pacemakers, with the song the Beatles had turned down, 'How Do You Do It', soon became number one. By March 1963, the Liverpool Sound was a phrase people in the pop business had started to use.

The success of 'Please Please Me' led, in April 1963, to their first LP, which had the same name. It included both sides of their first two records, plus 'Twist and Shout', 'A Taste of Honey' and others. This album remained in the LP charts for six months.

In April 1963 they brought out their third single, 'From Me To You'. This reached number one, like 'Please Please Me', and was awarded a Silver Disc.

Brian was still signing up other Liverpool artists. He took over Billy Kramer, put a J in the middle of his name and gave him a new backing group, the Dakotas from Manchester. John and Paul wrote a song for him, 'Do You Want To Know a Secret'. It became number one.

Already, even as early as April 1963, when their third record, 'From Me To You', came out, people were comparing their records and saying they'd gone off. Disc jockey Keith Fordyce wrote that the 'singing and harmonizing are good and there's plenty of sparkle. The lyric is commercial, but I don't rate the tune as being anything as good as on the last two discs by this group.'

John and Paul had composed this song while on a coach during the Helen Shapiro tour. They were writing simple and uncomplicated lyrics, as they'd always done, using easy audience-identifying words like 'me' and 'you' in the titles.

They were signed up for another national tour in May, this time with Roy Orbison. This was the only British tour Arthur Howes didn't do. He didn't have a tour going out at the time, but Brian thought they should keep touring and cash in on their record fame.

Ringo and Paul in a cheap Bournemouth hotel in 1963, while they were still touring the provinces and before full-scale Beatlemania set in.

Before they went off, they had a short holiday in Tenerife in the Canary Isles. This was at the holiday home of Klaus's father, their Hamburg friend, who they still kept in contact with. Paul was nearly killed on this holiday, when he swam out too far and got swept out to sea.

Whenever they could, during these tours or in any breaks, they all went home to Liverpool. 'We went around boasting,' says Ringo. 'Professional group, you know. Most groups were still going out to ordinary jobs.'

John felt slightly embarrassed and some-how self-conscious being back in Liverpool, despite their success.

'We couldn't say it, but we didn't really like going back to Liverpool. Being local heroes made us nervous. When we did shows there they were always full of people we knew. We felt embarrassed in our suits and being very clean. We were worried that friends might think we'd sold out. Which we had, in a way.'

During their third tour, with Roy Orbison in May 1963, they started causing riots, though not the sort which made many national papers, who were still ignoring them. This was their first tour as the stars of the show and they were beginning to have everywhere the sort of reaction they'd had in the Cavern in Liverpool.

Although Brian had made them more show business and polished, so John thought anyway, they were still larking around on stage, singing corny songs if anything went wrong and making funny introductions. 'And now for a song by that Red Hot Gospel-singing Mama, Victor Silvester.' In any interview they managed to get with the pop music writers, they were much the same. Maureen Cleave had said in her *Evening Standard* piece that it was like living it up with four Marx Brothers.

It was on this tour with Roy Orbison that a black market started in tickets. Jelly babies were thrown at them on stage – after George had been foolish enough to say he liked them – and they were mobbed in the theatre, at their hotel and everywhere they went.

Roy Orbison got equal billing with the Beatles, but he was the second to last act on the bill, with the Beatles following him, as the main stars of the show.

'It was terrible following him,' says Ringo. 'He'd slay them and they'd scream for more. In Glasgow we were all backstage, listening to the tremendous applause he was getting. He was just standing there singing, not moving or anything. As it got near our turn, we would hide behind the curtain whispering to each other – guess who's next folks, it's your favourite rave. But once we got on the stage, it was always OK.'

It wasn't OK for Neil Aspinall, their road manager, once the touring days began. It hadn't been so bad in Liverpool, round and round the same old places. But now it was a new road, a new hotel, a new theatre and new problems every day.

'There was always trouble with the mikes on every tour,' says John. 'No theatre ever got it how we liked it. Even rehearsing in the afternoon first and telling them how we wanted it, it still wouldn't be right. They'd either be in the wrong position or not loud enough. They would just set it up as they would for amateur talent night. Perhaps we had a chip about them not taking our music seriously. It drove us mad. Brian would sit up in the control room and we'd shout at him. He'd signal back that that was all they could do.'

They used to shout most of all at Neil. It was one of his jobs to get them and their gear everywhere at the right time and help set it up. As the fans started mobbing, endangering them physically as well as trying to steal bits of equipment, it became more and more impossible for Neil to do everything.

'In five weeks of touring I lost three stones in weight. No one will believe it, but it was true. I went down from eleven stone to eight stone. I just didn't eat or sleep for five weeks. There was no time.'

So Malcolm Evans, the bouncer from the Cavern, was taken on. He joined Neil as road manager and continued throughout their touring days. They are both still with them today, as their closest companions and friends.

Neil is thin, highly intelligent, quietly efficient but with very strong opinions and by no means a yes-man. He looks a bit like George. Mal is big and hefty, open-hearted, good-natured and easy-going. Neil gave up a career in accountancy to join the Beatles. Mal's job was less imposing, but he was completely settled into it.

Mal had been working for eleven years as a telecommunications engineer when the Beatles came along and changed his life. He was 27, married with one child, paying the mortgage on a terrace house in Allerton Road, Liverpool, the proud owner of his first car and on a good salary of £15 a week. He had absolute security, paid holidays and a pension when he retired. He looked obviously set for life.

One day in 1962 he came out of work at the Post Office and decided not to walk around the Pier Head, which is where he usually went for a walk in his lunch hours. 'I saw this little street called Mathew Street that I'd never noticed before. I walked down it and came to this club, the Cavern Club. I'd never been inside a club before. I heard this music coming, real rock it sounded, a bit like Elvis. So I paid me shilling and went in.' He went in so often after that it was suggested if he became a bouncer, guarding the door, he could get in for nothing.

He'd been bouncing part time for about three months, when, in the summer of 1963, Brian asked him to give up the Post Office and be their second road manager. Mal's job, during all the years of touring, was to drive the van containing the equipment to the next theatre, set it up and test it in time for them coming on. Afterwards, he packed it all up safely and looked after it till the next stop. Neil looked after the Beatles personally.

During his first week with the Beatles, Mal estimates he was sacked six times. 'I'd never seen a drum kit close up before. I didn't understand any of it. Neil helped me the first couple of days, but the first day I was on my own was terrible. It was a huge stage and my mind went a blank. I didn't know where to put anything. I asked a drummer from another group to help me. I didn't realize each drummer likes his cymbals at a special height. He did them his own way, but they were useless for Ringo.

'The worst of all was at the Finsbury Empire in London, when I lost John's guitar. It was one he'd had for years as well. It just disappeared. Where's my Jumbo, he said. I didn't know. It's still a mystery today. I fairly got it that day.

'It was great meeting all the people I'd seen on TV. I was really star-struck. I still am. I soon realized, of course, that people were being nice to me, trying to get to know me, just to use me to get to the Beatles. I soon got to spot them a mile off.'

'It was OK for him,' says Neil. 'Going out in front, getting the instruments ready. Dead popular he was. As they cheered and shouted at him, he talked to them and made jokes. He didn't have to physically fight them off, once it started.'

'My ideas about the fellows soon changed,' says Mal. 'Up to then, they'd been four beautiful people. I'd looked upon them as gods. I soon found out they were just ordinary blokes, not made of platinum. I got some bellyaching and I couldn't answer back. I just had to put up with it.'

The worst part of all touring, they both say, was the dressing room before a show. It would be jammed with reporters, police and theatre staff, while outside, fans were trying to break in. 'I had to look after all that,' says Neil, 'until we got a press man ourselves. And I was supposed to get food.

'When things got too much, if someone was going on a bit, John or one of them would shout "Cripples, Neil". This meant get rid of somebody. It originally had just meant cripples, but it came to mean anyone who was in the way.

'We always got masses of cripples, even from the first tours. They would be in the dressing room when we arrived at the theatre. The management would let them, thinking we'd love to see them, as we were supposed to be such lovely blokes. It was terrible. You couldn't move for them. What could you do? They wouldn't be able to move themselves so Mal or I usually had to carry them out. Mal got a claw stuck round his neck one night.

'As the Beatles' following got bigger, we got more and more. The image of the Beatles was so good and nice, for some reason. They thought we'd *want* to see them, or we'd be disappointed.'

Some even thought that being in the presence of the Beatles might miraculously cure them. It was one aspect of their adulation which never made the papers. Pictures of cripples being carried out of their dressing room would not have been very suitable.

Riots were starting on these early tours, as they travelled up and down the country, but they were still completely a Liverpool group, doing shows round their old Merseyside haunts between tours. They didn't do their last performance at the Cavern until 23 August 1963.

John was home in Liverpool for the birth of his son Julian – named after his mother, Julia. When he visited Cyn at Sefton General Hospital he had to wear a disguise so no-one would see him. This was still April 1963. They were household names in Liverpool, but unknown elsewhere. 'A few did recognize me. "Dere's one of dem", I heard someone shout, and I had to run for it.' A few days after the birth, John went on holiday to Spain with Brian.

Cyn moved out of the little flat they'd had in the centre of Liverpool and moved in with Mimi in Menlove Avenue. 'When I was pushing Julian in his pram round Woolton, people would come up to me and say, are you Cynthia Lennon? I'd say no.'

They were all still Liverpool based in June 1963, when it was Paul's 21st birthday. All the fans knew of course, so he couldn't have a party at his home in Forthlin Avenue. Instead he had it at his Aunt Jinny's, one of the two aunts who had helped a lot when his mother died.

This was a huge, drunken, noisy orgy, with all the other groups playing, as at Ringo's party, and as at all their welcome homes from Hamburg. The Fourmost, who had also been signed on by Brian, played, and so did the Scaffold, the Liverpool group that had just got going. This consisted of Roger McGough, the Liverpool poet, John Gorman, a comedian actor and boutique owner, and Michael McGear, formerly Michael McCartney, Paul's brother.

Michael was still working as a hairdresser, but had started appearing with the Scaffold in his spare time. Once Paul became famous in Liverpool, Michael had changed his name for any acting work, in case anyone felt he was cashing in. He also refused to sing.

During this party, John picked a fight with a local disc jockey, who at one time had done a lot, before Brian, to get them bookings.

'I smashed him up,' says John. 'I battered his bloody ribs for him. I was pissed at the time. I think he'd called me a queer.

'He sued me afterwards, for thumping him. I paid him £200 to settle it. That was probably the last real fight I've ever had.'

The end of an era, in many ways. It was the beginning of the end of John's violently aggressive, chip-on-the-shoulder attitude to life and everyone. And it was the beginning of the end of the whole Liverpool stage, as their touring was at long last receiving national attention.

Back in London, in August 1963, they produced their fourth single, 'She Loves You'. This was the start of 'Yeh Yeh' and the beginning of national fame. Liverpool was now where they had come from.

22

BEATLEMANIA

Beatlemania descended on the British Isles in October 1963, just as the Christine Keeler-Profumo scandal fizzled out.

It didn't lift for three years, by which time it had covered virtually the whole world. There was perpetual screaming and yeh yeh-ing from hysterical teenagers of every class and colour, few of whom could hear what was going on for the noise they were making. They became emotionally, mentally, or sexually excited. They foamed at the mouth, burst into tears, hurled themselves like lemmings in the direction of the Beatles, or just simply fainted.

Throughout the whole of the three years it was happening somewhere in the world. Each country witnessed the same scenes of mass emotion, scenes which had never been thought possible before and which are unlikely to be repeated. Today, it all sounds like fiction, yet it was only yesterday.

It is impossible to exaggerate Beatlemania, because Beatlemania was, in itself, an exaggeration. For those who can't believe it, every major newspaper in the world has miles of words and pictures in its cuttings library, giving blow-by-blow accounts of what happened when the Beatles descended on their part of the globe.

Once it had stopped, by 1967, and everyone was overcome by either exhaustion or boredom, it was difficult to believe it had all happened. Could everyone have been so mad? People of all ages and all intellects eventually succumbed, though perhaps not all as hysterically as the teenagers.

World leaders and famous personages, who had often started by warning or criticizing, fell over each other to drag in references to the Beatles, to show that they were in touch, to let people see that they also knew that a phenomenon of mass communication had occurred.

It occurred suddenly and dramatically in Britain in October 1963 and Brian Epstein

Opposite: Police control a queue for Beatles tickets in Lewisham, southeast London, on a wet day in November 1963. Almost as many teenage boys as girls were hoping to see them in the flesh at the Odeon Cinema two weeks later.

said he wasn't prepared for it. He was prepared for success, because they were already having it. What he wasn't prepared for was hysteria.

'She Loves You', which had come out at the end of August, also went to number one, following the pattern of their previous two singles. As early as June, even before it had a title, thousands of fans had already ordered the next Beatle single. The day before it went on sale, there were advance orders for it of 500,000.

By September the Beatles had reached a unique position in Britain. They had the top-selling LP record, *Please Please Me*. They had the top-selling EP record, 'Twist and Shout'. They had the top-selling single, 'She Loves You'.

But it wasn't until the night of 13 October 1963 that the Beatles stopped being simply an interesting pop music story and became front-page hard *news* in every national newspaper.

This was the night they topped the bill at the London Palladium, on a show that was televised as *Sunday Night At The London Palladium*. An estimated audience of 15 million viewers watched them that night.

Argyll Street, where the Palladium is situated, was besieged by fans all day long. Newspaper reporters started arriving, once they'd heard the stories of the crowds. The stage door was blocked by fans, mountains of presents and piles of telegrams. Inside, it was almost impossible to rehearse for the continual screams of the thousands of fans chanting outside in the streets.

Other TV companies turned up, from the news departments, to record the crowd scenes, even though the show was being put out by a rival network. The police, taken completely by surprise, were unable to control most of the crowd. It was decided that the Beatles' getaway car should be stationed at the front doors, as everyone expected them to leave afterwards by the stage door. Their car, by this time, was a chauffeur-driven Austin Princess. Neil's old van had long since been discarded, once the hit records started appearing.

The police, thinking they were clever, moved the car slightly away from the front door, trying to conceal it. This meant that when the Beatles did appear, shepherded by Neil, they had to search wildly for the car, then make a dash of 50 yards, almost being killed by the mobs in the process.

The front page of every newspaper next day had long news stories and large pictures of the hysterical crowd scenes. The stories weren't about how well or how badly the group had played their songs, but simply about the chaos they had caused.

'From that day on,' says Tony Barrow, their press officer, 'everything changed. My job was never the same again. From spending six months ringing up newspapers and getting no, I now had every national reporter and feature writer chasing *me*.'

His job entailed simply selecting, along with Brian and other press officers who were later used, journalists who were allowed to interview the Beatles.

'Even before that, I'd never been in any sense a publicist, the way most groups have publicists, thinking up publicity stunts. I didn't know about that, as I'd never been one. Brian anyway would have been against any stunts. We never used any and we never had to.'

The following Wednesday, Bernard Delfont announced the names for what is looked upon by most British show business people as the biggest show of the year – the Royal Variety Performance. Marlene Dietrich was also to be on the bill.

The Beatles were back on tour when this news came out. They were actually in Liverpool, about to appear at a Southport Ballroom, when the news came out. All the national newspapers sent reporters and photographers across from their Manchester offices to get the Beatles' reactions to the news. They were obviously hoping for some satirical remarks about the Royal Family, but to Brian's relief, there were none.

The Royal Variety Show was planned for 4 November. Before that, they continued touring in Britain and for the first time went abroad, to Sweden.

In Britain, each one-night stand was now resulting in the same hysterical crowd scenes. Every day the newspapers had, almost word for word, the same front-page news story as the day before, only the name of the town was different.

Even in smallish towns, like Carlisle, where earlier in the year they'd been ejected from a ball at a local hotel, the crowds were huge. On the night of 24 October, over 600 teenagers waited all night long in a queue for tickets. Most of them brought sleeping bags and slept. Some had been there for as long as 36 hours. When the box office opened and the queue moved forwards, shop windows were smashed and nine people were taken to hospital. In bigger towns the casualties ran into hundreds.

Young girls, with their pens and paper ready, waiting for the 'Fab Four' in 1963.

The Swedish tour, their first foreign trip since Hamburg, was a direct result of their record sales. 'She Loves You' soon reached the 1 million figure in Britain, for which it got a Gold Disc, and also sold well in Europe, which British pop stars had rarely done before.

They were in Sweden for five days, from 24 to 29 October. Day by day they made the British papers at home, as well as the Swedish press and TV. At a concert in Stockholm, police with police dogs tried to control the fans who couldn't get in. Inside, 40 policemen, with batons, stood guarding the stage, to stop fans climbing on. The fans did eventually break through the barrier of police and got on the stage. George was knocked over but the police managed to restore order before he was trodden on.

Swedish fans were already affecting Beatle hairstyles and clothes, as British fans had started to do. In Sweden, their hairstyle was known as the Hamlet style.

The Beatles themselves date the beginning of Beatlemania slightly later than the Palladium Show, when Brian and Tony Barrow first realized it. They weren't aware of their massive popularity until 31 October, when they arrived back at London Airport from Sweden.

They had, of course, been aware of the chaos at the Palladium two weeks previously, and all the other riots up and down the country. But this had been going on, building up

The Beatles get ready to rattle their smiles for the Queen Mother at the Royal Variety Performance – their second big London date after the Palladium – at London's Prince of Wales Theatre, 4 November, 1963.

all the time, though less publicized, since their Cavern days. They'd got into a pattern on tour of having to be smuggled in and out of theatres. They were trying to escape it, rather than face up to it and risk being killed.

But when they arrived back at London Airport the scale of their popularity suddenly hit them. It was their first triumphal arrival from anywhere, since the Cavern welcome homes. Thousands of screaming fans had been choking London Airport for hours. In the chaos surrounding their arrival, the car containing the Prime Minister, Sir Alec Douglas-Home, was held up. Miss World, who was also passing through London Airport, was completely ignored. These airport scenes became familiar pictures during the next three years.

The Royal Variety Performance, their second big London date, was held at the Prince of Wales Theatre on 4 November. The audience wasn't as big as at the Palladium show, but in theory much more select, as the seats were about four times the normal price. It was a charity show, full of show-business establishment, minor society and rag trade moguls, all hoping for a glimpse of the Royals. On this occasion they were the Queen Mother, Princess Margaret and Lord Snowdon. It's said to be a difficult audience to play to. There is the nauseating tradition of the audience craning to see what effect each act is having in the Royal Box before they clap or laugh.

Paul got a laugh all round from the beginning. The Beatles came on immediately after Sophie Tucker. Paul said how pleased they were to be following their favourite American group.

Musically, they did their usual act – causing hysterics just by announcing they were going to sing 'She Loves You'. Then they did 'Till There Was You' and 'Twist and Shout'.

John introduced one number. 'The ones in the cheap seats clap their hands,' he said. Nodding towards the Royal Box, he added: 'The rest of you just rattle your jewellery.'

This joke was on every front page the next day, everyone loving the implied, though very slight, joke at the Royals' expense. All completely harmless of course. But it was looked upon as being rather cheeky, but of course very lovable, because the Beatles had become so very lovable.

The Queen Mother, talking to them afterwards, showed that she was well aware of what they did. She even made her own jokey remark, though it probably wasn't meant to be jokey. She asked them where they were appearing next, and they said Slough. 'Oh,' said the Queen Mother, 'that's near us.'

The show was televised the following Sunday and had an audience of 26 million.

The front-page stories about their concerts became monotonously the same. Even papers like the *Daily Telegraph*, which up until then had considered itself too staid to cover pop stories, (although they now religiously publish the top ten each week), gave columns to every riot. For a long time, however, they still referred in their reports, as in one about a Newcastle concert on 28 October, to 'teenagers fighting to get tickets for the Beatles "pop" group...' They still felt it necessary to explain who the Beatles were.

There were questions in Parliament about the thousands of extra policemen all round the country being made to do extra and dangerous duties because of the Beatles. One MP suggested that the police should withdraw and see what happened. Luckily, no one took that suggestion seriously.

On 1 November they began another tour, this time billed simply as the Beatles Show. There was no other joint star, as there had been with Roy Orbison, because none was needed.

In the programme for this show, which toured till 13 December, there were several adverts for Beatle products. A firm in Peckham was offering Beatles sweaters 'designed specially for Beatle people by a leading British manufacturer with a top-quality two-tone Beatle badge'. All for 35 shillings each.

Manufacturers all over the country were by this time competing to get a concession to use the word Beatle on their products. Beatle jackets – the collarless ones, usually in corduroy, first worn by Stu in Hamburg – were on sale everywhere as early as September 1963.

Beatle wigs started appearing. A factory in Bethnal Green was working night and day to keep up with the demand. It announced it had orders from Eton College and from Buckingham Palace. Not from the Queen herself. Just a member of the staff.

Most teenage boys were growing their own Beatle-length hair. From November on there was a continuous stream of newspaper stories about schoolboys being sent home from school because of their long hair, or of apprentices not being allowed into factories.

The *Daily Telegraph*, on 2 November, produced the first leader criticizing the Beatles hysteria. It said the mass hysteria was simply filling empty heads, just as Hitler had done. The *Daily Mirror* jumped to the Beatles' defence. 'You have to be a real sour square not to love the nutty, noisy, happy, handsome Beatles.' They complimented the Beatles for not relying 'on off-colour jokes about homos for their fun.'

They were attacked and then defended in the Church Assembly, the annual meeting of leaders of the Church of England. One bishop said they were a 'psychopathetic group' and that one week of their wages could build a cathedral in Africa. But another speaker said he was a fan and that it was all healthy fun.

The *Daily Mirror* appears to have been the first paper to drag out a tame psychologist to try to explain what was happening. This was a practice that kept tame psychologists, especially Americans, in easy money for the next three years. This psychologist said the Beatles were 'relieving a sexual urge'. Doctors later came forward to say that girls had had orgasms during Beatle concerts.

On tour they arrived at Cheltenham, a very refined country town in Gloucestershire. The newspaper headlines next day announced 'Squaresville Falls', which was probably a headline the subeditors had got ready the day before. A local policeman was quoted as saying that it had been 'the craziest night since Mafeking'.

In Plymouth, on 14 November, hoses had to be turned on screaming fans to control them. There was great panic at Portsmouth, because Paul had slight flu and they had to miss a concert. Every paper gave hour-by-hour bulletins on his condition.

In Birmingham, on 11 November, they managed to escape the crowds disguised as policemen. On 18 November a Church of England vicar got a lot of space in the papers when he asked the Beatles to tape for him 'Oh Come All Ye Faithful, Yeh, Yeh,' for Christmas.

EMI sales were shooting up. When the story came out about Decca and all the other companies having turned them down, it was compared to 20th Century turning down *Gone With The Wind*.

At the end of November they brought out their fifth single, 'I Want to Hold Your Hand', which went direct to number one. It had advance orders in Britain of one million.

Their second LP, *With the Beatles*, came out a few days before. This had the stark, but very arty, photograph on the cover, showing their four heads and shoulders, dressed in black polo-neck sweaters. Their faces were cleverly lit so that one side was in the shade, as Astrid had photographed them in Hamburg. When this LP was announced, at the beginning of November, it had immediate advance orders of 250,000. It was noted at the time that this was the best advance for an LP record anywhere in the world. The best Elvis Presley had done was 200,000 for his *Blue Hawaii* album.

Every big by-lined feature writer in Britain was competing for an interview, waiting for hours and hours outside their dressing room, hoping for a word. Donald Zec of the *Daily Mirror* was one of the first to do a large interview with them, right at the beginning of their nationally famous days, on 10 September. Describing their hairstyle, which journalists still felt they had to do, he said it was a Stone-age cut.

By December 1963, the posh Sundays had at last got in on the act, doing long and very solemn investigations on the phenomenon, dragging out their own psychologists, but using even longer words. The *Observer* had a picture of a guitar-shaped Cycladic fertility goddess from Amorgos that it said 'dates the potency of the guitar as a sex symbol to about 4,800 years before the Beatle era'. The *Sunday Times* commented on how they had enlarged the English language, bringing Liverpool words like 'gear' (meaning good or great) into general usage. This rather put the Conservative politician, Edward Heath, in his place. Earlier he had criticized them by saying their language was 'unrecognizable as the Queen's English'. But Mr Heath redeemed himself slightly later, when he was reported as saying 'who could have forecast only a year ago that the Beatles would prove the salvation of the corduroy industry'.

Even the *Daily Worker*, the British Communist party newspaper, was getting its comment in. 'The Mersey Sound is the voice of 80,000 crumbling houses and 30,000 people on the dole.'

By early December they had seven of their records, singles as well as EPs, in the Top Twenty. On 11 December they went on the TV programme *Juke Box Jury*, the four of them taking over the complete jury, and gave the show the highest rating it had ever had.

A film deal was announced. Walter Shenson and George Ornstein, in association with United Artists, said they were going to star the Beatles in their first film, with a script by the Liverpool playwright, Alun Owen. Brian Epstein was in on this deal, making sure that the Beatles were to take a large percentage. He was, by now, doing the same with their tours, once it was obvious that their name alone was enough to guarantee a full house everywhere. The Beatles Tour, which had begun in November, was 'presented by Arthur Howes, by arrangement with Brian Epstein'.

In October Brian had moved his own office to London, joining Tony Barrow and the growing number of secretaries and assistants.

The fan club was also growing to huge proportions, and was soon completely unable to cope with the thousands of application forms. There were many stories in the newspapers about poor fans not having their letters answered for months, but the deluge was just too much. By the end of 1963, the official fan club had almost 80,000 paid-up members, compared with only a couple of thousand at the beginning of the year.

BBC TV did a half-hour show from the Northern Area Convention of the Beatles Fan Club from the Liverpool Empire.

At Christmas time the Beatles did a Christmas show, along with other Brian Epstein artists – Cilla Black, Billy J. Kramer, Tommy Quickly and the Fourmost. It opened in Bradford, then Liverpool, then came to London at the Finsbury Park Empire, which was where Mal lost John's favourite guitar, alas.

The intellectual following was now in full cry. The heavy papers were giving them as much space as the populars. They were on everyone's lips, in every paper, jokes were created about them, cartoons were full of them. The *Daily Mail* stopped using the word Beatle in headlines, and had the same little drawing of four Beatle haircuts, four mop tops as they were called, to illustrate every story.

Brian worried at first about his own name and personality becoming famous, but eventually he couldn't help it. He realized that it made things easier for him to get things done. 'I was worried about all of us becoming overexposed. At first sight, the endless discussion in the newspapers of the Beatles' habits, clothes, and views was exciting. The boys liked it at first and so did I. It was good for business. But finally it became an anxiety. How long could they maintain public interest? By carefully watching their bookings and press contacts, we just averted saturation point. But it was very close. Other artists have been destroyed by this very thing.'

At the time, judging by the newspaper and TV reports, it looked as though there was no control at all. Every paper, every day, had something on them. In one week, five national newspapers were serializing what they called the Beatles' life story, most of it taken from the old hand-outs. Almost anyone with any opinion on them, for or against, was guaranteed to be reported. They were so new in a jaded scene and so different from the usual show-business glitter, and they were British.

Several people said that Brian Epstein was the Svengali. He'd cleverly created and promoted them. Brian always denied this. 'In all our hand-outs,' says Tony Barrow, 'and in all our press dealings, Brian only stressed what was good about them. He never created any non-existent good points. The Beatles were four local lads from down the street, the sort you might have seen at the local church hall. This was the essence of their personal communication with the public. People identified with them from the beginning. Brian realized this and never tried to hide it.'

But Brian did, of course, create a smooth machinery, organized their lives meticulously, never let people down, which they had done when they were on their own.

From 1963 onwards, millions of words were written by people trying to analyse the Beatles' success. It could take a separate book just to cover all the theories that appeared. The first phase of the analyses was based on their sexual attraction. Then the pundits decided the Beatles were of social significance, symbolizing all the frustrations and ambitions of the new emergent, shadow-of-the-Bomb, classless, unmaterialistic, un-phoney teenagers. Then the intellectuals moved in, studying their words and music with great intensity, and coming up with some clever interpretations. All of it was true, and still is true. Any reason that anyone has for liking something is true.

To the ordinary newspaper reporter, back in 1963, the big attraction was to have a word, any word, with the Beatles. Every reporter knew that each interview would be different and funny. They didn't come out with the same jokes and comments each time, like most supposedly famous personages. Ringo turned out to be as funny as the rest of them. He was asked why he had so many rings on his fingers. He said he couldn't get them all through his nose.

'We were funny at press conferences because it was all a joke,' says John. 'They'd ask joke questions, so you'd give joke answers. But we weren't really funny at all. It was just Fifth-

Form humour, the sort you laugh at at school. They were putrid. If there were any good questions, about our music, we took them seriously. We *were* nervous, though I don't think people thought so. We were nervous at most functions.

'Our image was only a teeny part of us. It was created by the press and by us. It had to be wrong because you can't put over how you really are. Newspapers always get things wrong. Even when bits were true, it was always old. New images would catch on just as we were leaving them.'

In just twelve months, from the release of their first record, they had become an established part of the British way of life. Dora Bryan did a record about them at Christmas 1963, 'All I Want For Christmas Is A Beatle'. Even that got into the hit parade.

There was by now nobody else on the hit parade scene, unless you counted the other Liverpool groups, all of whom Brian Epstein managed, and all of whom were being recorded by George Martin.

In 1963, out of the 52 weeks in the year, a record produced by George Martin was at the top of the British hit parade for 37 weeks. This is an achievement no one has ever equalled, or is likely to.

The *New Musical Express*, in their end of the year charts, made the Beatles the world's top group. They polled 14,666 votes. The American group, the Everly Brothers, were runners-up with 3,232 votes.

In the British Vocal Section, the section they had been near the bottom of the year before, they polled 18,623 votes. The second group, the Searchers, were miles away with only 2,169 votes.

The two biggest selling singles of the year were 'She Loves You', with 1,300,000, and 'I Want To Hold Your Hand', with 1,250,000. Cliff Richard, with 'Bachelor Boy', was a long way down in third place.

The Times musical critic, William Mann, did a long and serious review of their music, in which he talked about their pandiatonic clusters and submediant key switches. He said John Lennon and Paul McCartney were 'the outstanding English composers of 1963'.

'I think I'll invite them down for the weekend, just to see what kind of fellas they are,' said Viscount Montgomery.

On 29 December, in the *Sunday Times*, Richard Buckle, reviewing John and Paul's music used in the ballet 'Mods and Rockers', said they were 'the greatest composers since Beethoven'.

23

USA

Sandi Stewart is an ordinary American Beatle fan, not silly, not half-witted, just nice and sensible. In early 1964 she was living with her parents in a wealthy middle-class small town in New Hampshire. She was 15 and in the ninth grade at high school.

'I was going to the supermarket in the car with my mother one day, in our Rolls, that's what we had at the time, though that's not important. Over the car radio came "I Want To Hold Your Hand". It was the first time I'd ever heard of the Beatles. I went, Wow! What a strange sound. I just couldn't get over it. No tune had ever affected me as much.

'I found a lot of the girls at school had also heard it and felt the same. I remember walking down the street with two of my friends and discussing them. We all said how ugly they looked in their photographs, especially with no collars on their jackets. The music was great, but we thought they did look ugly.

'Then slowly we changed our minds. I became really interested in pop music, which I'd never been before. I knew about everything they did. I read everything about them. I grew my hair long, because I read they said they liked girls with long hair.

'At the beginning I loved Paul most of all. He was so beautiful. I couldn't pinpoint it. He just seemed very beautiful.

'I didn't like George for some reason. I drew in a werewolf's fangs on his face because I didn't like him. I suppose the Beatles were outlets for love and hate. I eventually did like George a bit more.

Then I went more on John instead of Paul. He seemed so intelligent and witty. His body was very sexy. He became the one I loved passionately.

'I became obsessed about John. I dreamt about him all the time. We'd compare dreams at school. Tell each other what we did with our own favourite Beatle. I knew when I was depressed I could start a dream about John, just by lying there thinking about him, then

Opposite: The Beatles playing up to the cameras outside the Washington Coliseum, where they gave their first live performance in the USA in February 1964. There were 20,000 spectators at that concert.

falling asleep. Those dreams were absolutely beautiful. We did a lot of things together, John and I. He made love to me and I'd tell my friends next day. They weren't all sexual, but a lot were. They were so real.

'I talked and thought about them non-stop. My father was always telling me I'd get over them. I'd shout, Never, Never, Never!

'It was funny though. Even though I loved John so much, it didn't stop me chasing other boys at school. That was sort of different. But John was the most important person in my life.

'I read all the fan mags and listened to Murray the K all the time. He was the disc jockey who was the sort of Beatles expert.

'I got so desperate about John that I wrote a letter to Cynthia. I was very nice in the letter. I just told her I was very sorry, but I loved her husband. I never got a reply.

'I got all their records and had their photographs over my bedroom. When I saw a photograph of them in half shadows, my friends and I all went into town and got our photographs taken the same way.

'When absolutely nothing else in life was good, I'd go to my room and have the Beatles, especially my darling John. They all furnished something I desperately needed. The sort of rich community I lived in in New Hampshire gave me nothing. I didn't like school and didn't like home. They gave me something to live for when everything was black and depressing.

'When I heard they were coming to the Carnegie Hall in New York, I planned with two of my school friends to go and see them. We pleaded and pleaded, as we weren't allowed to go to New York on our own. No teenage girl is, from our sort of homes. We said it could be our special birthday treat, or we'd run away…'

The Carnegie Hall concert was to be promoted by Sid Bernstein, a short, tubby, ex-Columbia University student, ex-ballroom manager, ex-promoter who had become an agent with General Artists Corporation, one of the biggest agencies in America. Throughout his attempts to break into show business big time, he'd kept up his academic interests.

For ten years he'd gone to evening classes, specializing in English Government. 'I remember going to hear your Harold Laski give a lecture. He was one of the finest speakers I ever heard. After Churchill, of course.'

His interest in English Government led him to read the British newspapers. In mid-1963, something caught his attention. 'I kept on reading about these Beatles. I was supposed to be specializing in teenage music at GAC, yet I'd never heard of them. Nobody in the business bothered about the English scene.'

He took out subscriptions to all the English pop newspapers and decided to ring Brian Epstein. After a lot of difficulty, he got his home number in Liverpool. He said who he was, and Brian said he had never heard of him. He asked if he'd like his Beatles to appear at the Carnegie Hall, though he hadn't actually got the Carnegie Hall. 'Brian said when, and I said what about 12 February. I chose this day because it was Lincoln's birthday and I knew I'd be able to get it. I offered him 6,500 dollars for two shows.'

Brian didn't say yes immediately. It took some time to finalize, although the proposed date sounded fine, as he'd already fixed up two Ed Sullivan shows, for 9 and 16 February.

Sid Bernstein was made, just by getting in first as the New York promoter. He soon left agency work and branched out on his own with a partner. He went on to promote all their New York shows, except one. His story, of getting in first, could be duplicated all over the States, and all over the world.

But it wasn't all Sid Bernstein's doing, as far as New York was concerned. Brian had been working on launching the Beatles in America from the summer of 1963, though he wasn't sure if things were ready. At first the Beatles had been a failure in the States. In the first half of 1963 they'd had four records out in America, by two different record companies, and they'd got nowhere.

Once their success in Britain was assured, Brian went over to New York with Billy J. Kramer, in November 1963, the month that President Kennedy was assassinated.

'I wanted to find out why the biggest thing in British pop that anyone had ever known hadn't happened in America. It was like the early days in London. I started going the rounds of recording firms and television people.'

During this trip he met Geoffrey Ellis again, the friend who'd lived beside him in Liverpool, but had gone to Oxford and then into insurance in New York.

'I'd vaguely heard Brian was involved with some sort of beat group, but I didn't believe it. It sounded a lot of rubbish, not something shy little Brian would get mixed up in.

'I was walking down Broadway with Brian and Billy J. Kramer. We got to Times Square and Billy wanted to buy an awful shirt they have in those awful shops round there. Brian said no, he couldn't. He said "It's not your image, Billy." That was the first time I realized that Brian was seriously in all this. I realized then that he had changed.'

During this visit Brian arranged for Capitol records to issue the Beatles' records this time. Capitol, although a subsidiary of EMI, hadn't been very keen on the Beatles at first, which was why the two other American companies had issued them, though with little success.

Brian also got an appointment with Ed Sullivan, whose TV show is the biggest of its kind in the United States. His talent scouts had passed on the word about the Beatles' success in Britain. After a lot of discussion, Ed Sullivan agreed to book the Beatles for two of his shows.

Brian insisted that they should get top billing on both shows. 'This was contested vaguely by Ed Sullivan. He saw the coming importance of the Beatles, but he rejected my view that they were going to be the biggest thing in the world. He agreed in the end, but his producer later told me that Sullivan had said it was ridiculous to give a British group top billing when a British group had never made it big in the States before.'

The Beatles themselves were very nervous at the idea of America. George had been there for a short holiday earlier in 1963. He said the natives were quite human and he thought they might be all right. He'd been to see his sister Louise, who had married an American and emigrated from Liverpool to St Louis. Like her mother, Mrs Harrison, she is a devoted Beatle fan and rang up her local radio stations, requesting Beatle numbers.

But John was worried, because no British groups or singers had ever got through in America before. 'Cliff went there and died. He was 14th on the bill with Frankie Avalon.' George said he'd seen Cliff's film, *Summer Holiday*, reduced to the second feature in a drive-in in St Louis.

In January 1964, 'I Want To Hold Your Hand' entered the US charts at 83. In Britain it was at last knocked from the top, after two months, by what many people thought was going to be the new sensation – Dave Clark Five and 'Glad All Over'.

The London papers went to town on the story, glad of a local pop story for a change, after all the Liverpool successes. The *Daily Express* had a front-page headline that said: 'Tottenham Sound Has Crushed The Beatles.'

The cartoonists, after almost six months of having to think up Liverpool jokes, jumped at the idea of the Beatles being finished. Vicky in the London *Evening Standard* had the Cabinet in Beatle haircuts with the Prime Minister saying to them: 'How can I say you're with it, with old-fashioned haircuts like that?'

For a while the Beatles themselves were worried. 'We couldn't help it,' says John. 'Everyone was telling us, Dave Clark is coming, you've had it now. It worried us, but just for a minute, the way we'd worried in Liverpool that Gerry would beat us in the Mersey Beat poll.'

Before their American visit, Brian had arranged their second European trip. This was three weeks in France, playing at the Olympia in Paris, starting on 15 January.

Several thousand fans saw the three Beatles off from London Airport. Ringo had been delayed by fog in Liverpool and followed later. At London Airport he held up a sign saying TLES after the initials BEA on the side of the aeroplane. Osbert Lancaster in his *Daily Express* cartoon had Napoleon with a Beatles haircut.

The first concert at the Olympia was not a success, the first poor reception, in Beatle terms, they'd had in almost a year of touring. There was a fist fight involving photographers, French policemen and Brian Sommerville, the Beatles' new publicity man, who was now responsible for handling the press on tour. They did get a bit of clapping and John replied 'Mersey beaucoup'.

> *BBC Interviewer in Paris: How important is it for you to succeed here?*
> *PAUL: It is important to succeed anywhere.*
> *BBC: The French have not made up their minds about the Beatles. What do you think of them?*
> *JOHN: Oh, we like the Beatles. They're gear.*

In America, in its second week, 'I Want To Hold Your Hand' got to 42. Norman Weiss from GAC in New York came to see Brian, finalized the Carnegie Hall deal and became the Beatles' agent in America from then on.

In London, the *Daily Mail*, in its report from Vincent Mulchrone, who was with the Beatles, said: 'If Paris and the Beatles are going to have an affair, it's getting off to a slow start. Either the Champs-Elysées was not in mobbing mood today, or Beatlemania is still, like Britain's entry into the Common Market, a problem the French prefer to put off for a while.'

They were in their suite at the George V hotel in Paris when the news came through that 'I Want To Hold Your Hand' had got to number one in America. They had started writing this song, in the basement of Jane Asher's London house, with the aim of doing a mock-American gospel song, so it was apt that it became their first American success. They all had had a big dinner to celebrate. Brian was photographed eating his dinner with a chamber pot on his head.

American reporters and TV interviewers immediately started arriving in hordes. American Beatle fans, like Sandi Stewart, besieged the Carnegie Hall and Ed Sullivan for tickets. 'She Loves You', having lingered nowhere in the American hit parade, suddenly started climbing after 'I Want To Hold Your Hand'. In the LP charts, *Please Please Me* was just about to get to the top.

The American press, like the English press the previous year, were arriving late but in deadly earnest.

'Tell me about your hairdos,' asked an American reporter.

'You mean hair-don'ts,' said John.

'We were coming out of a swimming baths in Liverpool,' said George. 'And liked the way it looked.'

Sheilah Graham, the syndicated columnist, arrived and asked them which one was which. *Life* magazine came out with a six-page story on the Beatles.

To capitalize on all the free press publicity and the success of their records, Brian persuaded Capitol records to spend 50,000 dollars on what they called a 'crash publicity programme'. Five million 'The Beatles Are Coming' posters were plastered throughout the States, every disc jockey got a copy of every Beatles record brought out in Britain, they gave out a million copies of a four-page newspaper on the Beatles and they photographed their top executives wearing Beatle wigs.

'There was a lot of hype,' said Voyle Gilmore, Vice-President of Capitol records. 'But all the hype in the world isn't going to sell a bad product.'

The Ed Sullivan Show couldn't cope with the demand for tickets – 50,000 applied for

January 1964: dinner at the George V hotel in Paris to celebrate the news that 'I Want to Hold Your Hand' had got to No. 1 in the USA. Brian Epstein, naturally enough, dons a chamber pot. George Martin is on the right, his wife Judy, on the left.

728 seats. Sid Bernstein could have sold tickets for Carnegie Hall at twice the price. 'Even Mrs Nelson Rockefeller couldn't buy a ticket. I had to give her mine.'

Brian was offered another New York date, this time at Madison Square Garden, at double the fee for Carnegie Hall, but it was too late to fit it in.

As the Beatles left London Airport, on Pan Am flight 101, on 7 February 1964, station WMCA in New York made the first of a series of announcements. 'It is now 6.30 a.m. Beatle time. They left London 30 minutes ago. They're out over the Atlantic Ocean heading for New York. The temperature is 32 Beatle degrees.'

On the plane the Beatles were nervous. They hadn't heard details of all the promotion that was being done, but they had read reports of people criticizing them and saying they were ugly.

Cyn was on the plane with John, the first and only time she went on tour with them. The un-famous George Harrison was there from the *Liverpool Echo*. He thought he'd retired from national news for good, when, at the age of 45, in 1954, he'd left Fleet Street and London for Liverpool. Now he was setting off on his first of four coast-to-coast trips with a group he'd once refused to write about. He says they were all very dubious about what sort of reception they would get. 'They all said to me, "America's got everything, George, so why should they want us?"' People always call George by his Christian name in his stories.

George Harrison, the famous one, said he was feeling ill. 'I was worrying about my hair as well. I'd washed it, but when it dried it had gone up a bit.'

'We did all feel a bit sick that first time,' says Ringo. 'We always did, though we never showed it, before anything big. We'd felt a bit sick before the Palladium Show. Going to the States was a big step. People said just because we were popular in Britain, why should we be there.'

Neil and Mal were busy on the plane, forging Beatle signatures on photographs to give to any fans. Brian was also busy. Several British businessmen, having failed to get a second with him in London, had decided that 30,000 feet above the Atlantic was the best place to get him. They sent little notes to him, asking if he would endorse their products. They were all politely refused.

But all the doubts were swept away the minute they saw Kennedy Airport, when they landed at 1.35 in the afternoon. Over 10,000 screaming teenagers were choking the airport. They were all singing 'We Love You Beatles, Oh Yes We Do', a song, or at least a doggerel, peculiar to American Beatle fans.

Capitol was still pursuing its crash publicity, and handed each person who got off the aeroplane a 'Beatle Kit', complete with wig, autographed photo and a button saying 'I Like the Beatles'.

They fought their way eventually to the airport press lounge and faced the biggest press conference they'd ever had. John shouted at them all to shurrup. Everyone applauded him.

'Will you sing something for us?'

'We need money first,' said John.

'How do you account for your success?'

'We have a press agent.'

'What is your ambition?'

'To come to America.'

'Do you hope to get haircuts?'

'We had one yesterday.'

'Do you hope to take anything home with you?'

'The Rockefeller Centre.'

'Are you part of a social rebellion against the older generation?'

'It's a dirty lie.'

'What about the movement in Detroit to stamp out Beatles?'

'We have a campaign to stamp out Detroit.'

'What do you think of Beethoven?'

'I love him,' said Ringo. 'Especially his poems.'

It was chaos at the Plaza Hotel, a hotel that prides itself on its discreet exclusiveness and hadn't checked the professions of the five English businessmen who'd booked some months ago. When a Plaza executive saw his hotel besieged by thousands of screaming teenagers he went on radio and offered the Beatles to any New York hotel who wanted them.

Not that the Beatles were grateful. 'What made you pick the Plaza?' a reporter asked George. 'I didn't. Our manager did. All I can tell you is, I don't like the food.'

George was by this time ill in bed and looked like missing the Ed Sullivan Show. Neil stood in for the rehearsal, but George managed the show, filled up with dope. The screams echoed across America. The show had a record audience of 73 million.

In New York, during the show, not one hubcap from a car was stolen. Throughout America, so it was reported, not one major crime was committed by a teenager.

Elvis Presley sent them a congratulatory telegram. Next morning the *Herald Tribune* said they were '75 per cent publicity, 20 per cent haircut and 5 per cent lilting lament'. The *Daily News* said: 'The Presleyan gyrations and caterwauling were but lukewarm dandelion tea compared to the 100-proof elixir served up by the Beatles.'

Every paper gave them huge coverage. The analyses were long and complicated. There was another huge press conference. 'Do you have a leading lady for your film yet?' 'We're trying for the Queen,' said George. 'She sells.'

Billy Graham said he'd broken his strict rule and watched TV on the Sabbath, just to see them. 'They're a passing phase,' he said. 'All are symptoms of the uncertainty of the times and the confusion about us.' Then they set off by train for Washington.

'What happened in the States was just like Britain,' says Ringo, 'only ten times bigger. So I suppose it wasn't like Britain at all. That first Washington crowd was 20,000. We'd only been used to 2,000 at home.'

The Coliseum, where the Washington concert was held, their first one on American soil, is normally used as a boxing ring or baseball field. The Beatles were put on a revolving stage, so the whole audience could see. It meant they were hit from all angles by jelly babies.

'It was terrible,' says George. 'They hurt. They don't have soft jelly babies in America, but hard jelly beans like bullets. Some newspaper had dug out the old joke, which we'd forgotten about, when John once said I'd eaten all his jelly babies. Everywhere we went I got them thrown at me.'

Sir Alec Douglas-Home, the British Prime Minister, was due to arrive in Washington the same day. He put his arrival back to the day after, to avoid the Beatle chaos.

The Beatles meet Cassius Clay, as was, in February 1964 at his training camp for the world title in Miami, Florida, USA. The first of many posed pictures with world celebrities.

That evening they accepted their first, and last, embassy invitation. They'd already turned down dinner with Lady Dixon, wife of the British ambassador in Paris.

'We always tried to get out of those crap things,' said George. 'But that time we got caught. They were always full of snobby people who really loathe our type, but want to see us because we're rich and famous. It's all hypocrisy. They were just trying to get publicity for the embassy.'

Reports of what exactly happened at the Washington embassy party vary in detail, but Michael Braun, in his paperback book on the Beatles' early tours (*Love Me Do*, Penguin, 1964), says that it started off amicably enough.

'Hello John,' said Sir David Ormsby-Gore (now Lord Harlech) when they arrived.

'I'm not John,' said John. 'I'm Charlie. That's John.'

'Hello John,' said the ambassador to George.

'I'm not John,' said George. 'I'm Frank. That's John.'

'Oh dear,' said the ambassador.

Several elderly ladies, with glasses of drink in their hands, accosted the Beatles and demanded autographs. Officious junior officials started pushing them around, insisting they spoke to people and gave autographs. 'Sign this,' one said to John, who refused. 'You'll sign this and like it.' A young lady guest walked up to Ringo, removed a pair of nail scissors from her purse and started snipping off locks of his hair. John left early, but the others stayed on and saw it out. The ambassador and his wife said how sorry they were.

Even Brian's charm hadn't managed to calm things down. 'Both the ambassador and his wife were extremely nice,' he said later. 'But the Beatles loathed that reception. Since then they have refused every invitation of that type.'

Sir Alec Douglas-Home at last arrived to meet President Johnson. 'I liked your advance party,' said the President. 'But don't you feel they need haircuts.'

The Beatles started back for New York and their Carnegie Hall concert, under the usual barrage of press, TV and fans. The American wheeler-dealers were now out in strength, trying to get contracts for Beatles products, at any price. It was estimated that in 1964, 50 million dollars worth of Beatle goods was sold in the States. Several unauthorized tape-recorded interviews, which no one realized had been done, were brought out as LP records, billed heavily under the Beatles name, much to Brian's annoyance.

Over 6,000 were in the audience for each of the two Carnegie Hall concerts. Sid Bernstein had to turn down David Niven and Shirley MacLaine. Hysterical screams greeted and accompanied the Beatles' two appearances, each only 25 minutes long, so the papers reported next day.

Sandi Stewart, the 15-year-old fan from New Hampshire, made it, but she didn't think the screams were all that great. 'That first concert wasn't all that wild, I mean there wasn't much screaming, nothing like later concerts which were completely wild. I remember being very annoyed with George that first time, perhaps that was why I didn't like him. He seemed to be standing in the way of Ringo and we couldn't see him. We all shouted at him to get out of the way and let us see Ringo.

'You really do believe they can see you, just you alone, when they're up on the stage. That's why you scream, so they'll notice you. I always felt John could see me. It was like a dream. Just me and John together and no one else.

'Even when you're screaming, you can still hear. All the reporters in the papers always said you couldn't hear anything with all the noise, but you could, even when you were screaming. Their sexy movements made you scream even louder.

'They were being sexy with you personally. It was an outlet. But I don't think many girls got sexually excited, not at concerts anyway. I didn't myself.'

The Beatles then went by plane from New York down to Miami for the second Ed Sullivan Show. The pilot wore a Beatle wig. They met Cassius Clay, who said he was the greatest, but they were the most beautiful.

It was getting close to 25 February, George's 21st birthday. Even though Sandi Stewart didn't like George so much, she still decided to send him a present. 'We found out he was staying at the Deauville Hotel in Miami. We sent a registered parcel, figuring that was very clever, as he'd have to sign for it and we'd get his autograph. But we didn't.

'It didn't really matter. John was the one I was in love with. I gave him three whole years of my life from then on.'

24

BRITAIN AND BACK TO THE USA

Back in Liverpool, the Beatles' old schools were getting some strange requests. Teenagers from all over the world were writing for any old desks belonging to the Beatles, or old caps or old exercise books. There were soon scores of signed exercise books in circulation, far more than they could ever possibly have had.

'We were getting these very funny letters from girls, mainly in America,' said Mr Pobjoy of Quarry Bank. 'Asking if our boys would write to them. I thought they were howlingly funny. For the boys' amusement as well as mine, I used to read them out in the hall after morning prayers.

'The boys enjoyed them so much they were convinced for a long time that I was making them all up, but I gather that quite a few boys in the end did write to the wretched girls.'

The Beatles' parents were also being contacted by a lot of American fans, some of them turning up on their door step, having forced their parents to stop off on their European grand tours to fit in the Dingle and Woolton.

'I'd usually ask the ones who'd come a long way if they'd like some tea,' says Jim McCartney. 'When they said yes, I'd say, there's the kitchen. They'd go in and start screaming and shouting because they'd recognize the kitchen from photographs. They knew more about me than I did myself. Fans would make very good detectives.'

On George's 21st birthday, Mrs Harrison was unable to find room in her house for all the cards and presents. They came in mail vans by special deliveries.

Elsie and Harry, Ringo's parents, like the others, began to find themselves surrounded and barricaded in their own home, while fans camped outside and stole bits of the door or chalked on the walls.

'The first time I really noticed how well they were known,' says Elsie, 'was when we woke up one morning to find a bus-load of fans knocking at the front door. It was seven o'clock

Opposite: Remember Hush Puppies? They were always smart, back in the1960s, but not quite as smart or hilarious as the Beatles became after their first film, *A Hard Day's Night*, world-premiered at the London Pavilion on 6 July 1964.

on a Sunday morning. They'd travelled overnight from London. Well, what could I do. I fetched them all in and gave them tea and biscuits. I thought it was marvellous. All that way, just for Ritchie. They never ate anything. They wrapped them up to take back as souvenirs.

'They used to climb over the backyard wall, or sleep in the street for days. They were physical wrecks, most of them, but they were just too excited to rest or eat. They'd ask, which is his chair? I'd say, sit on them all love, he has. They always wanted to go up and see his bed as well. They'd lie on it, moaning.'

Cyn and Julian had by this time moved out of Mimi's house and into a place of their own. She was still avoiding the press as much as possible. 'A gang of reporters trailed me round for days, when they found out who I was. They cornered me one day when I was visiting my mother in Hoylake. This reporter chased me all over the place and besieged me in a shop. I managed to dart out the back and into a fruit shop next door, where I hid for half an hour till he'd gone.'

The Beatles came back from America to the usual hysterical scenes. The Prime Minister, Sir Alec Douglas-Home, called them 'our best exports' and 'a useful contribution to the balance of payments'. Mr Wilson, leader of the Labour Party and a Liverpool MP, didn't like the inference that a 14th Earl should be trying to cash in on the Liverpool Beatles. 'The Tories are trying to make the Beatles their secret weapon,' he said.

They were invited to dinner by the Master and dons of Brasenose College, Oxford, where they asked for jam butties. A Roman Catholic bishop called them a 'menace', but Prince Philip met them and thought them good chaps. He had a chat with John about books. They met Mr Wilson at last, at a Variety Club presentation, and called him Mr Dobson.

John's first book came out in March. It was called *In His Own Write*, a title suggested by Paul. They discarded another idea, *In His Own Write and Draw,* as the pun (right-hand drawer) was too complicated. Most literary experts and most publishers said it was a stunt that would fail – how could a beat group player write anything that was any good. It went to the top of the bestseller list, beating James Bond. The *Times Literary Supplement* said: 'It is worth the attention of anyone who fears for the impoverishment of the English language and the British imagination.' John was invited to be guest of honour at a Foyles literary lunch. He didn't speak, except to mutter 'Thank you, you've got a lucky face', and got a few boos for not doing so. But Brian Epstein made a very nice speech.

On 24 March, their sixth single, 'Can't Buy Me Love', came out. It went straight to number one. It also went immediately to number one in America. In Britain and America, before it had come out, the advance sales were 3 million, a world record. Not long after, they had the top six records on the United States hit parade.

Ringo was elected a Vice-President of Leeds University in preference to a former Lord Chief Justice. Madame Tussauds put wax effigies of all four Beatles on show. Paul Johnson, in the *New Statesman,* did an article headed 'The Menace of Beatlism'. A writer in the *Sunday Telegraph* said that the group would break up, because eventually they would all get married and 'the chance of four random women liking one another or even being able to get on with one another will be small indeed.'

In March they started shooting their first film. The title, *A Hard Day's Night,* wasn't decided until it was almost finished and Ringo came out with the phrase, though John had used it earlier in a poem.

Paul was by this time going out with Jane Asher, daughter of a Wimpole Street doctor. On the first day of the film, George met Pattie Boyd. Like Jane Asher, she has a a South of England background, completely different from the background of the girls in the other two Beatles' lives.

Pattie was working as a model, mainly in magazines, and did a TV commercial for Smiths Crisps, which was very successful. This was directed by Dick Lester, which was how she came to be auditioned for a part in the Beatles' film.

'I met them and they said hello. I couldn't believe it. They were so like how I'd imagined them to be. They were just like pictures of themselves coming to life. George hardly said hello. But the others came and chatted to us.

'When we started filming, I could feel George looking at me and I was a bit embarrassed. Ringo seemed the nicest and easiest to talk to, and so did Paul. But I was terrified of John. After that first day's shooting, I asked them all for their autograph, except John. I was too scared.

'When I was asking George for his, I said could he sign it for my two sisters as well. He signed his name and put two kisses each for them, but under mine he put seven kisses. I thought he must like me a little.'

He did and they started going out. 'I took him to Mummy's, then he took me to see this house in Esher he was interested in. I thought it was lovely. The next weekend was Easter. I went with George and John and Cynthia to Ireland for the weekend on a private plane. It was a dead secret, but it got out and there were hordes of pressmen at the hotel.

'This was my first experience of that sort of thing. The manager tapped their phones and we could hear them sending back the most awful things to Fleet Street. When we went out, they all followed us with cameras.

'It was impossible to get out. In the end Cyn and I had to dress as maids. They took us out a back way, put us in a laundry basket, and we were driven to the airport in a laundry van.'

Naturally, with all the publicity and gossip interest in her, she was offered even more modelling jobs. 'I took a lot, the ones I fancied, but George said I shouldn't. He didn't like it. They were just wanting me for the wrong reasons.'

She was very worried by the threatening letters and even physical attacks all the girlfriends and wives were getting from girl fans. 'The letters upset me a lot. They were really nasty and said awful things, especially from the States. I used to worry that perhaps I was nasty. They always said they were really George's girlfriend, I'd better leave him alone or they'd get me.'

They moved into George's new house in Esher. 'We lived together for about a year before we got married. My mother knew, but she never mentioned it.'

In the summer of 1964, the tours started again. They went to Europe first of all, starting with Denmark. In Amsterdam a crowd of 100,000 turned up in the streets to see them. Girls were diving into canals to get near them. Then they went to Hong Kong, Australia and New Zealand.

The American tours had, and always will have, the most publicity associated with them, simply because they were beating the Americans at what the Americans had always been leading the world in. But, surprisingly, the biggest ever crowd to turn out to watch the Beatles was in Adelaide. This was simply to watch the Beatles arrive. Every newspaper that day put the figure at over 300,000. Numbers like this never turned out to see them in New York, or even in Liverpool.

Back in London, on 6 July, *A Hard Day's Night* had its premiere, in front of Princess Margaret and Lord Snowdon. The LP of the film came out the following month.

On 19 August 1964 they left for their first major American tour. The trip in February had been a short, two-week trip, with only a couple of concerts and TV shows.

Not usually known for their fishing, the Beatles relax with some rods in Seattle during their US tour, August 1964.

This tour, in August and September, covered in all 32 days. It was the longest, biggest and most exhausting tour they ever did. They travelled in all 22,441 miles, spending a total of 60 hours, 25 minutes flying. They visited 24 cities in the United States and Canada. They gave a total of 30 performances, plus one charity show. 'During that American tour,' says Mal, the road manager, 'each of us lost one and a half stone in sweat.'

Norman Weiss of GAC, their American agent, spent six months planning this tour. 'It took about as much planning as the invasion of Normandy. Millions and millions of dollars must have changed hands. It would be impossible to work out what it all cost, from the Beatles' fees down to all the hot dogs sold and films used up.

'We could easily have charged three times the price and still sold out, but Brian said it was unfair to the fans. We had it written into all contracts, stating what the prices had to be. We dictated all the contracts, set the terms ourselves. Every promoter agreed, thankful to be putting them on.

'The Beatles and Elvis are both in show business. After that, any comparison is just a joke. No one, before or since, has had the crowds the Beatles had.'

Records were broken everywhere, but to the Beatles themselves, it all became meaningless. It was just like it had been yesterday. Even the questions were always the same – what did they think had caused their success and when did they think the bubble would burst. They almost got to screaming point, with the endless repetition.

They fled to a remote country town for a day's rest and the locals very kindly kept out of the way. But as they were boarding their plane to take off again, the sheriff and other town dignitaries could be seen coming across the tarmac towards them. Derek Taylor, the Beatles' press officer, was sent out to see what the locals wanted. They said they wanted autographs and photographs standing with the Beatles, which was the least they could do, as they'd been so kind and left them alone.

'I went back on to the plane to ask the boys,' says Derek. 'Paul was sitting beside the window, looking at them. He was smiling like mad at them, nodding his head wildly up and down, but he was saying to me, "Get out there quick. Tell them *we* want to go out and meet them, but *you* won't let us because we're too tired. Go on."'

Even George Harrison, the *Liverpool Echo* one, became numbed by it all. 'But I'll never forget this big noise from Kansas City coming to see Brian when we were in San Francisco. Kansas City wasn't on the tour. He was a millionaire, the owner of the local football club or something. He said he'd promised Kansas City that he would get the Beatles for them.

'Brian said no. They couldn't fit it in. This bloke said would 100,000 dollars change their minds. Brian said he'd go and ask the boys. They were all sitting playing cards and hardly looked up. Brian told them about the offer of 100,000, which is £30,000 in anybody's money. They said it's up to you, Brian, and went on playing.

'Brian went back and told the man he was terribly sorry. They couldn't give up a day off. The man said he'd promised Kansas City and he couldn't go back without them. He tore up the cheque for 100,000 dollars. Then he wrote out one for 150,000 dollars. This was the highest fee that had ever been offered to any artist in America. He was offering them £50,000 for 35 minutes. Brian could see the prestige value of beating all American artists would be fantastic. So he said all right. The Beatles didn't look up when Brian told them.

'So the bloke went home, dead happy. But he knew he couldn't possibly make any money. The ground wasn't big enough to get back anything like he'd had to pay, but he'd kept his promise to Kansas City.'

The pillowslips on which they slept in their Kansas City hotel were later sold to two Chicago businessmen for £375. They cut them into 160,000 one-inch squares, mounted them on certificates saying whose bed they had come from, and sold them at one dollar each. A New York syndicate offered Brian £3,715,000 for the Beatles, but he turned them down.

During all the shouting and screaming and boasting of all their record-breaking tours, in Britain and America, the Beatles were crouching somewhere inside the giant piece of machinery that was transporting them round and round the world. They'd retreated inside it in 1963, forced by all the pressures, and remained there, hermetically sealed.

They were trapped in their dressing room before a performance. Then, afterwards,

The Beatles in concert in the USA, August 1964, when their touring days were in full swing. During all the shouting and screaming and boasting of record-breaking tours, the Beatles were trapped somewhere inside the giant piece of machinery that was transporting them round and round the world.

there was the mad dash, guarded by hordes of police and bodyguards, to the hotel. There they stayed, with the outside world locked out, till the time came for the next move. They never went out in the street, to a restaurant or for a walk. Neil and Mal serviced them, bringing sandwiches, ciggies and drinks. Out of jealousy, and sometimes out of fear of being left unprotected, they wouldn't let Mal or Neil go out either. So they all sat in their hotel bedrooms, smoking, playing cards, playing their guitars, putting in the hours. Earning £1,000 or £10,000 or £100,000 for one-night stands was meaningless. Being rich and powerful and famous enough to enter any door was pointless. They were trapped.

For a long time, of course, there was great excitement. They had waited so long for this. They'd been playing for seven years together and getting nowhere, which at least meant they were physically and emotionally prepared for the terrible conditions of one-night

stands. Even the one-night stands weren't as strenuous as the Hamburg clubs, where they'd really learned to churn it out endlessly.

After the first record, so many stages came one after the other so quickly that they never got bored or complained about the slowness, at least for some time. They all remember the excitement of going from one peak to another. Getting a record in the charts, then a number one, then another, then TV shows, the Palladium, the Royal Variety Show and then, America.

Although John, Paul and George were not taken in or affected by all the publicity, they considered themselves good. They knew their music was good and were annoyed when anyone didn't take it seriously. They didn't for one minute consider, as so many people did, that they would just disappear. At last they were in, and they couldn't see any reason why they shouldn't stay in. This probably explains part of their attitude to the press. They didn't feel grateful or in any way humble. They didn't care about being funny or rude because they didn't consider they owed anything to anybody.

Only Ringo was in any way rubbing his eyes. It had all suddenly happened to him. He joined them, then immediately they were away.

'None of us ever worried about things like the future. I've always just taken chances myself and been lucky. I was lucky to get an apprenticeship when I did. I've always had a few bob in my pocket. But I always thought it was bound to come to an end some time.

'There were good nights and bad nights on the tours. But they were really all the same. The only fun part was the hotels in the evening, smoking pot and that.'

25

THE END OF TOURING

Throughout the next two years, 1965 and 1966, their life was dominated by touring, which really meant no life at all. They averaged three long tours a year – one British, one American and one other foreign tour taking in several countries. They produced around three singles a year and one LP. They also aimed to do one film a year, but after their second film, *Help!*, in 1965, they came to a halt. It wasn't until the end of this two year grind that their lives and their work began to settle down into new patterns.

The details of all their tours are in newspaper files somewhere, for anyone mad enough to want to look them up. The Beatles certainly can't remember. As always, they can only remember the laughs, such as their MBE.

On 12 June 1965 it was announced that the Beatles were to be made Members of the Order of the British Empire. There were immediate protests, from members of the House of Lords to ancient wartime fire watchers, who felt their MBE had been cheapened. A retired Colonel said he wasn't going to give the Labour Party a £11,000 bequest after all, or his twelve military medals. MBE medals were sent back from all over the world.

Brian was very pleased about the honour. He said later he never had any doubt that the Beatles would accept, but John says he seriously thought about saying no. Today his MBE sits on the TV in Mimi's bungalow.

'We thought being offered the MBE was as funny as everybody else thought it was. Why? What for? We didn't believe it. It was a part we didn't want.

'We all met and agreed it was daft. What do you think, we all said. Let's not. Then it all just seemed part of the game we'd agreed to play, like getting the Ivor Novello awards. We'd nothing to lose, except that bit of you that said you didn't believe in it. We agreed in order to annoy even more the people who were annoyed, like John Gordon. We were just getting at the people who believe in such things.

Opposite: In June 1966, the Beatles flew to Tokyo for their one and only series of appearances in Japan. For this event the Japanese organizers produced the most lavish and exhaustive programme of all their concerts anywhere.

'All we did when we were waiting in the Palace was giggle. We collapsed, the whole thing was so funny. There was this guardsman telling us how to march, how many steps, and how to curtsey when we met the Queen. We knew in our hearts she was just some woman, yet we were going through with it. We'd agreed to it.

'I really think the Queen believes in it all. She must. I don't believe in John Lennon, Beatle, being any different from anyone else, because I know he's not. I'm just a feller. But I'm sure the Queen must think she's different.

'I always hated all the social things. All the horrible events and presentations we had to go to. All false. You could see right through them all, and all the people there. I despised them. Perhaps it was partly from class. No it wasn't. It was because they really *were* all false.'

Some of the 1965–6 tours have to be mentioned, if only as a brief record, especially their two other American tours. Their third American tour began on 13 August 1965. It was decided to keep it to half the length of the previous one, as that had been too exhausting. This tour covered 17 days and they were insured for a million pounds, which was what the last tour had taken. It made even more money than the previous one, though it was half the length, because they concentrated on baseball grounds, which they had pioneered the time before.

The biggest event of this tour of America was on 15 August 1965. This was when they played at the Shea Stadium, New York. 'Over 55,000 people saw that show,' says Sid Bernstein. 'We took 304,000 dollars, the greatest gross ever in the history of show business.'

This is still a world record. It wasn't beaten during their subsequent American tour. Out of the 304,000 dollars, the Beatles got 160,000 dollars. Over 30,000 dollars went on the rent of the Stadium for the night. There were 1,300 police on duty, which cost 14,000. Insurance came to 11,000. After advertising, publicity and other expenses, Sid Bernstein's profit on the evening came to 7,000 dollars.

'I could still do it again today. The Beatles are as popular in the States as they ever were. I've offered them one million dollars for two shows at the Shea Stadium. That offer still stands. It would have to be exclusive in the USA. One million dollars. That's my offer.'

Exactly a year later, in August 1966, they did their fourth and final American tour. This was again a shorter one, but it made most money of all. Nat Weiss, who had been appointed head of Nemperor Artists in New York, helped to organize it. He had been practising as a divorce attorney in New York for 15 years when he met Brian Epstein, socially, and through him became interested in pop music. In June 1966 Brian decided to bring all the NEMS bits and pieces in America under one office. Nemperor was named after the cable address of Nems.

It was just before this tour that John's remark about Jesus Christ hit America. He had originally said that the Beatles 'were now more popular than Christ' several months previously in a Maureen Cleave interview in the London *Evening Standard*. No one had objected or remarked on it publicly. But when it was reproduced and went round America, out of context, it caused a furore.

'A friend rang me to say they were burning Beatle records in Nashville, Tennessee,' says Nat Weiss. 'I rang Brian and said I thought it serious enough to warrant his arrival in New York.'

Brian was very worried, as the Ku Klux Klan came out and Beatle effigies were burned throughout the Bible Belt. He considered cancelling several appearances, even though it would have meant paying back one million dollars. 'I didn't want any chance of the boys being harmed, whatever the cost.' But the promoters and mayors and local officials said there would be much more trouble from fans if any concerts were cancelled. A slight retraction was put out from John, saying he hadn't meant it, and the tour went off as planned. The concerts in the Bible Belt were the best of all.

Their other foreign tours during these two years included France, Italy, Spain and Germany (a huge welcome in Hamburg). From Germany, in June 1966, they flew to Tokyo for their one and only Japanese series of concerts. The Japanese Beatle fans turned out to be the most knowledgeable of all, judging by the programme they produced for the concerts. This was the most lavish and exhaustive programme from any of their concerts anywhere. It contained, amongst other academic information, the title of every song they'd ever sung up to that time and its chart position. Nobody in London had ever worked it out in such detail. Brian kept a copy of it in his desk as a work of reference.

From Japan, they returned home via Manila in the Philippines, and wished they hadn't. This visit resulted in the first and only scene of real violence throughout their touring career. All those times they'd nearly been killed in Britain and America was due to over-affection. In Manila they were kicked and punched by officials and police. This was the result of a supposed act of discourtesy towards the President's wife. She expected them to turn up at the Palace after she had invited them. They said they'd never been invited. The President's wife was very hurt.

In Britain, Beatlemania hardly abated. The switchboard at University College Hospital was jammed when Ringo had his tonsils out. Hourly bulletins were issued. Thousands of fans wrote asking for his old tonsils. Ringo announced that no one was getting them. They were to be burned.

In October 1965, the Queen and Prince Philip were on tour in Canada. One of the biggest stories of the tour in the British press was when Prince Philip was quoted as saying that the Beatles 'were on the wane'. This got headlines everywhere. The London *Evening Standard* did a poll to find out if it was true – five out of seven said it wasn't true. A couple of days later, Brian Epstein got a personal telegram from Prince Philip in which he explained that what he'd really said was 'I think the Beatles are away.'

It shows that famous personages were still coming out with Beatle references, and were very worried if they came out wrong. But more than that, it shows there was now a bit of wishful thinking around. Everybody was sure the Beatles must be on the wane. They couldn't possibly keep up the same pace.

But they were waxing as strongly as ever. After each wave of bubble-pricking, they brought out yet another record that went straight to number one. In December 1965, when 'Day Tripper' came out and went direct to number one, it was their tenth consecutive number-one record in the British charts.

That same month, December 1965, they started what was to become, although no one said so at the time, their last British tour. They did one concert after that, on 1 May 1966, at Wembley, which is the last live concert the Beatles have done in Britain.

At long last, one of their singles didn't immediately reach number one, although after a week it did. This was 'Paperback Writer' in June 1966. Even more surprisingly, because it was much better, 'Penny Lane' and 'Strawberry Fields', in February 1967, didn't get to number one at all. Perhaps by that time the fans knew they were never going to see the Beatles singing in the flesh again.

Their last live appearance anywhere in the world was at the end of their American tour, on 29 August 1966.

'During that last show in San Francisco,' says Nat Weiss, 'Brian was very sad and almost pathetic. It was the first time I'd ever seen him pathetic. He suddenly said, what do I do now? What happens to my life? That's it. Should I go back to school and learn something else?

'He was obviously greatly saddened. Then he took hold of himself and said no. He *would* carry on and do something.'

There was no denial or confirmation about giving up touring when they came back to England. This led to some confusion, and rumours began spreading that they were splitting up.

The fan club and *Beatles Monthly* were swamped by letters from fans. Mrs Harrison, George's mother, got so fed up answering the same query that she had several hundred copies of a letter duplicated, saying they were *not* splitting. She said they were very busy on an LP, which would keep them going all over Christmas. 'So I think this proves that they have no plans what-so-ever for parting company. All my best wishes. Louise Harrison. (Mrs)'

They had decided some time before to stop touring, but it was difficult, because of contractual arrangements, to say so straight away. Arthur Howes, for example, had been hoping for another British tour. British fans had felt out of it for a long time. Since their first number one days, they had been seen live by far more people in the States, on their four tours before huge open-air audiences, than on their seven tours round the smaller British halls and theatres.

There was no definite agreement with Arthur Howes that they had to get out of, just the natural expectation he had that they'd go on for a bit longer.

'In this field,' he says, 'I look upon the life of an artist as five years. I know, because that's how it always happens. After five years, their generation has grown up and there are new artists with new audiences. The Beatles are different. The Beatles will last for ever. They've no need to worry. But I did, when they stopped touring in 1965. They didn't even do three years of touring.'

In Britain a full house at the biggest theatres in Manchester, Birmingham or Glasgow is only around the 2,500 mark. The biggest theatre in Britain, of the type used for packaged shows, is the Hammersmith Odeon, which seats 4,000.

Even ten full houses in Hammersmith still wouldn't equal a full house at the Shea Stadium, which, as we have seen, attracted 55,000 for the Beatles' first concert there.

Because of the high percentage the Beatles took – 50 per cent in the end – and also because they toured for such a comparatively short time, Mr Howes made more from touring Cliff Richard than he made from the Beatles. Between October 1958 and February 1963, Cliff Richard did eleven tours with Arthur Howes. Between February 1963 and December 1965, the Beatles did seven tours, six of them with Arthur Howes.

'The biggest thing the Beatles did was to open up the American market to all British artists. Nobody had ever been able to get in before the Beatles. They alone did it. I had brought over lots of American stars, but nobody had gone over there. They just weren't interested. By opening up the States, the Beatles made an enormous amount of money for this country.'

John and Paul looking exhausted after a long journey to Tokyo, via an unscheduled nine-hour stop in Alaska, in June 1966, for concerts at the Nippon Budokan Hall. For a long time, the Beatles had felt tired and disillusioned with what they were doing – dragging themselves round the world and performing on stage in the same old way.

Once it was made clear to Arthur Howes and to various other people that touring was over, the Beatles let it be known publicly. One of the reasons given was that their music had developed so much, using full orchestras and electronic devices, that they couldn't possibly perform it on stage any more.

This is true, but the most important reason was that for a long, long time they had hated what they were doing. They disliked dragging round the world, appearing publicly in a glass box like a peep show. They disliked performing on stage in the same old way. They thought it was a farce, a mockery.

Neil and Mal, their road managers, disliked the tensions, the panic and chaos of it all.

'Open-air concerts in the States were terrible,' says Mal. 'We were in this baseball field once. There they were, stuck out on their own in the middle of the field with 30,000 kids screaming and waiting to hear them. I said to the promoter, where's the outlet, chief? He said, what. They play guitars, don't they? He hadn't realized they used *electric* guitars. We had a right panic getting electricians to lay on wires in time.

'When it looked like rain in the open air I used to be scared stiff. Rain on the wires and everybody would have been blown up, yet if they'd stopped the show, the kids would have stampeded.'

'We learned always to go on at the very last minute, if not later,' says Neil. 'If we went too early they just got mobbed on the way from the dressing room. But if they had to run like mad after they were supposed to be on, people would get out of the way and let them through. We did this with our first Ed Sullivan show in New York. He was sweating like a pig, convinced we were going to be late. It was a live show as well. He blamed me for it all, for just doing it.'

'Touring was dangerous sometimes,' says Ringo, 'but we never thought about it. A plane did catch fire once in Texas and scared everyone. We flew from Liverpool to London once with a window open. We were a bit worried when our death was predicted on a plane in the States. That wasn't nice.'

This was by a woman who had predicted President Kennedy's death. Some of the other acts refused to go on the Beatles' plane. Mal wrote his last letter to his wife, Lil, convinced he was going to die.

'There was one near escape at the Cow Palace in the States,' says Ringo. 'The crowds surged forward and got on the limousine we were supposed to be in. They squashed the roof in. We could have been killed, but we were safe in an ambulance with seven sailors. That's how they were smuggling us that time.

'It was just one long hustle. You'd have a hustle with the police, then the theatre people, then the hotel people. We always thought we were safe when we got into our hotel rooms, but we'd have to contend with the hotel staff as well, wanting autographs. You could see them thinking why not, what's the matter with you, you've only worked half an hour today. But we'd probably travelled 2,000 miles since the last half-hour concert and not eaten or slept properly for two weeks.

'The American police could be as bad as anybody, demanding autographs. I caught one once going through our pockets.'

George says that as early as the first big American tour, in August 1964, they were all beginning to dislike it. Even making the tours shorter, didn't make them any more enjoyable.

'It was like the end of a cycle. In Hamburg we had played for up to eight hours at a stretch, loving it all, getting to know each other and what we could do. It was a real freak-out in those days, the things we did were really wild.

'Back in Liverpool we were doing shorter hours, but it was still as enjoyable. We were part of the audience. We lived our lives with them. We never rehearsed an act. We had to get more polished eventually, but the Cavern was fantastic. It was so spontaneous, all jokes and laughs. It was so intimate.

'Then came touring which was great at first, doing an even shorter, more polished act and working out new songs. But it got played out. We got in a rut, going round the world. It was a different audience each day, but we were doing the same things. There was no satisfaction in it. Nobody could hear. It was just a bloody big row. We got worse as musicians, playing the same old junk every day. There was no satisfaction at all.'

'It was wrecking our playing,' says Ringo. 'The noise of the people just drowned anything. Eventually I just used to play the off beat, instead of a constant beat. I couldn't hear myself half the time, even on the amps, with all the noise.

'We'd get put in silly positions in the halls so we'd be too far away from each other. On stage we used to play things faster than on the records, mainly because we couldn't hear what we were doing. I used to come in at the wrong time sometimes because I'd no idea where we were at. We just used to mime half the time to the songs, especially if your throat was feeling rough.

'In the end no one enjoyed touring. You can't really. Once you've got to manufacture it, it doesn't work. You've got to give to receive. Some nights we'd feel it had been terrible. We didn't give anything. That was when we decided we should give it up, before others started disliking it as well.'

'When we were away from it for a while,' says John, 'it was like the school holidays. You hadn't done any work for a bit and you'd just remember the laughs. You'd quite look forward to it again. Until you got back and were fed up.

'It's like the army, whatever the army's like. One big sameness which you have to go through. One big mass. I can't remember any tours.

'We've had enough of performing for ever. I can't imagine any reason which would make us do any sort of tour ever again.'

Paul says they would do a live stage show, if they could think of a way of doing a stage show that was completely different. But nobody can think of a new way. It looks as if Sid Bernstein will be keeping his million dollars.

It was a brave step, in some ways, to give up doing what had made their name. Very few people, certainly in show business, have given up at the height of their adulation. People often say they intend to give up the public before the public gives up them, but they usually do it too late.

The Beatles had no hesitation. They saw it as the end of Chapter One. Being naive and simple, they did it without knowing what Chapter Two was going to be. All they knew was that it didn't include the drag of touring and the discomfort of Beatlemania.

26

THE DEATH OF BRIAN EPSTEIN

It was the end of a chapter when the Beatles stopped touring, as Brian Epstein had realized that time in San Francisco. But Brian was resolved, so he told Nat Weiss, to go on and do something else. Which he did, for a time.

NEMS Enterprises had grown into a huge organization, handling many other artists apart from the Beatles – Cilla Black, Gerry and the Pacemakers and many others. They moved into the agency business, they took on a theatre – the Saville – as well as continuing and expanding as artists' managers.

Although his staff had grown so much since the Liverpool days, the more important personnel were still old friends and contacts from Liverpool. Alistair Taylor, his assistant on the counter at NEMS, who had signed the original contract with the Beatles, rejoined the firm in 1963, after a spell with Pye records.

More important, Geoffrey Ellis and Peter Brown, his two oldest Liverpool friends, also joined NEMS Enterprises in London.

Geoffrey Ellis, the ex-Oxford insurance man in New York, saw a lot of Brian on his American trips and was eventually persuaded to join NEMS in London. His legal knowledge was invaluable in dealing with all contracts. He joined NEMS in October 1964 as a senior executive, becoming a director the following year.

Peter Brown didn't leave NEMS in Liverpool until mid-1965. He had nothing to do with the Beatle business up till then, continuing simply to manage the record stores in Liverpool, which Brian had given up. But in June 1964, Harry Epstein, Brian's father, decided to sell most of his shops, although his other son, Clive, stayed on as managing director.

Peter Brown stayed on as well for a while, but didn't see eye to eye with the new owners. Brian offered him a job instead in NEMS Enterprises in London. 'I was a bit worried at first, working so closely with Brian again, that it might lead to rows as it had done before. But it worked very well.' He became Brian's personal assistant, taking over from Wendy Hanson.

Opposite: Brian Epstein, framed by George and John, in Tokyo, 1966.

In early 1967 Brian bought a country home in Sussex, which Peter found for him. This was a large, historic country mansion at Kingsley Hill, near Heathfield. It cost £25,000.

He also took on a personal secretary, Joanne Newfield, a niece of Joe Loss. She worked from an office at the top of his London house in Chapel Street, Belgravia. This was necessary, as he did so much of his work at home.

This was the setting, then, of the life of Brian Epstein in the summer of 1967. He was 32, rich, good-looking, charming, popular and gay. He was a household name, known for spotting talent, associated by everyone with the success of the Beatles. He had many other artists and many other interests, particularly the Saville. His ventures there were getting a lot of attention from the press.

He was completely happy and fulfilled, as far as the public could see. According to the *Financial Times* in the summer of 1967, he was worth seven million pounds. The true figure turned out to be a great deal less, but Brian Epstein was rich enough not to have any money worries for the rest of his life.

Mrs Queenie Epstein, Brian's mother, arrived in London on 14 August 1967 to spend ten days with her elder son at his Belgravia home. She returned to Liverpool on Thursday, 24 August.

She was in rather a distressed state when she arrived. Her husband Harry had died the previous month, which had upset Brian a great deal as well. Brian went out of his way to make her stay as happy and pleasant as possible. He was organizing a flat for her in Knightsbridge, as it had been decided she should now move to London from Liverpool. He wanted her to be as near him as possible.

Brian altered his normal daily habits to suit and please his mother. Instead of rising very late and going to bed very late, which had become his habit, he managed to be awake and ready each morning when his mother came into his bedroom to draw his curtains. Round about ten o'clock, he and his mother had breakfast together in his bedroom. She then saw him off bright and early to his office in Mayfair, something else that hadn't been his normal habit for a long time.

Throughout the ten days of his mother's stay he went into his office every morning and worked there all day. He came home, at a normal coming-home-from-the-office time, and had a meal with his mother. Then they'd watch colour TV together, have a cup of hot chocolate, and go to bed, always well before midnight.

Both Joanne and Peter Brown say he didn't dislike doing all this. He obviously preferred his usual habits, but he knew it gave his mother pleasure. He loved her and knew that she loved him, so he wanted her to enjoy her stay.

I went to visit her after she'd been there five days, on Friday, 18 August. We had tea and talked about Brian's childhood. They were obviously very close and affectionate.

Brian showed me out. He talked about his forthcoming visit to the United States and Canada. He was going to appear on a big TV spectacular, as the compere, which he was obviously looking forward to. We made arrangements for me to spend the weekend with him in Sussex on his return.

His mother left the following Thursday for Liverpool. On Thursday evening he had his first night out for almost two weeks, but this was just a quiet dinner with Simon Napier-

Bell at Carrier's Restaurant in Islington. What he was looking forward to most of all was the long weekend, August Bank Holiday weekend, at his country house. He invited Simon Napier-Bell, but he said no, as he had to go to Ireland.

'Brian left on Friday about 3.30,' says Joanne. 'He was all smiling and happy. He told me to have a lovely weekend and he'd see me on Tuesday. I watched him drive off with the roof of his Bentley down, waving at me.'

She knew that his two oldest and closest friends and colleagues, Peter Brown and Geoffrey Ellis, were also due to go down to Sussex for the weekend with Brian. She heard from Peter, later in the afternoon, that he would be setting off much later than he'd intended. She realized that Brian would therefore be down there for a few hours on his own. She hoped Peter wouldn't be too late for dinner.

'I did get there in time for dinner,' says Peter Brown. 'We had a very good meal, just the three of us, with a bottle of wine and a couple of ports afterwards.

'I was supposed to be bringing some other people down with me, but at the last moment they hadn't turned up. Brian was very disappointed by this. It was his first weekend in the country for a while and he was looking forward to enjoying himself, meeting a few new people. He didn't really fancy just spending it with his two oldest and very familiar friends.'

Brian rang a few numbers in London, trying to contact people, but it was a Friday night before a long August Bank Holiday weekend and no one was available. Around ten o'clock, Brian decided to go back to London instead.

This wasn't such a strange decision as it might appear. It was typical of him to suddenly change his mind. He often walked out of his own parties in the middle, parties which he'd spent weeks preparing. As far as Brian was concerned, the weekend in Sussex was going to be boring, after looking forward to it for so long. London seemed the only place to find some excitement.

'I walked with him to the car,' says Peter Brown. 'I said he was soft going back to London at this time. He said I hadn't to worry. He'd be all right. He was slightly drunk, with the big meal, but nothing much. He said don't worry. He'd be back in the morning before I was up.'

Not long after Brian left, a party of visitors did arrive by cab from London, in answer to one of his calls. But it was too late, he'd gone, though Peter Brown half thought Brian had gone for a drive round the local countryside and would soon return. But at 12.30, when he hadn't, Geoffrey started ringing Chapel Street, to see if he'd arrived. Antonio answered the telephone. He and his wife Maria were Brian's Spanish butler and housekeeper at Chapel Street. Antonio said Brian had returned. He buzzed Brian's intercom in his bedroom to say Mr Ellis was on the phone, but he got no reply. Geoffrey and Peter weren't worried. They were satisfied Brian had arrived safely and was now, presumably, asleep.

Peter Brown and Geoffrey Ellis rose late the next morning, Saturday, in Sussex. Brian hadn't reappeared, but they didn't really expect him to. They didn't bother to ring him, assuming he was still sleeping. But Brian himself rang Peter about five o'clock on the Saturday afternoon.

'He was very apologetic for not having come back in the morning, as he'd said he would. He said he'd been sleeping all day and was still feeling drowsy. I said he'd better not drive back. If he got the train down to Lewes I'd meet him there. He agreed that was best, but he was still too dopey to start off. He was always drowsy when he woke up after taking sleeping pills. He said he'd ring back later, when he felt more like it, so I'd know when he was starting off. That was how we left it.' But Brian didn't ring back.

By Sunday lunch time at Chapel Street, as Brian hadn't woken, Antonio and his wife Maria began to get worried. It wasn't unusual for him to be still sleeping at lunch time, but he hadn't been out of his bedroom, as far as they knew, since he'd returned from Sussex on Friday evening. His Bentley stayed in the same position all weekend – they specially noticed it. They also never heard him moving about, apart from breakfast on Saturday until tea time, when he'd rung Peter. They say they would have done, if he'd got up or gone out after that.

At 12.30 they tried to ring Peter Brown at Sussex to tell him their worries, but he was out at the pub. So they rang Joanne at her home in Edgware.

'Maria spoke to me and sounded very worried. She said Brian had been in his bedroom for so long, which was very unusual. I was very worried. I phoned Peter but couldn't get him. So I rang Alistair Taylor and told him. I said I was driving across to Brian's and I'd meet him there. I tried to contact Brian's doctor, but he was in Spain, then I got my car out.'

Peter and Geoffrey got back from the pub just before two o'clock to find the house-keeper had several messages for them.

'I rang Chapel Street,' says Peter, 'and spoke to Antonio, who told me they were all very worried about Brian. He said Joanne and Alistair were on their way across. I told him there was nothing at all to worry about. I assumed Brian must have gone out on Saturday night and was sleeping late. I said they were all just panicking. I told him to stop Alistair coming if he could.'

Joanne arrived at Chapel Street. She found Antonio and Maria still very agitated, despite Peter's reassurances. She rang Peter. He told her there was still no need to panic, but perhaps she should ring his, Peter's, doctor and get him to come round, just in case.

When the doctor came, she rang Peter to say they were forcing the door. Peter stayed on the telephone, waiting to hear what happened.

'The doctor and I went in,' says Joanne. 'The room was dark and I saw Brian, lying on the bed. He was on his side with his back to us. The doctor pushed me out of the room. I came out and told Maria and Antonio that it was all right, Brian was just asleep.

'Then the doctor came out, all white and shaken, and said Brian was dead. He went to pick up Peter's phone to tell him.'

'He couldn't get any words out,' said Peter. 'So I knew what had happened.'

Peter and Geoffrey immediately contacted the Beatles in Bangor, where they were staying with Maharishi. In an hour from the body being found, the *Daily Express* was ringing to ask if it was true that Brian Epstein was dead. They were told it wasn't true.

The next day it was on the front page of every paper. *The Times* obituary was across three columns at the top of the page. The man in the street seemed to think it was suicide. It is always comforting for those who have never had wealth, fame, or power to believe that those who have are, of course, not *really* happy.

Brian Epstein could be very happy and he could be very unhappy. His unhappiness hadn't been caused by the Beatles or even by success. His unhappiness was part of an

Brian Epstein in a private moment with Paul. Brian was always very possessive of his artists, especially of the Beatles, to whom he felt particularly close.

illness, an illness that dated back many years.

'In Liverpool, he always had depressions,' says Peter Brown. 'Not as bad or as long as later, but they were there, long before the Beatles came along.'

The causes and origins of his mental state at the time of his death had been with him throughout his life. But it was during the year leading up to his death, in August 1967, that many things came to a head.

'When he was in a depressed state,' says Joanne, 'it would just take a little thing to finally knock him out. There was once when he was trying to contact Nat Weiss, who was over in London from New York. He went round to the Grosvenor House Hotel to see him, but couldn't find him. He came back furious and started ringing the hotel. For some reason I gave him the wrong number – I gave him MAY 6363 instead of GRO 6363. So he was getting nowhere. When I discovered my mistake, he was terribly angry.'

Peter Brown says one of the troubles was that Brian was a perfectionist. If anything went wrong, or people interfered or spoiled perfect plans, it could throw him completely. He was so meticulous, exact and organized himself. Those early memos to the Beatles, telling them which ballroom to be at and not to swear on stage, were models of efficiency.

As NEMS grew larger and Brian had to delegate, more things were bound to be not to his liking – especially as he had the habit of appointing people out of a sudden feeling, rather than because of their knowledge and experience. But he always tried to keep his main artists to himself. He was completely possessive about the Beatles, and even disliked secretaries becoming too familiar with them. It was only in the last few months before his death that he let Peter Brown, his personal assistant, have any personal dealing with them.

Since early 1967 he had given up most of the daily responsibility for the running of NEMS, apart from the Beatles. He brought in Robert Stigwood, an Australian, to be co-managing director. It was he who ran NEMS from day to day, along with the other directors, Vic Lewis, Bernard Lee, Geoffrey Ellis and his brother Clive Epstein.

The withdrawal from NEMS came not long after the Beatles stopped touring. Apart from the Saville theatre, which was never a success financially, nothing took the place in his affections of the Beatles. But he was still looking for something, as he'd been looking for something when he'd gone off to join RADA, then later when he left everything to manage the Beatles. It was the old creative urge coming out again. He was being tormented once more by an unfulfilled creative desire, but yearning with little possibility of satisfaction. This is what often happened with Brian, with his love affairs and with most of his pleasures.

There did come a chance to be creative, when John Fernald, the ex-boss of RADA, who had taken Brian in as a student and whom Brian took on later to work for him, fell ill during rehearsals of the play *A Smashing Day* and Brian took over as director.

'He'd been ill at the time, recovering from jaundice, but he threw himself into rehearsals completely,' says Joanne. 'I don't think I ever saw him as happy in all the three years I worked with him. He stayed up all night with the cast, waiting for the reviews and adored every minute of it.' But the play soon came off.

The urge to be creative never found another outlet. He didn't know what he was looking for, and nothing presented itself the way the Beatles had done. Instead it turned him more and more against a strictly business life. This was one of the reasons he withdrew so much from NEMS.

'He didn't really like being a businessman,' says Joanne. 'He didn't like business meetings. He so wanted to be a creator. He used to cancel even the most important meetings. Sometimes I had to say he was ill, or had an urgent conference. The real reason was that he was still in bed, having been awake with insomnia all night. It was awful. He would leave me notes telling me which meetings I had to get him out of. I had to cancel Bernard Delfont four times in one week. I don't know what he must have thought.'

But there were several things which did give him great pleasure. He loved Kingsley Hill, his house in Sussex. He also loved bullfighting. He backed a fighter and was financing a film about bullfighting at the time of his death.

The other things he took up were more occasional whims, like drugs and gambling. He took LSD several times, when he heard from the Beatles the effects it had had on them. But on not more than a handful of occasions. He seems to have given it up about the same time as the Beatles – which was well before his death.

He had spasms of gambling. He enjoyed it and was successful. Joanne often found a note waiting for her when she arrived in the morning with a pile of money, perhaps around £300, which he'd won the night before. 'He would say in his note that I had to go and bank his happiness.'

Peter Brown, who usually went with him, says he was a good gambler because he knew when to stop. 'This was because he wasn't really carried away by it. The whole point of gambling was somewhere to go very late at night and to meet people.'

Apart from the Beatles and Cilla Black, none of his artists lasted as big stars and many of them soon faded away completely. Quite a few, naturally, resented his over-attention to the Beatles and then, as he drew out of NEMS, his complete lack of work on their behalf. Brian regretted this as much as anyone. It would make him feel very guilty. 'He believed in so many of them really,' says Joanne. 'He honestly did. He would promise them great things, absolutely sincerely. They'd go away, feeling hopeful again. In a few months they'd be back, accusing him of having let them down.'

But the only really important row he had with any of his artists was, ironically, not with any of the ones who were doing badly, but with Cilla Black, his most successful single star.

She had felt for a long time that she wasn't getting the personal attention she'd had from Brian in the past and which she felt she deserved. At the beginning of the summer of 1967, she decided she'd had enough. Brian had gone off somewhere again, leaving her. So that was that. She was leaving him.

As Brian was away, Peter Brown was the first to hear the news of her decision. He knew how badly it would affect Brian and he was worried about telling him. He consulted Brian's doctor for advice, who told him to do it slowly and carefully. When Brian heard, he made the mistake of allowing others to go and try to pacify her first, but they eventually met in Chapel Street. After several hours of discussions with Cilla, and then agreements, it was all patched up. They became friendlier than they'd ever been and remained so, up until his death. Cilla realized she would never have left Brian anyway.

There were never ever any rows with any of the Beatles. He loved them all as much as ever, and they loved him. But with the end of touring, their main point of contact ceased to exist.

They still saw a lot of each other. Any business decision came through his hands. But at the end of 1966, when the touring stopped, their concern was with themselves, working out what sort of life they would lead, what they would do with themselves, what the point of it all was. This was when the drugs, and then religion, started to enter their lives. They almost became hermits for several months, seeing only each other.

Brian went his own way, a way which had always been completely different, in so many respects, to theirs. If he hadn't become their manager, it's unlikely they would ever have been friends. He was of a different age, class and background, with different attitudes and, most of all, different pleasures. But for five years his life had been his work for them. When that finished, the Beatles had each other, and their wives. He was alone, obsessed by himself, worrying about his worries, worries which he hadn't had much time to think about for five years.

The Beatles had no idea how he was leading his last year, how he had become increasingly dependent on pills, as his worries, real and imagined, took over and obsessed him. They were amazed to hear, a long time after his death, that he'd hardly been at his office for so many months and had rarely been up and out in daylight. They knew nothing either of his personal affairs.

They had heard he'd been mildly depressed early in 1967, but thought he'd got over it. When he was with them, he was certainly always happy. This was true. His greatest pleasure was to be with them. He loved doing anything for them.

'He had Pattie and me for a week's holiday in the south of France in 1966,' says George. 'When we arrived, he had every little thing worked out, each meal, each visit, each place we would go to, for the whole week. A private plane arrived one day, which he'd organized to take us to a bullfight.

'He was always like this. He so wanted to please people that he worked everything out, down to the last detail.' When he had a dinner party, he went to great lengths to know each person's favourite cigarettes and had them laid out by their plate at the table.

Pattie says she did once hear from Joanne about the amount of pills Brian was taking. 'I said why couldn't she or Peter stop him, but she said they couldn't. I said to George that he should speak to Brian himself, but he said it wouldn't do any good.'

Brian had at first been attracted most of all to John, from those early days in the Cavern. John was the only one he'd ever spent a holiday with alone, that time they went to Spain together, leaving Cyn in Liverpool.

His relationship with Paul was the most subtle and complicated, at least Brian felt it was. He felt he had to overcompensate towards Paul. He admitted it himself once. 'I think Paul thinks I'm closer to John than I am with him. It's not really true. It was earlier on, but now I love them all equally.' He always gave Paul particularly lavish presents. They rarely gave him any.

'Paul was the only one who ever gave him any little worries,' says Joanne, 'when he rang up to complain about something, or ask things. The others might ask exactly the same, but he always worried more about pleasing Paul. He could be upset by talking to Paul on the phone, but never by any of the others.'

This was probably because, in 1967, Paul, for the first time, had become interested in business affairs. Formerly, George had been the only one to cross-examine Brian on contracts, or how much they were getting, and couldn't he do better. But George, when his interest in religion arrived, stopped worrying completely about materialistic things.

Brian was always involved, but now and again didn't like the way they were doing things, such as the complicated – legally, economically and artistically – cover for *Sergeant Pepper*.

During the spring of 1967, when he was visiting New York, Nat Weiss says that Brian got a premonition he was going to die. At Kennedy Airport, he became convinced his plane was going to crash over the Atlantic. Just before take-off, he wrote a note on a scrap of paper, which he asked Nat Weiss to give the Beatles as his last wish. The note, which Nat Weiss still has, read: 'Brown Paper bags for Sergeant Pepper.'

As he didn't crash, the Beatles never found out how much he worried about the complications of the *Sergeant Pepper* cover, just as they never found out so many things about his last year.

On 8 September 1967, a Westminster coroner's court pronounced that Brian Epstein's death was accidental. He had died from the cumulative effect of bromide in a drug he had been taking for some time. The drug was Carbitral. The level of bromide in him was only a 'low fatal level', but he had taken repeated 'incautious self overdoses' which had had a cumulative effect, enough to kill him.

His body showed there had been no one immense dose, but a series of large ones. The court was told he took drugs, in the form of sleeping tablets, as he suffered from perpetual insomnia.

In his body were found an antidepressant drug and barbiturate, as well as bromide. The police reported that in his house they had found 17 bottles of tablets of some sort, seven by his bedside, eight in the bathroom and two in a briefcase.

Medical experts said that the amount of bromide he had been taking would have made him drowsy and could also have made him careless and injudicious. He had died from an accidental overdose.

There is not the slightest reason to doubt it. The medical evidence showed conclusively he had been dosing himself up for three days. With suicide, the practice is to take one large dose.

It's highly unlikely he would have deliberately committed suicide, not at that time, with his mother already recently bereaved. One or two small facts are still not clear, but there were no rows or specific reasons for depression, as far as is known. It was just an escalating depression as he thought his longed-for weekend would turn out boring.

The memorial service for Brian Epstein was held at the New London Synagogue, Abbey Road, St John's Wood on 17 October 1967.

It was an apt setting, just a few yards away from EMI's studios, where all the Beatles records up until Brian's death had been recorded, and just round the corner from Paul's house in Cavendish Avenue.

It was also not far away from St John's Wood underground station, which contains the nearest public telephones to Paul's house. Brian used these phones twice in his life. The first time was in 1962 when he rushed out of the EMI studios to cable the Beatles in Hamburg with some good news about their first record. The other time was five years later, just before his death. He'd been round to Paul's house but couldn't get in. Paul had been bothered by fans all day and had stopped answering the door. Brian had been forced to find a phone box and ring up Paul and tell him who it was before he was allowed in. Brian always thought this story was very symbolic.

George, when he heard of Brian's death, says it struck him like an old-fashioned film. 'You know, where they turn over the last page of one section to show you they've come to the end of it, before going on to the next. That was what Brian's death was like. The end of a chapter.'

Brian watching from the wings as his most successful group ever perform to a crowd of thousands in the USA.

27

THE BEATLES, FROM DRUGS TO MAHARISHI

When the touring was over, they had no idea what was going to be in the next chapter. They'd had ten years, from 1956 to 1966, of not just living a communal life but communally living the same life. They were still each other's greatest friends and they were still going to record together, but as individuals they felt it was time to look for a separate identity.

George was off first. The month after they stopped touring, in September 1966, he went to India with his wife. For the first time, he had found a serious interest not shared by the others.

John accepted a film part, in *How I Won The War*. He'd always liked Dick Lester, though he hadn't particularly enjoyed doing their two Beatle films. He said it felt like being an extra. But he still thought that perhaps acting was the new thing he was looking for. He also liked the idea of an anti-war film, a subject he's always felt strongly about.

Ringo, the most home- and family-minded of them all, started to expand his family and his home. Paul was the only one who felt out of it. He envied George. He wished he had something like Indian music to occupy himself. He did a bit of painting and decorated pieces of furniture, but without much interest. He tried hard to think about God, but nothing came. So he decided to do the music for a film, *The Family Way*, to see if he enjoyed writing film music, but he didn't. After that, he went off on a long trip across Africa.

George's passion grew, but John soon found that he didn't like acting and he didn't like most actors. He and Paul were both searching again. They had no intention of retiring from life, as 25-year-old millionaires, but they'd avoided so much formal discipline and knowledge, the sort a university might have given them, that they didn't know where to begin. Not that they wanted anyone to teach them anything. Materially and emotionally they were 100 years old. Which is where drugs came in. Through drugs they found out about themselves, by themselves.

Opposite: **John and Cynthia and Pattie and George with the Maharishi – peace and love and flowers.**

They'd taken pep pills, of varying strengths, ever since their Hamburg days. They'd had occasional marijuana cigarettes as other people have a drink. None of them drink, apart from wine with a meal now and then.

George and John were introduced to LSD, through a dental friend, in 1965, without realizing they had been given it. 'It was as if I'd never tasted, talked, seen, thought or heard properly before,' says George. 'For the first time in my life I wasn't conscious of ego.'

Taking drugs didn't stop their music. Now that they were all back together again, having found that things like acting didn't work, they began work on their most ambitious album so far, which showed traces of their interest in drugs. This was *Sergeant Pepper's Lonely Hearts Club Band*.

During this session, they also got the idea for a TV film. For over a year they'd been putting off doing their third film, at the same time as they were putting off other things they didn't care for, like touring and appearing. Many scripts had been written then rejected, one of them by the late Joe Orton. (He was an intense Beatle fan, and 'A Day In The Life' was played at his funeral.) Eventually, they came round to the idea of writing and doing a film by themselves, just to see if they could do it.

The Beatles first met Maharishi Yogi on 24 August, 1967, when they attended a lecture by him at the Hilton Hotel in London. The following weekend they went to Bangor in North Wales for his transcendental meditation conference.

Paul thought of the idea of a TV film in April, flying home from visiting Jane on her 21st birthday in the States, where she was on tour with the Old Vic. He thought they would all get onto a bus and just see what happened. It would be Magical, so they could do what they wanted. And Mysterious, as no one would know where they were going or what they were going to do. That was as far as he got then. The others agreed to it, but no further work was done on it for almost six months.

George, by this time, was well immersed in Indian music, which also shows in *Sergeant Pepper*, but he'd also become very knowledgeable about Indian religion. His wife Pattie was with him in all this. In fact, it was she who first had any contact with the Maharishi.

She says that their interest in religion had started by chance, during their trip to India in September 1966. This had been simply to study Indian music with Ravi Shankar, which

again had started by chance. During the film *Help!* there is a scene in which there are some unusual musical instruments. George, bored by filming, had amused himself by trying to play one of them, which turned out to be a sitar.

In India, apart from studying the sitar, George also met Ravi's spiritual guru, Tat Baba, who explained the law of Karma (the law of action and reaction). 'Meeting him and reading *Autobiography of a Yogi*, as well as the seven weeks with Ravi, were more spiritually rewarding than anything that had come before, even drugs.'

Back home, George and Pattie were reading many books about religion, an interest which had been first roused after George's first LSD experience. He had begun with Aldous Huxley and gradually moved further into Eastern concepts.

In February 1967 Pattie had become a member of the Spiritual Regeneration Movement, on her own. George did go once, around the same time, but wasn't initiated, as he didn't feel it was right for him. 'I'd been trying to teach myself meditation from books,' says Pattie, 'but only half doing it. One day a girlfriend told me about transcendental meditation and I went along to a lecture at the Caxton Hall. Maharishi himself wasn't there, just someone else talking about his work, but I joined the movement then. The lecture wasn't very inspiring, but transcendental meditation seemed an obvious and simple process. I got all the movement's literature from then on, so I knew about their summer conference at Bangor.'

George, in the meantime, was not only telling the others about what he was reading, he was now also looking round the world for some wise learned man to explain things and put him on the right track.

George even trailed down to a deserted part of Cornwall, after he'd read a book on cosmic communication, and spent several hours climbing a high hill, but nothing happened. He heard of many other people, Indian and Western, and their ideas, but no one seemed to him to be the right one, until Maharishi.

It is important to stress that all of them were already very knowledgeable, long before Maharishi came along. He didn't convert them, or reach out and direct them, or even tell them much they didn't know. He chanced upon their lives, just at a time when they were looking for him.

All this spiritual groping didn't stop them from doing their normal Beatle work. They did a song, 'All You Need Is Love', in July 1967 for a worldwide programme *Our World*, which was seen live by over 150 million people.

Their spiritual awakening did have one concrete effect. By August 1967 they had given up drugs. By actively thinking, reading and discussing spiritual matters, they decided that artificial stimulants like drugs were no real help. It was better to get there without them.

They don't regret having been on drugs. They say it was useful for them at the time, but is now no more. But it was nothing to do with Maharishi that they gave up drugs. They'd already done so on their own before they met him. He simply confirmed and gave more lucid reasons for their decision.

It was ironic that all the acres of heavy print from leader writers and doctors, warning about drugs – after Paul and then Brian admitted they'd had LSD – had been ignored, but their own gropings into religion had worked.

In mid-August 1967 it was suddenly advertised in several newspapers that Maharishi was in London and would be giving a public lecture. 'This seems to have been a sudden decision,' says Pattie. 'It wasn't in any of our literature that he was in London, or even coming to our Bangor conference. When I heard, I said to George, look, we've got to go.'

But by this time George had already heard, from other people, that Maharishi was in town. He contacted the others and said they must all go to his lecture at the Hilton Hotel.

This was on the Thursday evening, 24 August 1967. Afterwards, Maharishi invited them to join his movement's summer conference at Bangor on Saturday. They said yes.

They told Brian Epstein about Maharishi and his transcendental meditation movement and how impressed they were by it all. Brian said he was interested. He might come up later during the conference, which was scheduled to last ten days. But he was more concerned with having an exciting August Bank Holiday weekend at his country home with a few new friends.

The news leaked out that the Beatles were going to Bangor with the Maharishi. What they thought was going to be a private, spiritual experience, developed into a carnival. It was almost like their touring days again, which they thought they'd given up for ever a year ago.

Euston Station was crowded with thousands of sightseers and press, who had turned out to watch the Beatles off on what the *Daily Mirror* called next day, a 'Mystical Special', or the 3.50 stopping train to Bangor, North Wales.

There was such chaos that Cynthia Lennon was left behind on the station platform, unable to get through the crowds to join John. A policeman forcibly held her back, thinking she was a fan.

On the train, jammed tight in a first-class compartment, were John, Paul, George and Pattie and Ringo, plus Mick Jagger, Marianne Faithfull and Jennie Boyd, Pattie's sister. Ringo was a late starter. His wife Maureen had just had their second child and was still in hospital. It wasn't clear if he would join them. 'I rang Maureen in hospital. She said I had to go. I couldn't miss this.'

The decision to go had been very sudden. Brian Epstein knew about it, but he wasn't involved in any way. Even the ever-present Mal and Neil hadn't been brought along. For five years they'd never gone anywhere without Brian Epstein or someone looking after them. 'It's like going somewhere without your trousers on,' said John.

They sat tight for several hours, scared to go to the lavatory in case they got mobbed. They had no idea what had happened to their luggage. No one seemed to have any money. They wondered what Maharishi would tell them. John said perhaps he might just turn out to be another version of what they already knew, but on a different label. 'You know, like some are on EMI and some on Decca.'

Official publicity hand-out photograph of the Beatles from 1967.

Very seriously, George said he didn't think so. He was sure this was going to be it. Mick Jagger sat very quiet and serious. John said he hoped it would save him having to go on working as a Beatle, if the Maharishi told him to go off and sit in a cave in India for the rest of his life. 'But he won't, I bet. He'll just say go away and write "Lucy In The Sky With Diamonds".'

In another compartment, the Maharishi was sitting cross-legged on a white sheet laid out on the seat by his followers. He bounced up and down when he laughed, which was most of the time. He admitted he'd never heard any Beatle music in his life. He had been told they were very famous, and so was Mick Jagger, but he got very confused about him being a Rolling Stone. He didn't know what that meant.

The Beatles eventually went into his compartment. He laughed a great deal as he chatted with them. He illustrated his talk by taking a flower in his hand and saying it was really all sap. The petals on their own were an illusion, just like the physical life.

He said that transcendental meditation, which he would indoctrinate them into at Bangor, was simply a method of quickly and easily reaching a spiritual state. His meditations, once learned, need only be practised for half an hour every morning. That would be enough for the day. He said it was like a bank. You didn't need to carry money around with you if you had a bank, you just needed to pop in now and again to get what you wanted.

'What if you're greedy,' said John. 'And have another half hour's meditation after lunch, then slip in another half hour after tea?'

Everybody laughed. The Maharishi nearly bounced his head against the ceiling this time. The Beatles adjourned for tea while the girls and Mick Jagger had a turn with the Maharishi. The attendant roped off part of the dining room for them, but a few people managed to break through for autographs.

'What you going to Bangor for?' asked two teenage boys, unable to believe that anyone would want to go to Bangor, least of all the Beatles. 'Are you playing there?'

'That's right,' said Ringo. 'On the Pier Head at 8.30, Second House. See you.'

At Flint Station Ringo said that Flint had been the furthest he'd ever cycled on his bike from the Dingle.

Bangor was pandemonium. The Beatles considered going on to the next station, then getting a taxi back. But Maharishi said if they stayed beside him, they'd be all right.

On the platform, rather lost and bemused amongst all the screamings kids, was a handful of Maharishi's followers, waiting to welcome him to the conference. They were each clutching a flower, ready to hand to him. They were bowled aside by the crowds, screaming at the Beatles.

Bangor is a small seaside town on the north coast of Wales. It has a large training college, which was where the conference was being held. Over 300 meditators were already in residence, all unaware of the Beatles' arrival.

Maharishi himself seemed to be enjoying all the commotion and excitement. He was very kind and considerate to all the press and TV men. He very smartly agreed with them to have a press conference, after he'd spoken privately to the conference members.

Maharishi's philosophy, very simply, is that life consists of spiritual as well as materialistic values. He is not in favour of becoming a spiritual recluse, cutting oneself off from the world. But he says that without spiritual consciousness, it is impossible to lead a full life, or to fully enjoy materialism. In a way, it is a simple blend of Eastern mysticism and Western materialism. You don't have to give up money or even the pleasures of the flesh, within reason, to become one of his followers, but you have to learn his methods of spiritual realization. This helps you to transcend yourself, although still continuing to live an ordinary life.

At his private meeting he asked his 300 followers how they were getting on in their meditations. One man asked if it was possible still to hear motorcars during meditation.

The press conference, afterwards, was confused and unsatisfactory. The press, mainly local stringers of national papers, had little idea what was going on. They thought the Beatles must be involved in some publicity stunt. They couldn't believe they were serious about Maharishi, whoever he was. They were belligerent in their questions, almost as if they expected the Beatles to admit they were just doing it all for a laugh. The Beatles were cheered loudly by the congregation when they made it clear, at the expense of the press's ignorance, that they were very serious indeed.

John found a reporter's notes afterwards in one of the college's telephone booths. It had the heading 'Paul, George, Ringo, John Lennon and Jagger' plus details of what each had been wearing. 'You've taken over from me,' said John to Mick Jagger, pointing out to him how the reporter had named each of them. 'I just used be called Lennon when I was wicked. Now I'm John Lennon. I haven't yet reached the next stage of just being John. You're still Jagger.'

By midday on the Sunday they all had been indoctrinated. They were all resting, after their mental efforts, when the news about Brian Epstein's death came through. Maharishi saw them all again, to help and comfort them, to cheer them up and explain how little death meant. Then they all went back to London by car, missing the rest of the conference.

They were due, originally, to go out to India to be with the Maharishi in September 1967, but it was put back to February 1968 for various reasons, such as *The Magical Mystery Tour*.

Opposite: On a shoot for the *Magical Mystery Tour* film. Largely Paul's creation, the hour-long feature was slated by most British critics when it was shown on television by the BBC at Christmas time, 1967.

They and NEMS were a bit perturbed by the way various organizations suddenly sprouted up and tried to get them to give a press conference. They were even talking about selling press and TV rights to cover the Beatles' trip to India, and setting up an official press office, long before the Beatles had made up their minds when to go. Maharishi's public relations people were very keen on this.

An Indian official arrived, sent by the Indian Government, and went to NEMS saying he had organized visits for them to six Indian states, and that he was going to arrange for them to meet Mrs Gandhi, the Prime Minister of India. Any sort of publicity for their religion or anything else is the last thing the Beatles ever want, although no one will ever believe this.

There has always been a certain element, very often even governments, who try to turn the Beatles' presence or interest to their own advantage. The same sort of thing happened with Greece, around the same time in 1967. They were thinking of buying a Greek island. They'd seen it during a cruising holiday, and had even got the money organized. This was very difficult at the time because of the currency restrictions. But the Treasury gave them special dispensation to help them to take the money out of the country.

It was agreed that, as they'd brought so many millions into the country, they should be allowed to buy an island refuge. The price was agreed. They didn't care about the military regime that had just taken over in Greece. On one trip they were asked by an official if they would be kind enough to look at a very quiet little village. When they got there, they found hordes of press and TV people. It had been organized by the tourist people to use the Beatles as propaganda. They decided to forget about Greece.

It might seem far-fetched that governments should wish to court four members of a beat group. Many said the Labour Government did, by giving them an MBE. But it has always happened, since the beginning, from people trying to get them to go to embassy parties to state visits. Most governments see the Beatles as a way of keeping in with the young voters.

But all the wheeling-dealing that went on around the Maharishi didn't put them off him. Most of it had nothing to do with Maharishi anyway, although his natural enthusiasm to spread the word led him to be talked into lots of things by press and PR men. But the Beatles did want to help if possible. George and John even went on the David Frost TV show, the first time they agreed to talk on any TV programme for over two years.

George and John spent two months in India studying under Maharishi in the spring of 1968. Paul spent one month. Ringo managed ten days. He felt a bit homesick, even though, like the others, he took a consignment of baked beans with him. But all of them found their stay spiritually rewarding.

Despite everything, the year 1967, the year of LSD and meeting Maharishi, turned out to be their most creative year up to that time. In the first six months they recorded more new songs (16 in all) than in the first six months of 1963. This equalled what they'd done in the *whole* of 1966, which shows how much they gained from giving up touring.

Later in 1967, in November, they did another single, 'Hello, Goodbye', then the *Magical Mystery Tour* in December. This was their hour-long, colour TV film. They spent more time making the film than doing the songs for it.

They'd done no work on the film from April, when they thought of the idea and recorded the title song, until September, when they started shooting. They set off for Devon in a bus with 43 people on board, none of them, including the Beatles, knowing precisely what would happen. There was no script.

They did two weeks of shooting in all. They'd blithely expected to do a week in the studios at Shepperton after Devon, thinking you could just turn up. Instead they had to use an airfield in Kent.

The main work was done at the editing stage, which took eleven weeks in all, eleven times as long as they'd expected. Paul, as with the shooting, was the main inspiration. He directed every minute of the editing, along with the editor. The others were there most of the time, usually having a singsong with a drunken street singer who wandered into the cutting rooms.

They disregarded all the rules and conventions making this film, but just bashed on, unworried by their lack of film knowledge and experience. It was a completely new medium for them but most of all, for the first time ever, they were doing something on their own, with no Brian Epstein to stage manage things or George Martin to lend his accumulated wisdoms.

It was shown at Christmas time 1967 in Britain on the BBC, and was seen in most countries in Europe, South America, Australia and Japan. The lack of plot and experienced direction did show, and it was savagely criticized by most of the British TV critics. The *Daily Express* called it 'blatant rubbish' and 'tasteless nonsense'. The pre-publicity had made most people forget it was an experiment, and they possibly expected too much. It was the first time the Beatles had been criticized in five years. Most critics made the most of it.

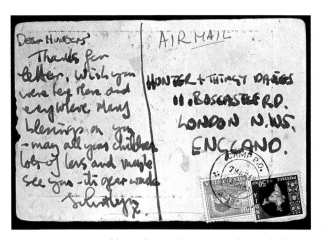

Postcard from John in India, 1968, out there with the Maharishi. Note the jokes. It is signed 'John and Cyn'.

Long before it was out, the Beatles had almost forgotten it, having learned their lessons, though Paul perhaps was still hoping it would be liked. But they'd gained enough to make them feel confident enough to have a go at a full-length feature film.

Apart from the TV film, it had been a good year. *Sergeant Pepper*, particularly, was looked upon as their biggest advance so far. *The Times* music critic, William Mann, took 30 inches to say it was more genuinely creative than anything else in pop music.

The year had begun with them searching as individuals, and ended with them as a group once more, though without a manager. But they'd found Maharishi. And as individuals they'd begun, at last, to put their own minds and own homes and own organizations into some sort of order. Which brings us, roughly, to where they are today in 1968.

PART THREE
1968

28

FRIENDS AND PARENTS

There are no blue plaques on the Beatle birthplaces in Liverpool today, though all the old homes get thousands of fans making pilgrimages to look at them every year. There is only one Beatle parent left living in Liverpool, but Liverpool does have an ex-Beatle – Pete Best.

Pete Best is married with two children. He lives in Liverpool with his in-laws and has a job slicing bread in a bakery for £18 a week. He did work in other groups after he left the Beatles, but in 1965 gave up show business for good. He did nothing for a year, refusing to see people, almost becoming a recluse. He turned down large sums for his life story. His memories of Hamburg, especially of their girls, drink and pills, would have been very lucrative.

'What good would that have done, apart from the money? It would just have seemed like sour grapes. I wanted to try to get a life of my own, but it took a long time.

'What I dreaded most was people's cruelty. When I met people, I knew what they were going to say or think. I was the bloke that was no good. It was the sort of psychological knowledge which got me down. People were rude and said awful things to me.'

He has lost a bit of heart. He looked very tired, slumped in front of the TV at his mother's home. He has a Beatle hairstyle at last, but he was still wearing a leather jacket and jeans, as they'd all done in their Hamburg days. Mrs Best has given up all show business work, but she's as forceful as ever. She still maintains the Beatles chucked Pete Best because they were jealous of him.

Pete says he knew all the time that they were good and obviously going to be successful. 'That was what was really disappointing, knowing what I was going to miss. I did regret everything at first. When they kicked me in the teeth I did wish I'd never set eyes on them. I'd have just had an ordinary job, perhaps teaching, and never known all this anxiety.

'But not now. I'm glad really. I've got a lot of happy memories. I had some great times. I'm grateful for them. Then the Day of Judgement came.'

Opposite: **Ringo with Astrid Kirchherr in 1964. Although Ringo did not play with the Beatles in Hamburg, he met them there while drumming for another group, Rory Storm and the Hurricanes, and, like them, became a friend of Astrid.**

In Hamburg, the clubs are still full of British groups, but Klaus is no longer there. He's joined a British group, Manfred Mann. His fascination for the Beatles led him to follow them back to England and to join a group, even though he could play no musical instrument, except the piano. He is still very friendly with them. George composed one of his songs in Klaus's house. Klaus also does a bit of drawing – he did the cover for the Beatles LP, *Revolver*.

Astrid is still in Hamburg, but she's no longer a photographer. She says she got sickened by the press and refused all offers for her memories of the Beatles.

Her last job was serving in a bar in one of Hamburg's small but strange night clubs. She is married, to Gibson Kemp, a Liverpool-born ex-beat group player. At one time he played in a trio with Klaus. Astrid still has Stu's room almost as it was. It is very dark and eerie. The candles are still burning.

Fred Lennon had no contact with John, or even bothered to go and see him or inquire about him, from 1945, when John was five, until 1964. Fred was then washing dishes at a hotel in Esher. 'One day the washing up woman said to me, "If that's not your son, Freddy, then I don't know what." She said there was a boy in this group with the same name as me and the same sort of voice, though he didn't sing as well as me. I'd never heard of them.'

Fred Lennon, John's father, aged 56 in 1968. He and John were finally reconciled that year, after more than two decades of estrangement.

John must have passed the hotel where his dad was washing dishes many times, without knowing it, going back and forward to his home in Weybridge.

When Fred realized it was his son, he was immediately appearing in all the newspapers, giving interviews. Fred says, of course, he didn't seek publicity. It just happened. It also just happened that *Tit Bits* paid him £40 for his life story, and that he made a record. He says that singing on this record didn't make him any money. 'I lost, if anything. They made me get my teeth seen to. It cost £109. I'm still paying it up, £10 a month.'

He had a short 20-minute meeting with John and then was shown out. He tried to see him again, by just arriving at his house one day, but had the door slammed in his face. He's surprisingly small, but almost dapper. He has thick greying hair, which is swept back lushly at the sides, like an ex-the-atrical. He's 55 but very cheerful and young-looking. 'I can still get the girls, you know. If they think I'm smashing, I must be OK. I know John has a horror of old age. But tell him this from me. I'm younger than he is.'

He has watched John's progress very carefully. 'He's only let me down twice. Once was accepting that MBE. I wouldn't have done it. Royalty can't buy me. The other time was not speaking at the Foyles literary lunch. I would definitely have given them a speech, and a song too.'

Since 1964 he said that his ambition was to meet John properly. 'Just to let him see what sort of bloke I *really* am.' And he wouldn't say no to any help. 'If John happened to offer it.'

When John heard that Fred Lennon was so full of memories of Julia and John's childhood, the great reconciliation took place. They met and became friends, much to Fred's delight. Since early 1968 he has stopped washing dishes and is now living in a smart flat, subsidized by John.

Mimi today lives alone in a luxury bungalow near Bournemouth, with her cat Tim, a stray that John brought home many years ago. The house is very white and sunny, with a magnificent setting, right beside the sea. It has its own little steps at the bottom of the garden, leading down to the sea. It cost £25,000.

The front and the back of the house are completely un-overlooked. Only in the summer, when steamers go up and down across Poole Bay, can she be in any way interrupted. As they go past the house, she can hear a megaphone on board announcing: 'And that is John Lennon's house with the striped blinds. That will be Mimi sitting there.' The first time she heard it, she was so furious that she ran down to the bottom of the garden, stood on her sea steps and shouted 'Shut up!' Everybody on the boat just laughed.

Apart from that, her life is fairly uninterrupted. A few lamps from the front of the house have been stolen by fans. Now and again, she's seen them snatching photographs of her and the house, but nothing much. She says she keeps her telephone number and address secret.

Most of the furniture is reproduction antique. It all looks very new, but most of it was brought from her old home in Liverpool. She did have some nice things there, she says. When a reporter came to see her once in her old house in Liverpool, he looked round at everything and said how nice it all was – 'Wasn't John good to buy it all for her.' She threw him out immediately.

There are lots of books around, mainly classics and biographies. She's just been reading *Max* by Lord David Cecil. She doesn't care for novels.

On the TV set she has John's MBE medal, though she is a bit worried some people might think it a slight on Royalty. John had arrived one day and pinned it on her, saying she deserved it more than him.

In the hall and on the walls of the bedrooms she has some of their Gold Discs, although not as many as the other parents. She has a large plaque, which John presented to her. Engraved on it is the phrase she used at him almost every day of his adolescent life: 'The guitar's all right as a hobby, John, but you'll never make a living with it.'

She had no strong desire to leave her house in Liverpool. 'I was very happy. It was a very comfortable house. I'd spent hundreds on it. But John went on at me for about two years, then he said OK, stay.

'Then he started again, when the other parents began to move into their new houses. "You silly little sausage," I said to him. "There's no need to lift me out of the mire."

'I was staying in London with him after the premiere of the first film. He came down to breakfast and said "OK, I'm going to find you a house. Where would you like it?"

'I said Bournemouth, just for something to say. He picked up the phone and called Anthony, his chauffeur. He told him to get the maps out for Bournemouth, we're leaving now.

'Well, I thought, it would be a run. We came down and got a list of houses from Rumsey's. We went round a lot, but I wanted one by the sea and there wasn't one. So I thought, that'll be it, now we can go home. Then the man suddenly remembered one that had just come up.

'The people were still living in it and I didn't want to go in, especially the way John was dressed. He had old jeans with holes in them and an old suede jacket I'd bought him years ago, which was miles too small for him. He had a silly yachting cap on as well.

'I said we shouldn't go in and just to land on them like this. John told me it was just a tuppeny ha'penny little bourgeois home. If I wasn't careful, I'd get a mind to match.

'He marched in and said how do you do, mind if I look round. The man and his wife just gaped at him. John said, "Do you like it, Mimi? If you don't, I'll have it." So he rang his accountant and bought it.'

Mimi moved in in October 1965. She sold her old house in Liverpool for £6,000, a good price, though, as she says, it was a good house in a good area.

The Bournemouth house is still in John's name, but it is Mimi's for as long as she wants it. He pays all the bills. He told her just to spend her £6,000, but she told him not to be so stupid.

'It's lovely down here. I had always vaguely thought of moving to the south coast when George retired. I haven't felt a winter since I arrived. I've had drinks with people, but that's about all. I've never tended to make many friends outside the family. I do a lot of walking and reading. The days are too short really.'

All the Beatle parents have had their material lives completely changed by their sons, and all of them have reacted to it in slightly different ways. But Mimi is probably the only one whose relationship has not really changed. She still, in many ways, treats John as she's always done, whereas with the others there is a hint of hero worship, almost reverence. Mimi still criticizes John's clothes and how he looks, as she did when he was a teenager. She tells him when he's looking fat and not to spend too much. 'He's too soft over money. He's an easy touch. Generous beyond belief. I'm always telling him.' The other parents never voice any criticism of their sons.

Mimi doesn't care for the way John speaks. She says he won't speak properly, never finishing sentences. 'And he's getting worse all the time. I often can't understand what he's talking about. His mind's jumping all over the place.'

She doesn't see him very regularly, but he always sends her funny letters when he's abroad, with a little drawing on the envelope, specially for her. She keeps them all carefully arranged in a bureau. When John visits her, he rakes through all her belongings, just to see what she's been doing while he's been away. She still has the old childhood books he used to write. She reads them now and again.

'It's just the same stuff that he's had published. Just his scribble, as I call it, which he's been doing for years. I think the first book was better, but I still burst out laughing at some of his poems.'

Her way of life isn't that different, despite the luxury of her setting. She says she would give up everything, her house and all their success, just to have John as her little boy again.

'I'd give up £2 million to be back again. It's very selfish, I know. I always think of him as a little boy. I know it's stupid. But nothing could compensate for the pleasure he gave me as a boy.'

She obviously would like to see him a lot more, but would never, in any way, let this be known, or hang on to him at all. 'It's not his fault I'm a widow. There's nothing worse for a boy to feel than that anyone's hanging on to him. He's got his own wife and family to think about. He knows I'm here. He comes to see me as often as he can. He sat up on the roof for four days in the summer. I ran up and down getting drinks for him. He never shows much emotion. He finds it hard to say sorry.

'But one night he said that even if he didn't come down to see me every day, or every month, he always thought about me at some time every day, wherever he was. That meant a great deal to me.'

The happiest day in Jim McCartney's life, so he says, occurred in 1964, when Paul told him he could give up work. Unlike some of the other parents, he needed no second telling. He was 62 at the time, with another three years before retiring. He'd worked for the same cotton firm since he was 14, and he'd had enough. His wage, despite all his years and his experience, was only £10 a week. The recession in the cotton trade had made his last years very uncomfortable. For years he'd had the fear that they would pay him off in favour of a younger man.

Paul found him a house, an £8,750 detached house in the Wirral in Cheshire. About a year after that, Jim found himself a new wife, after almost ten years of being a widower.

He'd met Angela only three times when he asked her to marry him. She was a widow, a good few years younger than himself, with a daughter, Ruth, aged five. She'd been living in one room in Kirby since the death of her husband in a road accident. 'We were two lonely people.'

They are obviously very happy. He dotes on Ruth, a highly intelligent young lady, who thinks the girls in her school who try to chat her up about her famous stepbrother are really rather silly. Angie is very bouncy, witty and high-spirited. She runs the large house with great efficiency and drives Jim's car, as he can't. She's given him a second youth. He now wears very fashionable, clinging polo-neck sweaters and well-tapered trousers, the type he used to shout at Paul for wearing not so long ago.

Michael, Paul's brother, is still living at home.

'I've just taken Mike up a lilo and three sheets of carbon paper,' says Angie.

'That's very sanitary of you,' said Jim.

'He now wants some more three-pound bags of flour. He's dropping the flour onto a bread board and tape-recording it. A gear bedroom, but what a mess. What do you think he's after?'

'The sound of three-pound bags of flour dropping onto a bread board,' said Jim.

Another £8,000 was spent on the house, after Paul had bought it, putting in central heating and completely furnishing and decorating it. The house has large grounds, with a view at the back towards the Dee estuary. Despite the newness of all the fittings, it has a homely, lived-in feeling. They're not scared to enjoy all the new luxury.

'I do miss Liverpool and some of my old friends, but not all that much. I was getting a bit fed up with people saying, "You must be very proud, what's it like?" That's all they ever asked, over and over again. I've cut myself off from people like that. But close friends and relations I often ring up and ask to come out here.'

Jim is on Christian names terms with his doctor – even using his nickname, Pip. Not in an affected, putting-it-on way, but perfectly naturally. He gets out the malt whisky the minute Pip calls. He has two part-time gardeners, but he looks after his vines in the large heated greenhouse himself. He's laid down his own wine, and always has a plentiful supply of drinks. He gets books out of the library on ornithology and knows exactly which birds are in his garden. He's also an expert on squirrels.

Apart from his slight Liverpool accent, to see his life, his clothes and his pleasures, it's impossible to imagine he's spent over 40 years in rooms or a council house, earning under £10 a week. Most of all when you see him at a race course. That's when he really looks one of nature's gents.

Leaving work, getting the house and, most of all, getting married again have all made him very happy. But his next biggest kick came on his 62nd birthday. It was the same night, 6 July 1964, as the premiere of the Beatles' first film.

'We all went to the Dorchester afterwards. Princess Margaret was there. I could see Paul signalling to somebody and he was handed a parcel. He gave it to me and said, "Here you are, all the best, Dad."

'I opened it and it was a picture of a horse. I said, "Very nice", but I was thinking, what the hell do I want with a picture of a horse.

'Paul must have seen my face. He said, "It's not just a picture. I've bought the bloody horse. It's yours and it's running at Chester on Saturday."'

The horse, Drake's Drum, a well-known gelding, cost £1,050. Paul also pays for its training fees, which come to around £60 a month. In the 1966 season, it won over £3,000 in prize money, including a £1,000 race at Newbury and the race before the Grand National at Aintree.

Jim wants for nothing now. Like all the Beatle parents, he has an account from which he can take anything he likes. He doesn't go in for any ostentation, but he seems to enjoy and savour the middle-class life even more than the others.

'The change was a bit sudden, coming as it did when I was 62. It took a while to get used to it. Now I've taken to it like a duck to water. I haven't started saying "glaas" or "baath", but I'm enjoying everything. It's as if I've always been used to it.'

Michael McCartney, Paul's brother, took longer to get used to the changes he's had imposed on his life. Paul has always been very close to his brother, in age and in taste, more than George has been with his brothers, which made it worse for Michael. 'I suppose I couldn't help being affected by our kid. He's always had success. He was the first boy, the best looking one, the one who got all the girls and then all the fame.'

He has been asked for some years for his autograph around Liverpool, being Paul's brother. He resolutely signs 'Michael McGear', much to their disappointment. He usually also denies any relationship. 'No, love, wish I was his brother. I'd be in the money then, wouldn't I?'

He's now making Michael McGear better known, though it's taken a long time and long spells out of work. He became Michael McGear when he joined the Scaffold group in 1962. They started off well, with a 27-week TV series, then nothing much happened, apart from local theatre shows, until 1967, when they got a record 'Thank U Very Much' in the Top Ten. This has led to other shows and records. He is a good singer and he can compose, but he's always played that down, preferring to try something different.

'I don't want to be famous. I just want to be a success at my job, as long as I'm making it on my own. What I always worried about was being like Sean Connery's brother, or Tommy Steele's brother, just trying to follow in their brothers' footsteps.'

The Harrisons now live just outside Warrington. They moved from Liverpool in 1965, when Mr Harrison stopped being a bus driver. Warrington isn't the sort of place Liverpool people usually move to when they make good. They prefer to move across the water, to the posh part of Cheshire, as Jim McCartney has done. Warrington is 15 miles from Liverpool and about the same distance from Manchester, one of Lancashire's endless industrial towns, where, on the sunniest day, the prevailing colour is always grey.

The Harrisons, however, don't live in Warrington itself, but in a village called Appleton, three or four miles out. Their house is in a forgotten rural oasis, surrounded completely by fields, with no other houses in sight. Of all the parents' houses, the Harrisons' is the most isolated and the hardest to find.

The McCartney family at the races, 1968. From left to right: Michael, Paul's stepmother Angela, Paul and his father Jim.

It's a large L-shaped bungalow, with three acres of garden, which until fairly recently was a farmer's field. A gardener works two days a week knocking it into shape. They call it a bungalow, but it does have one upstairs room. They call it a room, but it is, in fact, 32 feet long, stretching the length of the house. They use it for parties or cinema shows.

The house cost George £10,000. With all the additions and improvements, such as a new open-plan staircase and a sun room, it's easily worth £20,000. The same house, in Bournemouth, near Mimi, would probably fetch £40,000.

Inside it is full of brand new modern furniture, deep-pile carpets and bright knick-knacks from all over the world. Most of these presents from around the world have been sent not from their son, as in the other parents' homes, but personally to the Harrisons from fans. And unlike the other homes, you aren't too dazzled by the number of Gold and Silver Discs inscribed to the Beatles. Their walls are hung instead with presentations inscribed to Harold and Louise Harrison.

On one wall is an enormous gold plaque with the inscription: 'Presented to Harold and Louise Harrison for the time and effort they have shown towards Beatle people everywhere. United Beatles Fans. Pomona, California, 1965.'

The other Beatle parents think that Mrs Harrison must be a little bit daft, at least they can't understand why she spends so much of her time being so kind to fans when she doesn't have to. Mrs Harrison just happens to be fanatical about fans. She's a fans' fan.

Every spare minute of the day she's answering fan letters. Most evenings she sits up till two o'clock, writing away. She personally writes 200 letters a week. Not notes, but proper letters of about two pages each. This is apart from signing and sending photographs. Their stamp bill is enormous.

'I've always personally answered all letters, except from obvious cranks. If it's in a foreign language, like Spanish, say, I read through it carefully and pick out words like "admiro". I can then roughly tell what it's about, so I send them a signed photograph.' Mr Harrison travels to the Fan Club HQ in Liverpool each month to pick up a new load of photographs. They get through 2,000 a month.

'From the beginning I used to get such lovely letters from fans, or more often the fan's mum. "Dear Mrs Harrison, you'll never realize what your letter has meant. After years of writing to phoney fan club addresses and never hearing anything back, a personal letter from George's mum! My daughter went through the roof." So you see, I just have to go on.

'Of course, at one time it was just physically impossible to answer all letters. In 1963 and '64, we were getting 450 a day from all over the world. On George's 21st birthday we had 30,000 cards and scores of screaming fans. They had to put a policeman on duty outside. He couldn't get over the kids kissing the door knob. "Have you got to put up with this all the time?" the policeman said. "I'd go mad." For years the post office always sent a special van with our mail, but things have settled down a lot now. I find 200 letters a week enough to cope with, if I don't slack.'

Fans she has corresponded with have a habit of suddenly turning up. She'd just had a family of Americans, who had come specially to see her. 'They were doing Europe and the Holy City in a fortnight. They were missing out Britain, but they decided to fly from Paris to Manchester, then get a taxi from Manchester, just to see us. It's a good job we were in.'

Mrs Harrison has always been a keen letter writer, long before George became a Beatle. She's got two pen pals she's corresponded with for 30 years. She got their names through the *Woman's Companion*. One lives in Barnsley, the other lives in Australia. With both these pen pals, she's swapped all family gossip since 1936. When the Beatles went to Australia, pictures of George as a little boy started appearing in the Australian press. Nobody could work out where they had come from. George himself had never seen them before. It was Mrs Harrison's pen pal, who had dug out the snaps she'd been sent many years ago.

'People always think we must be different now, because of George. We went to a fan's wedding the other day, and people said "How can you enjoy yourselves with the likes of us." They expect us to wear mink all the time.

'They *want* you to be different, I don't know why. When Harry was still working, people used to say to him, don't tell me *you're* still working. Now that he's not, they're sure we must be different. You can't win.'

Mr Harrison gave up working in 1965, after 31 years on the buses. 'I was driving the big 500. That's the limited stop bus that goes right across Liverpool, very quick, you can't afford to be caught in any traffic. "How much are you getting for driving that 500?" George said to me one day. "Ten pounds two shillings," I said. He said was that a day. I said no, a week. He said what a bloody liberty. I'll give you three times that to do nothing. It'll put another ten years on your life.'

Every summer they both open garden fêtes up and down the country, usually Roman Catholic Church ones. Mrs Harrison doesn't go to church, but as she was born a Catholic she thinks she should help them if she can.

'We've been as far south as Salisbury. What was that place north of London, Harry? Oh flippin' heck. I've forgotten. Harpenden, that was it. They advertised us in the local paper that we were going to open their fête. They usually do that.

'We judge beauty contests as well. We've done it for spastics, blind people, as well as churches. I don't care what it's for really.

'I usually say when I'm making my little opening speech that I'm quite pleased to be here to help them. I say how George and the boys wish to be remembered to them and send their best wishes. Then we get besieged when we go round the stalls. We enjoy it. Well, anything to help.'

Ringo's real father, who is also called Ritchie Starkey, has seen very little of Ringo since he separated from his mother when Ringo was five years old.

As far as Ringo can recall, after his early childhood he has only seen his father once. This was in 1962, before he was with the Beatles and still with Rory Storm's group.

'He happened to be at the Starkey's one day when I called,' says Ringo. 'I wasn't so childish by that time and didn't feel anything against him. He said to me, "I see you've got a car." I'd just got the Zodiac. I said, "Do you want to come outside and have a look at it?" He said yes. So we went out and had a look at my car. And that was all. I haven't seen him since or had any contact.'

His father later moved away from Liverpool. He now lives in Crewe, where he works as a confectioner in a bakery. He also has a part-time job as a window cleaner. He has remarried but has no children. Ringo is his only son, and Ringo's children his only grand-children. He collects their photographs, tearing them out of newspapers every time they appear. He doesn't feel any envy at what his son has done, although he wishes his father had been alive as he was always so fond of Little Ritchie. He is referred to in his family as Big Ritchie and Ringo as Little Ritchie.

Since Ringo's earliest days of fame he has remained hidden from any publicity and from Ringo, which is highly commendable. On the occasions when people have noticed his name and asked if he was any connection, he has said he was an uncle. But he does admit he would like to set his eyes on his son again. 'But I'm slow. I want kicking to do anything.' He gets annoyed when, now and again, Harry Graves, Ringo's stepfather, through no fault of his own, appears in the papers simply as 'Ringo's father'. He would like to correct it, but on the other hand he doesn't want the Press to find out who he is and where he lives. He has no wish to get involved in Ringo's fame.

Like Ringo, he's quiet and self-deprecating. He has many of Ringo's features, particularly the nose. And like Ringo, he hates onions, which is strange, considering they have not spent their lives together.

Ringo's mother Elsie and his stepfather, Harry Graves, now live in a luxury, Ideal Home

Exhibition bungalow in a very select part of Woolton in Liverpool. It cost £8,000. Marie Maguire, Ringo's childhood girlfriend from the Dingle, helped his parents find it. It's not far from the part of Woolton, the best part, where the Epsteins used to live. Elsie and Harry are the only Beatle parents still living in Liverpool.

The bungalow is set well back from the road, in almost an acre of land and is surrounded by lush lawns and rose bushes. It's in the sort of posh suburban neighbourhood where all the houses look as if they're uninhabited exhibition models, unlike the Dingle, where you can't get moving for human beings hanging out of windows or congregating on doorsteps.

Inside, it is all lushly furnished, in good taste, G-plan style, all bought by Ringo. There are three Gold Discs and two Silver Discs of Beatle records on the wall, all expensively framed. Over the TV is a wedding picture of Ritchie and Maureen and one of the children.

'Looking back,' says Elsie, 'I think the biggest thrill was going down to the Palladium that first time. Sitting in the audience and listening to all the London people cheering. 'Course, the two film premieres were nice. And the civic reception in Liverpool. They were all lovely. Everything was.

'I will say this, he's never got bigheaded. He's never changed his life. Maureen's very quiet, very natural.'

'I think I preferred their earlier music best,' says Harry. 'The rock and roll stuff. But they've got to change, haven't they? You've got to in this business. You've got to listen to their tunes properly now, more than once.'

Ringo's parents were the last of the parents to be moved into a new house. 'I always said I'd never ever move. I liked my neighbours so much down the Dingle. Even when the boys became famous, the neighbours never changed towards us. We never felt out of place. But the fans became too much. I couldn't stand it in the end. It's not so bad now, especially here.

'It's still very difficult for the boys though. I've seen Ritchie sit in here till it's dark because he's scared to go out in the light. Isn't it terrible? But you can't have everything, can you?

'I thought I'd get more privacy up here. I've always

Ringo, with his mother Elsie and stepfather Harry Graves, in their Liverpool home in 1964.

hated any publicity, reporters coming to see me, people asking me to go places, open things. Up here it really is quiet. Nobody knows our phone number up here.'

All the parents dislike publicity. None of them ever gives interviews. They wouldn't like to say anything which would annoy their sons in any way. Elsie and Harry most of all. Ringo had to ring up and tell his mother not to say that the sun shone out of his eyes all the time.

While the Harrisons love being nice to fans, Jim McCartney loves all the new good things in life and Mimi loves her dream world of John as a little boy, Elsie and Harry, in some ways, haven't yet come to terms with it all. It's almost as if they can't believe it. They still tend to think twice about doing anything, although they do enjoy themselves.

Harry gave up painting and decorating for Liverpool Corporation in 1965 at the age of 51. 'I could have gone on another 14 years if I'd wanted to. The Corporation were very good. They were almost as proud of the boys as I am. I had to take jokes of course. "*You* don't have to queue up for your wages, do you!" That sort of thing.

'Ritchie was at me for a long time to retire, but I didn't think I should. Then one day one of his mates saw me up a 40-ft ladder in the snow painting a council house, and he forced me to give up.

'Time does drag by a bit. I've decorated the house. I might do it again now, or get somebody to do it, now we can afford it. I've had to get used to a new sort of life. But I think I'm settling to it now. I've always got the garden. Or little inside jobs.'

In the evenings, they watch the TV, play bingo or go to dinner dances. Dinner dances are new things for them and they go a lot. They've made friends with several business people in the area who take them to their works dances. It usually comes out who they are and they have to sign autographs. Harry quite likes it, but Elsie doesn't.

'When I was down at Romford recently, seeing my relations,' says Harry, 'I went to a school do with my nephew. They had a sort of concert. It came out who I was, you know how it is, and I ended up signing about 300 autographs. I never saw the concert yet.'

Harry has always done a bit of singing, in pubs, usually imitating Billy Daniels. Since the Beatles, he always puts in a few of their numbers.

'It rained for three days the other week and we just sat here, looking out at the rain. Just to give myself something to do, I thought I'd write a few songs. Do you want to see them? Here's one, "They sit all day, thinking alone, Waiting for a ring on the telephone." I've done about five songs now. I sent them to Ritchie, hoping he might put some music to them. It's all they need, just a bit of nice music to go with them. But he sent them back. He says he can only play one instrument, so he couldn't do any music. Well, it's something to do, isn't it?

'It's funny, after all these years, not wanting for money. After all the years of pushing along. We still go second class on trains. You get just as good a seat.

'We do miss our old friends, but we often go and see them. Sometimes I go round the Corporation sites, if I'm passing. I look up at the lads and they all shout down at me. I shout back, "That's how it goes, lads. Keep the brush going."'

'It's all out of this world, isn't it?' says Elsie. 'There's not much more they can do. They've done everything. The last five years has been like a fairy story. But I still worry about him, about his health, after all he went through. I know he's a man, with little children of his own. But I still worry.'

PADDINGTON
STREET W.

THE BEATLES' EMPIRE

After the death of Brian Epstein, there was some reorganization done to NEMS Enterprises. Until then they had still been an expanding business, as managers, agents and theatre owners. It had then to be decided whether to go on, or whether to stop short and consolidate what they had. With the death of Brian, even though he hadn't done as much personally in the last year, the figurehead of the firm had gone. He'd been the main talent spotter. He'd created everything in the first place.

His mother, Mrs Queenie Epstein, inherited the bulk of his fortune while his younger brother, Clive, took over as chairman. He'd always had shares in NEMS Enterprises, from those very early Liverpool days. Of 10,000 one-pound shares in NEMS Enterprises, Brian had owned 7,000, Clive 2,000 and the Beatles 250 each.

But Clive had continued in the television business, doing little on the show business side of NEMS. He has Brian's good looks, and many of his mannerisms – his habit of looking slightly away while talking to you – but he is strikingly fair-haired while Brian was dark-haired.

Unlike Brian, he has always led a much quieter and less exhausting life, professionally and privately. He likes to spend as much time as possible with his wife and two children.

Robert Stigwood left the firm soon after Clive took over, which in one way solved the problem of whether to expand as a management. Stigwood had been brought in to do just this, to use his flair to find new groups and promote them. He left taking the groups he'd brought with him.

NEMS Enterprises is now, basically, a management and agency organization, whose managing director is Vic Lewis. Geoffrey Ellis, Brian's old friend, is still there as a director. A lot of the Beatles' interest, and money, now go into Apple rather than NEMS. Apple is the company they themselves have set up, which they alone control. It was being started, mainly thanks to Paul, before Brian died, but only began to be properly organized in 1968.

Opposite: The Apple boutique in Baker Street, London, opened in December 1967, attracting crowds of onlookers, who came to gape at the psychedelic mural. It closed seven months later, having lost around £200,000.

Peter Brown, who was Brian's closest friend and personal assistant, has taken over most of the personal handling of the Beatles, although it was laid down by Clive Epstein that the Beatles were free to decide all their own affairs from then on. He and NEMS would not try to take Brian's place in that respect. This is what the Beatles now do. They run themselves. But Peter is their link with NEMS and with the outside world. Anybody wanting them, if they're not fobbed off immediately, has to go through Peter. He does all the arranging and fixing that they want him to do. He has an ex-directory phone, his Beatles phone, whose number only they know.

Tony Barrow is still their senior press officer, although he also heads his own independent PR organization – Tony Barrow International. He is still writing Disker for the *Liverpool Echo*. He also does a lot of work coordinating the Fan Club, whose secretary is still Freda Kelly. It costs seven and six a year to be in the Fan Club, for which members get a regular bulletin and a Christmas present. There has always been a special Christmas record, made by the Beatles, exclusively for the Fan Club. They usually do little sketches and sing a few corny songs, as in their old Cavern days. The membership of the Fan Club is now just over 40,000. In 1965, at its height, it had twice that number. There are 40 regional secretaries, all voluntary, and 40 overseas branches.

The Fan Club runs at a loss and always has done. The cost of sending out 40,000 bulletins and posters several times a year alone uses up most of the subscriptions. On top of that there is the cost of the contents – the special *Sergeant Pepper* colour photo which everyone got cost £700 – plus the salaries of the two full-time Fan Club officials.

The *Beatles Monthly* makes a good profit. This is separate from the Fan Club, though most Fan Club members buy it, and a lot more besides. It costs two shillings a month and has a sale in Britain of 80,000. In America it comes as a supplement in *Datebook* magazine.

John and Paul at London Airport, May 1968, with their press spokesman and close friend, Derek Taylor. He later worked with Apple, the company the Beatles set up to look after their interests.

It has been going since August 1963 and is the longest-running fan magazine in Britain. It is not produced by NEMS but by a firm called Beat Publications, who pay for the privilege. Instead of taking a lot of the profits out of it, NEMS insists on its quality being maintained by having, for example, many-full colour pictures. It is an excellent publication. The best photographs of the Beatles appear in it, much better than any that appear in newspapers.

Very few new people have moved into the Beatles' magic circle. Professionally, they are still associated with those who first gave them their chance when they arrived in London in 1962.

Outside NEMS and Apple, their most important adviser and friend is George Martin. But in five years his position has almost been reversed. In 1962 he was the God figure

from Parlophone, the great A and R man, upon whom everything depended. Today, they depend on nobody.

George Martin left EMI in August 1965 after 15 long years. During this time he saw Parlophone saved and the profits of EMI itself soar to immense heights.

'I never made any money out of the Beatles' successes. I just got my same EMI salary, which I would have done anyway, as I was under contract. I never participated at all in their huge profits. I'm glad of this, because I've always been able to speak freely. No one could say I rode on the backs of the Beatles.

'But at EMI everyone always thought I *must* be in on their profits somehow, through one of their many companies. And the Beatles always thought I must be OK, because EMI must be looking after me.'

During that first phenomenal year of Beatlemania, 1963, he was probably the only person at all connected with the Beatles who did not make a lot of money because of them. Dick James, their music publisher, certainly did.

In 1963 George Martin was responsible for more number-one records than any other record producer in the history of British pop music, which, admittedly, hasn't a very long history. Most of his successes, during his 37 weeks with a number one, were by the Beatles. But he was also responsible for all the hit records by Cilla Black, Gerry and the Pacemakers, Billy J. Kramer, Matt Monro and others.

In 1964 his salary went up to £3,000 but this was as part of his contract with EMI, made before the Beatles came along. He started negotiating for some sort of incentive scheme. 'I thought the person doing all the hard work should be entitled to some recompense. But EMI were very unhappy about this.'

So he decided to leave, which didn't make EMI any happier either, because he took two other A and R men with him, John Burgess and Ron Richards. Along with a fourth, Peter Sullivan from Decca, they began their own company, Associated Independent Recordings, AIR for short.

It was a big chance to take at the time, as everyone told them. It was going against the traditional pattern of the record industry. Independent A and R men just need one flop to fold up completely, whereas a big record company, with a huge staff, can afford lots of flops.

But the biggest chance George Martin was taking was whether or not he could retain the Beatles. Legally, their contract was still with EMI. George Martin was simply EMI's staff A and R man employed on Beatles records. If he was no longer on their staff and became a freelance, EMI need no longer give him any more work at all – unless of course the Beatles particularly requested him to be their A and R man.

'I didn't consult the boys about leaving. I just took the chance that they still wanted me.' Which they did. And EMI agreed. EMI still produce Beatles records, but George now looks after them, not as an EMI man but as a freelance. They have to pay him for his services, very highly. 'I suppose now I am earning more than the managing director of EMI records.'

Today, AIR have, in their own little way, transformed the British record industry. Many of the best and most creative brains have opted out of the big corporations, selling back their services for double and treble what they got before.

In early 1968, AIR produced such artists as the Beatles, Cilla Black, Gerry and the Pacemakers, Shirley Bassey, Adam Faith, Lulu, Tom Jones, Manfred Mann and many others.

George Martin, with his 23 Gold Discs behind him, has at last got few financial worries. He now lives in style in a large, brand new, luxury town house near Hyde Park, and has a country cottage in Wiltshire. He and his wife Judy have a baby daughter called Lucy, no connection with 'Lucy In The Sky'. She has a full-time nanny to look after her.

He is trying to cut down more and get on with his own composing, which slightly amuses the Beatles, as they tend to think that only young people can write pop music. He has done several film scores on his own and did most of the knocking together of Paul's score for the film *The Family Way*. He composed the BBC's Radio One signature tune and has contracts to do more film music.

When the Beatles' plan, through Apple, to have their own recording studios and A and R men, gets properly organized, this might in some ways affect George Martin's position. But whatever happens, his own company's success seems solid enough. They have an interest in Playtape, a system which he says will one day replace gramophone records completely.

Musically, George Martin now tends to keep in the wings when they're doing their records, as we shall see in Chapter 30. They have now grown so sure of themselves as composers, and even as arrangers, that they make jokes about Big George.

Dick James, their music publisher, has no such ambivalent position. His relationship with them is purely business, though they are very fond of him.

Dick James is, on paper, a millionaire, thanks not simply to the Beatles, but also to the fact that he built up his firm so well and attracted many other artists.

Today, his one-room office days are far behind. He has his own posh block of offices in New Oxford Street – Dick James House, no less. The ground floor also contains a branch of the Midland Bank. Very handy. From this building Northern Songs, Dick James Music and many other companies operate. He now has a staff of 32 people and 6,000 square feet of office space on four floors.

Dick James still has a lot to do for the Beatles, plugging and selling their records. He says no one is so good that the release and promotion of their work doesn't need to be properly worked out. But his main job is collecting their royalties. It's up to him to fight for good terms, even though many percentages are laid down by agreements in the trade.

When they brought out their *Magical Mystery Tour* records, in a unique package, of two extended players inside a book, he had to do a lot of haggling with EMI over what their royalties would be for that. This entailed endless discussions over fractions of a farthing. Multiplied by millions, fractions of a farthing matter.

Dick James has also branched out, as most of the old sheet music people have had to. He now does every aspect of record work, even hiring recording studios and producing his own records, then leasing them to the big companies to sell. Like George Martin, he was enormously affected by the Beatles and then went on to make his mark in his own part of the show business industry.

The Beatles' personal buddies are all Liverpool lads like themselves. Many people have appeared or been connected with them at different stages of their lives, but only one or two have retained links. Alex Marda, the electronics expert, Robert Fraser, the art gallery owner, and Victor Spinetti, the actor who was in their film *Help!* are still friends, but most people are dropped completely once any contract is finished, such as the making of a film or a record. Even when they're looking for someone new to do something, they tend to dig out an even older mate from the past, such as Pete Shotton.

Pete Shotton was John's best friend from the age of about three. They were the bad lads at Quarry Bank together. But Pete went into the police force from school and lost contact with John. He gave up the police after three years, realizing that it was completely against his nature, and drifted into a series of dead-ends jobs, such as looking after a café that went bust.

In 1965, when Pete had no job and no money, he met John again by chance in Liverpool. John said he would back Pete in any enterprise he wanted to start. 'I was on holiday in Hampshire when I noticed this supermarket on Hayling Island. I liked the look of it. So John bought it for me to run. It cost £20,000.'

On the face of it, John was taking a big chance, investing so much money in Pete, with no proof of his competence, more the opposite if anything. But Pete managed the supermarket for almost two years, very successfully, making good profits. He increased its value and expanded it to include a menswear department.

'If John hadn't come along then, I might have ended up a crook. This is what John says he might have ended up himself. I had no money at all. I was getting into lots of shady deals and meeting bad people through the cafés.'

In the autumn of 1967, John asked Pete to leave the supermarket in Hayling Island – Pete's mother took it over as manager – and come up to London to work for Apple. He opened the first Apple Boutique, in Baker Street, and became the manager.

Terry Doran, another Liverpool friend, is also employed by Apple. He runs their music publishing department. Terry was originally in Brian's Liverpool circle, but got to know the others from the earliest days. When their success started, Brian set Terry up with his own car firm – he'd originally been a car salesman in Liverpool. This was called Brydor Cars (after Brian and Doran). It sold cars to the Beatles, among others, but eventually closed.

Alistair Taylor, who was with NEMS (the shop) in Liverpool and then with NEMS Enterprises (the show business agency) and witnessed the original Beatles' contract, is now also working for Apple as office manager.

John's other childhood friend, Ivan Vaughan, is not employed by the Beatles in any way, but is still a close friend. He went to school with Paul, and it was he who introduced Paul to John and his Quarrymen skiffle group. He is now training to be an educational psychiatrist.

The Beatles' two closest, ever-present and most important helpers and buddies are Neil and Mal. Neil (or Nell) Aspinall was their first road manager. Mal Evans joined them later, after a spot of bouncing at the Cavern club. Both, alone, were their road managers during all their big tours round the world.

Even in those days, they didn't like the term road manager. They did anything and everything. Now that they don't tour, it is even less applicable. Their relationship with the Beatles is very subtle, almost medieval. They are paid retainers, they do humble fetching and carrying, yet there is no master-servant relationship. They're just mates, who happen to get paid for being mates, whenever or wherever any Beatle decides he wants a mate.

Mal is big and well built, very bland and good natured, solid and sensible. Neil is smaller, slender, clever and outspoken. He would obviously be prepared to give it all up any time and just leave, if there was ever a serious disagreement. He does say no if he doesn't want to do something, though he could only think of one time when he said he didn't want to go anywhere. This was when John said he would be coming with him to Spain for the filming of *How I Won The War*. In the end, Neil gave in and went, hanging around the set for days, so that John would have someone to talk to afterwards, apart from the actors, with whom they didn't have much in common.

Mal, on the other hand, with his years of doing a regular job, sees everything as part of his job and has no complaints about anything he has to do.

'In America we were constantly being asked, "What will you do when the bubble bursts?"' says Neil. 'It never worried me then and still doesn't. I'll be doing something else, that's all. I've no idea what I'm going to do for the rest of my life. It never worries me.'

When the touring came to an end in 1966, they had a less strenuous life. But during recordings or TV or film work, Mal and Neil still go back to the old routine, getting them to and from the studios and making sure the instruments and equipment are ready.

They both follow Beatle fashion, growing moustaches and long sideboards when the others did, or wearing long neckerchiefs. They are completely part of the group. They look and talk the same.

When the Beatles are not recording, then Mal and Neil's life is much more irregular with long periods of doing nothing, but they are always expected to be on call. 'We're supposed to take alternate weeks, but we just both always seem to be around.'

When any of the Beatles individually has to go somewhere on his own, Mal or Neil accompanies him. Neil went with John on his film. Mal went with Paul to the USA to see Jane and with Ringo to Rome for his film. In February 1968 he was the one who went with them to India to see Maharishi.

They also do a lot of work liaising between the Beatles and people like Dick James, especially Neil. It's his job to make sure the words of a song are written down correctly and get sent to Dick James. They also help out sometimes by actually playing maraccas, triangles or anything else. John often asks Neil for ideas for the last lines of songs. They both appeared in *Magical Mystery Tour*. Mal was one of the five magicians. They write regular Beatle chat for *Beatles Monthly*. Mal is also a good photographer.

Neil is a bachelor and lives in a large luxury flat in a new block of flats in Sloane Street, opposite the Carlton Towers Hotel. He spends some of his spare time painting, a hobby he shares with the Beatles. He has a piano in his flat, though he can't play, with a piano exercise book opened at the second lesson.

For a long time, Neil was slightly under-used – after all he has more O levels than the rest of them put together – just because the Beatles valued him so much at what he was doing already. But since 1968 he has been director of Apple Corps, the central organization run by the Beatles, which looks after all their Apple branches. He has a large plush office in Wigmore Street where he sits in executive style.

Mal, who is married with two children, shared Neil's flat for a long time when they first all moved to London, commuting to Liverpool when possible. In 1967 he bought a house in Sunbury and moved in with his family. He chose the house to be within reasonable distance of the homes of John, Ringo and George. He has also now got an executive position – as manager of Apple Records.

What Mal and Neil have never been able to understand is the marvellous image the Beatles have always had. 'It wasn't really Brian's doing,' says Neil. 'He did make them smarter, put them in suits and got organized. But they've always come across as being so good and kind and nice, when they're not particularly, not more than other people. I think people *wanted* them to be like that. Fans made up the image for themselves. I don't know why. That's just what the fans wanted.

'They're now appearing to the public more like they really were before Brian came along, all individuals, doing and saying what they like.

'The public still think they're as nice, but perhaps they're a bit "eccentric" now, that's all. It's strange, isn't it, how people take to an image.'

'I'm always being asked which Beatle I like best,' says Mal. 'I usually say whichever one has just been nice to me.'

30

THE BEATLES AND THEIR MUSIC

It's all been a continual development. Now and again they appeared to be marking time, but not for long, then they were off and away again. They are always too bored by what they have just done ever to consider repeating it, however successful.

But with each new step they've laced the progressive with the traditional, like 'Eleanor Rigby' and 'Yellow Submarine', or 'I Am The Walrus' and 'Hello, Goodbye'.

There are lots of recognizable steps, if you like looking for recognizable steps. The first rock and roll stage was finished around the spring of 1964, after 'Can't Buy Me Love'. The end of the simple beat group line-up came in August 1965, with 'Yesterday' and the introduction of new instruments. The really serious experimentation started in August 1966, with the last track on *Revolver*, and was continued in *Sergeant Pepper*.

Even apparent anomalies can be explained, like 'All You Need Is Love'. This came out in mid-1967 and seemed to fit more into the 1963–4 period. But it wasn't, because it was satirical, poking fun at themselves, which is a stage they didn't reach in their music till 1967. 'Lady Madonna', in early 1968, wasn't really a throw-back to 1963 but mock-rock.

But trying to explain it all, slicing it up into nice pieces, is for the musicologists. It's not just Mr Mann of the London *Times* who's gone to town on each stage in their career. Serious American musical criticism of the Beatles could fill a book, and probably has done.

The simplest way to look at how they make their music, rather than trying to analyse it, is to split it into the touring days and the post-touring days.

John and Paul had had over six years together, writing and playing their music, by the time they started seriously recording in 1962. In those pre-1962 years they wrote hundreds of songs, most of them now forgotten or lost. Paul still has an exercise book full of them, but they don't show much. The words are of the simple 'Love Me Do', 'You Know I Love You' pattern. For the music, all they wrote was a few Do Ray Mes. Only they could work out at the time how the tune was supposed to go. They've forgotten now.

Opposite: The Beatles at Chiswick House, London, making the promotional film for 'Paperback Writer' and 'Rain', 1966.

It was more vanity, or frustrated professionalism on Paul's part, that made them write down all their 'Lennon-McCartney originals'. They knew them all anyway, with playing them hundreds of times in the Cavern.

Once 'Love Me Do' – a very old one, from the Quarrymen skiffle days – was recorded, they could have used up their old songs, but they didn't. They'd done so many already that it was comparatively easy for them to think up new ones for their next records.

They were composed, in those days, by Paul and John playing together on their guitars, just to see what came, either in hotels or on the road. 'She Loves You' was written on a coach in Yorkshire. They each tried out their own chords and own bits and pieces, following their own thoughts, until they liked something the other was doing. They then joined in, pushing it forward, then back for the other to have a go.

They deny today that they were deliberately concentrating on simple emotive words like 'I' and 'Me' and 'You'. That was just how it happened. They think the words of 'Love Me Do' are just as philosophical or poetic as, say, 'Eleanor Rigby'.

But their songs were simpler in those days. The Beatles were simpler lads, writing songs to play to screaming fans on one-night stands and wanting a simple and immediate reaction.

The songs were written, worked out and perfected on tour. By the time they got into the recording studio they knew them backwards.

'We were held back in our development,' says George, 'by having to go on stage all the time and do it, with the same old guitars, drums and bass. We just had to stick to the basic instruments.

'For a long time we didn't know what else you could do. We were just lads down from the North being allowed to make music in the big EMI studios. It was all done very quickly, in one go, on one track, as "Love Me Do" was. We used to do "Love Me Do" better on stage than we did on the record.'

Their first LP, *Please Please Me*, took just one day to record and cost £400. *Sergeant Pepper* took four months and cost £25,000.

Today, now that they have stopped touring, their recording sessions are long and highly complicated.

'Now that we only play in the studios, and not anywhere else,' says George, 'we haven't got a clue about what we're going to do. We have to start from scratch, thrashing it out in the studio, doing it the hard way. If Paul has written a song, he comes into the studio with it in his head. It's very hard for him to give it to us and for us to get it. When we suggest something, it might not be what he wants because he hasn't got it in his head. So it takes a long time. Nobody knows what the tunes sound like till we've recorded them, then listened to them afterwards.'

Nobody knows either how tunes come into their heads in the first place. They don't know, or can't remember, how and why they did something. Cross-examining them, unless it is very recent, is impossible, because it's all gone. The only way is to be there, except that with this method you still can't see into their heads, but only what is coming out.

'A LITTLE HELP FROM MY FRIENDS'

In March 1967 they were getting towards the end of the *Sergeant Pepper* album. They were halfway through a song for Ringo, a Ringo sort of song, which they'd begun the day before.

At two o'clock in the afternoon John arrived at Paul's house in St John's Wood. They both went up to Paul's work room at the top of the house. It is a narrow, rectangular room, full of stereophonic equipment and amplifiers. There is a large triptych of Jane Asher on the wall and a large silver piece of sculpture by Paolozzi, shaped like a fireplace with Dalek heads on top.

John started playing his guitar and Paul started banging on the piano. For a couple of hours, they both banged away. Each of them seemed to be in a trance till the other came up with something good and he would pluck it out of a mass of noises and try it himself.

They'd already got the tune the previous afternoon, a gentle lilting tune, and its name, 'A Little Help From My Friends'. Now they were trying to polish up the melody and think of some words to go with it.

'*Are you afraid when you turn out the light*,' sang John. Paul sang it after him and nodded. John said they could use that idea for all the verses, if they could think of some more questions on those lines.

'*Do you believe in love at first sight*,' sang John. 'No,' he said, stopping singing. 'It hasn't got the right number of syllables. What do you think? Can we split it up and have a pause to give it an extra syllable?'

John then sang the line, breaking it in the middle: '*Do you believe – ugh – in love at first sight*.'

'How about,' said Paul, '*Do you believe in a love at first sight*.'

John sang it over and accepted it. In singing it, he added the next line, '*Yes, I'm certain it happens all the time*.'

They both then sang the two lines to themselves, la la-ing all the other lines. Apart from this, all they'd got was the chorus. '*I'll get by with a little help from my friends*.' John found himself singing '*Would you believe*,' which he thought was better.

Then they changed the order round, singing the two lines '*Would you believe in a love at first sight Yes/I'm certain it happens all the time*', before going on to '*Are you afraid when you turn out the light*', but they still had to la la the fourth line, which they couldn't think of.

It was now about five o'clock. Cynthia, John's wife arrived, wearing sunglasses, accompanied by Terry Doran, one of their (and Brian Epstein's) old Liverpool friends. John and Paul kept on playing. Cyn picked up a paperback book and started reading. Terry produced a magazine about horoscopes.

John and Paul were singing their three lines over and over again, searching for a fourth.

'What's a rhyme for time?' said John. '*Yes, I'm certain it happens all the time*. It's got to rhyme with that line.'

'How about, "I just feel fine",' suggested Cyn.

'No,' said John. 'You never use the word just. It's meaningless. It's a fill-in word.'

John sang '*I know it's mine*' but nobody took much notice. It didn't make much sense, coming after '*Are you afraid when you turn out the light*'. Somebody said it sounded obscene.

Terry asked what my birthday was. I said 7 January. Paul stopped playing, although it had looked as if he was completely concentrating on the song, and said, 'Heh, that's our kid's birthday as well.' He listened while Terry read out the horoscope. Then he went back to doodling on the piano.

In the middle of the doodling, Paul suddenly started to play 'Can't Buy Me Love'. John joined in, singing it very loudly, laughing and shouting. Then Paul began another song on the piano, 'Tequila'. They both joined in again, shouting and laughing even louder. Terry and Cyn went on reading.

'Remember in Germany,' said John. 'We used to shout out anything.'

They played the song again. This time John shouted out different things in each pause in the music. 'Knickers' and 'Duke of Edinburgh' and 'tit' and 'Hitler'.

Paul, John and George making music in Abbey Road: playing together sparked each other off to higher, better things, and sometimes just to play around, muck around, making it up as they went along.

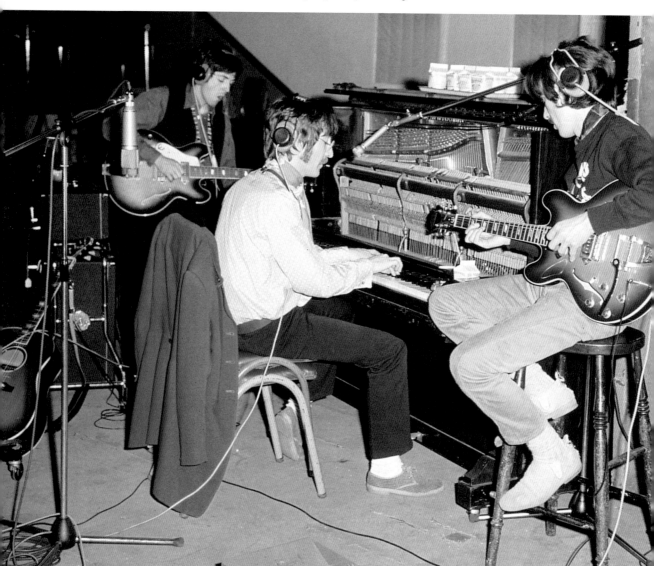

They both stopped all the shouting and larking around, as suddenly as they'd begun it. They went back, very quietly to the song they were supposed to be working on. '*What do you see when you turn out the light,*' sang John, trying slightly new words to their existing line, missing out 'afraid'. Then he followed it with another line, '*I can't tell you, but I know it's mine.*' By slightly rewording it, he'd made it fit in.

Paul said yes, that would do. He wrote down the finished four lines on a sheet of exercise paper propped up in front of him on his piano. They now had one whole verse, as well as the chorus. Paul got up and wandered round the room. John moved to the piano.

'How about a piece of amazing cake from Basingstoke,' said Paul, taking down a piece of rock-hard cake from a shelf. 'It'll do for a trifle,' said John. Paul made a face. Terry and Cynthia were still quietly reading.

Paul got a sitar from a corner and sat down and started to tune it, shushing John to keep quiet for a minute. John sat still at the piano, looking blankly out of the window.

Outside in the front courtyard of Paul's house, the eyes and foreheads of six girls could just be seen peering over the front wall. Then the girls dropped, exhausted, on to the pavement beyond. A few minutes later they appeared again, hanging on till their strength gave way. John peered vacantly into space through his round, wire spectacles. Then he began to play a hymn on the piano, singing words that he made up as he went along.

'Backs to the wall, if you want to see His Face.'

Then he seemed to jump in the air and started banging out a hearty rugby song. 'Let's write a rugby song, eh.' No one listened to him.

Paul had got his sitar tuned and was playing some notes on it, the same ones over and over again. He got up again and wandered round the room. John picked up the sitar this time, but he couldn't get comfortable with it. Paul told him that he had to sit on the floor with his legs crossed and place it in the bowl of his foot. Paul said that George did it that way; it felt uncomfortable at first, but after a few centuries you got used to it. John tried it, then gave up and placed it against a chair.

'Heh,' said John to Terry, 'did you get to the place?'

'Yeh, I got you three coats, like George's.'

'Great,' said John, very excited. 'Where are they then?'

'I paid by cheque and they wouldn't let me have them till tomorrow.'

'Oh,' said John. 'Couldn't you have said who they were for? You should have said they were for Godfrey Winn. I want them now.'

'They'll be OK tomorrow,' said Paul. 'There's some more stuff to get tomorrow. Don't worry.'

Paul then went back to his guitar and started to sing and play a very slow, beautiful song about a foolish man sitting on the hill. John listened to it quietly, staring blankly out of the window, almost as if he wasn't listening. Paul sang it many times, la la-ing words he hadn't thought of yet. When at last he finished, John said he'd better write the words down or he'd forget them. Paul said it was OK. He wouldn't forget them. It was the first time Paul had played it for John. There was no discussion.

It was getting near seven o'clock, almost time to go round the corner to the EMI recording studios. They decided to ring Ringo, to tell him his song was finished – which it wasn't – and that they would record it that evening. John picked up the phone. After a lot of playing around, he finally got through, but it was engaged. 'If I hold on, does that mean I eventually get through?'

'No, you have to hang up,' said Paul.

'IT'S GETTING BETTER'

Another afternoon – it was the first afternoon of spring – and Paul went for a walk with his dog Martha. John still hadn't arrived for their latest recording work on *Sergeant Pepper*.

He pushed Martha into his Aston Martin and got in beside her and started the car, but it wouldn't start. He gave it a few bangs, hoping that would do it, then he gave up and got out of the Aston Martin and into his black-windowed Mini Cooper. He revved up first time. His housekeeper opened the large black doors and he shot through, catching all the fans by surprise. He was away before they realized he'd come out.

He drove to Primrose Hill, where he parked the car and left it, without locking it. He never locks his cars.

Martha ran around and the sun came out. Paul thought it really was spring at last. 'It's getting better,' he said to himself.

He meant the weather, but the phrase made him smile because it was one of Jimmy Nichols' phrases, one which they used to mock all the time in Australia.

When Ringo was once ill and unable to play, Jimmy Nichols deputised for him on part of their Australian tour. Every time one of them asked Jimmy how he was getting on, if he was liking it and was he managing OK, all he ever replied was 'It's getting better'.

That day at two o'clock, when John came round to write a new song, Paul suggested: 'Let's do a song called, "It's getting better".' So they got going, both playing, singing, improvising and messing around. When the tune was at last taking shape, Paul said, 'You've got to admit, it is getting better.'

'Did you say, "You've got to admit, it's getting better"?'

Then John sang that as well. So it went on till two in the morning. People came to see Paul, some by appointment. They were left waiting downstairs, reading, or were sent away. They stopped once for a meal, a quick fry-up.

The next evening, Paul and John went to the recording studio. Paul played the new song on the piano, la la-ing the accompaniment or banging in tune to his words, to give the others an idea of what it sounded like. Ringo and George said they liked it, as did George Martin.

The first stage in the layer cake system that they now use in recording songs was to get the backing recorded on one track.

They discussed what the general sound would be like and what sort of instruments to use. They also chatted about other things. When they got bored, they went off and played on their own on any instruments lying around. There was an electronic piano in the corner of the studio, left over from someone else's recording session. Someone doodled on it and it was decided to use it.

Ringo sat at his drums and played what he thought would be a good drum backing, with Paul singing the song to him in his ear. Because of the noise, Paul had to shout in Ringo's ear as he explained everything.

After about two hours of trying out little bits and pieces, they had the elements of a backing. George Martin and two studio technicians, who'd been sitting around just waiting up until then, went up into their sound-proof glass control room, where they continued to sit around and wait for the Beatles to get themselves organized.

Neil and Mal got the instruments and microphones arranged in one corner of the studio and the four of them at last started to sing and play, 'It's Getting Better'. Ringo looked a bit lost, sitting slightly apart on his own, surrounded by his drums. The other three had their heads together over one microphone.

They played the song over about ten times. All that was being recorded, up in the sound-proof box, were the instruments, not their voices. From time to time, Paul said 'Once more, let's try it this way,' or 'Let's have less bass, or more drums.' By midnight they had recorded the backing.

The next day John and George assembled at Paul's house. Ringo wasn't there. They were just going to do the singing track for 'It's Getting Better' and he wouldn't be needed. Ivan Vaughan, the schoolfriend of John and Paul, was also at Paul's house. At 7.30 they all moved round to EMI, where George Martin, like a very understanding housemaster, was ready and waiting for them.

The backing for 'It's Getting Better', which they'd recorded the night before, was played over and over again for them to listen to. George Harrison and Ivan went off to chat in a corner, but Paul and John listened carefully. Paul instructed the technician on which levers to press, telling him what he wanted, how it should be done, which bits he liked best. George Martin looked on, giving advice where necessary. John stared into space.

Dick James, their song publisher, arrived wearing a camel coat. He said hello to them all, very jolly and breezy. He made a joke about there being no truth in the rumour that EMI were buying Northern Songs.

He listened to the backing of 'It's Getting Better' and showed no expression. Then they played him one of their other songs, about a girl leaving home. George Martin said this was the one that almost made him cry. Dick James listened and said yes, it was very good. He could do with more of them. 'You mean you don't like the freak-out stuff?' Dick James said no, no, he didn't mean that. Then he left.

They played the backing track of 'It's Getting Better' for what seemed like the hundredth time, but Paul said he wasn't happy about it. They'd better get Ringo in and they would do it all again. Someone went to ring for Ringo.

Peter Brown arrived. He'd just returned from a trip to America. He gave them some new American LPs which they all jumped upon. They played him 'She's Leaving Home' and a few other of the *Sergeant Pepper* songs, already recorded. Then they played him the backing track of 'It's Getting Better'. As it was being played, Paul talked to one of the technicians and told him to try yet a different sound mix. He did so, and Paul said that was much better. It would do. They didn't need to bring Ringo in now after all.

'And we've just ordered Ringo on toast,' said John. But Ringo was cancelled in time and the studio was got ready to record the sound track, the voices. As it was being set up by Neil, Mal brought in tea and orange juice drinks on a tray.

Paul let his tea go cold while he played with an oscillating box he found in a corner. By playing around with the switches, he managed to produce six different noises. He said to one of the sound engineers that if someone could produce oscillating boxes with the sounds controlled and in order, it would be a new electronic instrument.

They were ready at last. The three of them held their heads round one microphone and sang 'It's Getting Better' while, up in the control box, George Martin and his two assistants got it all down on track. The three Beatles were singing, not playing, but through headphones strapped to their ears they could hear the recording of the backing track. They were simply singing to their already recorded accompaniment.

In the studio itself, all that could be heard were the unaccompanied, un-electrified voices of the Beatles singing, without any backing. It all sounded flat and out of key.

They ran through the song about four times and John said he didn't feel well. He could do with some fresh air. Someone went to open the back door of the studio. There was the sound of loud banging and cheering on the other side. The door began to move slightly inwards, under the strain of a gang of fans who'd somehow managed to get inside the building.

George Martin came down from his box and told John he would be better to go up on the roof and get some air, rather than go outside.

'How's John?' Paul asked into the microphone to George Martin up in the control box.

'He's looking at the stars,' said George Martin.

'You mean Vince Hill?' said Paul. He and George started singing Edelweiss and laughing. Then John came back.

In the corner of the studios, Mal and Neil and Ivan, the friend, couldn't hear the jokes over the headphones. They'd finished their tea. Ivan was writing a letter home to his mother. Neil was filling in his diary. He'd only started it two weeks previously. He said he should have started one about five years ago.

A man in a purple shirt called Norman arrived. He used to be one of their recording engineers and now had a group of his own. The Pink Floyd. Very politely he asked George Martin if his boys could possibly pop in to see the Beatles at work. George smiled, unhelpfully. Norman said perhaps he should ask John personally, as a favour. George Martin said no, that wouldn't work. But if by chance he and his boys popped in about eleven o'clock, he might just be able to see what he could do.

They did pop in, around 11.00, and exchanged a few half-hearted hellos. The Beatles were still going through the singing of 'It's Getting Better', for what now seemed the thousandth time. By two o'clock they'd got it at least to a stage which didn't make them unhappy.

'MAGICAL MYSTERY TOUR'

The tune and all the words of 'It's Getting Better' had been worked out before they got into the recording studio but when they arrived at the EMI studios at 7.30 one evening to record 'Magical Mystery Tour' all they had was the title and a few bars of the music.

There was the usual crowd of fans waiting for them as they went in. Not screaming. Just quiet and contrite, like humble subjects, subdued by the presence. As they went in, one girl very shyly gave George a button badge which said 'George for PM'.

'Why would Paul McCartney want you,' said John to George.

Paul played the opening bars of 'Magical Mystery Tour' on the piano, showing the others how it would go. He gestured a lot with his hands and shouted 'Flash, Flash', saying it would be like a commercial. John was wearing an orange cardigan, purple velvet trousers and a sporran. He opened the sporran and took out a cigarette, which he lit. Someone shouted that Anthony, John's chauffeur, wanted him on the phone.

They leaned round the piano while Paul was playing, going over and over the opening. Paul told Mal to write down the order of how they would do the song. In a very slow schoolboy hand, Mal wrote down the title and got ready for Paul's instructions. Paul said Trumpets, yes they'd have some trumpets at the beginning, a sort of fanfare, to go with 'Roll Up, Roll Up, for the Magical Mystery Tour'. Mal had better write that line down as well, as it was the only line they'd got. Paul told Mal to write down DAE, the first three chords of the song. Mal sucked his pencil, waiting for more of Paul's inspired words, but nothing came.

The instruments were then set up and they got ready to record the backing, which as usual was to be the first track they would do. John came back and asked Mal if he'd got in touch with Terry yet. Mal said he couldn't get through to him. John said it was his job to get through. Just keep on until he did.

It took a couple of hours to work out the first backing track and get it recorded. After it was done, Paul went up to see George Martin in the control room. Paul had the track played back to him, again, and again.

Below in the studio, while Paul got the technicians to do things upstairs, George got a set of crayons out of his painted sheepskin jacket and started to draw a picture. Ringo stared into space, smoking, looking very unhappy, which is his natural expression when he's not talking. John was at the piano, sometimes playing quietly, other times jumping up, pretending to be a spastic, or thumping out loud corny tunes. No one was watching him. He smiled fiendishly to himself through his spectacles, like a Japanese gnome. Neil was reading a pile of *Occult Weeklies*, which they'd all been thumbing through earlier in the evening. Mal had disappeared.

Paul was at last satisfied with the sound of the first track. He came back down and said he thought they could now add a few more things to it.

Mal reappeared carrying a big brown paper bag full of socks, all in bright colours. He passed the bag to John first. He grabbed it in great delight. He chose several pairs of orange terry towelling socks, then passed the bag round for the others to have a dip. The previous night he had said, just in passing, 'Socks, Mal.'

After the socks had been handed out, Paul asked Mal if he'd managed to get any real mystery tour posters. Mal said he had been round the bus stations all day looking for them. But he couldn't find any.

They had hoped that some real posters would have given them some ideas for the words of the song. Instead they all tried again to think of some good words, apart from Roll Up, Roll Up, which was still all they'd got.

As they shouted out ideas, Mal wrote them all down. 'Reservation', 'Invitation', 'Trip of a lifetime', 'Satisfaction guaranteed'. But they soon got fed up. They decided they would just sing any words that came into their heads, just to see what happened. So they did.

When they'd finished that, Paul decided that on the next track he would add a bit of bass to the backing. He put on the headphones, so that he could hear what they'd done so far, and strapped on his bass guitar. After that he said they should add even more instruments. All of them, Paul, Ringo, John, George, Neil and Mal, then picked up any old instruments that were lying around – maraccas, bells, tambourines. George Martin didn't play anything, though he has done on many of their records. They all put on headphones and banged and played them to the music.

By two o'clock, they had recorded a basic backing, and had layered onto it a bass track, a lot of shouting and disjointed words, and some percussion instruments. 'Magical Mystery Tour' was then forgotten about for almost six months.

The Beatles do seem to record their music in apparent chaos. It is certainly an expensive trial-and-error method, making

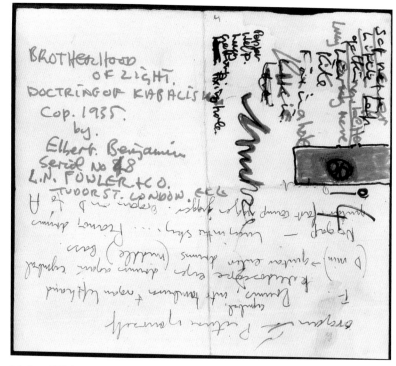

John's scribbled notes about 'Lucy in the Sky'. The full title of the song has been said, wrongly, to stand for LSD.

it all up as they go along. At one time, their songs were recorded at one go and on one track or at the most two. Now it takes at least four tracks, as they continually think of another instrument or effects to add. And when a 40-piece orchestra is used, as in 'A Day In The Life', the expense is enormous.

Listening to each stage of their recording, once they've done the first couple of tracks, it's often hard to see what they're still looking for, as it sounds so complete. Often the final complicated, well-layered versions seem to have drowned the initial simple melody. But they know it's not right, even if they can't put it into words. Their dedication is impressive, gnawing away at the same song for stretches of up to ten hours.

Paul often appears to be the leader in all this. This is mainly because someone has to say it's not good enough, let's do it once again. They all know it. But someone has to voice the instructions. Paul does it best, as he's still the keeny. But they all have a say in any big decisions. When it's John's song, he does most of the directing, and the same with George. George, most of all, is in complete charge of his own songs.

The recording of all their songs follows roughly the above pattern. But there is no pattern to the writing and creating of the songs in the first place. That can happen in many ways.

'The last four songs of an album are usually pure slog,' says Paul. 'If we need four more we just have to get down and do them. They're not necessarily worse than ones done out of imagination. They're often better, because by that stage in an LP we know what sort of songs we want.'

About a third of their songs are written like this, because they've got to write a song and can't wait for any sort of inspiration. John and Paul can do these slog songs on their own, but mostly they do them together, starting at two in the afternoon and giving themselves a day to complete it.

The rest of their songs owe something, even if it's very little, to inspiration of some kind. But even when an idea has suddenly come to them, they rarely sit down and work it all out. Very often they put it away at the back of their head till they need it. Even if they are in the process of doing an album, they still tend to bring out the song for the other one to hear, or bring it to the studio, still half finished. It's due to laziness as much as anything else. They want to get the others to help.

Paul's song 'Eleanor Rigby' came to him when he was looking at a shop window in Bristol and liked the name – Daisy Hawkins. Playing with the name in his head, it turned into a rhythm, and then into Eleanor Rigby. He saw the tune all through his head, but he still hadn't finished the words by the time it was recorded. The last verse was thought of by all of them, making suggestions at the last minute in the studio.

The only song either of them can think of that came straight out and was then recorded unaltered was John's 'Nowhere Man'. He's not particularly proud of it.

'I was just sitting, trying to think of a song, and I thought of myself sitting there, doing nothing and going nowhere. Once I'd thought of that, it was easy. It all came out. No, I remember now, I'd actually stopped trying to think of something. Nothing would come. I was cheesed off and went for a lie down, having given up. Then I thought of myself as Nowhere Man – sitting in his nowhere land.'

Very little inspiration comes simply out of the air. But a lot comes out of their immediate environment, past (like 'Penny Lane') or present ('Lovely Rita'). John, particularly, has taken many ideas from the media surrounding him at the time he's been looking for a song.

'Mr Kite was a straight lift. I had all the words staring me in the face one day when I was looking for a song.

'It was from this old poster I'd bought at an antique shop. We'd been down in Surrey or somewhere filming a TV piece to go with 'Strawberry Fields For Ever'. There was a break and I went into this shop and bought an old poster advertising a variety show that starred Mr Kite.

'It said the Hendersons would also be there, late of Pablo Fanques Fair. There would be hoops and horses and someone going through a hogshead of real fire. Then there was Henry the Horse. The band would start at ten to six. All at Bishopsgate. Look, there's the bill, with Mr Kite topping it. I hardly made up a word, just connecting the lists together. Word for word really.

'I wasn't very proud of that. There was no real work. I was just going through the motions because we needed a new song for *Sergeant Pepper* at that moment.'

Almost the same sort of lifted inspiration caused what many people thought was their best song on the *Sergeant Pepper* LP, 'A Day In The Life'.

This was the one banned by the BBC on the grounds that it contained references to drugs – 'I'd love to turn you on.' Even John himself is quite pleased with this song.

Most of the words of the first section – the verses that begin with 'I read the news today, oh boy' – came from genuine pieces of news John was reading the day he wrote the song.

'I was writing the song with the *Daily Mail* propped up in front of me on the piano. I had it open at their News in Brief, or Far and Near, whatever they call it. There was a paragraph about 4,000 holes in Blackburn, Lancashire, being discovered. There was still a word missing in that verse when we came to record. I knew the line had to go "Now they know how many holes it takes to... something, the Albert Hall." It was a nonsense verse really, but for some reason I couldn't think of the verb. What did the holes do to the Albert Hall?

'It was Terry who said "fill" the Albert Hall. And that was it. Perhaps I was looking for that word all the time, but couldn't put my tongue on it. Other people don't necessarily *give* you a word or a line, they just throw in the word you're looking for anyway.'

The film mentioned in the song wasn't in the newspaper, but was a reference to his own film, which he'd just finished acting in – *How I Won The War*. The film is about the English army winning the war. It was originally a book.

'The lucky man who made the grade' in a car accident was based, rather indirectly, on the death of a friend of John's, and of all the Beatles – Tara Brown. Michael McCartney, Paul's brother, was a particularly close friend of his. There was a reference to his death in the paper on the day John was writing the song.

'I didn't copy the accident. Tara didn't blow his mind out. But it was in my mind when I was writing that verse.' Tara wasn't from the House of Lords either, but he was the son of a peer, Lord Oranmore and Browne, and a member of the Guinness family, which is the next best thing.

'Goodmorning, Goodmorning' was sparked off by listening to a cornflakes advertisement on TV. 'I often sit at the piano, working at songs, with the telly on low in the background. If I'm a bit low and not getting much done, then the words on the telly come through. That's when I heard Goodmorning, Goodmorning.'

Many times the first starting point of John's songs is a basic piece of rhythm, then words are fitted to it so that the rhythm, which originally consisted of only three or four notes, can be gone over and over and developed, either in his head or at the piano.

One day, down at his home in Weybridge John had just heard a police car going past in the distance with its siren shrieking. This consists of two notes, up and down, repeated over and over again, like a primitive wailing. The rhythm had stayed in his head and he was playing with putting words to it.

'*Mis-ter, Ci-ty, p'lice-man, sit-tin, pre-tty.*'

He'd got as far as trying the words in a slightly different order. '– Sitting pretty, like a policeman', but hadn't got much further. He said it would be a basis for a song, but there was no need to develop now. It could be dragged out next time he needed a song. 'I've written it down on a piece of paper somewhere. I'm always sure I'll forget it, so I write it down, but I wouldn't.'

He'd written down another few words that day, just daft words, to put to another bit of rhythm. 'Sitting on a cornflake, waiting for the man to come.' I thought he said 'van to come', which he hadn't, but he liked it better and said he'd use it instead.

He also had another piece of tune in his head. This had started from the phrase, 'sitting in an English country garden'. This is what he does for at least two hours every day, sitting on the step outside his window looking at his garden. This time, thinking about himself doing it, he'd repeated the phrase over and over again, till he'd put a tune to it.

'I don't know how it will all end up. Perhaps they'll turn out to be different parts of the same song – sitting in an English country garden, waiting for the van to come. I don't know.'

Which is what did happen. He put all the pieces together and made 'I Am The Walrus'. In the backing to the song can be heard the insistent rhythm of a police siren, which had sparked the song off in the first place. This very often happens. Bits of songs which have started off separately end up as the one song, when the time comes to empty his head and find a new song.

John is sparked off by rhythms, but more and more he is setting his own poetry, or often simply disconnected thoughts, to music. With Paul, the tune usually comes first. John woke up at seven o'clock one morning and couldn't get back to sleep. He found the words 'pools of sorrow, waves of joy' going through his head. He got up and wrote them out, writing about ten lines in all which eventually became 'Across the Universe'. In this first, early morning version, when he knew he was writing down some sloppy, corny phrases, just to get himself on to the next line, his handwriting got worse and more illegible, out of embarrassment, in case anyone should see lines he didn't like. This is what he did in his poems as a boy, or in letters to Stu, trying to cover up his soft sentimental thoughts in case Mimi or anyone should read them.

He wasn't really pleased with the song in the end. He said it didn't come out as he'd heard it in his head. When they came back from India in April 1968 he decided to try to record it again, having thought of new ideas.

When John is talking to George Martin, on a John song, there is a lot of whooshing and wow wow wow, as he tries to let George Martin hear what he can hear in his head. He's also not as definite as Paul, or doesn't appear to be, asking the others what they think when they've just heard a track played back. Paul tends to say straight away, let's do it again.

'Heh Bulldog' was another John song which began simply with a set of words to which music was put. This is probably one of the quickest post-touring songs they've ever recorded. It was done, in February 1968, almost in a day, from start to finish. They had to come into the studio one Sunday to be filmed for a three-minute promotional film to go with 'Lady Madonna', Paul's song, the A side of their single in March 1968.

'Paul said we should do a real song in the studio, to save wasting time. Could I whip one off. I had a few words lying around at home so I brought them in.' Along with Neil and the others, the words were finished in the studio. John told them roughly how he heard the song and they all created the backing between them, just by getting their instruments and playing together, while the film people filmed them.

The words changed, even as they sang them, as Paul misread John's handwriting. One line had 'measured out in news', which came out as 'measured out in you', which they agreed sounded better. There was no reference anywhere to bulldog when they started recording the song. There was a mention of bullfrog, which made Paul, as a joke, start barking, just to make John laugh. They kept the barking in and changed the title. John said the idea of a dog fitted very well. It could be a dog that barks away, worrying at you, trying to pull you, just like the girl in the song. He then picked up a sitar and started singing the words in a Lancashire voice, strumming on the sitar like George Formby, but they couldn't work that in.

Most of John's composing is done at the piano, just doodling over it for hours, letting his mind wander, almost in a trance, while his fingers look for bits of tunes. 'I've got another one here, a few words, I think I got them from an advert – "Cry baby cry, make your mother buy". I've been playing it over on the piano. I've let it go now. It'll come back if I really want it. I do get up from the piano as if I have been in a trance. Sometimes I know I've let a few things slip away, which I could have caught if I'd been wanting something.'

Paul tends to work on whole songs, rather than little bits. But very often songs are left unfinished. And even when they are finished, they are sometimes left around for a long time. 'When I'm Sixty Four' (the age is in honour of Paul's Dad) was written in the Cavern days before it popped up and was revised as being ideal for *Sergeant Pepper*.

Sometimes, when they both have a half-finished song, they meld them together, to make one new whole one. The classic example of this was 'A Day In The Life'.

'I'd written the first section and I let Paul hear it. I said to him what we want now is a middle eight bars. He said what about this – "Woke up, Fell out of bed, dragged a comb across my head." This was a song he'd written on his own, with no idea of what I was working on. I said yeh, that's it.

'Then we thought we needed some sort of connection bit, a growing noise to lead back into the first bit. We wanted to think of a good end and we had to decide what sort of backing and instruments would sound good. Like all our songs, they never become an entity until the very end. They are developed all the time as we go along.

'Often the backing I think of early on never comes off. With "Tomorrow Never Knows" I'd imagined in my head that in the background you would hear thousands of monks chanting. That was impractical, of course, and we did something different. I should have tried to get near my original idea, the monks singing. I realize now that was what it wanted.'

Their long stay in India with Maharishi in the spring of 1968 proved an ideal environment for writing songs – and not Indian ones either. The strange, foreign environment of Hamburg produced from within themselves a Liverpool sound. (Marshall McLuhan, who fancies himself as a Beatle expert, says this proves his theory that when a new environment goes round an old environment, the old one becomes an art form). India had a similar effect, at least with Paul, making him go back to his boyhood influences, like Hollywood musicals and westerns.

Anyway, when they came back, both John and Paul had written about six or seven songs each, enough for a new LP. They even came back with an idea for its format – the LP would consist of the songs from the sound track of a non-existent musical. It was original-ly going to be called *Doll's House* – Doll being a girl's name, and her house being a house of pleasure, where all the people in the fictional musical would congregate. But they found that *Doll's House* had already been used as a title.

Paul came back and played his songs, with Jane singing a la la accompaniment, to all the friends who dropped in, especially when they were going to launch into some saga of the things that had gone wrong when he'd been away. 'No, no, don't tell me, listen to this instead.' Then he began a song about Rocky Racoon checking into his room and finding only a Gideon Bible. At the rhyming of 'Bible' with 'rival' he gave an apologetic grimace.

He'd also written a song about junk in a junk yard. He paused in the middle of singing a line about 'broken hearted jubilee mug' to say wasn't 'jubilee' a lovely word to sing. Then he had a song about a girl sitting in the distance with a red umbrella. It had few words but lots of la las. He enjoyed most of all singing to everyone a mock folksy-American song about it being great to be back in the USSR. He put on a Beach Boy voice for the chorus. Mike, his brother, said why didn't they get the Beach Boys themselves to sing the chorus, but Paul said no. Although Paul still obviously had many gaps to fill in the songs, in singing them to others he was not looking for suggestions, the way John might do, or even to show off. He was just sharing the enjoyment he was having in beginning some new songs, before he'd finished and forgotten them for ever.

It is hard enough for John, Paul and George to get the sound they think they can hear in their heads, but it can be even harder for George Martin. They leave him with bits of tracks that can't sometimes be tied together, or present him with problems that can't be solved, at least at short notice. Just as they thought they could hire Shepperton studios to film *Magical Mystery Tour* at a week's notice, so they still decide overnight that they'd like a 40-piece orchestra for the next evening. George Martin is expected to get it for them.

He is sometimes slightly amused by their lack of musical knowledge. 'They ask for such things as violins to play an F below middle C, which, of course, violins can't do.'

But he approves and enjoys their method of piling track upon track until they get the sound they like. He's always enjoyed the electronic side of recordings, since the days of trying funny noises for his Peter Sellers records. He thinks that they could often do with 64 tracks, not just four, in order to add on everything they think of.

'I once saw a film of Picasso at work. He starts with an idea, then he overlays it with something else. He still has the same basic idea, but he changes it by putting something else over it. Sometimes the original idea can get obliterated.'

Complications arise when it's not just a matter of adding something to an existing track, but taking bits out of two separate tracks. 'Strawberry Fields' was one of the more complicated creations, in a technical sense. They did the usual basic tracks, then John, playing it at home, decided it wasn't what he'd wanted.

'He'd wanted it as a gentle dreaming song, but he said it had come out too raucous. He said could I do him a new line-up with the strings. So I wrote a new score and we recorded that. But he didn't like it. It still wasn't right. What he would now like was the first half from the early recording, plus the second half of the new recording. Would I put them together for him? I said it was impossible. They were in different keys and different tempos.'

While George Martin was trying to puzzle out a way of getting round this, without having to do the whole recording session all over again, he noticed that by speeding up the slower tempo recording by five per cent, it not only brought it to the same tempo as the other one, it brought it in the same key. By chance, he was able to join both together, without too much trouble.

The Beatles have never worried about being told things were impossible, nor have they worried when George has told them that new ideas they've thought of were very old hat. They got an idea at the end of 'She Loves You', which they thought was really new. This was to go down on the last yeh yeh to an added sixth. 'I told them it was corny. Glenn Miller was doing it 20 years ago. They said so what. That was what they wanted.'

George Martin sees his work with them as having been in two stages. 'At first, they needed me enormously. They knew nothing and they relied on me to produce their sound, the deafening sound they'd produced in the Cavern, but which nobody was doing on record. People like Cliff and the Shadows were very quiet and subdued.

'The second stage is now, when they know what they want to put in a record, but they rely on me to arrange it for them.

'In between, I've changed from being the gaffer to four Herberts from Liverpool to what I am now, clinging on to the last vestiges of recording power.'

This is a half joke, he hopes. There is a bit of teasing on both sides. The Beatles tend to mock him slightly. He in turn is slightly amused by their innocence and naivety. He is worried that it might one day make them go too far, not in music, but in films perhaps, refusing to rely on anyone experienced, such as himself. He did think they were taking on too much with their TV film. From the response of the British TV critics, he was right.

He thinks Paul has the most all-round musical talent, with an ability to turn out tunes almost to order. 'He's the sort of Rodgers and Hart of the two. He can turn out excellent potboilers. I don't think he's particularly proud of this. All the time he's trying to do better, especially trying to equal John's talent for words. Meeting John has made him try for deeper lyrics. But for meeting John, I doubt if Paul could have written "Eleanor Rigby".

'Paul needs an audience, but John doesn't. John is very lazy, unlike Paul. Without Paul he would often give up. John writes for his own amusement. He would be content to play his tunes to Cyn. Paul likes a public.

'John's concept of music is very interesting. I was once playing Ravel's "Daphne and Chloë" to him. He said he couldn't grasp it because the melodic lines were too long. He said he looked upon writing music as doing little bits, which you then join up.'

Both Paul and John do have natural musical talent and originality, but they both have it in different ways. Paul can produce easy, sweet music, like 'Michelle' and 'Yesterday', while John's music is much bumpier and more aggressive, like 'I Am The Walrus'. In a way, it comes out of their personalities. As people, long before they started writing songs, John was always the rough, aggressive one and Paul the sweeter and the smoother.

But perhaps the most interesting thing about them as composers is that despite writing so closely together for over ten years they are still strong individuals. Each has retained his own flavour.

If anything, their individuality has got stronger over the years. In their rock and roll days, both were writing the same sort of songs, but since 'Yesterday', a Paul or a John song is fairly easily identifiable. They've influenced each other, in that Paul has been spurred on to try harder with his lyrics, while John has been spurred on by Paul's keenness and dedication. But they are still very different.

Their music has been constantly analysed and praised and interpreted, right from the beginning in 1963, when *The Times* music man had admired their 'pandiatonic clusters'.

Opposite: **Paul and George Martin during a composing and smoking session. In addition to producing records for the Beatles as their A and R man, Martin wrote his own music, including a number of film scores.**

They are said to have been influenced by everything, from Negro blues to Magyar dances.

References to drugs have been seen everywhere, once it was known they took drugs. Even the 'help' in Ringo's 'A Little Help From My Friends' was said to mean pot. 'Lucy in the Sky with Diamonds' was said to stand for LSD, which was just a coincidence. John's son Julian had drawn a picture for John showing Lucy, a girl in his class, in the sky. In America it was said that 'meeting a man from the motor trade' obviously meant an abortionist. It was in fact a joke reference to their friend Terry Doran, who used to be a car salesman.

They have used drug slang in their songs, but not as much as people have said. Strangely enough, several deliberate slang obscenities have gone unnoticed. In 'Penny Lane', for example, the finger pie referred to is an old Liverpool obscenity, used by Liverpool lads about Liverpool lasses.

They are amused by all the interpretations. John deliberately let all the verbal jokes and stream-of-consciousness nonsense stuff stay as they had come out of his head in 'I Am The Walrus', knowing a lot of people would have fun trying to analyse them.

But whether they are the greatest song writers in the world today, as some have said, or even better than Schubert, doesn't interest them. They never discuss or try to evaluate or appreciate their music. When forced to talk about it, Paul says simply that it must obviously get better all the time.

'Each time we just want to do something different. After "Please Please Me", we decided we must do something different for the next song. We'd put on one funny hat, so we took it off and looked for another one to put on.

'Why should we ever want to go back? That would be soft. It would be like sticking to grey suits all your life.

'I suppose everybody would like to do this, try something different every time they do any work. We do, because it's just a hobby, that's all. We put our feet up and enjoy it all the time.'

George doesn't think they've done many songs worth talking about yet (his song writing is discussed separately later).

But now and again George does yearn for the old days. 'I often think it would be nice to play together again. We've never done it since we stopped touring. Perhaps one day we might hire a studio, just to play in for ourselves.'

'They're good songs,' says John, 'but nothing brilliant. I just feel indifferent when I hear them on the radio. I never listen to them properly. Maybe if someone was attacking them, saying they were rotten, then maybe I'd work up some reaction to them.'

They never play their own records, except perhaps when they're about to start a new album. Then they might play the previous one through, just to see where they got up to last time. None of them sings their own songs, either before they've recorded them or afterwards. When John, or the others, break into a chorus of 'She Loves You', it's as if they're ridiculing a corny song written by someone else.

'We did all the proper listening to them, over and over again, when we wrote them,' says John. 'When it's finished, it doesn't matter any more.

'I actively dislike hearing bits of them that didn't come out right. There are bits of "Lucy in the Sky" I don't like. Some of the sound in "Mr Kite" isn't right. I like "A Day in the Life", but it's still not half as nice as I thought it was when we were doing it. I suppose we could have worked harder on it. But I couldn't be arsed doing any more.

'I don't think our old songs are all that different from our new ones, as people are always saying. The words are different, but that's because they're done up differently. The tunes are much the same.

'I suppose I'm so indifferent about our music because other people take it so seriously. It can be pleasing in a way, but most of it gets my back up.

'It's nice when people like it, but when they start "appreciating" it, getting great deep things out of it, making a thing of it, then it's a lot of shit. It proves what we've always thought about most sorts of so-called art. It's all a lot of shit. We hated all the shit they wrote and talked about Beethoven and ballet, all kidding themselves it was important. Now it's happening to us. None of it is important. It just takes a few people to get going, and they con themselves into thinking it's important. It all becomes a big con.

'We're a con as well. We know we're conning them, because we know people want to be conned. They've given us the freedom to con them. Let's stick that in there, we say, that'll start them puzzling. I'm sure all artists do, when they realize it's a con. I bet Picasso sticks things in. I bet he's been laughing his balls off for the last 80 years.

'It's sad though. When we're not laughing, we're conning ourselves into thinking we are important. People won't take anything as a laugh. If we said when we wrote "She's Leaving Home" we were actually thinking about bananas, nobody would believe you. They don't want to believe you.

'It is depressing to realize we were right in what we always thought, all these years ago. Beethoven is a con, just like we are now. He was just knocking out a bit of work, that was all.

'The thing is, do Beethoven and these sort of people realize they're a con? Or do they really think they're important? Does the Prime Minister realize he's just a bloke? I don't know. Perhaps he's taken in by all this pretending to know what he's doing. The drag is he sounds as if he really thinks he knows what's going on, when he doesn't.

'People think the Beatles know what's going on. We don't. We're just doing it. People want to know what the inner meaning of "Mr Kite" was. There wasn't any. I just did it. I shoved a lot of words together, then shoved some noise on. I didn't dig that song when I wrote it. I didn't believe in it when we were recording it. But nobody will believe it. They don't want to. They want it to be important.'

31

JOHN

John lives in a large mock-Tudor house on a private estate full of mock-Tudor houses in Weybridge, Surrey. Ringo lives on the same estate. John's house cost him in all £60,000, although it was only £20,000 to buy. He spent the other £40,000 doing it up, knocking rooms around, decorating and furnishing, landscaping the garden and building a swimming pool. He has spent too much on it, which he knows. 'I suppose I'd only get half the money back if I sold it, about £30,000. I'll need to find a pop singer to sell it to, someone soft anyway.'

In the garden he has a psychedelically painted caravan, which was done to match the patterns of his painted Rolls Royce. The house is on a slight hill, with the grounds rolling beneath. There is a full-time gardener, a housekeeper called Dot and a chauffeur called Anthony. None of them lives in.

Inside, the front hall is dark and book-ridden, but the rooms beyond are bright and large and lushly decorated. There are long plush sofas and huge pile carpets and elegant drapes, all of which look brand new and unused, like a Hollywood set. But amongst them are scattered irrelevant ornaments, old posters and bits of antiques. They look highly used and personal, obviously chosen by John, rather than an interior decorator, but just dumped and forgotten about once the initial whim wore off.

These reception rooms might as well be corridors. Nobody ever seems to use them, although they are kept beautifully dusted. They just walk through them to get out. All the living is done in one little rectangular room at the back of the house. It has one wall completely made of glass and looks over the garden and trees beyond.

John, his wife Cynthia and their son Julian (born 8 April 1963) spend most of their time in this living room and kitchen. The surrounding opulence seems to have nothing to do with them. Dot looks after that.

Inside their quarters, Cyn looks after her family on her own, doing all the cooking for the three of them – though John sometimes makes tea. She looks after Julian by herself.

Opposite: **John on location for the** *Magical Mystery Tour* **film, 1967.**

She has never had a nanny, although Dot does a lot of baby-sitting. It was she who looked after Julian while John and Cyn were in India in early 1968.

Cyn gets worried now and again by the expense of having and not using such a big house. John, when he thinks about it, finds it a laugh.

'Everything seems to cost a fortune,' she says. 'John spends impetuously and it's catching. I'm always feeling guilty. I have to pull myself together now and again, when I realize how much something would mean to some people. Our food and drink bill is amazing. It's mostly bread, tea, sugar, milk, cat food and soft drinks, as we don't drink. Yet it somehow comes to £120 a month. I don't know how.'

They have five cats. Their names chart the stages in John's life. There's Mimi, after his aunt, and Nel and Mal, after their road managers. One kitten, born in the summer of 1967, at the height of their Yogi summer, is called Babidji.

A lot of the regular bills, like gas and electricity, are paid direct by their accountant. Cyn pays the rest.

'I sometimes open them when they arrive,' says John. 'If I don't like the look of them I put them away and forget about them till they start complaining. Now and again I do query them, but they just go on about "Well, sir, it's like this sir." You never get anywhere.'

All the Beatles receive a weekly sum of £50 in fivers to cover any personal expenses, like staff. They rarely carry any money personally.

'I don't know how much money I've got,' says John. 'I'm not conscious of having a treasure chest full of it at the bottom of the garden. It's all hypothetical, but I know it's not as much as some people think.

'It's all tied up in things, in various forms. I did ask the accountant once how much it came to. I wrote it down on a bit of paper. But I've lost the bit of paper.'

Their little rectangular living room is crammed high with posters, ornaments and photographs. A large notice pinned on one wall says 'Milk is Harmless'.

They eat in this room, watch telly in this room, and when it's cold or rainy John spends most of his time, when he's not recording or writing a song, curled up on a small sofa in this room, doing nothing. The sofa is far too small for him. He would obviously be more comfortable on one of the lush ones from the other room. But he curls his legs round and can lie for hours.

When it's fine, he opens the sliding glass door and goes out and sits on a step in the garden, looking down at his swimming pool and his English country garden.

Anthony or Dot usually answer the front door, though if he's in the mood, John does. He rarely answers the telephone. It is almost impossible to get him on the telephone anyway, as he has an answerphone system that takes messages. This in itself puts off most people trying to get through to him. There is a recorded voice that says 'This is Weybridge Four, Five, Wubbleyoo, Dubbleyoo, please leave your message now.'

His ex-directory number is always being changed, which is supposed to be one way of keeping it secret. It's a secret from John anyway. He can never remember it.

An ordinary evening at the Lennons is ordinary. This particular ordinary evening, two door-to-door salesmen had come to the door, saying they were Australian students selling magazines. John happened to open the door and let them in. They said they were in a competition to see who could get most subscriptions. The prize would help their studies.

That was their story anyway. John said yeh, very good, come on then, what do you want me to do. They got out the list of magazines and asked John to tick the ones he would like to read. He ticked a lot and the two salesmen-students said it would come to £74. John said OK, hold on till I find some money. He could only find the packet with the £50 housekeeping cash. He gave them that. They said that would do fine. They thanked him very much and left.

Cyn made the evening meal for her family. They started with a slice of melon followed by a plate of cold meat with vegetables. John didn't have the meat, as he'd become a vegetarian. They all drank cold milk with it.

John had a filling coming out of his tooth, which he constantly played with, making a sluicing noise as he ate his food. He went to the fridge in the kitchen to get some more milk. He drank it ice cold from the bottle. Cyn said that wouldn't do his tooth any good.

Throughout the meal, the television was on. They all turned their seats to watch it. Now and again Cyn or John would change the station. They never seemed to watch any programme for more than ten minutes. John stared silently at it, lost and abstracted, through his specs. Cyn was reading the *Daily Mirror* at the same time. Julian watched it and chattered. Then he got down from the table and lay on the carpet and started to do a drawing. Cyn got him some coloured biros. They both watched him, asking him what his drawing was. He said it was a bird cage, like the one in the garden. He explained all the things happening in his drawing. John and Cyn smiled at him as he did so.

John then opened the large sliding window, and sat on a step to get some fresh air, looking down upon the pool. On the surface of the pool the automatic filter buzzed round and round, like a space ship that had just landed. Julian came out and went down to the pool. He threw some oars in, then got them out again and came back to the house. Cynthia cleared up.

Terry Doran arrived and was greeted warmly by all, including Julian who sat on his knee.

'Do you want your Dad to put you to bed?' said Cyn, smiling at John, who grinned back. 'Or do you want Terry.' Julian said he wanted Terry. But she picked up Julian herself and put him to bed.

'Are you going to roll us a few then?' said John to Terry. Terry said yes. John got up and brought out a tin tool box which he opened for Terry. Inside was some tobacco, wrapped in tin foil, plus some cigarette papers. Terry rolled a couple of cigarettes, which they smoked, sharing them between them. This was during the pot-taking period, which is now over.

Cyn came back. The television was still on. They all sat and watched it, still changing programmes all the time, until about midnight when Cyn made some cocoa. Terry left and John and Cyn went to bed. John said he was going to read a paperback book someone had given them. Cyn said oh, she wanted to read that first.

'I'm pleased I made it young. Making it young means that I've now got the rest of my life to do what I really want. It would have been terrible to spend your whole life before you finally make it, just to find out it's meaningless. We knew it was anyway, but we had to find out for ourselves.

'For a long time we always had specific little aims, we never really looked far ahead. It was all a series of goals, to get a record made, to get a number one, to do another one, to do a film and so on. We just sort of glimpsed it all in stages. We never thought about any

John and Cynthia Lennon, with their son Julian, in 1968. One of four world-exclusive photographs taken by Ringo for the first edition of this book. John met Cynthia for the first time in 1958, when they were at the Art College together.

big things. Now I can. I'm not interested in little stages now. Acting doesn't interest me any more. It's a waste of time for me. Writing, I've done that. I wanted to do a book and I produced one, so that was it.

'I suppose now what I'm interested in is a Nirvana, the Buddhist heaven. I don't know much about it, or really understand it enough to explain it. George knows more.

'Studying religion has made me try to improve relationships, not to be unpleasant. It's not a conscious move to change my personality. Perhaps it is. I don't know. I'm just trying to be how I want to be, and how I'd like others to be.

'Drugs probably helped the understanding of myself better, but not much. Not pot. That just used to be a harmless giggle. LSD was the self-knowledge that pointed the way in the first place. I was suddenly struck by great visions when I first took acid. But you've got to be looking for it, before you can possibly find it. Perhaps I was looking, without realizing it, and would have found it anyway. It would just have taken longer.

'That first time we took acid really was an accident. Me and George were at dinner and someone gave it to us when we didn't know much about it. We'd taken pot, but that was all. We hadn't heard of the horrors of LSD. And we weren't supervised, which you should be. We did think we were going barmy.

'But there are much better ways of getting there. I've nothing really against the ideas of Christianity and their ways. I suppose I wouldn't make that remark about Jesus today. I think about things differently. I think Buddhism is simple and more logical than Christianity, but I've nothing against Jesus. I'll let Julian learn all about Jesus when he goes to school, but I'll also tell him there have been lots of other Jesuses, I'll tell him about the Buddhist ones, they're good men as well.

'When I made the Jesus remarks, lots of people sent me books about Jesus. I read a lot of them and found out things. I've found out for example that the Church of England isn't very religious. There's too much politics. You can't be both. You can't be powerful and pure. Perhaps I'll find out that the gurus are like that as well, full of politics. I don't know. All I know is that I am being made more aware by it all. I just want to be told more.

'I don't know if you have to be poor or not. I feel I could give up all this. It does waste a lot of energy. But I have to wait and see what I'd be giving it up for, what I was replacing it for. I might give up all this material stuff in the end. But at the moment I want to find myself.'

Cyn said she had noticed a difference in him. Perhaps he was nicer. He was quieter and more tolerant. But he still didn't communicate very much. 'Perhaps I'm being selfish,' she said. 'It's just easier for me if he tells me things.'

John admitted he'd never be one for communicating. He'd read an interview with his chauffeur Anthony in a colour supplement, in which Anthony had been quoted as saying that he'd driven John for hours and hours across Spain for his film and John had never spoken to him. 'I hadn't realized till then that I hadn't.'

John's record for not speaking, just doing nothing and not communicating to anyone, is three days. He was doing it long before meditation came along. 'I'm an expert at it. I can get up and start doing nothing straight away. I just sit on the step and look into space and think until it's time to go to bed.'

He doesn't consider this frittering his time away. He frittered it away even more, immediately after they stopped touring, when he never got out of bed till three in the afternoon. Now at least he tries to get up and see a bit of daylight. He says if he's doing nothing he might as well be doing it when there's some sun around.

Even when he is trying to communicate, Cyn, like his aunt Mimi, often finds it difficult to know what he's on about, although he makes more of an effort these days, since Maharishi arrived, taking over from the Buddhism.

'I do find it hard to pass the time of day with people. There's no point in that sort of talk. Now and again I do it, as a game, to see if I can. How are you? What's the time? How are we getting on? Those sort of pointless things.

'The main thing is, there's nothing to talk about any more. I *think* communication all the time like mad, but putting it into words is a waste of time.

'We talk in code to each other as Beatles. We always did that, when we had so many strangers round us on tours. We never really communicated with other people. Now that we don't meet strangers at all, there is no need for any communication. We understand each other. It doesn't matter about the rest.

'Now and again, even though we feel each other, we do have a talking communication session, when we have to say things out loud, or otherwise we forget what we know we've decided amongst ourselves.

'I do daydream a lot. That's in the same class as idle conversation, so I suppose I shouldn't really condemn idle conversation. Just the normal daydreams, what am I going to do today, shall I get up or not, shall I write that song or not, no I'm not going to answer that phone.

'Talking is the slowest form of communicating anyway. Music is much better. We're communicating to the outside world through our music. The office in America say they listen to *Sergeant Pepper* over and over so that they know what we're thinking in London.

'I do have little spasms of talking. I go and chat to Dot or Anthony, or the gardener, just to see if I can do it. It surprises them.'

The biggest change in John is the decline in his aggression. All his close friends have noticed. They all believe it has been brought about by success.

'It took a long long time,' says Ivan Vaughan, his friend from school. 'Even a couple of years ago, the old animosities were still there, refusing to talk to anybody, being rude, slamming the door. Now he's just as likely to say to people come in, sit down.'

Pete Shotton, the other boyhood friend who opened the Apple Boutique, agrees that all the chips have been smoothed down.

'The good I always saw in him is now at the top. It was only people like schoolmasters who thought he was all bad. No one would ever believe what I saw in him at the time.

'It's great that he's so happy. He spent his whole childhood and all his youth trying all the time to be number one. He had to be the leader at all times, either by fighting everyone or, if they were big, by undermining them by abuse or sarcasm.

'Today John is not trying to prove anything, he doesn't have to be number one, that's why he's happy. You can even *see* the change. He used to walk like this at school and at the Art College, all hunched up, his eyes and head down, like a scared rabbit, driven into a corner, but ready to lash out. You can see it in all the old pictures of him. Now he can smile in pictures. He's now learning because he wants to learn. At school you are forced to learn because you have to fit into society.

'But John hasn't changed in some things. He's not bigheaded or vain, and he's as generous as ever. When John had a dozen sweets in a bag and there were three of us round him, he'd share them all out, three sweets each. He made me more generous, just by being with him.'

John doesn't see why success should have made him bigheaded or changed him in any way. Apart from thinking that success is meaningless, he also thinks anybody can do it, which is what Paul also thinks.

Both he and Paul feel that the most important thing about success is willpower.

'Everyone can be a success. If you keep saying that enough times to yourself you can be.

We're no better than anybody else. We're all the same. We're as good as Beethoven. Everyone's the same inside.

'You need the desire and the right circumstances, but it's nothing to do with talent, or with training or education. You get primitive painters, and writers, don't you. Nobody told them how to do it. They told themselves they could do it and just did it.

'What's talent? I don't know. Are you born with it, do you discover you have it later on? The basic talent is believing you can do something. Me and Paul were always drawing, but George wouldn't even try because he said he couldn't draw. It took us a long time to persuade him anyone could draw. Now he's drawing all the time. And he's getting better.

'We knew that the GCE wasn't the opening to anything. We could have ground through all that and gone further, but not for me. I believed something was going to happen which I'd have to get through. And I knew it wasn't GCE.

'Up to the age of 15 I was no different from any other little cunt of 15. Then I decided I'd write a little song, and I did. But it didn't make me any different. That's a load of crap that I discovered a talent. I just did it. I've no talent, except a talent for being happy or a talent for skiving.

'Someone wants to bust open this whole talent myth, wise everybody up. Politicians have no talent. It's all a con.

'Perhaps my guru will tell me what my real talent is, something else that I really should be doing.

'I never felt any responsibility, being a so-called idol. It's wrong of people to expect it. What they are doing is putting their responsibilities on us, as Paul said to the newspapers when he admitted taking LSD. If they were worried about him being responsible, they should have been responsible enough and not printed it, if they were genuinely worried about people copying.

'I only felt responsible to the public in that we tried to be as natural as we could. We did put on our social faces, but that was to be expected. But given the circumstances, we were as natural as we could be. Being asked the same questions at the same sort of places all over the world, all about the four mop tops. That was boring. And having to be social to so many people and Lord Mayors' wives. All those tasteless people who determine tastes. All those people with no standards, setting all the standards.

'Even from the beginning I hated such things as meeting the promoter's wife. People were always saying you had to go through with all the false social things. You just couldn't be yourself. They wouldn't understand if you said what you wanted to say. All you could do was make jokes, which I was expected to do anyway after a while. I don't really believe people are like that. Yet why do they go through with it all?

'I don't have to go anywhere now, perhaps a club now and again. Cyn cons me into it. We went to some opening the other night, some old friend. David Jacobs was everywhere. I went with George. He realized what it was going to be like the minute we got to the door but I didn't. I looked round and he'd gone. He never even went inside. But I was in and was stuck. It was horrible.

'I'm never conscious of being a Beatle. Never. I'm just me. I'm not famous. It's other people that do it. Until they come up and react, you've forgotten. Oh, yes, that's why they're behaving so strange, then I remember I'm a Beatle. I was more used to it a year or so ago, when we were in the thick of it, moving round the country, meeting people all the time who you knew were going to stare. I don't move around now, except with people I know, so I forget, till I go somewhere new and people stare.

'People did stare at us before we were famous. Going on a bus to the Cavern, all in leather and carrying guitars. We liked it then. It was our bit of rebellion, just to annoy all the Annie Walkers sitting in the Kardomah.

'I miss playing soft jokes on people. I used to do it on trains, go into people's compartments and pretend to be soft, or in shops. I still feel an urge to do that, but you can't. It would be Beatles Play Tricks. This Will Give You A Laugh.

'We were on the way to Wembley once in the van. We wrote on a piece of paper, "Which Way to Wembley". We spoke in a foreign language and pointed to a map of Wales. Everybody went mad putting us right.

'We did all think of disguises once, so we could get around. George and I went through the customs in long coats and beards thinking no one would recognize us, but they all did. Paul was the best. He pretended to be a weird photographer, coming out with a lot of psychological gibberish. He even fooled Brian.'

Most of all, John misses just going out and about and being ordinary. Even though Beatlemania is long since over, it is impossible for him or any of the Beatles to go anywhere and not be recognized. Cyn can manage on her own. Her years of avoiding all publicity have now paid off. 'But we can't do a simple thing together as a family, like going for a walk. It's terrible. Sometimes I wish it had never all happened.'

Of all the Beatles John is the one who most detests not being able to be a private citizen. When he thinks that perhaps he is doomed for ever to be well known, whatever he does from now on, it almost makes him scream.

'No! You don't think that could happen do you? Not famous for ever? What if we disappeared for years and years, wouldn't that work? I suppose we'd then just become famous in another way, like Greta Garbo. Perhaps a new group will come along and take over from us? It would be so nice to be completely forgotten.'

Towards the end of 1967 and in early 1968 they did start trying to make contact with the real world again. They found that their faces had become so famous that, like the Royal Family, people don't expect to see them in the street or in a Wimpy Bar. They managed quite easily to go to little cafés in Soho during the cutting of the *Magical Mystery Tour*. So many people at the time looked like the Beatles anyway, with sideboards and moustaches, that few believed they were the real ones.

'I did a trial run with Ringo the other day. We went to the pictures, the first time for years and years, since we lived in Liverpool. We went to see a Morecambe and Wise film in Esher. We chose a matinée, thinking it would be quiet, but we forgot the schools were off and it was packed. We didn't see the whole film. We had an ice cream, then left. Nobody bothered us. It was just a practice run. I might go more often now.

'Brian used to take us to a West End theatre now and again. We'd go in a party and that would be OK. People would stare, but we wouldn't be bothered too much. But I don't care about the theatre, so I'm not worried about missing that. It's just five blokes on the stage pretending to be somewhere else. But I miss the cinema. I spent all my time in Liverpool at the pictures.

'Ringo and I also went on a bus. We just decided to try it, to see if we could do it. I've never been on a London bus before. It was on the Embankment. We were on the bus 20 minutes. It was great. We got recognized, but it didn't matter too much. We were in the mood for it. We started filming all the people on the bus. The conductress told us dirty jokes. Most people didn't really believe it was us.

'Some newspaper rang up the office the next day. They said some woman was claiming she'd seen us on a bus. I told them to say she was wrong. It wasn't us. The next thing would have been the newspaper ringing up and saying what was it like John, going on a bus after all these years? I couldn't be arsed with all that.

'What I'd like is to be completely left alone. I'm not a mixer. I've got enough friends to see me through. I just want to be left alone.

'My so-called outgoing character is all false. I kept it up for years, but I'm not a loud-mouth. It was a part I put on, as a defence. I cried wolf and I'm paying for it now. I know it sounds like a moan. Perhaps it's just because the grass is always greener.'

Paul and George do tend to go and see people now and again, but John rarely makes an attempt, to give out or make contact. Things have to come to him, or else he doesn't care about them. And the way his life is ordered, it is hard for anything to get through to him, except on the telly, which he has on non-stop.

'A couple of weeks of telly watching is as good as pot. When I used to watch it a few years ago I couldn't stand people like Hughie Green, now he doesn't annoy me. He amuses me. He and Michael Miles are my favourites. Everything's the same. It's like a newspaper. You read all the stories and they go into your head as one.

'I think a lot when I'm watching telly. It's like looking into the fire and daydreaming. You're watching it, but your mind's not on it.'

The only live stimulus he gets is from the other Beatles. No one has been within light years of taking their place in his life.

At first, they naturally repelled all boarders, because they were so busy going their own way, doing their own things together. When they became famous and people deliberately tried to get into their circle, usually for the wrong reasons, they actively and brutally repulsed all advances.

Most show business stars change their friends as they change the size of the billing. Apart from Mick Jagger of the Rolling Stones, the Beatles have picked up no friends from the pop music world. In their normal daily life, there is still only each other or Mal, Neil and Terry.

'We have met some new people since we've become famous, but we've never been able to stand them for more than two days. Some hang on a bit longer, perhaps a few weeks, but that's all. Most people don't get across to us.'

John sees Ringo most of all, as he lives just round the corner. He pops round to his place when he's bored, to mess around in Ringo's garden or play with Ringo's expensive toys. They never make dates or proper arrangements. Things are just done as the mood takes them. Everything's on a basis of if I see you, I see you.

John most of all can't be without the other three for very long, which is hard luck on Cyn. He doesn't mean it in any way nastily, as he doesn't mean not talking to her or going into a semi-trance to be an insult to her. That's just him, which she has to accept.

'If I am on my own for three days, doing nothing, I almost leave myself completely. I'm just not here. Cyn doesn't realize it. I'm up there watching myself, or I'm at the back of my head. I can see my hands and realize they're moving, but it's a robot who's doing it.

'Ringo understands it. I can discuss it with him. I have to see the others to see myself. I realize then there is someone else like me, so it's satisfying and reassuring. It's frightening really, when it gets too bad. I have to see them to establish contact with myself again and come down.

'Sometimes I don't come down. We were recording the other night and I just wasn't there. Neither was Paul. We were like two robots, going through the motions.

'We do need each other a lot. When we used to meet again after an interval we always used to be embarrassed about touching each other. We'd do an elaborate hand shake, just to hide the embarrassment. Or we did mad dances. Then we got to hugging each other. Now we do the Buddhist bit, arms around. It's just saying hello, that's all.'

Now and again he gets the desire to go off somewhere, with Cyn and Julian, and of course the Beatles as well. The Greek island idea, which John was particularly keen on, greatly appealed to him at the time. 'We're all going to live there, perhaps for ever, just coming home for visits. Or it might just be six months a year. It'll be fantastic, all on our own on this island. There's some little houses which we'll do up and knock together and live sort of communally.

'I'm not worried about the political situation in Greece, as long as it doesn't affect us. I don't care if the government is all fascist, or Communist. I don't care. They're all as bad as here, worse most of them. I've seen England and the USA, and I don't care for either of their governments. They're all the same. Look what they do here. They stopped Radio Caroline and tried to put the Stones away, while they're spending billions on nuclear armaments and the place is full of US bases that no one knows about. They're all over North Wales.'

But the Greek idea came to nothing, as did other mad ideas John's had from time to time in the last two years. One day he was all set to go to India in his caravan, though the caravan doesn't look strong enough to take him into Weybridge. He and Cyn and Julian were going to live inside it, so he said, while Anthony, his chauffeur, pulled them in the Rolls. Another idea was to go off and live on an island off the coast of Ireland. He did buy the island. 'No, I can't remember where. Just somewhere off Ireland.'

But the Greek idea was discussed for many weeks. It even got to the stage of trying to work out what to do about Julian and his schooling.

John has some strong theories about the sort of schooling he wants Julian to have, but he usually forgets about them when he's contemplating six months on a deserted Greek island.

'He could go to a school in Greece,' he told Cyn, who was obviously much more realistic about the problem than John. 'What's wrong with that? He'd just spend six months of the year there and the rest here at his English school. These little Greek village schools are very good, you know. Why can't Julian go along with them? He'll soon pick up the language.'

Opposite: John and Cynthia, off on another adventure with the rest of the Beatles. At one time the group were going to buy a Greek island and all go off and live there together, but it never came to pass.

Cynthia said the chopping and changing around wouldn't do him any good. John then thought of sending him to the English school in Athens, where all the British diplomats and others send their kids. Cyn pointed out that would mean him boarding in Athens. They were both against that. Neither wants him to go away to boarding school.

John would prefer a council school, if possible. He'd just found out that the local nursery school Julian was going to wasn't a council one, as he'd thought. Cynthia explained to him that there wasn't a council nursery school she could get him into, that was why she'd done it.

'I don't know,' said John. 'I suppose the fee-paying schools are no worse than the others. As long as he's happy. What does it matter if you have to pay? But I definitely won't send him to a boarding school. I wouldn't send him to Eton. They'd teach him to believe all that shit if he went to Eton. Perhaps a Buddhist school, if there is one. Or a day school, a progressive one, not far from Weybridge, that's all we want.

'We've been thinking of Julian's schooling for some time. I even got a book out about all the schools in England. All they went on about was that they could offer football and tennis. Ridiculous, isn't it? They've got all their priorities wrong. He's got to be taught to be aware of other people, that's all. He doesn't want to know how Sir Francis Drake killed all the Spaniards and that Britain invented television and all that shit fool nationalistic stuff. He wants to know how to live in this world.

'If we do go abroad, then I suppose it'll have to be a tutor, but we'll have to make sure there are other kids for him to play with. I had a happy childhood. I liked being at school. It was just that the teachers hated me and I hated teachers. But I liked school. When we're all talking about our memories, it's sometimes us as the Beatles, but more often it's remembering about our school days.

'I don't think Julian could go to the sort of school I went to. I have to admit a council school might be tough for him now, thanks to me. He'd be laughed at. Millionaire pop singer's son. They'd all point at him. At least that wouldn't matter so much in a fee-paying school, where all they think about is money.'

Cyn is stronger than she looks. She's been through it all before and knows where she is. She understands John's often apparent lack of consideration. He can be selfish, but not deliberately, just without thinking.

All the rows they had in their early Liverpool days are long since over. They are very happy, though she still says that, but for her becoming pregnant, they would probably never have married. John agrees.

'John never thought of settling down in any way, just as he never thought of taking a proper job. If I hadn't got pregnant and then married, we would just have drifted apart as he started touring round the world. I would have stuck in at the Art College and probably become a teacher. But for Julian, it would never have happened. It kept us tied together.'

She doesn't think any such thing as love would have kept them going if they'd been so far apart. 'His love was for the Beatles. Without the baby he would just have gone off with the Beatles for ever.'

They both say they are glad the baby did happen, keeping them together. They also think it was meant to happen. It was fate. John, particularly, believes in fate.

Cyn now and again would like to try something new, to have a job, perhaps use her art college training in some way. She and Pattie, George's wife, discussed the idea once of opening a boutique together in Esher, but it never came to anything.

'I am becoming a bit frustrated. I don't really want to have another child at the moment, now that we can get around so much. I know that might mean leaving it too late and I would never want another.

'But I'm frustrated really, because I'd like something to *do*. I do a bit of painting and dressmaking, but I often think I'd like a job. Not now, but later on. I've never had a job. I might do some designing, or perhaps teaching.'

She teases him about his dependence on the Beatles, and is obviously hurt by it sometimes.

'I do find I suggest something and he just ignores it at the time, or says it's wrong. Then a few weeks later Ringo suggests the same thing and he's all for it. But I don't worry. I can't put it into words, but I feel strong. It's a sense. I understand things.

'What I would like is a holiday on our own, without the Beatles. Just John, Julian and me.'

'You what?' said John, smiling. 'Not even with our Beatle buddies?'

'Yes, John. Don't you remember we were talking about it last week?'

'What did we say?'

'We said the three of us could just go off somewhere, not with your buddies.'

'But it's nice to have your mates around.'

'That really offends me. He does think it's not enough just to go with his family.'

He smiled at her. She shook her head at him.

'They seem to need you less than you need them,' she said.

Before he could reply to this one she got in with an example she'd obviously had all ready.

'George went off to Los Angeles, just with Pattie, didn't he? *He* didn't need to get everyone to go with him?'

John smiled. He agreed it did seem to be true. 'I did try to go my own way after we stopped touring. I had a few good laughs and games of monopoly on my film, but it didn't work. I was never so glad to see the others. Seeing them made me feel normal again.' Cyn looked soulfully at him.

'OK, I know, we'll all retire to a little cottage on a cliff in Cornwall, all right?

'No, but I can't retire. I've got these bloody songs to write. I have to work, to justify living.'

32

PAUL

While the other three moved out into stockbroker Surrey, Paul remained the only London Beatle. He took a large, detached, three-storey house in St John's Wood, near Lord's cricket ground and just round the corner from EMI's recording studios. He bought it at the end of 1966 for £40,000. He didn't do much knocking about, compared with John and Ringo. The garden became a jungle, completely overgrown, inhabited only by the prowling Martha. When he'd moved in, it had been very pretty. Everybody kept on at him, especially his Dad, to do something about it. He seemed to delight in its wildness and the way it annoyed some people. But at the end of 1967 he decided to start having it tarted up. He got the idea of building a magical house in it, a sort of pagoda on a raised platform with an open glass roof onto the skies. When he got that finished, he and Jane started thinking about moving to a smaller house in the country.

The house is guarded by a high brick wall and large double black gates, which are controlled from the house. You speak into a microphone, someone inside answers and, if you say the right thing, the doors swing open and then clank shut again to keep out the fans.

All the Beatle homes have fans hanging around, but Paul has most, being Paul and also being in London. They keep up a permanent watch outside, usually sitting in rows on the wall of the house opposite. From there they can just see over the wall and make out any movements around the front door. Coming into the street you can tell Paul's house by the rows of girls hanging precariously from his wall, a couple of feet off the ground, craning to look over.

The basement of the house contains a staff flat. He had a couple for a long time, Mr and Mrs Kelly, who both lived there. She did the housekeeping and he was the sort of butler, but both really mucked in and were just there. Since them, he's had a succession of people. They just seem to arrive at random and he keeps them on sometimes, however unsuitable. He could really do with a secretary, to organize his house and his visitors, but he says he

Opposite: Paul and Jane Asher, to whom he was briefly engaged, with their dog, Martha, photographed in 1968 by Ringo.

would never do that. Very often he has nobody living in the house, and when he's been abroad his dad Jim sometimes has come down to look after the house and Martha.

Not that Paul worries about it. It doesn't bother him that people he's promised to see arrive, and he's gone off to Africa or America. All he likes around is a nice motherly lady to serve up a fried breakfast at about one o'clock and at other hours of the day as required. When Jane is not working, she does a lot of the cooking and is very good.

The ground floor contains the kitchen, which is very large and well appointed, a large haughty dining room which looks completely unused, and his living room at the back, which is the most used of any Beatle room. This is very large and comfy with french windows opening on to the back garden. It has a large soft green Edwardian suite, nicely faded. There is a large wooden table in this living room where most meals are served, rather than in the dining-room. It is usually covered with a white lace tablecloth, very working-class posh. The room is usually in chaos, with stuff piled everywhere, ornaments, flashing lights, packages, newspapers and bits of equipment. This is where the Beatles and Mal and Neil and others congregate before recording sessions and, in fact, most times they are in London. It has an unpretentious lived-in feeling. 'Everywhere I've lived always ends up like this. At Forthlin it was the same. Things might look a bit different now, like a big colour TV, but the atmosphere's always the same.'

On the first floor is his bedroom, a large L-shaped room with an extravagant bed with a large carved headboard. Jane helped him to furnish this room. There are two other bedrooms. On the top floor is his work room, where he and John do most of their hard slog together when they need some more songs to fill up an album. This is where he has the Paolozzi sculpture. Very interesting, that piece. Paolozzi was Stu Sutcliffe's hero and teacher.

The famous Martha (if you don't think she's famous you should read *Beatles Monthly*) is a very large, shaggy, good-natured old English sheep dog. She's good-natured even when she has a few fleas. She has her own trap door into the garden for her regular prowls, but Paul tries to take her for a proper walk as often as he can. He usually goes to Primrose Hill or Regent's Park. He did go to Hampstead Heath once, but Martha had a fit and he hasn't taken her back. There are also several cats, and kittens, which seem to vary in number from day to day. All the Beatles have cats, and all their births are faithfully reported in *Beatles Monthly*.

Paul manages his walks with Martha with surprising lack of recognition. The fans never realize where he's going, when he rushes out. And in the park, he usually has his jacket collar up and walks round the remotest parts with Martha, meeting only elderly dog lovers who are more interested in the enormous Martha than Paul.

He exchanges the time of day with other people and makes polite dog chat. He even shouts out at people he vaguely recognizes, something the other Beatles wouldn't do, not being as sociable as Paul. He was on the top of Primrose Hill one day when he saw an actor he slightly knew. He shouted at him, but the actor walked past, as if to say I don't know you so please don't shout, there's a good chap. He was a terribly upper-class young English type actor. He gave a great backwards Hello, when he at last recognized Paul. Paul had met him once through Jane. He'd been acting in the same play and had invited Jane and Paul to his house for dinner.

Paul asked him how he was doing, then. The actor said, very coyly, that he had a chance of a play in New York. 'Oh aye,' said Paul. 'What?'

'Can't tell,' said the actor, going even coyer. 'Sorry. Never do. When there's something in the offing one might spoil it by talking about it, mightn't one? Don't you find that, hmm?' Paul smiled and said yeh, he supposed so. 'Well, bye then,' said the actor. He breezed off, swinging his arms, looking up and breathing heavily at the lovely day. You could almost see him reading the stage directions.

'Strange, isn't it,' said Paul, walking back to the car. 'How somebody like that just can't relax. It's impossible for him to be natural. Yet he's OK, he's a nice enough bloke, once he relaxes and has a few drinks. By the end of that dinner we had with him he was almost normal. I feel sorry for people like that, really. It's the way they've been conditioned.

'When I was a kid of 16, all adolescent and awkward and shy, I was dying to be an actor like that, all smooth and in command, always coming on dead confident. But it was worth going through that awkward stage, just to be natural now. Jane has a little bit of the same trouble, with her background. She can't help it. It's how they've been brought up.'

Jane and Paul make a very loving and lovely couple. Everyone agrees on this. From the very beginning, Jim said nothing would make him happier than their marriage.

Jane Asher comes from a professional London family. Her father is a doctor. Her mother, a professor of music, taught George Martin to play the oboe. Jane began acting, in films and on stage, as a child. She met Paul in May 1963 at a pop concert at the Albert Hall. She was then 17, and had been appearing on the TV pop record programme *Juke Box Jury*. The *Radio Times* asked her to go along to the concert with a reporter and give her comments, as a teenager, on the groups. She said the only one worth screaming over was the Beatles. The Beatle she liked the look of most, when she caught sight of them in the corridors afterwards, was George.

But it was Paul, who always was a star spotter, who recognized her and shouted after her, which brought the rest of them rushing round her, chatting her up. 'We all said, "Will you marry me",' says Paul, 'which was what we said to every girl at the time.' They invited her back to their hotel, the Royal Court, for a drink. 'A rave London bird, the sort we'd always heard about. We thought we were set.'

The others left Paul alone in the bedroom with Jane, after a lot of winking. They spent the evening talking about gravy and what their favourite meal was. 'I realized this was the girl for me. I hadn't tried to grab her or make her. I told her, "It appears you're a nice girl."'

'They couldn't believe I was a virgin,' says Jane.

They went out many times in the next few weeks, often just walking round Soho together. Nobody yet recognized Paul, in early 1963, though a lot knew Jane. When he came back from a short holiday in Rome, Jane and her mother met him at London Airport. He missed a connection back to Liverpool, but Mrs Asher said he could stay the night with them. Paul didn't want to. He didn't like the idea of staying with a girl's family. It's not the sort of thing working-class lads do. But he agreed in the end, just to stay the night. The night turned into three nights, then into three weeks, then into three years. Unbeknown to fans, Paul lived all his London life at Jane's house, until, at the end of 1966, he got his own house in St John's Wood.

An evening with them, once again, is like an evening with any other young couple. Jane made the dinner. It was all vegetarian; Paul was one at the time, like John and George. The first course was avocado vinaigrette, followed by a casserole of vegetables, nuts and spices.

They shared a half-bottle of white wine, which had been opened for cooking. They were just finishing it up.

Throughout the meal, fans were ringing the door bell. It was a time when Paul was between staff. Each time Jane answered them, speaking through the intercom. She was very polite. She got up nicely from her meal each time, not at all angry, and asked them if they would mind waiting as they were still eating. Paul, at this stage in the day, after dozens of door bell fans, wouldn't have bothered. He would have stopped answering by then, as he had done that time Brian Epstein called and couldn't get in. In the end, she made Paul go, even before he'd finished his meal. He gave a twisted smile, but went out and signed for all the girls who'd been waiting.

After dinner, they got out some photographs that had been taken on a Scottish holiday they'd just had. Paul has a house in a remote part of Argyllshire, where they usually spend at least one week a year. Then they watched colour TV and went to bed.

It was perhaps a quieter than normal evening. Paul often has some friends dropping in. People do tend to drop in a lot to see Paul, which he encourages. It happened a lot during the five months in 1967 when Jane was acting in America. It rarely happens to the others, partly because they live farther out.

During a new album, people are coming and going all the time. Paul is now so much the leader, as he was even before Brian died, in organizing many of their affairs that most things happen from his house.

Peter Blake, the artist, came to Paul's house during the discussions for the *Sergeant Pepper* cover. John was usually there as well, and so was Terry Doran. Just after Peter Blake left one afternoon, Paul's man, the one who was working in the house at the time, came into the living room to say that a parson was at the front gate. They all laughed.

Someone said it must be a gag. Paul looked at John. John obviously didn't want to see any parson. Paul said to his man to get rid of him. Terry said it was probably a TV actor, dressed up. They laughed. Paul said perhaps Terry should be the one to go and tell him politely that Paul was out. As Terry was halfway across the room, Paul said no, we'll let him in, eh? If he looks all right, he might be interesting. Terry came back from the front gate and said, he's foony, honest. So the electronic gates were allowed to swing open, allowing the parson to enter.

The parson, middle-aged and well scrubbed, entered the living room, very nervously. Everybody smiled politely at him. Paul told him to sit down. He apologized for coming in on them when he knew they must be so busy, so frightfully busy, he knew that. He was already making their excuses for them. He was obviously so surprised to get in. He knew it couldn't last long and he'd be straight out. Paul asked what he wanted.

The parson turned to face Paul, having realized he must be Mr McCartney. He'd been peering round, trying hard, but obviously unable to recognize anybody. Holding his hands together, he said it was just that they were having a garden fête and he was wondering if Paul could come along, just pop in for a second. Of course he knew how busy they were. It was marvellous, all they had done. They must be very busy people, he knew that.

'No, I never do that,' said Paul. 'Of course, of course,' said the parson, hurriedly, 'I couldn't expect it. You're so busy. I knew it. So busy…'

'No we're not,' said Paul. 'It's not that at all. It just wouldn't be right, would it, as I don't believe. You know?' Paul was smiling. The parson smiled back not listening, just nodding in agreement with everything Paul said.

'Why don't you make the product better,' said Paul, still smiling kindly, 'instead of getting gimmicks like us?' 'Oh, you're quite right, quite right. We are trying. We're trying hard to get all together. We've got an interdenominational service next week.'

'That'll be good,' said Paul, 'for a start. Of course, if we got going on this, we'd be here all night, wouldn't we.'

'You're quite right,' said the parson. 'And you're so busy. I couldn't expect you to come, you're so busy…'

Paul didn't bother to explain again, that that was not the reason. The parson started to get up, smiling, and so did everyone else in the room. He went round them all, smiling earnestly and thanking them for all their time. He stared hard at everyone, trying to place them, knowing they must be placeable. Paul went with him to the door. As he left the room, he turned round again and said to everyone, 'I suppose you're *all* world famous.' Then he left.

When he'd gone, everyone said how nice he was. John particularly was pleased at not being recognized. He said it was funny how people always got worried when they didn't recognize you straight away, as if you would be hurt, not realizing it was the opposite.

It was about five o'clock. Mrs Mills, Paul's housekeeper at the time, served breakfast all round. Fried eggs, bacon and black pudding. She brought in a big pile of sliced bread, already buttered, and endless tea. George and Ringo, then Neil and Mal arrived, and they all in turn got a cup of tea. Then they went off to the recording studio.

Apart from Beatle people, or people associated in some way with the record they're working on, Paul often has a lot of his Liverpool relations staying with him. His dad and stepmother Angie and stepsister Ruth, plus his aunts and uncles often have a week with him. Paul goes up to Liverpool most of all the Beatles. John doesn't go at all, since Mimi moved to Bournemouth. George goes up to Warrington quite a lot to see his folks, and so does Ringo. But Paul is always going up for the weekend on a sudden whim, if Jane is away and there's no work on. Jane often goes with him as well.

Michael McCartney, Paul's brother, is probably the most frequent Liverpool visitor, especially since his own records and work began to have a London success.

The phone never seems to stop ringing. There are two numbers, both ex-directory, but no matter how often the numbers are changed, fans still find out. Paul answers the phone himself, always with a funny voice. It's easy to tell a fan by the frightened silence, in which case he hangs up without speaking.

'Oh, yeh, hi,' he said on the phone, still keeping up his funny voice, but admitting who it was by the way he was speaking. It was a well known disc jockey, inviting him to come down on Sunday and do some horse riding. 'Yeh, I might at that,' said Paul, politely, but not definitely promising anything. He made faces down the phone as the other person smarmed on about the excellent riding. 'Yeh, great, yeh. OK, then. I might see you. Cheerio.'

The phone rang again and it was his dad, asking about his proposed trip up to Liverpool at the weekend. 'What time do you think you'll be coming, son?' said Jim. 'Just so I can get ready.'

'Ready for what?' said Paul.

'Oh you know, just get things ready.'

'Don't be so stupid, Dad. I don't want you to get ready for anything. I'll arrive when I arrive.'

Astrid in Germany was always a bit suspicious of Paul at first, though his relationship with Stu was also bound up in this. 'It used to frighten me that someone could be so nice all the time. Which is silly. It's ridiculous to feel at home with nasty people, just because you feel that at least you know where you are with them. It's silly to be wary of nice people.'

A lot of Paul's niceness comes from his dad. His brother Michael has it as well. At 17, when the others were in revolt against their parents, Paul was the only one who listened to his dad and his little homilies, and was mocked by the others for doing so.

Paul is the easiest to get to know for an outsider, but in the end he is the hardest to get to know. There is a feeling that he is holding things back, that he is one jump ahead, aware of the impression he is giving. He is self-conscious, which the others are not. John doesn't care, either way, what people think. Ringo is too adult to think about such things, and George in many ways isn't conscious. He is above it all.

Paul himself has come to terms with himself, having gone through a stage of trying not to be so nice or to appear keen. 'I do find it more of an effort *not* to make an effort. It's more false for me not to. So I might as well make the effort.'

Paul's way of making an effort, by being polite and hard working, was essential to the group. It was his PR approach that Brian Epstein brought out. Even before that, Paul gave them any gloss they had, writing little hand-out letters and making little speeches.

His way of making an effort has been especially vital to them since Brian Epstein died. Paul today makes most of the running. This is why it is true to say that, in some ways, Paul is the leader today, not John, though talking seriously about a leader of the Beatles is as pointless as it ever

Jane Asher with Paul, shortly before their relationship collapsed. Jane has never spoken about it since.

was. Paul is the business man, he's the pusher, he gets things done and wheedles the rest along with him. But no big decisions are ever taken unless they all agree.

Once they are taken, Paul starts moving and doesn't put up with inefficiencies. There was some hold up over a proof of the *Sergeant Pepper* cover. He hadn't got one when he should have done, so he rang EMI and went through department after department till he found the person whose fault it was. He told them exactly what he thought of them. It was brought round immediately by car, covered by apologies.

Another time, during some other discussions with EMI, Paul rang up the boss himself, Chairman Sir Joseph Lockwood. Sir Joseph told Paul on the phone to sit tight. Then he jumped into his Rolls Royce and came round to Paul's house personally to settle everything. He says that Paul has the sort of mind that could have made him a good lawyer.

Paul is keen, he wants things to go well. He also still has a slight residue of resentment, which they all had at one time. This came from being pushed around and looked upon as pretty stupid because they were just beat-group players. He hates any insinuation that he is thick. He came back from a meeting with the NEMS people one day, after he'd been trying to persuade them what a good idea Apple would be, furious at their attitude. 'They think we're all thick,' he said, walking round and round his living room.

The whole Apple idea and impetus is Paul's. It got going before Brian died, but it was still all Paul's creation. John and the others agree with everything and are there for all the big meetings. Paul sees it as a huge corporation, with shops, clubs, studios and the best people in the business, from cameramen and engineers to artists, writers and composers.

'We want to make it an environment. An umbrella where people can do things in the way they want. There's thousands and thousands of pounds going through NEMS and not being properly used. They've got it all tied up for us in the Bingley Building Society or somewhere.

'But it's all just a hobby, really, like our music. We do that with our feet up. When we get Apple going big, we'll do that with our feet up. You can have business meetings which are an uplift not a bring-down.'

The *Magical Mystery Tour* would never have got off the ground without Paul. He put his whole life into it for the 15 weeks, directing every stage. So it was a disappointment to him at first, when the British reviews were so bad. 'We knew from the beginning we were just practising. We knew we weren't taking time or doing things properly, but when you've spent a long time on something, even when it's not good enough, you begin to feel perhaps it is better than you know it is.

'I'm glad now it was badly received. It would have been bad to have got away with all that. It's now a challenge to do something properly.'

Paul went straight from *Magical Mystery Tour* into thinking of subjects for full-length films. He and Jane went to see *A Man For All Seasons* and were inspired to do something with a big, lush setting. Then he thought of doing a love story. Why should they always be expected to always lark around. Then he thought of doing some realism, such as Liverpool during the Depression.

Paul and Jane have more time together, on their own, than probably the other Beatle couples. They do get away together, to places like their Scottish home, thanks to Jane. They were the first to want to move to the country for good, to a quieter smaller house, which John and George now also want to do.

'I always wanted to beat Jane down,' says Paul. 'I wanted her to give up work completely.'

'I refused. I've been brought up to be always doing something. And I enjoy acting. I didn't want to give that up.'

'I know now I was just being silly,' says Paul. 'It was a game, trying to beat you down.'

At various times, one of them wanted to get married, but the other didn't. Jane says it was usually something happening with the Beatles, just when it looked all settled, which made her change her mind. Paul says it was her acting, although he agreed when the big tour of America came up, that she had to go on that.

'When I came back after five months, Paul had changed so much. He was on LSD, which I hadn't shared. I was jealous of all the spiritual experiences he'd had with John. There were 15 people dropping in all day long. The house had changed and was full of stuff I didn't know about.'

His life is much quieter and more ordered now. Paul is very communicative about himself, unlike the others. He talks everything over with Jane. She knows what he's thinking.

'Another problem,' says Paul, 'was that my whole existence for so long centred round a bachelor life. I didn't treat women as most people do. I've always had a lot around, even when I've had a steady girl. My life generally has always been very lax, and not normal.

'I knew it was selfish. It caused a few rows. Jane left me once and went off to Bristol to act. I said OK then, leave, I'll find someone else. It was shattering to be without her.'

This was when he wrote 'I'm Looking Through You'. Jane has inspired several of his more beautiful songs, such as 'And I Love Her'.

When they got engaged, on Christmas Day 1967, all these problems were in the past. Maharishi, for a long time, was the only little point of difference, although it was all amicable. Jane didn't fall for him when the others did, although she understood the attraction. She would obviously have preferred to try to reach a spiritual state on their own. Paul wasn't as committed as George and John when he went with Jane to India in 1968, but he felt there was something there that would help him, that might answer his questions. So Jane agreed to go with him. In the end they both had a rewarding and happy time in India.

'As Beatles, we've gone through millions of superficial changes, which mean nothing and haven't changed us,' says Paul.

'It's like in posh places, you get to like avocado and spinach and other way-out foods, so you have them every time. You learn about wine and that's the scene for a while. When you've done all that, then you can go back. You realize the waiter's just there to ask you what you want, not what anyone expects you to want. So if you feel like cornflakes for lunch, you ask for them, without feeling like a Northern comedian.

'These sort of cycles are coming and going all the time. Like the moustache. I had one to amaze people, as a fun thing. I had all the fun then one day took it off. Now I'm back to where I was. Like food, I got through it and realized what it was and came back.

'It's like meeting famous stars. You go through the being amazed stage when you first meet them, then find out he's just like Harry Bloggs. You knew all the time he was just Harry Bloggs, but you had to go through with it to find out.

'We always come back to ourselves because we never change. We might be A plus One, when One equals grey suits. That would be the grey suit cycle. Then A plus Two, when it's floral shirts. But we're always there all the time as A. Then you finish up A plus Dead. Excuse all the clever stuff. I just get carried away talking.

'But all the changes, you see, the physical ones are superficial. You go into a cycle, but you don't get carried away for ever by it, because the more you know, the less you know. And there's always each other as safety valves.

'The thing is, we're all really the same person. We're just four parts of the one. We're individuals, but we make up together The Mates, which is one person. If one of us, one side of the mates, leans over one way we all go with him or we pull him back. We all add something different to the whole.

'Ringo – he's got a great sentimental thing. He likes soul music and always has, though we didn't see that scene for a long time, till he showed us. I suppose that's why we write those sort of songs for him, with sentimental things in them, like "A Little Help from My Friends".

'George – he's very definite about things and dedicated when he's decided. It makes the four of us more definite about things, just because of George. We adapt what's in him to our own use. We all take out of each of us what we want or need.

'John – he's got movement. He's a very fast mover. He sees new things happening and he's away.

'Me – I'm conservative. I feel I need to check things. I was last to try pot and LSD and floral clothes. I'm slower than John, the least likely to succeed in class.

'When a new fender guitar came along, John and George would rush out and buy one. John because it was new and George because he'd decided definitely he'd wanted one. Me. I'd hang around thinking, check I had the money, then wait a bit.

'I'm just the conservative of the four of us. Not compared with outside people. Compared to my family I'm a freak-out.

'We still have the same basic roles, because that's what we are. But all of us will always appear to be changing, just because we don't conform. It's this not conforming, wanting to do something different all the time, which keeps our music different.

'The last generation worked all the time to attain a status in life, get certain clothes and a certain pigeon hole and that was it. We were lucky that by the age of 25 we realized we could achieve any pigeon hole we fancied. I could now sit back and be a company director till I'm 70, but I wouldn't learn as much as I would by trying new things. You *can* learn as much about life just by ploughing one furrow all the time, but it tends to make you narrow-minded.

'We've always not conformed. People told us we needed to channel ourselves, but we never believed them. People said we had to wear the school blazer. If you've enough confidence, you don't have to wear a school blazer through life, as so many people think you have to.

'We're not learning to be architects, or painters or writers. We're learning to be. That's all.'

33

GEORGE

George has a very long, low, single-storeyed, brightly painted bungalow at Esher. It's on a private estate, owned by the National Trust, very similar to the estate where John and Ringo live. You enter the estate through a gateway from the main road, then pass into what looks like the wooded gardens of a stately home. You can't see any houses at first. They are hidden from the roadway, all very secluded and lush looking. They're named, not numbered, so it's impossible to find any of them. George's is the hardest to find. The name of his house, Kinfauns, is not even on his house or in his garden. The driveway to it looks at first to be part of another house.

The bungalow has two wings to it, which enclose a rectangular courtyard at the back. In this he has a heated swimming pool. All the outside walls of the house have been painted by George, or at least sprayed, in bright luminous-looking colours. From his gardens, the house looks like a psychedelic mirage.

Inside, the kitchen area is beautifully done with lots of pinewood furniture and walls and Habitat-type utensils. It looks as if it's straight out of a colour supplement guide to a 1968 kitchen. The main living room has two huge windows, completely circular. They start at floor level and go up to the ceiling.

He has no Beatle Gold Discs or souvenirs in sight. The house might belong to a very contemporary young architect or fashion designer who has spent some time in the East. In the centre of the living room are some very low tables. There are cushions on the floor beside them, for sitting on, Arab fashion. There are no chairs anywhere in sight.

There is an ornate hookah beside one table. George was sitting on the floor, cross-legged, putting new strings on his sitar. He was wearing a long white Indian shirt. A joss stick was burning in an ornamental holder on the table, filling the room with a sweet smell of incense.

'I don't personally enjoy being a Beatle any more. All that sort of Beatle thing is trivial and unimportant. I'm fed up with all this me, us, I, stuff and all the meaningless things we

Opposite: **George and his wife Pattie – another snap by ace photographer Ringo, taken for the 1968 edition.**

do. I'm trying to work out solutions to the more important things in life.

'Thinking about being a Beatle is going backwards. I'm more concerned with the future, but it would take six months of just talking to tell you exactly what I believe in – all the Hindu theories, the Eastern philosophies, reincarnation, transcendental meditation. It's when you begin to understand those things that you realize how pointless the other stuff is. To the ordinary believer in God, I know it sounds very far-out.'

The telephone rang. George picked it up. There was a muffled giggling noise. 'Esher wine store,' said George, gruffly and impatiently. 'No, sorry.' And he hung up.

In the kitchen, Pattie and her sister Jennie, who had just dropped in, were embroidering. They were both wearing Eastern Apple Boutique clothes. They sat half smiling, very quietly and solemnly, working away at their embroidery. The noise of George beginning his sitar lessons next door could be heard. The setting was somehow medieval.

Pattie has the least help in the house of any of the wives, though when she has children she will doubtless have more help. They have a housekeeper, Margaret. She usually has most meals with them, as part of the family.

Margaret does most of the cleaning and Pattie does all the cooking. Pattie usually dries all the dishes and also helps to tidy up. 'It's not as big a house as it looks. It's so full of junk. If I had any more staff to help, they would just be more bother than their worth.'

Pattie also does all the shopping herself, at a local supermarket. She'd just bought a bar of chocolate, which she said tasted like soap. She'd sent it back with a letter of complaint. She didn't put her own name on it – she's at last learned from George to avoid any possibility of publicity. She used Margaret's. She was hoping for some free bars as compensation.

Of all the wives, she is perhaps the most co-equal with her husband. They're both very modern in their marriage, the way the magazines are always telling us modern marrieds are. More than the other Beatle wives, she shares her husband's interests. She was in at the very beginning of the interest in Indian culture and shared all those developments.

But she does retain some freedom and independence on her own, still doing a little bit of modelling work.

Everybody who has been close to the Beatles over the years says that George is the one who has changed most of all. Even fans, who have followed George's progress over a relatively short time, say he has changed. He was looked upon by many as the most handsome Beatle at one time. Now fans are always complaining about George letting his hair grow too unruly and untidy.

That is a superficial change. The inner ones are much more important. George, through being the youngest, was, for a long time, always considered the youngest in every sense. In comparison with John and Paul, most people who knew all three always looked upon George as just a boy. John and Paul were precocious, physically, sexually, and in their talent. They were writing songs long before George ever thought about it.

George did have a slight inferiority complex, although nothing serious. Cyn remembers him always hanging around when she wanted John on his own. So does Astrid, when she was trying to be alone with Stu.

George wasn't academic at school and didn't show many signs of being clever the way Paul did. Taking an ordinary apprenticeship, compared to Paul, the bright Sixth Former, and John, the art student, made people unfairly think George wasn't as good as the others.

Julia, John's mother, was horrified when John dragged along another baby-faced friend to meet her. She'd already thought Paul just a kid.

'He was a lovely little boy,' says Astrid, talking of their Hamburg days. 'He was just little George. We never judged him in any way, the way we used to work out how intelligent or clever Stu, John and Paul were. He didn't develop as quickly as the others had done.

'But he wasn't stupid. No one thought that for one minute. He made lovely jokes at his own expense, sending himself up for being young. I gave them all their Christmas presents one year, all wrapped up. John opened his first and it was an Olympia Press version of the Marquis de Sade. George picked up his and said, "What's in mine then, comics?"'

George, of course, always had his guitar, if apparently nothing else. He was even more fanatical about mastering it than Paul or John, and was much better than they were. He hardly smiled on stage, he was so busy concentrating. But he wouldn't try to do anything else for a long time, such as drawing. He thought he wasn't clever enough.

But now, since the end of 1966, George is the one with so much. He was the first to rise right out and beyond Beatlemania. They all envied him his new passions in life, when they themselves could find so little. He even became the leader in many things. Not by going out of his way to lead, the way John did in the Quarrymen days. The others came to George, following his interests.

George today is the Beatle who needs the other Beatles least. The others admit they all missed each other, during those go-it-alone post-touring months. 'I didn't miss them at all,' he says. 'But it was great to get home from India and tell them all about it.'

'George doesn't miss anyone,' Pattie says. 'He's very independent and he's breaking out more and more. He's found something stronger than the Beatles, though he still wants them to share it. He's the source, but he wants them to join it.'

Because George's abiding passions in life today are Indian religion and Indian music, all the other trappings of being a Beatle pass over him. Yet at one time, he was the most obsessed by all the money and by the business of being a millionaire. He was the one who cross-examined Brian Epstein on all the contracts.

But he can't avoid some things like autographs and the telephone. When that happens, he is often the only one who can be rude. He forgets for a minute why it has happened, and is simply irritated by perfect strangers interrupting his life. On the train to Bangor he was very angry when his tea was being spoiled by women asking for his autograph. The others, who were resignedly signing away, had to restrain him and tell him not to get angry, however aggressive the fans were.

George is the one who has an absolute mania about any publicity of any sort. Anything getting into the papers about him personally makes him furious, as Pattie knows if she accidentally causes any.

Even after more than two years of marriage, Pattie is still not used to all the publicity and press attention. 'I keep thinking, this time it will be OK. No one will know and even if they do, they won't care. That trip to Los Angeles last year, I thought that would be OK. To my horror, there were TV cameras and hundreds of girls screaming.

'In 1964 when we went to Tahiti, Beatlemania was at its height and we expected it. So we went to great lengths to go secretly. Neil and I flew first to Amsterdam, under assumed names, then we flew back towards Tahiti to meet George. Even then, people still found out.

'Things are slightly better today, but it always seems to be worse out of England. You might get on a plane fairly quietly at London Airport, but the English press wire the press at the other end and everyone turns out.

'At night it's not too bad. We have come out of a restaurant and walked down a couple of streets without being pursued.

'But I can't get over the fans always hanging round the house, even now. They come into the garden and rush around. They even come into the house. They got into our bedroom the other day and stole a pair of my trousers and George's pyjamas.'

Although George has warned her, she has, on occasions, inadvertently caused publicity. She received a letter through the post one day from an old man asking people to send him used spectacle frames. He said he was getting bundles of them to send to people in Africa.

She thought it seemed a good cause, so she went out and searched round the shops and bought up all the old spectacles she could find. She took out the glass and sent the old man the frames.

'The next thing there was a story in the *Daily Mirror* about what I'd done. The old man even wrote and thanked me. He said the publicity had done his work a lot of good. George was furious.'

Like all the other wives, she has come up against physical danger, purely through being a Beatle wife.

The worst time was the Christmas of 1965. They were doing their Christmas Show at Hammersmith. I went with Terry. I scraped my hair back so that I would look completely different and no one would recognize me. I don't know how anyone did, but a few did and started punching me. They took their shoes off and shouted, 'Let's go and get her.' I was hemmed in and couldn't get out. They threw things at me and screamed. Terry managed to drag me towards a side exit, with the girls kicking me as we forced a way through. Some followed me out and started kicking me again. I told them to stop. 'Who do you think you are,' they said. Then we all started fighting this time. I punched one in the face and Terry got one against a wall and held her tight. They were all shouting and swearing. Luckily, we got away in the end. They were just horrid little girls. They were so tiny, only 13 or 14 years old. I don't know where they were from.

'It's not so bad these days, but it happens. Cyn was attacked not long ago in the street. Some girl kicked her on the legs and said she had to leave John alone, or else. Isn't it amazing, after all the years that John and Cyn have been married.

'I'm still very frightened when I see a gang of girls in the street. I can't face them. I have to go the other way. I always think perhaps they're going to hit me.'

Being a Beatle wife, like being a Beatle, produces difficult relationships with old friends, as well as new ones. Her sister Jennie – who works in the Apple Boutique – is very close to her and spends a lot of time with her at the house. She is also very interested in Indian religion and culture. But apart from Jennie, Pattie has few close friends.

'People will suddenly make a snide remark – "It's all right for you, you can afford to do that." That sort of thing. Old friends you would think wouldn't come out with such silly things.

'It comes out with new people you meet as well. You think, here's a nice person, then they say something that shows they think I'm different. The other day I was doing a bit of work for *Vogue* and a woman said, 'I don't think of you as a model now, you're more of a celebrity.' I'm not an actress or a star or anything. I'm just me, as I always was.

'The wives have got to do something, when they're hours and hours in the recording studio. We have ideas, but the next thing, we're all leaving Esher anyway, going off to our hundred-acres estate in the country, and then it was Greece or somewhere. There's always these mad ideas around.

'I would like to do something, on my own. I took up the piano and went to lessons for a time. But it was going to take too long to be any good. I do believe you can do anything you want, if you spend enough time at it, but that was too late.

'Then I went to a clairvoyant, who said my grandmother had played the violin and that I was meant to play it as well. I don't know how she knew my grandmother was a violinist. So I thought I'd try. I went to lessons for a while. But that was worse. You've really got to start the violin young.

'I'm now learning the dilruba – that's an Indian instrument. I'm also going to Indian dancing classes under Ram Gopal. It's lovely. Jennie and I go every day before he does his ballet rehearsals.

'I just don't want to be the little wife sitting at home. I want to do something worthwhile.'

Pattie is involved in all things Indian, but George, as with everything he has always taken up, does it almost with a fanaticism. He used to practise the guitar till his fingers bled. Now he sometimes plays the sitar all day long. When he's not doing that, he is reading book after book on religion.

He's not cranky about it. As he goes on and learns more, he becomes more humble and more light-hearted about it. He doesn't preach as much, although there is always the danger, when he is being quoted, of making him appear more fanatical than he is. Paul and John would have been the first to cut down his pretensions or to mock his illusions, if there had been any.

Even from the first, before Maharishi came along, as George was discovering Buddhism and yoga for himself, the others were as fascinated to hear what he'd found as he was.

'Look at this book. An Indian gave us each a copy of it when we were in the Bahamas. It's signed and dated 25 February 1965. My birthday. I've only recently opened it, since I became interested in India. It's fantastic. That Indian really was something. You can tell by his name, it's really a title, showing you how learned he is.

'I now know it was part of a pattern. It was all planned that I should read it now. It all follows a path, just like our path. John, Paul and George converged, then a little later Ringo. We were part of that action, which led to the next reaction. We're all just little cogs in an action which everyone is part of.

'The only thing which is important in life is Karma, that means, roughly, actions. Every action has a reaction, which is equal and opposite. Everything that's done has a reaction, like dropping this cushion down, see, there's a dent in it.

'Your Samsara is the recurrence of all your lives and deaths. We've been here before. I don't know what as, though the friends you had in the previous life are likely to be the friends you have in this life. You hate all the people you hated last time. As long as you hate, there will be people to hate. You go on being reincarnated, till you reach the absolute truth. But heaven and hell are just a state of mind. Whatever it is, you create it.

'We were made John, Paul, George and Ringo because of what we did last time, it was all there for us, on a plate. We're reaping what we sowed last time, whatever it was.

'The reason why we're all here is to achieve perfection, to become Christ-like. Each soul is potentially divine. This actual world is an illusion. It's been created by worldliness and identification with objects. It doesn't matter what happens, the plan can't be affected, even having wars or dropping an H-bomb. None of it matters. Of course, it *does* matter to the people concerned, and a bomb would be terrible, but it's only what happens in ourselves that ultimately matters.

'I used to laugh when I read about Cliff Richard being a Christian. I still cringe when I hear about it, but I know that religion and God are the only things that exist. I know some people think I must be a nutcase. I find it hard not to myself sometimes, because I still see so many things in an ordinary way. But I know that when you believe, it's real and nice. Not believing, it's all confusion and emptiness.

'Life will all work out, as long as you don't bullshit. That's what I'm trying to do. I've blacked out most things that happened to me before I was about 19. I've got so much going forward now. I see so many possibilities. I'm beginning to know that all I know is that I know nothing.'

Transcendental meditation came along just at this stage. He was looking for something and someone to tie all the ends together. He has never missed a day's meditation since he started, unlike the others. Now and again they forget, or are too busy.

The other big part of George's life is his music. John and Paul were knocking out songs together from the day they met. But George never got round to it for a long time, although he helped with an instrumental piece they did on their Hamburg records. His songs have always been created separately from John and Paul's. He does them completely on his own. In this, as in other recent things, he has influenced them – making them aware of Eastern rhythms and instruments.

George's first song did not appear till their second long-playing record, *With The*

George's first meeting with Pattie Boyd took place while they were filming *A Hard Day's Night* in 1964. A model at the time, Pattie acted the part of a young schoolgirl.

Beatles, in the November of 1963. It was called 'Don't Bother Me'. He wrote it in a Bournemouth hotel during a tour. He had been ill and was resting.

'I was a bit run-down and was supposed to be having some sort of tonic, taking it easy for a few days. I decided to try to write a song, just for a laugh. I got out my guitar and just played around till a song came. I forgot all about it till we came to record the next LP. It was a fairly crappy song. I forgot about it completely once it was on the album.'

He forgot about writing songs for almost two years after that. 'I was involved in so many other things that I never got round to it.'

George rather plays down his Beatle songs, considering them a very minor sideline. He can't remember how many he's written and isn't even clear which albums he did songs for.

His next songs were on the LP *Help!*, which appeared in the August of 1965. He did two for this, 'I Need You' and 'You Like Me Too Much'.

He did two songs for *Rubber Soul* in the December of 1965 – 'Think For Yourself' and 'If I Needed Someone'. When he was trying to think of the LPs he'd written songs for he forgot to mention this. Both of these were well up to the standards of the rest of the songs on that album.

For *Revolver*, which appeared in August 1966, he wrote his biggest number of songs so far on one LP. He did three – 'Taxman', 'I Want To Tell You' and 'Love You Too'. This last one was one of the first using Indian instruments, in this case the tabla, a fashion which was soon copied by hundreds of pop groups in Britain and America.

His songs after this were much more Indian, reflecting his growing knowledge of the sitar and of Indian music. 'Within You, Without You', which has good words as well as haunting music, is perhaps his finest song to date. This appeared on *Sergeant Pepper* in June 1967. It was followed, at Christmas time 1967, by 'Blue Jay Way' for *Magical Mystery Tour*, and, in March 1968, by his first song for a Beatle single, 'The Inner Light'.

'I began to write more songs when I had more time, especially when we began to stop touring. Having the Indian things so much in my head it was bound to come out.' He has great difficulty getting the right sort of trained Indian musicians for studio sessions in London. For 'Within You, Without You' and 'Blue Jay Way' he spent weeks finding and auditioning people who could play Indian instruments. There were no full-time professionals in England playing the instruments he wanted.

'They have jobs like bus-driving during the day and only play in the evening, so some of them just weren't good enough, but we still had to use them. They were much better than any Western musician could do, because it at least is their natural style, but it made things very difficult. We spent hours just rehearsing and rehearsing.'

George's sessions take even longer than the Lennon-McCartney songs. As with theirs, George Martin also helps, and so do they, but George is in charge. Groups of very strange-looking Indian gentlemen with very strange-looking instruments come into the studio and sit cross-legged and play to George so that he can hear what they can do.

Up until now, there's also been the problem of writing down the music for them to play. Most of them can't read Western music.

For George's early Indian songs, the Indian musicians just had to pick up the tunes by watching George play them. Not even Big George Martin can read Indian music.

Now George is very well versed in Indian script. He has taught himself to write down his songs in Indian script, so that the Indian musicians can play them.

'Instead of quavers and dots written across lines, Indian music is written down very simply, like our tonic sol-fa. Instead of Doh, Ray, Me and so on, they sing Sa, Re, Ga, Ma, Pa, Dha, Ni, Sa. Often they don't have words for songs, but just sing those notes. You indicate how high or low, or how long each one is by putting little marks under each note.

'The first notes of "Within You", to go with the words "We were, talking", would go Ga Ma Pa Ni. You just need to write the first letter, that's enough. Now I can go to the Indian musicians, give them the music, play it through to let them hear it, and they can do it themselves.'

George spends at least three hours a day practising his sitar, sitting cross-legged with the end resting on the instep of his left foot, in the Indian manner. He has notebooks full of Indian music, written down in the Indian notation. These are the lessons he has to practise. His teacher, Ravi Shankar, has sent him some tape-recorded exercises, which he has on most of the time he isn't playing, even during meals. He is obviously very dedicated and hard working. But he says Indian music will take him years and years before he is any good. He is so busy learning Indian music properly that his Beatle songs are usually written in a rush. He still forgets about his own compositions until a new LP is approaching – then he thinks he should write one.

'Within You, Without You' was written at a friend's house after dinner one night – Klaus Voorman, the friend from Germany, who now plays with Manfred Mann.

'Klaus had a harmonium in his house, which I hadn't played before. I was doodling on it, playing to amuse myself, when "Within You" started to come. The tune came first, then I got the first sentence. It came out of what we'd been doing that evening – "We were talking". That's as far as I got that night. I finished the rest of the words later at home.

'The words are always a bit of a hang-up for me. I'm not very poetic. My lyrics are poor really. But I don't take any of it seriously. It's just a joke. A personal joke. It's great if someone else likes it, but I don't take it too seriously myself.'

A lot of critics didn't understand why there was sudden laughter after 'Within You, Without You' on *Sergeant Pepper*. Some said it must have been put in by the others, to mock George's Indian music. It was completely George's idea.

'Well, after all that long Indian stuff you want some light relief. It's a release after five minutes of sad music. You haven't got to take it all that seriously, you know. You were supposed to hear the audience anyway, as they listen to Sergeant Pepper's Show. That was the style of the album.'

His song for the *Magical Mystery Tour*, 'Blue Jay Way', was written during his visit to California in the early summer of 1967. The title comes from the street in Los Angeles in which he and Pattie had rented a house. They had just flown in from London and were waiting for their friend Derek Taylor (ex-Beatle press officer, now with Apple) to come and see them.

'Derek got held up. He rang to say he'd be late. I told him on the phone that the house was in Blue Jay Way. He said he'd find it OK, he could always ask a cop.

'I waited and waited. I felt really nackered with the flight, but I didn't want to go to sleep till he came. There was a fog and it got later and later. To keep myself awake, just as a joke, to fill in time, I wrote a song about waiting for him in Blue Jay Way.

'There was a little Hammond organ in the corner of this rented house, which I hadn't noticed. I messed around on this and the song came.'

All the words directly relate to him waiting for Derek Taylor – 'There's a fog upon LA, and my friends have lost their way…' When he came home to Esher, he perfected the song. There is still an organ effect, very deep and booming, in the backing to the song.

In January 1968 George agreed to write his first screen music for the film *Wonderwall*. He has been asked to do more single songs, but he has usually refused. One day he was working on one for Marianne Faithfull. She'd asked him to write one for her to sing, something like 'Within You, Without You'. He wasn't sure how it was going to turn out. He'd got the song in his head, but the words were becoming jokier and jokier. He thought they might end up too silly and he'd have to dump them.

'I've got "You can't love me with an artichoke heart", which is not bad.' He sang and played the song on his Hammond organ. 'But I'm not sure about continuing the joke – "You can't listen with your cauliflower ear" or "don't be an apricot fool". I don't know. I'll just see how it turns out.

'I've got no vocal range, so I've got to keep all my songs simple. Marianne is the same, so that's all right.'

His voice doesn't have much range, but it has a sizeable following from the fans, judging from the letters in *Beatles Monthly*. Fans are always asking why don't John and Paul let him sing more. 'It's not true they don't let me. I would if I wanted to. I just can't be bothered.'

He looks upon John and Paul as the composers and writers. He feels he needn't bother when they are so good, unless he happens to have something in his head.

George's song, 'Blue Jay Way', written on a scrap of paper while he waited for Derek Taylor in Los Angeles, 1967.

'I'm not sure which way I want to go now. Real Indian classical songs are so much different from the sort of Indian-influenced pop songs that have been turned out over here. They're just ordinary pop songs, with a little bit of Indian background.

'I'm not sure about the ones I've written. Looked at from another person's point of view, as pop songs, I like them. But looked at from my point of view, from what I really want to do, I don't like what I've done so far. I always seem to be rushed. I see things afterwards that I should have done.'

He's amused by people who take Beatle music too seriously. He says the words of 'Within You, Without You' were meant to be true, but it was still a joke. 'That's what people don't understand. Like John's "I Am The Walrus" – "I am he as you are he as you are me". It's true but it's still a joke. People looked for all sort of hidden meanings. It's serious and it's not serious.'

George thinks they could all go a lot further and probably will in music and words. He thought John's line about taking her knickers down in 'I Am The Walrus' was great.

'Why can't you have people fucking as well? It's going on everywhere in the world, all the time. So why can't you mention it? It's just a word, made up by people. It's meaningless in itself. Keep saying it – Fuck, fuck, fuck, fuck, fuck, fuck, fuck. See, it doesn't mean a thing, so why can't you use it in a song? We will eventually. We haven't started yet.'

This would follow on Kenneth Tynan's theory that the Beatle songs are in direct line from medieval English songs. They were all full of arses, shit and fucking. So in one way, it is true. George, John and Paul haven't really done anything yet in their songs.

Meanwhile, back at the George Harrison ranch. It does look a bit like a ranch, with all that low-slung white wood. The telephone rang. It wasn't a fan but an ex-employee with a long complicated story about how he'd loaned Jayne Mansfield £250 and she'd died without repaying it and he was about to be evicted and could George help. George said yes, of course. He put down the phone and said 'Well, what's £250.'

George is still a Beatle. It's his job and, as with all jobs, everyone has to think about it now and again, and of the future. He is now beginning to think he has a duty to do it well. He might even have some sort of social responsibilities as a pop idol, which is something none of them considered for one minute not so very long ago.

He is still umbilically connected with the others, despite all the sitar exercises and higher thoughts. They're his greatest friends. As they shared his religious interest, he shares all their passions, however mundane, from long neckerchiefs to cameras.

'If one experiences something, the others all have to know about it,' says Pattie. 'They have crazes, just like you have crazes at school. But it keeps them all happy.

'They do waste a lot, when they take up a new craze. They buy a lot of stuff they're never going to use, but it often turns out useful. They spent a lot on cameras and film equipment, but it showed them they could make films, without having to know a lot.

'I know now that they are all part of one thing. I didn't realize it when I was first married. They all belong to each other. No one person belongs to one other person. It's no use trying to cling on or you would just become miserable. George is my husband, but he's got to be free to go with them if he wants. It's important to him to be free.

'George has a lot with the others that I can never know about. Nobody, not even the wives, can break through it or even comprehend it.

'It used to hurt me at first, as I slowly began to learn there was a part I could never be part of. Cyn talked to me about it. She said they would always be a part of each other.'

There is only one other minor aspect of Beatle life that Pattie in any way criticizes. Unlike the Beatles themselves, Pattie feels they should do something with their money in the way of helping some charitable cause. (Since the summer of 1968 they have started to donate the profits of a few songs to certain charities. 'Across the Universe' went to the World Wildlife Fund.)

'I know they say a lot of these charities are just keeping the officials in money. There must be something we can do, the way Marlon Brando helps homeless children.

'The thing with the Beatles was that they were plagued by charities in the early days, wanting them to do things. All those crowds of crippled children that were taken to see them in their dressing rooms, as if they were faith healers. This somehow sickened them.

'I wouldn't mind organizing some charity, but there again the publicity would come out all wrong and spoil everything, as George says. It always does. People would think we were doing it for the wrong reasons, the way some people couldn't believe they were genuinely interested in going to listen to Maharishi. It's difficult to know what to do.'

George himself says he knows what he is going to do. He has no worries about the future.

His interest in spiritual things will last for ever, he says. The cynics will be proved wrong. The whole interest in Indian cultures is not a passing phase.

'Reaching a blissful state is the most important thing, but I've still got to do a job, being a Beatle.

'We've got to do that job because we *can* do things now. We're in a position to try things, to show people. We can jump around and try new things, which others can't or won't. Like drugs. People doing ordinary jobs just couldn't give the time we did to looking into all that.

'If Mick (Jagger) had gone to jail for taking pot he would have been the best person it could have happened to. It would have been much better than if it had happened to someone with no money, who it could have ruined. Being rich and famous makes it easier to go through with that sort of thing.

'We've just really started making films. *Magical Mystery Tour* was nothing. But we'll show it can be done. Anyone can make films, you don't have to do all this messing around with backers and companies and hundreds of technicians and scripts worked out to the last word.

'We'll make perhaps one or two films a year ourselves, not necessarily with us in them. We'll hire out our studios and people to anyone who wants them. We'll lend our money as well. If we ever have to use backers, we'll make sure they have no influence.

'We'll go round and round in circles, doing films, trying out new things. Then after films we'll try something new. I don't know what. We didn't know we were going to make films when we started making records.

'It'll just be the same sort of scene, trying to do something new each time, going on a bit. Then we die and go on to a new life, where we try again, to get better all the time. That's life. That's death.

'But as for this life, we haven't done anything yet.'

34

RINGO

Ringo lives round the corner from John on the same private estate in Weybridge, Surrey. It is also a large mock-Tudor house. It was built in 1925 and is called Sunny Heights. It cost him £37,000, plus £40,000 to do it up. It hasn't got a swimming pool like John's or George's, but it has much bigger grounds, with lots of trees and shrubs. It backs on to St George's Hill golf course. Neither he nor John is a member of the club and has never asked to be. But when they moved in one newspaper reporter asked the club if the Beatles could be members. He was told no, there was a long waiting list. Ringo says he wouldn't join anyway. He doesn't dig walking.

Ringo's garden has had a lot of very expensive landscaping done to it. At the back, the house now looks down into a huge amphitheatre, dug out of the ground. It has lots of brick terraces and ponds, which you walk down and into from the french windows of the main drawing room. There are little woods at either side of this amphitheatre, still part of Ringo's garden. Up one tree there is a large playhouse.

Part of the rebuilding at the back, a semicircular wall, brought in a bill for £10,000, to Ringo's amazement. Like all the Beatles, for years he never asked for estimates, which of course was just leaving themselves wide open. It's not that people necessarily tried to take them for a ride. They just made sure they provided their most expensive goods and services.

'When I walk round,' said Ringo, standing looking at his vast gardens, 'I often think, what's a scruff like me doing with this lot? But it soon passes. You get used to it. You get ready to argue with anyone who is trying to get too much of my money.'

In the summer of 1967 he had a large extension built on the house, containing extra living rooms, guests' rooms, a work-room and one very long room, which is used as a cinema or billiard room. The work was done by a building firm that he half owned. This was about the only investment he has made on his own. Unfortunately, it had to close in

Opposite: **Ringo tries out his educated left foot, during the filming of *Magical Mystery Tour*, 1967.**

mid-1967, thanks to the credit squeeze. 'We built a lot of very good houses, but nobody had the money to buy them. I didn't lose money when the firm closed, except that I was left with a dozen new flats and houses, which stood empty for a long time.'

Inside, the main drawing room is perhaps the nicest of all the Beatles' living rooms, though it's a shade dark on the garden side, as there is a terrace that obscures some light. It is beautifully furnished. It has a deep brown Wilton carpet which covers the whole room. This cost a fortune. It was made especially for him in one piece, which is why it cost so much. He now shudders to think what he paid for it. He doesn't want the price repeated. It was about double what normal people pay when they're buying an entire house.

One room is a bar, all very olde-worlde and very corny, though it has genuine bar bits and pieces. He has a cowboy holster hanging up in it, which Elvis gave him.

There are various Golden Discs and other awards scattered throughout the house, but not too many. In his main room he has a couple of sparse book shelves. They contain mostly well-thumbed paperbacks, some new but used-looking books on Indian religions and some new but highly unused-looking volumes of history and Dickens. Of all the Beatles, John is the only one with proper book shelves.

Ringo has a couple of rooms devoted to his own toys. They're very expensive ones, mainly film camera equipment. He has made some excellent and ingenious films, though he is very shy about showing them and doesn't really think they're all that good. He has one 20-minute film in colour, which consists mainly of close-ups of Maureen's eye, with a background of electronic music. In it there is a scene filmed while driving down the M1, with shots through a car window into the headlights of approaching cars. There is another excellent sequence he did by sitting on a garden swing with his camera, then shooting at the house and garden as he swung up and down. He did all the shooting, cutting and editing of the film himself. He used expensive equipment, but even so the results were very interesting. One or two shots in *Magical Mystery Tour* were done by Ringo, using his own cameras.

He also does a bit of painting, but not much. His wife Maureen spends hours doing very intricate patterns and designs. She's done one based on the *Sergeant Pepper* symbol, all in sequins, hundreds and hundreds of them. It took her six weeks, on and off, while she was waiting to have Jason.

Zak, their first son, was born in September 1965, and Jason in August 1967. Ringo doesn't think they'll have any more for a bit. He wants to give Maureen a rest.

They have a living-in nanny for the children and a daily woman for cleaning, but like John and Cyn, Ringo and his family live their self-contained life in the middle of the house. There is no outward sign of being attended on. Maureen does all the cooking for Ringo. But unlike the Lennons', the whole house has a lived-in feeling.

They both tend just to potter around, when Ringo's not working. Like John, they have pop records and the TV going all the time, even in rooms they're not in. They watch TV a lot. They have six sets. From the main couch in the drawing room Ringo can change channels without getting up, just by operating a knob on the couch.

Ringo will give a smile, or just nod, when a Beatles song comes on the TV or radio, if there is anyone else with him. John and Paul don't appear to notice. George doesn't watch telly or play pop records.

'I don't play our songs myself. Maureen puts them on sometimes. She's a Beatles fan and Frank Sinatra. In the old days we used to celebrate like mad every time we were on the radio.

'I don't mind if people attack us. We're so popular it doesn't matter now, but the critics can kill some records, when a lot of people might have enjoyed them.

'When you're coming up, everyone is all for you. When you've made it, they want to knock you if they can. If only 30 people turn up at the airport to see you, people say, that wasn't much of a crowd, you must be finished. They expect things to be the same as when we were touring. They think, ah the Beatles, there must be a million people round them.'

'He is as amused as the others by those who try to see hidden meanings in their records, particularly in America. 'It's bound to happen there. They have a hundred fellers doing what ten fellers do here. They're all looking for something different.'

Like all of them, he is trying to lead a private life for a change. He thinks that as they've stopped touring and stopped being public property, people should leave them alone. 'But people just stare at us everywhere, as if we were a circus. I can understand it when I'm Ringo the Beatle. But when I'm Ritchie the person, I should be freer.

'I suppose you can't expect it. They've heard so much. They want to see you. Fame, that's what it is. They don't realize we've stopped playing. They still want to gape.'

He and John were coming back from London one night, being driven by John's chauffeur in John's Rolls, when they passed a pub all lit up, with people sitting around in their shirt sleeves drinking. They couldn't get over it. To them it was like a scene from a fairy tale they'd dimly forgotten about.

'It looked great. We were past before it had really hit us. We were in suits and felt a bit stiff. We'd been to visit Queenie (Mrs Epstein). It wasn't long after Brian had died. When we got home, we decided to change and go and have a drink. I took Maureen round to Cyn's to sit with her while me and John went to the pub. It was just like the old days. We brought them back crisps and Babycham.

'The pub itself hadn't changed. It was just like pubs when we used to know them, straight out of Coronation Street. The barman was very pleased when he recognized us. We had a bottle of brown each. We had to sign a few autographs, but it wasn't too bad.'

He thinks now, having done it once, they should be able to pop in for a quick drink more often. He's never tried going for a walk on his own, because, of course, he doesn't go in for walking. None of the Beatles takes any exercise whatsoever, except Paul when taking Martha for a walk.

Playing billiards or his one-armed bandit is about Ringo's only exercise. 'There's the garden. What's wrong with that? I often walk round the garden.' He appears to need no exercise to keep fit, and has kept his same weight – between nine stone and nine stone six – for the last six years. Considering the unhealthy life he led touring, and his years of illness as a child, it is surprising. But they are all somehow fit, though rather pale-looking. They've had regular medical checkups for each new film and other big contracts, and nothing has been found wrong with them. John put on weight when they stopped touring, but he soon slimmed it off.

Ringo at last passed his driving test, after failing three times and driving without a licence for two years. He now has three cars, a Mini Cooper, a Land-Rover and a Facel Vega. 'Don't ask me how you spell it. I was away from school when they had spelling.'

Apart from his parents, he has helped other relations and friends, loaning them money to buy their own house.

'I do have a load of rubbish. I leap out and buy something, then it doesn't last a week. Camera stuff, I'm always getting it. I want something better or extra, so I'm changing cameras all the time. I don't know how much I'm worth. If I said give us my money tomorrow, I want it in me hand, I've no idea what it would come to.'

He doesn't carry cash around with him. 'Tell me, what do those pound note thingies look like? And do they still make those cute-like half-crowns? Maureen does the shopping, but she just uses a card that says, this is money.'

When they sign a bill in a shop it is sent on to their accountant's office. He sends it back to them, for their confirmation, before he pays it. 'Mine comes to about £1,000 a month. Last month it was £1,600, but I'd bought a new lens.

'I've only been caught once. We were at Brian's and me and Maureen decided to come home early. We'd come in someone else's car, so Peter (Brown) gave us his car to drive home.

'Halfway home, on the dual carriageway, miles from anywhere, in the middle of a Sunday night, we ran out of petrol. There was no garage and even if there had been, I had no money.

'I flagged a car down and told him I'd run out of petrol. I said could he lend us five bob so I could buy a gallon to get us home. He said are you Ringo? I said yeh. He said it would be no use loaning me money as there was no garage open anywhere around, but he'd drive us home in his car, which he did. It was great. He only turned out to be a journalist, from the *Daily Telegraph*. Well, it's those sort of unimportant things that are always getting in the papers that you don't want in. I took him into the house and gave him an LP. He never wrote about it.'

They were all given cheque books at one stage several years ago, to help in emergencies, but they never use them. 'I've never signed a cheque in my life,' says Ringo. 'I don't know how to. I lost my cheque book the minute I got it.

'I've never been refused in a shop yet, when I've asked to sign the bill, even in shops I haven't been in before. No one's asked me yet to prove that I really am Ringo.'

He doesn't feel any urge or necessity to give money to charity and doesn't see why they should. 'Brian gave stuff now and again, on behalf of us. John did Oxfam a Christmas card, didn't he? That made them a lot of money.

'I don't fancy it, really. Most of the people running charities are not nice people. What good did the Aberfan Fund do, except for all the lawyers? They gave each person £5,000 for losing a child. Ridiculous. Five million quid doesn't equal losing a child. I think a lot of people are making money out of charities. No, they're not for me.

'The Government's taking over 90 per cent of all our money anyway – we're left with 1s. 9d. in the pound. The Government spends it on helping people, doesn't it. That's like helping charities.

'Not that the Governments are any good. They can't make anything work. Buses, trains. None of them work. I was in the car yesterday going to town and I passed five Number 7 buses, one lined up behind the other, all with just two people on. Why couldn't they all be on one bus?

'The Government takes too much on taxes. There's no initiative, you get taxed right through life. When they've left nobody rich, no one will have any money to give the Government.

'Everything the Government does turns to crap, not gold. The railways made profits when they were private firms, didn't they. It's like Victorian England, our Government. Outdated.

'All Governments are the same, Labour or Tory. Neither of them offers me anything. All they do is oppose each other. One says one thing, and the other has to say something different. They both do it. That's all they do. Why can't they all get together and work for the country?'

They all say that Ringo is the sentimental one, although they all have bits of Ringo in them. One of the things Ringo is sentimental about is preferring England, which is something they say they don't care about. When the Greek island and other foreign ideas were being discussed, Ringo was the only one who wasn't very keen. He would have liked living all together on a hundred-acre site in Devon, but he doesn't fancy going away for a long time to a foreign country. The others say they could do it easily.

'I couldn't live anywhere but England. That's where I'm from. That's where my family is. England's no better than anywhere else, I know that. It's just that I'm comfortable here.'

He does take holidays abroad and he likes to be with the others, usually John. He and Maureen wouldn't go off alone to California on a whim the way George and Pattie did. Like John, he prefers going places with his Beatles buddies. 'It's nice to be together.'

He's lost none of the old-fashioned Northern idea of marriage, of the man being the master at home. 'That's how it is. My grandfather (Starkey) always had his seat in his house, which only he sat in. I'm the same I suppose.' Both he and John have a bit of Andy Capp in them. Paul and George are much more middle class in their domestic setting.

But Ringo is a bit alarmed that he appears more of the lord and master than he thinks he is. 'Maureen was telling me the other day that the cleaning woman fears me. I don't plan or expect it. I think it's just Maureen rushing around saying we must get this ready or that done for me coming in.'

When they're out, he squires Maureen in the traditional working-class way. Some years ago they once went out for dinner at Woburn Abbey, the home of the Duke of Bedford. Ringo had been friendly with his son, Rudolph, a keen pop fan. 'I thought it would be a good laugh, to see how the others lived, that's why I went.'

He was sat down at the baronial dining table, miles away from his wife Maureen, in the middle-and-upper-class way, much to his alarm.

'I said oh no. Come over here, luv. They were trying to make us sit apart. Very funny people.

'I don't think women like to be equal. They like to be protected, and, in turn, they like looking after men. That's how it is.'

They gave up London some time ago and rarely go out at nights. 'Swinging London was OK before it became swinging London. When we were just becoming famous it was nice to go around and see people knowing you, which is how all famous show biz people are supposed to do. But it was a drag.'

They don't entertain people in any formal sense at their home. He has one or two friends, like Roy Trafford, from his early Liverpool days. John is the main person who pops in, then sits down for tea or whatever's going.

February 1968: Paul, with girlfriend Jane Asher, and Ringo and his wife Maureen leave London Airport to join the other Beatles and their wives for two months of transcendental meditation at the Maharishi's academy in Rishikesh, India. Ringo, feeling homesick, returned home after only ten days.

Maureen prefers the quiet life, although her life is really Ringo's. Anything he wants to do, she wants to do. They are very happy.

She is the only Beatle wife who stays up for her husband and waits for him, no matter how late or in what condition he's likely to arrive.

'When he's recording I often stay up till 4.30 in the morning. He's usually got up late the day before and perhaps not had a proper meal before going out. So I try to have something for him when he comes home, however late. Then I know at least he's got a meal inside him. They all just peck at things when they're working.

'If it turns out he has eaten a proper meal at work, or with the boys, then it doesn't matter. I can easily use up the potatoes. Nothing's wasted. But I usually give him a meal. He might eat it quickly, as he's tired, but he does like something when he comes home.

'I don't mind staying up for him. I might change the furniture round, to put the hours in. I just mess around really. I spent two hours the other night deciding where to move a lamp. I might make things, curtains or clothes. I put sequins on an old lampshade the other day.'

She spends a lot of time answering correspondence. Maureen takes great interest in all Ringo's fan mail. Perhaps through having been a fan herself, she knows how much it means. Apart from Mrs Harrison, George's mother, she is the only one in the Beatle circle who bothers. She doesn't do as much as Mrs Harrison, as she has a large house and two young children to look after.

When people send birthday cards, she still drops a little note saying thank you, adding that Ritchie is too busy working to write himself. She always calls him Ritchie, never Ringo, even writing to people who only know him as Ringo. 'I don't know why, really, Ringo just seems funny. His name is Ritchie.'

In odd moments she gets him to sign big batches of autographs. She doesn't send them to everyone who writes, because that would take too long. She just drops in his autograph, with her little letter of reply, when people seem really nice and polite.

'I like answering the letters. I've been doing it for five years now. I get some lovely replies back from the parents.

'I do get behind sometimes. When I was having Jason I got behind for a few weeks and had three shopping bags full of them.

'I don't do it just because people are polite. I know that if I liked someone enough to write a nice letter to them I would like some sort of reply. I've had letters from fans saying this is their 15th letter. They must feel awful. What they've been doing is writing to the office. The office gets thousands and just can't cope. Not that I want any more sent to me than I get now, thank you.'

She makes quite a lot of clothes, when she is filling in the hours waiting. 'I like instamatic things. I'm in such a hurry that I never use patterns. I might start off making a dress, but keep going wrong, cutting it down and down, till I've ended up making a handkerchief.'

When she knows she's just going to have a go at something, she always buys cheap remnants, so there won't be much waste. She's very careful, when it comes to money. All her shopping is done at a Weybridge supermarket. She always gets Pink Shield trading stamps with everything she buys, which appears rather pointless, when she could buy anything she wanted anyway. She likes sticking the stamps in the pages. She gets out her little book now and again to see how much she's got.

Ringo thinks it's a bit of a joke, but he's proud of the way she manages the house and looks after him. He's also very pleased by things she's made, such as the sequined Sergeant Pepper design.

They haven't started thinking about Zak's or Jason's education, as they're so young. Like John, Ringo would like them to go to an ordinary council school. 'But Zak's not ordinary, is he? They wouldn't let him alone. It's eased off now a bit, but he'd still get picked upon. If the only way to get him a bit of peace is to pay for it, then we'll have to. If they want to go to a boarding school, then I'll let them. But I'd rather have them at home. I just want them to be as free as possible and love one another.

'I say all those sort of things, of course, but I don't know how I'll turn out when they get older. But I don't want them to have the restrictions I had, you know, your mother telling you not to play near the window, or watch you don't break anything. You never know, do you, when it's your turn to be a parent.'

But he wouldn't like them to have the sort of education he had, or, at least, lack of education. Those lost years of illness have had some effect on him, not in any serious way, at least not what he would call serious. His spelling, for example, is non-existent, but it doesn't worry him. His knowledge of where towns and places are is also very strange.

'I know I can't spell, but I can read anything you want to give me. English is hard for anybody to spell. My maths aren't bad. But I'm best really with my hands. I can do most little jobs, if I'm just left on my own. I can eventually work things out on my own. It's when things are written down I'm no good.'

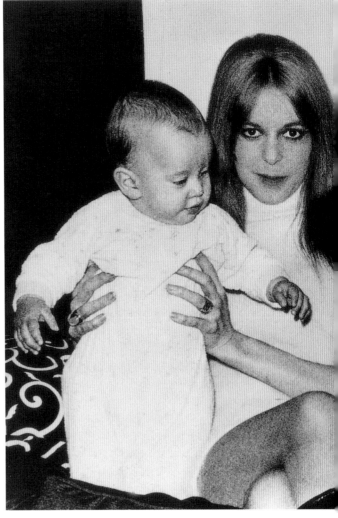

The Ringo Starrs, self-portrait: Jason, Maureen, Zak and Ringo, 1968.

Ringo came into the group last, long after all the others were settled in their positions and personalities. He felt it was all a marvellous stroke of luck. He moved in with them at the second they took off. The others never looked upon it as luck for one minute. They all knew they could be a success.

When they are all together, he does tend to be the withdrawn one, stuck out on drums while the rest crowd the microphone. He's always said he wasn't the talking one. But his jokes and observations were as wise and witty as theirs. The difference is that he doesn't keep up the patter, the way Paul can, or the way George does when he's on his hobbyhorse, or the way John can make daft jokes and observations all the time. Ringo keeps quiet, until he's spoken to.

In repose he does *look* withdrawn and worried. His grey streak is now greyer than it used to be. Apart from the left side of the front of his hair, it has now affected his right

eyebrow as well. Some doctors think there might be psychological reasons for premature greyness, but most agree it is meaningless.

His nose isn't as big as it can look in photographs, or, of course, in caricatures. It has been taken by many people as a sign that he must be Jewish. 'I never realized I had a big nose till I was famous. I never even thought people were thinking I was Jewish, till one day a bloke from the *Jewish Chronicle* rang me up. I had to tell him I wasn't.

'I'm beginning to see now that I am what I am because of the sort of upbringing I had, with no father and with my mother always out at work. It did make me very quiet and inverted. I'm only figuring myself out now, though I was very happy at the time. I saw a programme on TV the other day about the effect a long period in hospital can have on a child. It can make them very withdrawn.'

Ringo isn't withdrawn. He is completely open and friendly, the sweetest of them all really. He is not self-centred in any way. His wife Maureen thinks he could make more of himself, if he wanted to.

'It was his idea to do it with sequins, didn't he tell you? I know it's rubbish really, but he never takes credit for things.

'I think he often underestimates himself. He does forget what good ideas he has had, because he thinks he's not creative. He says it's for the others to have the good ideas. But he is good at many things. He's a good painter. I think films will be very good for him, so I hope they come off. He's great at all things. He's a lovely dancer.'

Ringo is a much stronger personality than he has appeared. He's also much handsomer in real life, with rich blue eyes. He is in no sense the buffoon of the group, or even their pet mascot. His opinions are as valid as theirs. But in the light of Paul and John's more obvious talents, he has kept himself even quieter than he is. But they rely on him a great deal. He is a vital part of the four, contributing elements that they need – that old sentimentality again, but also a strong common sense, the ordinary human touch. He has some good ideas and opinions about the Beatles, and about himself.

'I think four of us together, all sort of equal, made us one whole. We're different from each other, yet alike.

'When you have a single star, or a leader and a backing group, you either take him or leave him. With four, you can associate with one of us, yet still like the rest of us. If you didn't like Elvis, that was that. With four of us, there's more to go on.

'There was never any competition between us, either privately or publicly, though we all have our special fans.

'If all four of us had to stand up there in front of a million fans and they had to line up behind the one they liked best, I think Paul would get most. John and George would be joint second. Ringo would be last. That's what I think. You can tell, from the letters and the fans screaming and mobbing.

'With John and Paul, their own fans tend not to like the other one as much. But with me, I get John fans and Paul fans as well. They all like me at the same time as their own special favourites. So perhaps if you counted second votes, I might win.

'They all want to mother me. I know that. It brings out the maternal bit, sentimental little Ritchie. I've always had it, as a kid. Old women like me as well as girls. Paul has a bit of this as well.

'That's me, I know it. Why change it. Now and again I do feel like being different. When people keep on asking me to do films, I think I'll pick a part as a right bastard. That would be nice. Just to see the reaction.

'I'm not the creative one. I know that. But people expect I must want to be. They write and say why don't I try. I did try, a couple of years ago, to write two little songs, but they were such pinches, without me really realizing it.

'It can get you down, not being creative. You know people are thinking you're not the creative one. But out of four people you wouldn't expect them *all* to be creative, would you? Fifty per cent is enough. Think of all the groups, good groups, who can't write anything at all.

'I'd love to be able to, of course. It's a bit of a bind when I realize I can't. I've got a piano, but I can't play it really. I often get a feeling. I just feel like writing a lovely song today, but I go and I can't. I don't know how to. I can knock out things in C, as long as it's 12-bar. That's a musical joke. It means nothing.

'I do sometimes feel out of it, sitting there on the drums, only playing what they tell me to play. Often when other drummers of groups say to me, that was great, that bit, I know the others have usually told me what to do, though I've got the credit.

'Making films is OK, but I get cheesed off with it sometimes. It's just guessing, isn't it, hoping it's going to come off and you've got something good.

'But I'm quite interested in films, seeing as how I'm not writing or creating that way. I might as well get in there if I can.

'I know people said I was OK in *A Hard Day's Night*, but I had no idea what was going on. That little scene with the little boy on the canal that they said was good, I was stoned out of my mind when I did that. I had a real thick head. I'd been up all the night before. I just came on with me mac on, feeling dead weary. I couldn't hardly move. Dick had to shout everything at me. But it did turn out OK. That bit where I kicked the stone along, that was my gag. Yeh, it was. But everything else was Dick's idea. I was still in a haze.

'I had lots of films offered after that, but they were all big star things, expecting me to carry the show. I nearly agreed to one about Sherlock Holmes, with me as Dr Watson, but

I thought it was too big. I don't want to try and carry anything yet. It would be awful if it was a flop. But a minor part would be OK, then I wouldn't have the responsibility. If that was OK, I could try bigger stuff.

'I took *Candy* because it wasn't too big a part, and there was them other stars – Marlon Brando and Richard Burton. I thought, they'll be carrying the film, not me, and I'll learn from them. It was only a ten-day part, as the Spanish gardener, with not much dialogue.

'I can't act of course. I don't know how to. I watch these actors on television. You can *tell* they're actors, because their faces are going all the time. You should see their eyes. I can't do all that. I just don't do anything. I don't know. Perhaps that's acting.'

He says he wouldn't mind if it all just disappeared tomorrow. He still feels he's lucky and would be able to earn a bit of bread somehow, even if it meant going back to being a fitter.

'No, I probably wouldn't have been a fitter today. I gave that up before I finished my time, to join the groups. If Rory Storm hadn't come along and then the Beatles, I'd have continued running around in the Teddy Boy gangs. Today, well, I'd probably just be a labourer.

'I'm glad I'm not, of course. It'll be nice to be part of history, some sort of history anyway. What I'd like to be is in school history books and be read by kids.'

END BIT

Doing a biography of living people has the difficulty that it is all still happening. It is very dangerous to pin down facts and opinions, because they are shifting all the time. They probably won't believe half the things they said in the last four chapters by the time you've read them. They might have found new houses as well.

But at least with living people you can get it all first-hand, as long as they are willing to give up the time. In this case they were, though having to think about their Beatlemania days bored them stiff. Luckily, this is the most chronicled part of their lives so far, but as this is meant primarily to be a book of record, I have tried to give an outline of those Beatlemania years.

I've tried to keep myself out of the book as much as possible, though I'm sure my prejudices have crept in all over the place. I've also tried to resist the temptation to analyse. Too many millions of words have already been trotted out by the interpreters. Someone can do a critical biography of them in 50 years' time, if anyone remembers them by then.

Naturally, I think they will do. I wouldn't have done all this lot otherwise. But their immediate future is still very hazy. Will they do more films on their own? Will Apple come off? What will happen to Maharishi? Will they get bored and just pack it all in?

Perhaps by the time this book is out, some of these questions will be answered. They have gone through so many stages that there is no reason to doubt that there are more to come.

They are confident that they can succeed in films and in anything else they might try, but in the history of show business, no one has yet repeated a phenomenon. Elvis Presley stood still almost immediately. Charlie Chaplin went on to direct some very professional films, but no one can say they were phenomenal. As with Beatlemania, his little man, bewildered by the big new corporations, was right for the times. Can the Beatles be right again?

Opposite: The Beatles at the press party to launch *Sergeant Pepper,* held at Brian Epstein's home in London, May 1967.

It remains to be seen whether the Beatles will be handicapped by living such isolated lives. Is art affected by lack of stimuli? According to some art experts, if Picasso had gone off and seen new people and new places, he wouldn't have messed around doing little drawings on menus.

But Apple is at least providing some new stimuli, though their private lives are as private as ever. Apple is perhaps their most constructive stage so far. After years of being anti-help and anti-most organizations, like benevolent despots, they are now pouring back their money and power into helping and backing others. And whatever one thinks of transcendental meditation, their interest in religion is also positive and only for the good, which is again a reversal of their early attitudes. Having scorned the idea that pop idols should have responsibilities, they are now almost missionary, in spiritual and in materialistic matters. If their boast that they haven't started yet comes true, their biographer in 50 years' time will have more than just the records of a beat group to write about.

It now remains to be seen whether, and in which ways, they can go on alone. They had Brian Epstein when they were emerging as personalities, and George Martin when they were emerging as composers.

All the experts can't see them doing it again, not in a new medium and not without help.

'In their music,' says George Martin, 'they have an instinctive awareness of what to do. They are always ahead of everyone else. But in much of their other thinking, they tend to be juvenile psychologists.

'They are very like children in many ways. They love anything magical. If I had to clap my hands in front of John and produce a vase of flowers, John would be knocked out and fantastically impressed and I would be able to do anything with him.

'They like everything to be like instant coffee. They want instant recording, instant films, instant everything.

'I think they do need an organizer round them. This would allow them to be more outlandish. If they try to do everything on their own, things could go wrong.'

They are very young, no one can deny that, which is good, because they still want to do things on their own. It's to be hoped they keep on trying.

But they could and might pack up tomorrow, live on their millions and contemplate their navels. They haven't done badly so far. They've given us quite a lot. And in return, they have got their MBEs.

HUNTER DAVIES
Gozo, May 1968

POSTSCRIPT 1985

When that little End Bit was written, I carefully did not predict what I thought would happen to them. There seemed so many exciting possibilities, such as films, and exciting new creations, such as Apple. They had already stopped appearing in public, and had started to go their separate ways, living separate lives, but I never thought for one moment that a final split was imminent. I hadn't realized that, in fact, I had recorded the growth and rise of the Beatles and had captured them at their peak. All that was to come was the end. And rather petty and nasty it turned out to be.

In the meantime, back in 1968, I rewarded myself with a year abroad. After the book was finished, and all the boring arguments with Apple executives settled, and the Beatles and their respective families pacified about the contents, I went off with my wife and family, first of all to Gozo in Malta, and then to Portugal. We had two children at the time, aged four and two when we set off, so it seemed a good time to travel, before they started school. I wrote a novel abroad, and so did my wife. I never went back to the *Class of '68*, which was what my pre-Beatles book had become. The student sit-ins and radical movements had started, and all my interviews and material, gathered in 1966, had become very out of date.

One night in December 1968, while we were staying in a rented house in Praia da Luz in the Algarve, we were woken by a tremendous banging and shouting on the outside gate. We thought at first it was some fishermen on the way home, having drunk too much. Our house was right on the beach, formerly a sardine factory, with a large garden and high wall all the way round. I then realized my name was being shouted out, by someone with a strong Liverpool accent. 'Wake up Hunter Davies, you bugger.' I thought at first it might be John, as the voice was so raucous. I got up and went into the garden and opened up the big gates, and there was Paul, standing with a strange woman I had never seen before and a young girl, of about five or six.

That evening, back in London, Paul simply decided that he would come out and have a holiday with me. I had been in touch with all of them, and had sent Paul a postcard

On holiday in Portugal in 1968. From left to right: Hunter Davies, holding his son Jake, Linda, Paul, Linda's daughter Heather, Margaret Davies and daughter Caitlin.

inviting him to stay, so he knew where I was, though we were not on the telephone. When the idea had suddenly come into his head, Neil was detailed to get plane times. There were none that evening. Paul, of course, could not wait for the next day. Having thought of the plan, he wanted it *now*. Instant satisfaction. So a private plane was hired and told to be ready for Paul's pleasure. It landed at Faro in the middle of the night, much to everyone's surprise. Faro airport had opened only the previous year and was still pretty primitive, hardly used to scheduled flights, never mind private executive jets.

Paul's decision was so impulsive that he set off without any Portuguese currency, though he brought some bottles of whisky on the plane with him, as a present for me. In Faro airport, which was almost deserted, he eventually found some official and gave him £50 in English money, asking him to change it into escudos. Then he forgot all about it.

He suddenly noticed a taxi, which, luckily, happened to be there, jumped in and gave our address. On their arrival, I paid off the driver.

It turned out to be a very jolly arrival. Our two children, Caitlin and Jake, got up, hearing all the noise. Caitlin was charmed to see that a little girl of her own age, called Heather, had come to stay. My wife and I, though, were rather confused by this blonde American girl called Linda. We had never heard of her. When we left England, Jane Asher was the girl in Paul's life, and we got on with her very well. Was this Linda a one-night stand or was his relationship with Jane Asher finished?

It took us a while to find out the answers, as they slept in late next morning, despite the arrival at lunch time of the local press. I couldn't work out how they could possibly know Paul had arrived. We were in a very remote part of the Algarve and it was the dead of winter. I discovered later that rumours started when the official at the airport, to whom Paul had given £50 in notes, told everybody next morning about this strange English bloke with long hair who had arrived in the middle of the night and was giving money away.

The day after, the Lisbon press arrived – the big shots from the capital – and Paul agreed to hold a little press conference on the beach. Then he asked them not to reveal his address and to leave him alone, as he was on holiday, which they all did. For days afterwards, tradesmen and hoteliers from Lagos, the local town, kept on arriving with presents, baskets of fruit and food, invitations to parties and restaurants. I had never actually witnessed this effect on people before, though in John's house I had seen him ripping open parcels, looking for free things. It was strange to see it happening in a remote country, the most backward in Western Europe. Fame has its own reward. Those who have get showered with more.

Linda was, naturally, rather wary of us. I suppose she realized we had been friendly with Jane and would perhaps be critical of her. She also wanted to get Paul to herself, as it was the first stages in their romance, while Paul was keen on long, late-night talks and philosophical discussions. Paul always likes talking and explaining and giving his views.

At first, it seemed to us that Linda was very much a yes girl, who was overdoing her adoration of Paul, clinging on to him all the time, hanging on his every word. We couldn't see it lasting. We couldn't see what she was giving Paul. At times, during the ten days or so they stayed with us, there were some frosty moments.

We often went off on expeditions together, in one big party. Caitlin usually drove with Paul and Linda and Heather, in a car they hired. We learned later that Caitlin was being allowed to take the wheel, much to our horror, sitting on Paul's knee. That started the first of several little clashes over the upbringing of children. Another time, Jake started playing with a huge carving knife, so I grabbed it off him. Paul said that was not the way to train them. They should discover danger for themselves. It was how they learned. I said that as parents you had to look ahead, anticipate the results of actions that children could not see, otherwise they might end up with fingers missing. Heh ho. Such trivial little arguments, though, at the time, we discussed them for hours.

Paul was very good with the children, and with others who came to the house, and made a point of being friends, letting them do things and express themselves. I suppose our two did seem a bit house-trained and restrained. Heather had had rather a disturbed childhood so far, so we gathered, passed across the Atlantic between Linda and her father, and had been allowed to run fairly wild, at least that's how it seemed to our rather staid and conservative eyes.

One day we went up into the mountains at Monchique. We parked the car in the village and we were walking down a hill track when Paul spotted a man with a donkey coming up. He persuaded him to let Caitlin and Heather have little rides, lifting them up in turn on to the donkey's back. Caitlin had had a ride, and been lifted down by Paul, when the donkey suddenly stepped backwards – straight on to her foot. The screams were appalling. When we tore off her sock and shoe, we could see her foot was badly damaged and that the nail of her big toe was off.

We were miles from anywhere, on an empty hillside track. Paul decided at once to set off running, up the hill towards the village of Monchique. He eventually managed to flag down a car and came back for us. Paul and I then took Caitlin to the local little cottage hospital in Monchique, where they cleaned up the foot and gave her a tetanus injection, just in case. To cheer her up, for being a brave little girl, Paul bought a purple shawl in the village. When we all met up with Linda and my wife again, Heather burst into tears when she saw Caitlin had been given a present. So Paul bought her a shawl, just to keep things fair.

We did in the end get to know and understand Linda better, after some uneasy times. I suppose it was a difficult stage for her, not yet being sure of Paul, having somehow to compete. Being stuck with us, at that time, was probably the last thing she wanted.

I was, of course, completely wrong. Linda proved to be much more relaxed and friendly on our subsequent meetings, and her marriage to Paul has been a great success. They

Postcard from Paul, sent to me in Portugal. Paul arrived at our Algarve holiday home unannounced one December night in 1968, with his new girlfriend, Linda.

have the little rows we all have, on the usual trivial bringing-up-children and other family topics, but after 16 years, since they married in 1969, they appear pretty secure.

Linda has given Paul the moral support he always needed. John had, of course, been critical during his relationship with Paul, and often very cruel. Jane Asher had been very much her own woman, with her own career. Linda has been prepared to devote all her energies and emotions to Paul and their family and, if necessary, to his work, if that was what he felt he needed.

When I got back to England in 1969, I still kept in touch, going round to Paul's, to Abbey Road and the new Apple offices. I found that the empire, both the old one and the new one, was crumbling. During his stay in Portugal, I had lots of talks with Paul about the Beatles and learned about various disagreements they had during the making of the *Double White* album. Paul himself was still busy composing, so I presumed the albums at least would go on. I remember one tune he played to me in Portugal, which he had written on the lavatory (he rarely went there without his guitar) and was called 'There You Go Eddie'. Just a short verse, and I don't think he ever completed it. He discovered that my first Christian name is Edward, something I've always kept quiet.

In London, it was soon clear that the music making was now a secondary concern. Apple was in chaos, and so were their financial and business affairs, and they were quarrelling amongst themselves, about each other, and about what to do next.

I had never imagined that the end of the Beatles, whenever it happened, would simply come in a welter of legal tangles, financial quibbling, trivial personality clashes, slanging matches, ridiculous recriminations, juvenile insults and silly squabbles. In the end, alas, they finished the way many show business partnerships have ended – in pathos. Gilbert and Sullivan, Britain's other great song-writing partnership, finally descended to rows and sulks. How sad that Lennon and McCartney ended their joint days as just another pair of run-of-the-mill, archetypal, bickering ex-partners. Their rise has to be called phenomenal, as I hope the book showed, but the end was really rather sordid.

As sordid tales go, they don't even have the virtue of being worth retelling for the dirt. They became highly complicated and utterly confusing. Basically, they revolved round who owned whom and what, and for almost a decade they kept lawyers in high fees and newspaper libraries deep in reports of the latest court case. These legal rows were thought by many observers at the time to be the reason for the Beatles splitting. They were a result not a cause, though the personality clashes which ensued for a while were real enough. So what caused the split?

The Beatles themselves were not much help in giving exact reasons. At one time, they had contradictory theories – Paul was being blamed by the others for causing the split while he in turn blamed them. They even argued about who actually left the Beatles first. My theory, arrived at with the benefit of hindsight, was that the split had been happening for a long time. Rereading the book makes this abundantly clear, though I can't say I realized it at the time. If there was one simple reason why they split up when they did, it was not the argument over who should run their affairs, but the arrival into John's life of Yoko Ono. That's my explanation anyway.

The Beatles started to break up as Beatles as far back as 1966, when they gave up touring and stopped living communal lives. With living apart so much, the Lennon-McCartney numbers, however successful, became something of a fraud. They were no longer *joint* numbers in the way they'd been in the old days, knocked out together in the back of a van. It was very easy for the fans to recognize a Lennon song or a McCartney song, despite them getting equal credit. As the descriptions of *Sergeant Pepper* showed, they were, by now, each coming to the studio with almost every number worked out – at least in their heads.

Working in the new way was fine, as long as they were still mates and nobody was getting fed up or wanting to move off in a completely different direction, but petty rows did begin, based on boredom as much as anything else. In 1968 Ringo walked out on the Beatles double album. He said he was fed up being their drummer. Watching him so many times in the studio over the years, it was a pretty fed up-making process. On stage, he was equally involved and important and had his own little special bits to do and acquired his own faithful following amongst the fans. In the studio, he was often virtually ignored. John and Paul would break off sometimes for hours at a time, working on an arrangement or the words or the mixing. There was often no need for Ringo to be there at all – his contribution could be dubbed on at any time. However, he only walked out for a day and was persuaded to come back.

During *Let It Be*, it was George who left, after an argument with the others. He always had a part to play, though not as much as John and Paul, bringing in his own songs, which he did most painstakingly. During the Indian phase, he was also influencing the nature of the others' compositions. George had always been the least in love with being a Beatle and was the first to put equal energy into other interests, such as religion and Indian music. He in turn was persuaded to come back.

Paul was really the mainstay of the group in these later years, from about 1967 until 1969, keeping them going as composers, pushing them into new ideas, such as *Magical Mystery Tour*. He had many ideas for films and for expanding the Apple organization. He loved being a Beatle and didn't want it to change. While in Portugal in 1968, he was still full of plans to get them all performing in public again. He wasn't thinking of touring. That had gone stale for them all. He missed appearing in public – playing complete songs for a change, all together, in front of a live audience, trying to recapture some of the fun they had had in the early days. George was all against this. The others weren't very keen either. Paul, at the time, had high hopes of persuading them.

John, meanwhile, was letting Paul get on with directing most Beatle activities, unable to think of anything better to do. He was pretty bored being a Beatle, but he couldn't actually think of anything else he wanted to do with his life. It was obvious during the time I spent at his home (see Chapter 31), where he would sit for days dreaming, saying nothing, that he was utterly bored. His marriage had become a habit. Cynthia, as she was the first to admit, was never really on John's wavelength. She very honestly revealed in the book that but for her becoming pregnant, John would never have married her. (This remark was almost chucked out of Chapter 31, because of pressure from family and business friends.) She knew he'd always loved the Beatles more than her, but they'd been through so much together. John couldn't think of how else he'd like to live his life. Nothing better had turned up.

Then along came Yoko. At last he had found a kindred spirit, if of a very unusual kind. John was immediately sparked into life. He was away on a new plane, realizing at once that Paul, who until then had been his buddy, his soul mate, was in many ways as conventional as Cynthia. Together, John and Yoko discovered new and all-consuming aims. The rest of the Beatles didn't matter any more. When Paul came up with an idea for, say, a live TV show, John wasn't really interested.

Opposite: **Although the Beatles were starting to break up as a group in 1969, they presented a united front for this photograph. Not long after it was taken, they recorded their last album, *Let It Be*, which was released in May 1970.**

Yoko moved into John's life and into his work – sitting with him during the final Beatle sessions. The others weren't exactly thrilled at her influence over John or her continual presence in the studio. George and Ringo had become bored anyway, and this took the remaining fun out of it. John and Yoko's own fun was moving in new and different directions. Making music as Beatles finally finished in 1969. *Let It Be* came out in 1970, but it had been recorded almost a year before.

Around the same time as John was moving into a new, exciting life with Yoko, Paul met Linda. She came along at the right time for Paul, just as John was moving off, and encouraged Paul not to feel inferior, to be his own man, he could do anything if he tried. She took him over, without in any way becoming a rival. When the arguments started over Apple, both John and Paul were supported by their new mates.

The Beatles' financial and business affairs had been in some confusion since Brian Epstein's death – though it was his death that revealed the confusions rather than caused them. The creation of Apple had made things even more complicated. Someone was needed to straighten things out and organize their business lives. Allen Klein, an American accountant, was brought in by John and Yoko, with the backing of George and Ringo. Paul never liked him, and instead wanted his affairs to be handled by Lee Eastman, an eminent

Make love, not war: John and Yoko, recently married, receive the world's press in their hotel bedroom in Amsterdam, in March 1969. They stayed in bed for seven days as a protest against war and violence.

New York lawyer, who also happened to be Linda's dad. The others thought Paul was just trying to introduce his in-laws, which greatly upset Paul. He maintained they should have known him better than that. To break free from Apple, Paul realized he couldn't sue Klein. He had to sue John, George and Ringo.

Paul had discovered the fact that none of the Beatles had control of themselves. They were owned, including their own songs, by other people and other companies. Paul maintained he was doing it all for their sake – not just his own. To the other three, it looked as if Paul was causing all the trouble. At this stage, they still believed Klein to be their saviour. It was a very nasty few years.

The arrival of Klein was the event that finally and officially led to the split of the Beatles, but the differences between John and Paul, opened up by the arrival of Yoko, were already apparent.

It took up so much of their energy, both physical and creative, being caught in court cases for much of the next ten years. They also had their own individual court cases at different times – either divorces, drug offences, being sued or suing other record companies, immigration problems and such like.

The only fun, at least for the onlookers, was the madness of Apple. They seemed either unaware, or even to be enjoying the fact, that they were being ripped off. Millions of pounds were thrown away on daft schemes, shops, businesses, pandering to eccentric notions and strange people. It was almost a morality tale, as if to point up the pointlessness of big business: getting and spending we lay waste our powers, so let's go out with a mad spending spree. They took on some luxury offices in Savile Row in London, stocked them full of fine furnishings and equipment, and naturally half the Western hippy world flocked to try to take advantage of them, plus a few smart advisers who were supposed to be helping them sort everything out.

I used to pop into Savile Row, just to hear about the latest excesses, or for the pleasure of Derek Taylor's company. He had been with them since 1964, firstly as Brian's assistant, then as their press officer during the Beatlemania days. He had then gone off to America for a few years, but had now returned. One day, when I went in to have lunch with him, he declared it was his birthday. A very debutante-looking assistant was then summoned to bring in some birthday cake, still steaming from the oven, as they had their own kitchens, and I was offered a piece to celebrate. Derek insisted I had two slices and later, over lunch in a Mayfair restaurant, I practically passed out. It was a marijuana cake and they never told me, the rotten lot – one of Savile Row's specialities, baked on the premises. Although it did all end in tears, the late 1960s and early 1970s, there were a few moments to remember.

But most of that period, when the Beatles disintegrated, I now prefer to forget. It was exhaustively chronicled at the time, particularly the legal rows and arguments. Many of the nasty things they said about each other have now, fortunately, been forgotten.

It was a bad time for each of them, when in 1970, having lived such joint lives for so long, they set out to go forward alone.

John took all the headlines in the first few years. He did some songs with Yoko, forming the Plastic Ono Band, and had himself and Yoko photographed naked for 'Two Virgins' (1969), which amazed and amused the pop world. They had bed-ins in different hotels round the world, giving interviews about the world's ills and how they should be cured. He forsook the puns and the whimsy of some of his Beatle songs and earlier writings, and went headlong into the avant-garde. He took to defending causes of all sorts, such as the Hanratty murder case, and filled his new Yoko-songs with emotional outbursts, class struggles and political slogans. The layman was, in the main, amused by John's latest exploits, while there was a great deal of critical praise for several of the songs he was producing on his own, such as 'Imagine' (1971).

John married Yoko in 1969 and eventually moved permanently to New York, after a long legal fight to become a resident. I talked to him at the time and he denied that it was the arrival of Yoko that had broken up his marriage to Cynthia. 'That had already gone,' he said. It was interesting that when the Beatles split became inevitable, he announced to Paul, George and Ringo: 'I want a divorce – just like I had from Cynthia.' His relationship with them, particularly with Paul, had for so many years been similar to a marriage.

During 1974, John left Yoko for about a year – a year of drugs and drink and self-abuse, which has since been well chronicled – but from 1975, after the birth of their son Sean, he settled down to family life. He had produced ten albums in all, since ceasing to be a Beatle, but after *Shaved Fish* in 1975, he said he was going to take five years off work, and play with his baby.

He had just come back to record-making in late 1980, bringing out a new album, *Double Fantasy*, in time for Sean's fifth birthday, when he was murdered. It happened on 8 December 1980, on his return from the recording studios, outside the Dakota building in New York, where he lived.

The assassin, Mark David Chapman, had been waiting all day outside the building. On John's departure for the studios, Chapman thrust a copy of *Double Fantasy* into his hands and John had obligingly signed it, 'John Lennon, 1980'. On John's return, much later that night, Chapman fired five shots into him, from a distance of five feet. The world was stunned.

For a while, reaction did verge on the hysterical, especially in America, and especially when Yoko called for a round-the-world silent vigil. The worldwide grief was genuine. In Britain, some people were rather puzzled and surprised by the intensity of the mourning, unaware that since the end of the Beatles there had arisen two John Lennons, each with a different character and image.

In Britain, John Lennon was felt to have become a harmless eccentric, an oddball who had gone off with that funny woman and was doing funny things and producing occasional funny music. As a leader of pop music, or of fashion or anything else, his days appeared to be over, part of an era that had passed, a faded 1960s figure, though he was still well enough loved. Visiting British pop stars always tried to look him up in America, as if to pay homage to a Grand Old Man, now retired, perhaps now a bit soft in the head, yet someone who had influenced them all in their youth.

In America, as we all immediately became aware on his death, there had emerged a different John Lennon during the last decade, someone who had become an active spiritual leader, a symbol of a new generation's struggles and hopes, who could still communicate with millions of young people, even when, for those five years or so, he had hardly been seen or heard. 'Give Peace a Chance', which he had virtually written on the spot, after one of his bed-ins in Montreal in 1969, had become an inspiration for the Vietnam generation, a permanent anthem for the peace movement, still being sung today, long after his more contrived happenings and campaigns of the early 1970s have been forgotten.

The death of John highlighted his enormous contribution to popular music and to the youth of the West. It also brought to an end any suggestion that the Beatles would ever get together again. The Beatles had died emotionally by 1970. In 1980, there was the first burial.

One of the effects of John's death was that the three remaining ex-Beatles immediately became highly concerned about security matters. They had tried to live fairly private lives

Crowds of mourners for John outside the Dakota, New York, where he was shot and killed on 8 December, 1980.

after the split, and go their various ways. Since 1980, they have realized that even as private figures they must take great care.

Ringo today lives behind the well-guarded gates of Tittenhurst Park, a 17th-century stately home with some 74 acres, near Ascot in Berkshire. His personal life became rather complicated after the Beatles finished, and he has changed homes and countries several times.

Not long after the book came out, he and his wife Maureen moved away from Weybridge to Highgate, in North London, and while there I saw them quite often. But in 1975 they were divorced, by which time they had had a third child, a daughter called Lee. It was a rather messy, acrimonious divorce, and after it, Ringo started a wandering life, partly because of the break-up of his marriage. He was seen in various foreign countries, with various foreign girls. For several years he was technically based in Monte Carlo, though he seemed to spend much of his time in the States.

He returned to England in 1981, after six years abroad, stunned by the death of John, worried that it could happen to him.

'On the day John was killed, I flew from LA to New York to be with Yoko. I was given two bodyguards, and there were two of Yoko's supposed to be looking after me, but in that huge block we lost all the bodyguards. I ended up getting lost and walking out into the street by the wrong door on my own.

'Afterwards, I did have several threats on my own life, and I had to have guards living with me. I hated it. I always felt safe in America until John was shot. But you can't go on living in fear. If the President himself can't stay properly protected, what chances do other people have. They even got the Pope.'

One of the attractions of returning to England, and moving into his old home, Tittenhurst Park (the house where John and Yoko used to live before they went to the States), was that he was within 40 minutes of his ex-wife Maureen and his three children. They are now friends once again, although not particularly close.

Ringo returned to England with a new lady in his life, Barbara Bach, an American actress, who he married in London, at Marylebone register office, in April 1981. George and Paul came to the wedding, and so did his mother, Elsie.

Barbara Bach, who is seven years younger than Ringo, was previously married to an Italian and has two children, Gianni, aged 13, and Francesca, 16. She has appeared in *Playboy* magazine, and had a good part in a James Bond film, *The Spy Who Loved Me*. She has been in 30 films altogether, some with great titles – such as *The Humanoid, Free Range Male* and *Caveman* – though few of them won many awards. It was in *Caveman*, in 1980, that she met Ringo.

In 1984, they acted together in Paul's film *Give My Regards to Broad Street*, at least they appeared together in the film. Their parts did not call for any great exertions. It is noticeable how Ringo has remained good friends with Paul and George, better friends, in fact, than they are with each other, and when John was alive, Ringo was always close to him as well.

I went to see Ringo in March 1985, to have tea with him and his new wife at their London home, a small mews house in Chelsea, which also doubles as their office. He was looking very fit and well, rather spruce in a suit and clean-shaven. He had just that day taken off his beard for the first time in around ten years. He kept on feeling his smooth chin, as if to reassure himself that he still had a face.

He was wearing the usual handful of rings, as he always had in the '60s, plus a glittering blue earring in his left ear. It looked a bit incongruous. A gentleman of 45 in a suit wearing a punky style earring. He had also acquired a tattoo in recent years, a star and moon on his left arm, which he rolled up for me to inspect. His wife Barbara has an identical one on her thigh. 'On the fleshy bit,' said Ringo, but she refused to display it. The phone rang and she went to talk to Ringo's stepfather, Harry. Ringo's mother, Elsie, had had a heart attack just a couple of days previously. Ringo and Barbara had rushed up to Liverpool to see her in hospital and she now appeared to be recovering. Elsie is now 70, the same age as Harry, and they live in the same bungalow as they did in 1968, when I visited them.

Ringo bustled around their little kitchen, opening cupboards, looking for something to make for tea. I admired his fine head of lush, dark hair, but I wondered where the grey bits had gone, especially that grey patch at the front he has had all his life. Dyed it out, he said, just as for years he dyed out all the white bits in his beard. That's what had really made him shave it off. He could have lived with a pepper and salt beard, but huge white patches were appearing and he was fed up having to dye them. He pulled back his hair to prove it was all genuine, no bald patches, not even any receding bits at the edges. 'Not like some people I could mention,' he said. 'How old are you now, Hunt, hmm?'

He looked fitter and healthier than he did in 1968, despite a slight thickening of the waistline and the suspicion of a heavy jowl. Most of all, he was decidedly happier and chirpier. In 1968, when I used to go and visit him, he often seemed so edgy, prowling around, constantly on edge, as if bugged by something, or worried about the future, either his marriage or his future life with the Beatles.

Barbara finished talking on the telephone and came into the kitchen to see what he was making for tea. She felt his chin, another check on its smoothness. She had never in her life seen him clean-shaven, at least not close up.

'I did see Ringo first in 1966. I took my younger sister to the Beatles' Shea Stadium concert. I was about 19 at the time. My sister had a Beatles wig and was a real Beatles fan. I wasn't really interested. All I can remember about their performance was that it was rather short – and rather loud.'

When they first met in 1980, during the filming of *Caveman*, Ringo says he fell in love with her from the moment he saw her getting off the aeroplane.

'She gave me a hard time for two months, just picking on me. Oh, I don't know, little things. I threw a party for St Valentine's day and she kept on saying but what *is* the point of the party, what are you doing it for? She kept on cross-examining me. Either that or she ignored me.

'When we decided to get married, I said come on then, where do you want to live?'

'I wanted to go back to Europe,' said Barbara. 'But Ritchie can only speak English, so that meant England.'

'I wanted to go to England as well. It's the least police state I know. I feel secure here. I have no bodyguards at all. I feel so English. Not British. Just English. It's the fish and chips.'

Ringo eventually found a tin of salmon in one of the kitchen cupboards and was opening it, pouring on some vinegar to give extra taste, then he mixed it all up and dished out

Ringo with his new wife, the 36-year-old American actress Barbara Bach, after their marriage at Marylebone register office, London, April 1981.

three bowls. Not *smoked* salmon, I said? I thought you superstars lived on smoked salmon.

'I'll tell you something about that smoked salmon stuff,' he said, putting on a strong Liverpool voice. 'They don't cook it...

'I remember the very first time I had it. It was when Brian brought us to London and he insisted that we all tasted smoked salmon for the first time in our lives. We never had it in the Dingle. It was Brian's treat. We all went ugh, awful. I quite like it really.'

All the same, judging by Ringo's tea, and by meals I have had at other Beatle homes, none of them can exactly be described as foodies, though Ringo at home likes to think he at least does his bit, making the breakfast on Sunday morning for himself and Barbara.

I asked her about her *Playboy* appearance. Had it been, er, on the centrefold?

'It was on the *cover*, do you mind,' she said.

'She's still hoping to make the centrefold,' said Ringo. 'When she's 50. That will be in a year's time.'

'He lies all the time about my age.'

'Well you work it out, Hunt. She's 29, and she's got a kid of 31. You went to school.'

'It's a few years yet till I'm 50,' said Barbara.

'I can't wait. They're all the fashion, women of 50. When she gets to 50, she'll be the Joan Collins of Ascot... oh, no, stop it...'

Barbara had grabbed him and was hitting him with a tea towel. Oh, these marital scenes. So I made an excuse and left the kitchen and wandered round the office, admiring his decorations. On one wall was a huge photograph of John and Paul, a snap taken by Ringo and blown up. They each had lots of side whiskers and longish hair. In the foreground I could just see the top of Martha's back. It was taken in Cavendish Terrace, around 1968. Ringo was a budding photographer in those days and he took the four photographs that appear on pages 326, 336, 346 and 366–7. I remember he was pleased with the ones he took of John and Cyn, Paul and Jane, George and Pattie, but always hated the one of himself and his family. He made a mess of it, using an automatic button and having to rush back into his place after he had set the camera.

On a wall was a printed notice. 'The trouble with always keeping both feet firmly on the ground is that you can never take your pants off.'

Ringo is still keen on gadgets and jokey things. His main home is filled with all the latest TV and hi-fi equipment, and he still has five motor cars, including his special Pullman Mercedes, which has three rows of seats and is just two inches shorter than a London bus.

'In 1965, I sold all my five cars. It was ridiculous. You can only ride in one at a time. But then I started buying cars again. So I'm back to five. No, we've got six. I've forgotten Barb's Jaguar.'

He is the least affluent of the remaining Beatles, at least in terms of income, but he says he has no money problems. 'I'm mad on spending. I do it all the time. But it doesn't matter how much I spend, I won't run out of money in my lifetime.'

Nothing really new or creative has happened to Ringo since the split, not in an artistic or business sense. The single most amazing event in his life, which was being asked to join the Beatles, is not likely to be repeated. He has a market garden, employing ten people, adjoining his country estate. 'I walk round pointing at daffodils, saying that's daffodils, but I don't know anything.' He has also invested in a Liverpool cable TV firm and various other smallish enterprises.

As for his musical career, he produced some nice sing-along albums and singles after the Beatles split, avoiding the temptation to be too clever, but his recording career appears to have come to an end for the moment. His latest album, *Old Wave*, came out in 1984, but only in Canada. It was turned down in both Britain and the USA, the first musical failure for any of the Beatles.

'How do you think I felt? I was furious. I go round saying it's now very big in Afghanistan or wherever, oh yeh, Canada, I keep forgetting, but I was very disappointed. I liked the album. I thought it was the best I'd done. I called it *Old Wave* as a joke, as opposed to "New Wave". I suppose I am the old wave generation now. A bloke in LA did want to see me recently about releasing in the States, but he cancelled when his Mum fell ill.'

Unlike Paul, Ringo does not seem to need adulation as a musician, and he didn't seem too depressed that his singing and drumming career has come to a halt. 'I think Paul does love it still. I've heard the applause. It was very loud, but I've heard it, and I don't think I want it now. One day the clapping has to stop.'

He was now putting on his Lawrence Olivier voice. As an actor, he has done surprisingly well. At least, he is still constantly in business, being offered parts, 15 years after the Beatles finished, which has surprised many people. After all these years, he has proved he can do it, on his own, not just on his fame as an ex-Beatle. 'I like acting. It's because I'm a show-off.'

His part in *Caveman* was not very taxing, as all he did was grunt and groan, and the whole film contained only 15 words. But in other films, he did have quite good cameo roles, such as in *Candy* (1968), *Magic Christian* (1970), *That'll Be The Day* (1973), *Listo-mania* (1975), *Sextet* (1977) and *Princess Daisy* (1983). In 1984, he did the narrator's voice in a children's TV series, *Thomas the Tank Engine*. In 1985, he was getting ready to take the part of the Mock Turtle in a lavish six-part, American TV production of *Alice in Wonderland*.

'When we got married, we really semi-retired,' said Barbara. 'I had done three films the year I met him. I've done very little since.'

'Since we got married,' said Ringo, 'we have not spent one day apart in over four years. The most apart we've been is two hours.

'We had this terrible car crash in 1981. We were going *to* a party, that was the daft thing. Coming *from* a party, you can understand. I just lost control of the car going up the A3, I think it was. We were both very close to losing our lives. I woke up in hospital feeling awful. Barbara was in a rotten state as well. This nurse brought us round and was saying here you are, dear, a nice cup of tea. That's England for you. Tea cures everything. It only cost us £12.50 for that hospital. In the States, I'd still be paying.'

He also had a serious operation on his stomach, for the same complaint he suffered from for so many years as a child. This was when he lived in Monte Carlo and he collapsed with intestinal pains. 'They cut me to pieces and took away five feet of gut.'

Despite these frights, he still lives a rather hectic life, for a gentleman of his mature years, going out regularly to night clubs and parties.

'I *lived* in night clubs for 20 years. I still stay up all night, because I can't help it. It's nothing to do with those years on tour or playing in Hamburg. That's just the way I am. Even as a child I never closed my eyes till dawn. I still don't. I don't think in my whole life I've had more than four hours sleep in any one night. Barbara was horrified when we started going out. When it gets dark, she thinks it's time to go to bed, being a good little actress. When it gets dark, I think it's time to go out. I prefer going to bed at four. She prefers ten o'clock.

'So we don't go out *that* much now. I'm always getting at George because he's supposed to be the "recluse". When George is in England, he can be out at dinner four times a week, but nobody ever knows. He's probably just as sociable as me, but he does it all privately. I do it publicly. I love going to things like premieres. I like wearing a bow tie. I don't feel I'm dressed till I'm in a bow tie.'

'We've just been to Hawaii to see George's new place,' said Barbara. 'It's fantastic. He's got these thousands of acres of jungle which he's converting into a tropical garden. He took us round, saying there will be a bridge there, a little lake there. He's just like a kid.'

If George's new passion in life is gardening, what is Ringo's? Did he not miss having something like that to devote his energies to?

'What do you mean? That's my passion there. Barbara. I'm in love, man. And it's amazing. Better than a garden. You don't have to water her every day. I never thought it would happen to me again. It's the best thing in my life. I've never been happier.'

He didn't mind talking about the Beatle years, and says they were happy too, but he doesn't particularly want them back. 'I had a lot of good times. I wouldn't like to cancel them out. But I couldn't do it again. It was great doing all that at 20. I couldn't do it at 45. It was only eight years of my life anyway. That's all.'

His ambition in the old days was to end up with his name in school text books, and this has basically come true. 'The group just happens to be one which goes on from generation to generation. You can't stop it now. But I am a bit sickened by all the present-day Beatles commercialization. I feel sorry for kids being ripped off by the *new* souvenirs being manufactured. Then you get people stealing old Golden Discs and flogging them to some Japanese for £13,000.

'I got sent an autograph book the other day which had John's, Paul's and George's signature in. They wanted mine. So I put it in, then added "1985". I knew at once that would ruin the price. They couldn't pass it off as a genuine 1960's autograph.'

Ringo is the only one of the remaining three who has not done any sort of book, or allowed others to do one about his life, his times or his music.

George presented him recently with a special, leather-bound volume, which said on the cover, 'Ringo Starr: greatest drummer on earth'. Inside, all the pages were blank.

'George told me to start writing, to fill it up. I haven't even written January 1st. I'll never do a book about being a Beatle. I might write that we had three cups of tea on a certain day, then someone will say no, you had four cups of tea. I know what I know, so that's it. Why bother?'

Ringo missed his three children growing up, as he was wandering round the world for most of the '70s, but now he is closer to them. Zak, his oldest, now aged 19, and his other son Jason, now 17, were sent to well-known English public schools, to Haileybury and to Highgate. Lee, his daughter, now aged 14, is still at school, at Queen's College in Harley Street, London. 'Oh, I paid for the best, but it didn't do much good. The boys both wanted to leave at 16. What could I say? I wanted them to stay, but I left school at 13.'

The two sons are both drummers. He thinks Zak is very good and Jason could be good, but he's shy. 'I've been telling Jason he'll have to get over that, if he wants to appear on stage. The other day he came to me and said he had this idea. He would play the drums in one room, on his own, while they filmed him on video, then he could be shown with the group on stage. He had it all worked out.

'Zak is always finding new music that he thinks I've never heard of before. He'll come across a Blues tape and say Daddy, listen to this. Or a soul thing and say this is great,

Daddy. Of course he calls me Daddy. That's what I am. The other day he put on this really great thing he'd discovered – and it was Ray Charles. No, it doesn't make me feel old, though Zak does refer to me as the "Old Hippy". I'm just amused.'

Zak is currently (1985) playing with a group called Night Flight but not doing all that well. At first, when he started his drumming career, he appeared to hate being Ringo's son or at least being always linked with him.

'He would be mentioned in a newspaper as "Zak Starr, son of Ringo Starr" and he would get furious. I told him that I didn't ring up the papers, telling them to put my name in, but he seemed to think it *was* my fault. He just didn't understand how newspapers work. Then he came to me one day and said he thought the group was just using him, for his name. Son, I said, you've got a lot to learn.'

For a while, Zak lived with Ringo and Barbara at Tittenhurst Park, in the same house, but that led to scenes.

'Oh, the usual, parent-child rows. I'm sure you've been through them. I always loved him, I know that, but I didn't always like his attitude. It didn't get very friendly, living all together. In the end, I threw him out after a row. It was all stupid and trivial. We just began to feel that we were being ignored by this teenager. He would eat and sleep at home, but not talk to us at all. So I chucked him out. He left for about six months, then he came back. He now lives in a cottage on the estate and we're much closer.'

In February 1985, Zak rang Ringo at his office, at the mews house in London, asking him when he would be home from work.

'I said I wasn't sure, probably about 7.30. He said in that case pop in and see me, I've got a surprise for you. I thought it must be some recording deal. When I got home, it turned out that he'd got married that morning…'

Ringo laughed. Wasn't he at all worried, being the father of a 19-year-old, without a regular job or qualifications, who had just got married to a girl six years older than himself?

'Not at all. We've known the girl, Sarah [Menikides], for some time. We didn't *expect* them to get married, not just then, but I was quite glad he'd done it secretly, with no fuss. I couldn't be more pleased. She's very nice. They're like chalk and cheese, but so are me and Barbara, but it works. Barbara's not musical, doesn't like staying up late. Basically she's quiet, yet she's married a rock drummer. You know how noisy they can be. Sarah's done the same thing.'

Although it was a secret wedding, with no photographs in the newspapers, Ringo knows that the next stage will be very hard to keep quiet.

'I was telling them only last night about their "global" baby. When they get round to having one, it's bound to be global news. I think it will be great. Fabulous. I'm dying to be a grandfather. I'll spoil the shit out of my grandson. Of course it will be a boy. I've already told Zak that. And I want him to be called little Richard, after me. They're not very keen on Richard.

'When Zak was born, I really wanted to call him "XL". I thought names were boring for people. Letters would be much better, but Maureen refused. So we agreed on a short name that couldn't be abbreviated. It was the old cowboy in me, calling him Zak.

'Yes I know Jason is two syllables, but we usually call him Jay. He's an inch taller than me now, so he says, but I deny it. Zak is about my height. I deny that as well. I'm bigger than both of them and always will be.'

It will be interesting to see if any of Ringo's children make it as pop musicians. Paul has three children, yet to emerge into the public glare, and perhaps one of them will inherit his musical ability, just as he inherited some from his own father. In 1985, it was Julian Lennon, of the second generation Beatles, who was doing best in the pop world, with a successful album behind him and a song that got into the Top Twenty. His voice does have overtones of John and he can write pleasant tunes.

But as Ringo well knows, it will be the arrival of a third generation Beatle that will most amuse the world at large. It is hard to imagine, but it will happen soon that a still small voice will be able to say, 'My Grandad's a Beatle.'

George started off in great style after the Beatles split, obviously thankful to be on his own at last, in charge of his own destiny, able to concentrate on his new passion, which was Indian music and mysticism. *All Things Must Pass* in 1970 was highly acclaimed and so was his concert for Bangladesh in 1971. An enormous amount was raised for refugees, some ten million dollars, although not without several law cases. There were further legal problems when it was alleged he had 'subconsciously plagiarised' bits from someone else's song in 'My Sweet Lord'. This case dragged on for years, in Britain and in the US, and George was eventually fined a large amount. By which time, oh dreadful irony, he had to pay up money to a company run by Allen Klein, of all people, who had bought up the copyright of the original song, the one from which George is supposed to have taken bits.

George had vowed he would never tour again, but he did so in 1974, across the States, which was not a huge success. He was criticized for being too experimental, though people were mainly disappointed because he refused to play many Beatle numbers. It exhausted George, mentally and physically, and in 1974 he came close to having a mental breakdown.

He had started so well in 1969, moving off quickly and freeing himself from the worst of the Apple madnesses, but he was in a fairly depressed and unhappy state by the mid-'70s. His marriage to Pattie was collapsing, which he admits was becoming evident as early as 1972, when he wrote 'Sad Song'. 'It *is* so sad,' he said. 'It was at the time I was splitting up with Pattie.' They were divorced in 1977. They had had no children. Pattie later married George's friend, the guitarist Eric Clapton.

In 1978, George married Olivia Arrias, a Mexican-Californian, from a Roman Catholic family, who had originally come to work as a secretary in his record company, Dark Horse Records. They had lived together for about four years before they married. (All four Beatles ended up marrying foreign girls, all American-based, three of them divorcées. And three Beatles themselves got divorced and then remarried.)

Their first, and so far only child, was born on 1 August 1978, a boy named Dhani. He has brown eyes and dark hair, very like his mother. It was George's first child, born when he was 35, rather old to become a dad for the first time, but then George did always very sensibly take his time.

They live in an enormous Victorian Gothic mansion, Friar Park, at Henley-on-Thames, in Oxfordshire, which he and Pattie moved into in 1969, buying it at a time when it looked as if it might be demolished, since the nuns who were living there could no longer afford its upkeep. This house, in the last ten years, has become a major passion in his life. He has had his own record studio built on to it, plus a temple, but the main energies have been put into the 36-acre garden. He has a staff of ten gardeners, growing and caring for exotic flowers and plants. His two older brothers, Harry and Peter, work for him on the estate, supervising the garden and the house, one living in the gatehouse lodge and one nearby. (Louise, George's mother, died in 1972 and his father in 1978.) At the entrance to the house is a wooden signpost that says 'Private: Keep Out' in ten different languages. There's even an American English version which reads 'get your ass outa here'.

George's book *I Me Mine* (published in 1980 by Genesis Publications, and in 1982 by W. H. Allen) was dedicated to 'gardeners everywhere' and in it he says that he now looks upon himself as a gardener. 'I'm really quite simple. I don't want to be in the business full time, because I'm a gardener. I plant flowers and watch them grow. I don't go out to clubs and partying. I stay at home and watch the river flow.'

The latter is certainly true, as he lives a private life, but he is not a recluse, as some people have described him. A recluse, of the Howard Hughes variety, implies an eccentric, if not someone tinged with madness, which George is certainly not. He is sensible, well balanced, witty, aware of himself, aware of the world, honest and forthright, kind and generous and idealistic. He can also be grumpy, harsh and unfair and harbour resentment. In many ways, holed up in that Gothic folly, he leads a more 'ordinary' life than Paul, in that, unlike Paul, he no longer plays the public part of a rock and roll superstar.

He keeps out of the limelight because he knows, only too well, that the lime wants to alight on his old Beatle days, a subject he hates talking about. Even at the time, back in the late 1960s, writing my book, I found it hard to get George to talk about being a Beatle. It was a shame, as he has the best memory of the four and saw things very clearly.

With John, I often felt that his rubbishing of his Beatle days was partly for effect, to be contrary, to be provocative, and also to cover up his own guilt. Given the right interviewer, and the right atmosphere, John could always be talked into going over it all, once again. Paul will very easily talk about the past. But George was always matter of fact, quick and dismissive. Fifteen years later, he has many more engrossing topics to concern himself with. No outsider has trapped George, in the last 15 years, into talking properly about his Beatle days, either for or against them. It is only in passing, in brief conversations, or quick asides, that he will mention them.

'There were a lot of things we had to do collectively that didn't grab me personally that deeply,' so he wrote in his book. 'There was never anything, in any of the Beatle experiences, really, that good; even the best thrill soon got tiring. You don't really laugh twice at the same joke, do you, unless you really get silly.

'There was more good than evil in being a Beatle, but it was awful being on the front page of everyone's life, every day. What an intrusion into our lives. Dick Lester's version made it look fun and games, a good romp. That was fair in the films, but in the real world, there was never any doubt. The Beatles were doomed. Your own space, man, it's so important. That's why we were doomed, because we didn't have any. You know, everything needs to be left alone.'

Any success on the scale of the Beatles is of course doomed. How can it continue at that rate? Once you get to the peak, where can you go? And by definition, in Beatle terms, even standing still at the top is failure. George always knew their days were numbered and wanted to get out before anyone else realized it.

George's own life, after those mid-'70s problems, was helped by his house and garden, by his marriage and first child, and also by having a few laughs. This is one of the many paradoxes about George. He can appear to be preaching at you, bending your ear back with Indian philosophy, or gardening, or history, and just as you're beginning to think he's gone a bit loony, taking himself and life far too seriously, he then stops and laughs at himself.

He was always a fan of the Monty Python comedy team, as so many millions of people were in the 1970s, both here and in the States. He became friendly with them, especially with Eric Idle and Michael Palin. The Pythons come from rather different worlds than the Beatles, proper middle-class English boys, mostly educated at Oxbridge, far more serious and erudite in real life than their image might suggest, although they were working against the system, trying to do things their way, just as the Beatles did.

George loved *The Ruttles*, a television parody of the Beatles' story, which was done mainly by Eric Idle. He even appeared in the show, heavily disguised, as a reporter. In 1978, George heard that the Python team was having trouble with EMI over their proposed film, *Life of Brian*. Lord Delfont, then head of EMI, thought it was in very bad taste, making fun of the life of Jesus.

George asked his business partner, Denis O'Brien, who had been helping him with his affairs since the Apple fiasco, if perhaps they could manage to raise the two million pounds needed to get the film floated. They did, and the film was a huge success. The result was Handmade Films. George took the title from some handmade paper he had been given when he went to visit an old paper mill in Somerset.

Since 1978, Handmade Films had become one of the big successes of the British film industry. Not exactly a strong field, though David Puttnam during the same period has also done very well. They have now produced or backed ten major films, including *The Long Good Friday, Time Bandits, The Missionary, Privates on Parade, Water, Private Function*. They have one thing in common – all have British settings or British inspiration. It was partly by trying to ape America, and do mid-Atlantic films, that Lords Grade and Delfont eventually came to grief.

George takes an active part in the company, with his name often appearing as 'producer', and there are a lot more films in the pipeline, but he says that Denis O'Brien is the real businessman, the one with the financial flare, who makes sure the films get made on time and on budget.

'It's difficult being a film producer. I've been the one who's said of the people with the money, "What do they know?" and now I'm that person. But I know that unless you give an artist as much freedom as possible, there's no point in using that artist. On the whole, most of our relationships are still intact.'

I have talked to several of the people involved in making Handmade films and they all say George has been an ideal boss to work for, concerned, helpful, yet at the same time decently remote. Despite being 'friends' with the Pythons, he is not one of them, not their type, nor is he really in tune with the more artistic pretensions of some of the creators. He lets them get on with it.

One has to admire George for what he has done with Handmade Films, a creation of which he can be proud, and it must give him a lot of satisfaction. He has done it without using his 'Beatle' persona in any way. He has not insisted on star-studded premieres, lent his name to gala shows, turned up in person to promote his films, or gone on tour to publicize his own investments. He has been a background backer, a figure in the wings, content to let the product speak for itself.

I am not so sure that his book *I Me Mine* was such an admirable decision. He has gone to great lengths to distance himself from his Beatle days, yet the selling point of this book was presumably his boyhood and Beatle memories, and the presentation of the original manuscripts of his songs. It was all harmless enough, and fairly brief as far as the words went, revealing very little. It was the cost that was ridiculous. Each book, in the limited 1980 edition of 2,000 signed copies, cost £148. In it, he does confess to qualms about his reasons for doing such a book, but he never satisfactorily explains them, except that it was keeping alive the craft of hand-tooled, leather-bound, terribly expensive books.

In his spiritual searches, George, as I understand it, has been trying to rise above himself, to relate to greater gods and more constant truths, yet the contents of the book were an exercise in pure ego. The title makes that clear, though that could have been a double irony.

We should perhaps look upon it as yet further proof of the paradoxical George. While denying his fame, he provides for it. While casting off the Beatles, there are times when he appears to be calling for them again. 'The fab four were good because if one was in a bad mood, the others would cover. We protected each other. Now, you have to be more on your guard when you're alone. I miss them at times. We had great love for each other.'

George has discovered, as they all quickly did, that being famous attracts people who like you for being famous. It is very hard to find people you can trust. Nice people hold back. Pushers push forward. At least with three others, all in the same position, they had their brutal honesty to fall back on. In their present happy marriages, it is to be hoped that George, Paul and Ringo are getting the *real* truth, the ice-cold advice, the unpleasant criticisms, which John could give them, or they in turn could give John and each other.

I was also intrigued to learn, from George's book, that he had been back to Liverpool. It was when he first met his new wife, Olivia, to show her the house where he was born in Arnold Grove and then his old school, the Institute, to take her into his old classrooms. A normal enough thing to do. Yet this was the school George went through life hating. And in the book he still says he hated it. Has he protested too much?

George still hates flying, as he did in his Beatle years, when he could be almost physically sick in a plane or at an airport, and yet he has taken up fast driving in recent years, even in racing cars. He is still a vegetarian, still interested in India, in Hare Krishna and in things of the spirit.

As with the others, he has become obsessive about protection since John's death. Paul's fear is that there will be someone lurking in his bushes, who will spring out at him when he's jogging. He once imagined that someone was hiding in his garden, smoking a cigarette. It turned out to be a distant street lamp. George's fear is that the danger will come from a photographer, pointing a loaded camera at him, which is why he hates anyone suddenly snapping at him.

As for music, George at present appears to have come to a stop as a public composer or performer. In the last 15 years, he has produced regular albums, though his 1982 album, *Gone Troppo*, did not do very well. In 1984, he said he had retired from popular music. This does not mean he no longer makes music. He does, at home, but for his own amusement.

It is to be hoped this is only a temporary situation. George was different from John and Paul in music making, in that, while they wrote songs, he wrote feelings. 'Writing a song was like going to confession,' so he wrote in his book. It was when the spirit moved him, for good or ill, that George felt compelled to compose, which was why it took him so long to get going and why he always held back, till he had something to say. With Paul, making music is as natural as getting up and walking, eating and sleeping.

It is hard to tell which way George will go in future. Turning out to be a successful film producer has been a big surprise, at least to those who first met him as the baby of the group, shy and backward, compared with John and Paul. With George, there could be more surprises yet to come, new artistic or business endeavours. Or he might suddenly up

George with some of India's leading instrumentalists, including Ravi Shankar (third from right, on sitar), at a press reception at the Royal Festival Hall, September 1970. George became friends with Shankar in 1966.

and off to Hawaii, to the estate he has recently bought, to cultivate a tropical garden for a change, which would keep him well away from any dangerous photographers.

Unlike the other three, Paul started off his independent life very shakily indeed. His wife Linda wasn't exactly loved by all and Paul took the brunt of the legal troubles, being hated by the other three for starting it, and being disliked by the fans, who mistakenly thought he'd broken up the group. He too became a recluse, very fashionable for superstars in the early '70s. You had to get away and find yourself, just to prove you existed. There were rumours at one time that Paul was dead. He had in fact retreated to a small farm he'd bought, and still owns, in Argyllshire, Scotland.

'When the Beatles split up, I felt on the rocks. I was accused of walking out on them, but I never did. I think we were all pretty weird at the time of the court cases. I'd ring John and he'd say don't bother me. I rang George and he came out with effing and blinding, not at all Hare Krishna.'

He did odd songs for other people, and for films, then slowly he realized that he should do what he'd always enjoyed most in life – playing with a group on stage. This had always been his ambition for the Beatles, to get them out of the studio again, at least for occasional shows. So he decided to form his own group, Wings, along with Linda, his lady wife, who had no previous musical experience. The pop world had a jolly chuckle at this. They started off very quietly, arriving unannounced on university campuses, but it still didn't stop Linda being loudly derided by the experts for her lousy voice and daring to muscle into Paul's group. One of Wings' early singles was called 'Mary Had a Little Lamb', which wasn't very inspired. John was quoted as saying that Paul sounded like Engelbert Humperdinck, beyond which there is no nastier comparison. He went on to have a go at Paul in several of his own albums. In 'Imagine' he refers to Paul as 'Muzak to my ears' and talks about a 'pretty face may last a year or two'.

Very slowly, Wings got better. On their tours, Paul wasn't above throwing in the odd Beatles number, which everyone loved. Then, with 'Band on the Run' and 'Venus and Mars', he started producing world number ones again and almost, if not quite, repeating some of his Beatle success. His 1976 tour of the States was a sell-out and at last proved that Wings, Linda notwithstanding, was a very successful pop group.

Paul's songs haven't perhaps reached the heights of 'Yesterday' or 'Eleanor Rigby' but, commercially, Paul is far and away the most successful of the Beatles. 'Mull of Kintyre' in 1977 beat any Beatle single. Paul says he made more money with Wings than he did in the whole of his Beatle career. This isn't too hard to believe, as so many people had shares in their lives as Beatles.

Wings has now come to an end. And several people who worked with him in that strange, ad hoc group have since made capital out of saying how awful he was to work with, how bossy, how nasty he could be. Probably some truth in it. Paul is a perfectionist and can drive assistants mad with his demands. And working with Paul, or so it seems since the Beatles finished, you have to be an 'assistant', not a co-leader. Paul in turn now says he is fed up with running a band. 'I hate groups – it's like being stuck with bad relations.'

Paul today is still the public Beatle, giving interviews at fairly regular intervals, being open and honest about himself and his past, his worries and his pleasures. Naturally, as ever, there are people who suspect his motives, putting him down for being too charming. Paul may be a bit of an actor, acting the part of Paul McCartney, the charming superstar, still loved by every mum, which can make him sound rather prissy at times, but I believe he does tell the truth about himself.

He gave countless interviews during 1984 to promote his film *Give My Regards to Broad Street*, a film which was criticized, if not abused, by many reviewers. I always thought the criticism of *Magical Mystery Tour* was unfair – and it was Paul who was mostly blamed for that, being the main instigator. But it did have some good songs and was a modest, made-for-TV production. We all expected so much more from *Broad Street*, a full-length feature film with a good cast, but Paul's script was so tame it gave little scope. Perhaps, now he has created his own film, he will stick to composing and singing, and even acting, well now and again, and find experts to help on things like screenplays. I'm surprised he hasn't tried an original stage musical. Think what a director like Trevor Nunn could do with Paul's tunes.

Paul continues as a composer and singer on his own, even though Wings have flown, and will have many more Top Twenty hits. It would be impossible to imagine him doing anything else. He is also still very much a businessman, running his own company, McCartney Promotions Limited, which has offices in Soho Square, London. It handles all his own creations, plus other things they have bought, such as *Annie* and *Grease*, and scores of individual songs. He has at least put his money into music, rather than boring assets like property companies.

He has told the world often enough that what he cares for most is his family life. Heather, their oldest daughter (by Linda's first marriage), is now 22 and working as a photographer's assistant. Then there is Mary, 17, an attractive brunette, Stella who is 15 and red-headed, and James who is seven and fair-haired. All have gone to state schools, which is surprising, considering the many pressures. They live and play and stay together as one family, without nannies and without servants.

From the outside, their new home in Sussex can seem rather daunting, with searchlights and security fences, but all this is understandable, after what happened to John. The locals know it as Paulditz. But inside, it is surprisingly small, with only five bedrooms, and they live a modest, relaxed life with the usual family clutter. Linda was never the most house-proud of mothers, though she is a keen cook.

They moved there from an even smaller house nearby, knocking two old cottages together to get more security. They still have their London home in St John's Wood, dear to all those Apple scruffs and '60s Abbey Road groupies, and also their farm in Argyll in Scotland. Paul is a vegetarian, a non cigarette smoker, and does a bit of jogging, a bit of pottery, loves drawing and painting, watches a lot of TV. The influence of his heavy TV viewing was noticeable in *Broad Street* – all that glossy commercial stuff and the Children's Hour Dickensian period flavour.

As with George, there are endless contradictions. For a clever and supposedly devious person, he has been very silly to get caught four times in the last ten years or so for soft drug offences. Walking into a Japanese airport carrying £1,000 of marijuana was utterly daft. For a supposedly concerned father, getting caught taking drugs at all, even soft ones, is hard to reconcile.

He has let his hair start to go grey, yet watch him when a photographer arrives, and he pulls in his stomach. His self-consciousness extends to his physical body as well. He often moans at what people write about him, yet he gives interviews. He should know the consequences, after all these years. He is upset by the mad rush to buy and sell Beatle memorabilia, yet he himself has bid at Sotheby's. (He wanted a postcard that he had sent to John, but someone else outbid him.) Both he and George have, in fact, contributed to the present craze for Beatle artefacts, by putting out *more* material, such as Paul's book of drawings and George's book containing the originals of his songs.

Oh, what a complicated man he is, what convolutions, what self-justifications, what fears, how vulnerable he is. How could we, in the 1960s, have taken Paul for a simple, lovable soul, or accepted George as a quiet little boy? In the end, I think both of them are much harder to explain and understand than John. He was so much up front, to the point of brutality, quick to reveal himself and his opinions. Paul and George have so many layers. They both get upset when outsiders think they know them, when they are described in black and white terms, which of course is never completely true of any of us.

Not long after John's death, I had some strange conversations with Paul. He seemed so upset by so many things, not least of all John's death. This was in May 1981, and I jotted down in a diary some of the things he told me.

John's death had grown into a sort of cult, with instant books already appearing, and the papers were still full of it. Many people, in praising John, were at the same time putting down Paul, or so it appeared. He felt he had already been criticized in a book just out written by Philip Norman, a fine writer and formerly a colleague of mine on the *Sunday Times*. I had helped him, and let him see all my files, when he had come to talk to me, saying he was writing a book about the 1960s as a whole. None of the Beatles had in fact given him any interviews for his book, which was subtitled 'The True Story of the Beatles'.

Paul rang me on 3 May 1981, and went on for over an hour, all about how hurt he was. He had already been moaning at length to my wife, as I was out walking on Hampstead Heath when he first rang. He said he was fed up with all these people going on about him and John and getting it all wrong. Only he knew the truth. It wasn't anything like the things being said.

Paul criticized me, for having gone on some TV news programme after John's death. In my tribute to him, I said that John was more the hard man, with the cutting edge, while Paul was softer and more melodic.

But what had really got him upset that day was an interview with Yoko, in which Yoko was quoted as saying that Paul had hurt John more than any other person. Paul thought they were some of the cruellest words he had ever read.

'No one ever goes on about the times John hurt *me*,' said Paul. 'When he called my music Muzak. People keep on saying I hurt him, but where's the examples, when did I do it? No one ever says. It's just always the same, blaming me. Could I have hurt John *more* than anyone in the world? More than the person who ran down Julia in his car?'

'We were always in competition. I wrote "Penny Lane", so he wrote "Strawberry Fields". That was how it was. But that was in compositions. I can't understand why Yoko is saying this. The last time I spoke to her she was great. She told me she and John had just been playing one of my albums and had cried.'

So why don't you ring her up, I suggested, and find out if she really made that remark?

'I'm not ringing her up on that. It's too trivial. It's not the time. I wouldn't just ring up on that.'

What did you think then might have hurt John?

'There's only one incident I can think of that John has mentioned publicly. It was when I went off with Ringo and did "Why Don't We Do It In The Road". It wasn't a deliberate thing. John and George were tied up finishing something and me and Ringo were free, just hanging around, so I said to Ringo let's go and do this.

'I did hear him some time later singing it. He liked the song and I suppose he'd wanted to do it with me. It was a very John sort of song anyway. That's why he liked it, I suppose. It was very John, the idea of it, not me. I wrote it as a ricochet off John.

'Perhaps I have hurt people by default. I never realized at the time John would mind. At Ringo's wedding [the previous week] Neil happened to say to me that Mimi was upset I'd never contacted her after John's death. I'd never even thought of it. I don't know Mimi. I probably haven't seen her for about 20 years, since Menlove Avenue. I was just the little kid that hung around with John. We didn't get into her house.

'Anyway, I rang her up, in case she really was upset, and apologized for not ringing, saying I hadn't got her phone number, and she was terrific and we had a good chat. We discussed Philip Norman's book and she didn't like it either. She said I should write and complain. I told her I'd been writing letters constantly, but I'd torn them all up. She said I should do something about it, to stop this sort of thing.

'"In an earthquake you get many different versions of what happened by all the people that saw it. And they're all true." That's what I wrote in one letter. But how can you get the full story from someone who *wasn't* there? But I tore that up as well.

'Nobody knows how much I *helped* John. Me and Linda went to California and talked him out of his so-called lost weekend, when he was full of drugs. We told him to go back to Yoko and not long after he did. I went all the way to LA to see the bastard. He never gave me an inch, but he took so many yards and feet.

'He always suspected me. He accused me of scheming to buy over Northern Songs without telling him. I was thinking of something to invest in, and Peter Brown said what about Northern Songs, invest in yourself, so I bought a few shares, about 1,000 I think. John went mad, suspecting some plot. Then he bought some. He was always thinking I was cunning and devious. That's my reputation, someone's who's charming, but a clever lad.

'It happened the other day at Ringo's wedding. I was saying to Cilla [Black] that I liked Bobby [her husband]. That's all I said. Bobby's a nice bloke. Ah, but what do you *really* think, Paul? You don't mean that, do you, you're getting at something? I was being absolutely straight. But she couldn't believe it. No one ever does. They think I'm calculating all the time.

'I do stand back at times, unlike John. I look ahead. I'm careful. John would go for the free guitar and just accept it straight away, in a mad rush. I would stand back and think, but what's this bloke really after, what will it mean? I was always the one that told Klein to put money away for tax.

'I don't *like* being the careful one. I'd rather be immediate like John. He was all action. John was always the loudest in any crowd. He had the loudest voice. He was the cock who crowed the loudest. Me and George used to call him the cockerel in the studio. I was never out to screw him, never. He could be a manoeuvring swine, which no one ever realized. Now, since his death, he's become Martin Luther Lennon. But that really wasn't him either. He wasn't some sort of holy saint. He was still really a debunker.

'For ten years together he took my songs apart. He was paranoiac about my songs. We had great screaming sessions about them.

'In the beginning he was a sort of fairground hero. He was the big lad riding the dodgems and we thought he was great. We were younger, me and George, and that mattered. It was teenage hero worship. I've often said how my first impression of him was his boozy breath all over me – but that was just a cute story. That was me being cute. It was true, but only an eighth of the truth. I just used to say that later when people asked me for my first memory of John. My first reaction was very simple – that he was great, that he was a great bloke, and a great singer. My *really* first impression was that it was amazing how he was making up the words.

'He was singing "Come Go With Me to the Penitentiary" and he didn't know *one* of the words. He was making up every one as he went along. I thought it was great.

'He became so jealous in the end. You know he wouldn't let me even touch his baby. He got really crazy with jealousy at times. I suppose I've inherited some of that…

'It's true I didn't care for Stu, but I wasn't against him personally. He just couldn't play bass. That was all there was to it. I had a functional, ambitious-for-the-group sort of objection to him. He knew he couldn't play. I was the one who told him to keep his back to the audience, as that photograph (see pages 50–1) shows. I didn't want him out to get the bass job. Stu himself left us, to stay on in Hamburg. John asked George first to play bass. I've checked that with George the other day. He remembers it well. George refused. So he asked me. I got lumbered with playing bass. It wasn't my scheme.

'It was the same with Pete Best. I wasn't jealous of him, because he was handsome. He just couldn't play. Ringo was so much better. We wanted him out for that reason.

'The idea of Brian's murder is crazy, but all that merchandising trouble is true. We got screwed for millions, but in the end it wasn't worth suing everybody. We'd never get it all back and it would take such time. We knew most of them would still in the end get away with it. It was all Brian's fault. He was green. I always said that about Brian. Green.

'We knew he was gay, but it didn't matter. For a while he didn't know that we knew, and we pretended it that way. It didn't matter. We never discussed it with him. He kept it very private. It didn't matter. We might make faces at each other behind his back, you know if someone was dressed up in drag. We'd try to catch Brian's eye, to see if he was blushing. But we didn't say anything. It was all affectionate. As for that drawing with Brian in the middle of a row of kids in the Cavern, *salivating*. That is not true. I've heard of artistic licence, but that's ridiculous. The other drawings were meant to be true, as they started with one based on a photograph, so you took this as being true. It's just part of trying to build up Brian's gay thing. He *never* sat in the Cavern. He never mixed anyway. He just stood at the very back, so no one could see him or knew he was there. There was no salivating.

'I idolized John. He was the big guy in the chip shop. I was the little guy. As I matured and grew up, I started sharing in things with him. I got up to his level. I wrote songs as he did and sometimes they were as good as his. We grew to be equals. It made him insecure. He always was, really. He was insecure with women. You know, he told me when he first met Yoko not to make a play for her.

'I saw somewhere that he says he helped on "Eleanor Rigby". Yeh. About half a line. He also forgot completely that I wrote the tune for "In My Life". That was my tune. But perhaps he just made a mistake on that. Forgot.

'I understood what happened when he met Yoko. He had to clear the decks of his old emotions. He went through all his old affairs, confessed them all. Me and Linda did that when we first met. You prove how much you love someone by confessing all the old stuff. John's method was to slag me off.

'I've never come at him, not at all, but I can't hide my anger about all the things he said at the time, about the Muzak, about me singing like Englebert Humperdinck...

'If we had to start listing all the times when *he* hurt me. Doing that one little song on my own, compared with what he said about *me*...

'When you think about it, I've done nothing really to him, compared with that. Anyway, he did the same with "Revolution 9". He went off and made that without me. No one ever says all that. John is now the nice guy and I'm the bastard. It gets repeated all the time.'

But until John's death, I said, the general image was that you were the nice guy and that John was the bastard. Neither of course was true, not completely. Things will soon shake down. Don't worry. Keep cool.

'But people are printing *facts* about me and John. They're *not* facts. But it will go down in the records. It will become part of history. It will be there for always. People will believe it all.

'Anyway, me, George and Ringo have promised to be nice guys to each other from now on. When we meet and talk now I never mention Apple. I've learned that. Any mention of Apple just leads to rows and slagging off...

'I apparently hurt George Martin by default as well. I didn't know that till I read his book. I didn't let him do "She's Leaving Home". I rang him up, but he was busy, couldn't make it for two days, or two weeks or something, so I thought what the hell, if he can't fit me in, I'll get someone else. *I* was hurt at the time, which was why I got someone else. Now he says I deliberately hurt him. Well, if that's the only hurt I've done him...

'John and I were really Army buddies. That's what it was like really. I realize now we never got to the bottom of each other's souls. We didn't know the truth. Some fathers turn out to hate their sons. You never know.

'At Ringo's wedding, I happened to go to the toilet, and I met Ringo there, at the same time, just the two of us. He said there were two times in his life in which I had done him in. Then he said that he'd done himself in *three* times. I happened to be spitting something out, and by chance the spit fell on his jacket. I said there you go, now I've done you three times. We're equal. I laughed it off. It was all affectionate. It wasn't a row. It wasn't slagging off. He just suddenly said it, and we moved on. But *now*, I keep thinking all the time, what are the two times that Ringo thinks I put him down...?

'I suppose we all do that. We never publicly come out with little hurts. George told me the other day of a time I'd hurt him. He's done worse, I think, like when he said he would never play bass with me again.

'I was very upset when they said I was just trying to bring in Lee Eastman, because he's my in-law. In the end, they brought in Klein. As if I'd just bring in a member of the family, for no other reason. They'd known me 20 years, yet they thought that. I couldn't believe it. John said, "*Magical Mystery Tour* was just a big ego trip for Paul." God! It was for their sake, to keep us together, keep us going, give us something new to do.

'Legally, we were mugs. I still have Lee Eastman, and he's made a fortune. For me. I was forced to sue the Beatles, in order to prove what I knew. I didn't want to. I went up to Scotland and agonized for three months, cut myself off, before I decided it was the only way. To sue the Beatles. It was a terrible decision.

'I still get slagged off for it. In the history books, I'm still the one who broke up the Beatles.

'I didn't hate John. People said to me when he came out with those things on his record about me, you must hate him, but I didn't. I don't. We were once having a right slagging session and I remember how he took off his granny glasses. I can still see him. He put them down and said, "It's only me, Paul". Then he put them back on again, and we continued slagging… That phrase keeps coming back to me all the time. "It's only me." It's become a mantra in my mind.

'I have some juicy stuff I could tell about John. But I wouldn't. Not when Yoko's alive, or Cynthia. John would. He would grab, go for the action, say the first thing in his head. We admired him for that. It was honesty, but it could hurt. And it wasn't really all *that* honest. He *knew* he could hurt. He could be wicked. But I'm always sensible. That's me. I would never say the things he said.

'No one else knows the truth, such as it is, that's the trouble. I was talking to Neil the other day, having a laugh and remembering some incident, a funny story. We remembered everything exactly, what we said, what I was wearing, that someone had a fan. We were absolutely exact on 75 per cent of the story, except on one vital thing. I said it took place in Piccadilly and Neil said it was Savile Row. I can see it so clearly, every detail as it happened – and so can Neil, yet it's in different places.

'Until I was about 30, I thought the world was an exact place. Now I know that life just splutters along. John knew that. He was the great debunker. He'd be debunking all his death thing now.

'I can't really remember the 1960s anyway. I went through it in a sort of purple haze. The other day we were at a place, me and Linda, and this gorgeous blonde came up to me and flung her arms round my neck. 'Remember me, Paul?' I said hmm, yeh, now, let me see, but I had no knowledge of ever seeing her before. 'But Paul, we made love in LA…" "Oh," I said. "Really. Meet the wife. This is Linda… 'Scuse us, we'll have to go…"

'It's happened before of course. It was before I was married. It can be dodgy, but Linda's a good skin.'

I suggested that he should write it all down, or tape it, record in his words what he thinks was the relationship with John, exorcise it once and for all, then stick it in a drawer and forget it.

'I might. I did that after being in jail. I've written my feelings about that. I wasn't allowed pencil and paper in jail, and it was all I wanted, so when I came home I wrote it straight out. I don't know what to do with it. I don't want that usual publishing scene. It's just for me. It's about 20,000 words. Linda and one or two other people have read it and think it's good. I got a private printer, just to print for me one copy, one only. I've got it. I just wanted a plain white cover and, inside, just black words on white paper. On cheap white paper. I wanted it like an Olympia press book. Just a cheap little thing. It fits in the pocket, just six inches by about four. I did for a time think of publishing a few and selling them off the back of a barrow. Telling no one, just suddenly selling them in the street, for a few bob. But I don't want a big thing. Then I heard that some pop musician had already done this, so I didn't want it to look like copying. So I just have the one copy. I'll let you read it sometime. Tell me what you think.

'As for me and John, yeh, I might write it down. You know I helped him with his first book. That's never been mentioned by anyone. Not by John anyway…'

As for the other characters in the Beatle drama, Neil Aspinall, their roadie, went on to be an executive in Apple and produced the *Let It Be* film. He's still there, though Apple these days seems to have less to do and produce. He is married with five children. Mal Evans, on the other hand, who always seemed so relaxed and contented, compared with the rather nervy Neil, ended his life in tragedy. He'd left his wife and family and had moved to America when he was shot in an incident with the police in Los Angeles in 1976. Paul's father Jim had also died, so has John's father Fred, and George's mum, Louise. Ivan Vaughan, the boy who first brought John and Paul together (see Chapter 2), is now a semi-invalid, suffering from Parkinson's disease.

George Martin went on to become a successful independent music producer, which he still is, though without discovering anyone on the scale of the Beatles. His remark in the original End Bit, warning that they could go wrong on their own, was, in some ways, prophetic.

Cynthia Lennon married an Italian after her divorce from John. That marriage ended in divorce. And so did a third marriage. She now has a new man in her life and is living very quietly in Cumbria, near Penrith, taking up her interest in art again, which she neglected since her art college days with John. At the age of 45, with her son Julian beginning to be established in the pop music world, she is considering various new careers, such as fashion and television interviewing.

Pete Best dragged himself out of that depressive state he was in when I last met him, in 1968 at his mother's home. He got himself a respectable job, working at a Jobcentre in Liverpool, and after 16 years of it, he is earning £8,500 a year. His book about his days with the Beatles eventually came out in 1985. It even managed a favourable report in *The Times*.

After doing very little for a decade to commemorate or recognize their most famous sons, Liverpool has jumped into neo-Beatle life, with statues, exhibitions, tours and other excitements to interest the tourists (see Appendix).

One legal and business row still lumbers on – the battle by Paul, mainly, to get control of Northern Songs. It does seem unfair that the Beatles, in essence, still do not own themselves. When Paul was making *Broad Street*, he even had to ask permission to record 'Yesterday'. It's a very long story (see Chapter 20 for its origins), which started with Dick James and his firm owning 50 per cent of all Beatle numbers, as their music publisher. It then passed to Lew Grade's ATV empire, then to the Australian, Holmes a'Court. Paul at one time tried to buy it back for £10 million, but failed, and at the time of writing he is reported to be offering £20 million. Northern Songs owns the copyright of over 200 Lennon-McCartney compositions, virtually the complete Beatle canon. You can see the attraction.

If you are ever tempted to feel envious of millionaires, then realize how they too can be thwarted and put down, just like the rest of us. Even all their millions cannot always give them what they want. It has at least united Paul and Yoko, after several years of a somewhat strained relationship. Yoko is just as smart in business as Paul, if not smarter. Together, I am sure they will get what they want in the end.

What about the creative future of Paul, George and Ringo? There seems little evidence of them keeping up with new developments in literature, art, theatre or even popular music. But then again, there never was. They prided themselves on being uneducated, untouched, uninfluenced. They provided their own stimuli, the four of them sparking each other, getting out of themselves what was there. If they want to remain independent creative artists, working on their own, where will the stimuli come from? Who will provide the sparks?

They are now of course middle-aged men, so why should we expect it. Ringo is 45 this year, Paul is 43 and George, the baby, is 42. They have their children or their gardens to contemplate, time to put their feet up and relax, though in Paul's case he is not built for relaxation. Linda knows this well. She is the one pulling inwardly more, into the bosum of the family, but there is a part of Paul that would still like to be up there, still one of the superstars, singing along with Stevie Wonder, or Michael Jackson, or whoever the next flavour of the year will be, just to show he can still do it. The glitter still attracts him, despite his genuine love of family life.

Looking back over the last 15 years, I am surprised that no one has taken their place. Some people will argue with this. Seven years ago, it was said the Osmonds were making more money. Now it is said to be Michael Jackson. Probably, dollar for dollar, it is true. In five years' time, some other singing sensation will astound the world, sell more records, and will be said to be bigger than the Beatles.

There will also be composers who will come along and write individual tunes that will earn more money. Andrew Lloyd Webber is probably already on the way to doing this. There will be pop stars to come who will capture the imagination of the times, who will have wide social effects, create new fashions, new attitudes. As I write, Boy George is on the radio in my younger daughter's room. He has certainly made an impression, right across the so-called civilized world. Will we still be impressed by him in 15 years' or even five years' time?

As an entity, as a group who could compose and perform and influence their generation, it is hard to think of any rival in the last 15 years. With the Beatles, we got those three elements in one. They will be a hard act to beat.

But this is not meant to be a winning game, trying to prove they are better or more successful than anyone else. They were. They did. They have been. So let us celebrate. Let us forget those draggy Apple days, those pathetic squabbles and rows, and most of all, let us try to rise above the awful tragedy of John's death. He, and the Beatles, left us more than enough to rejoice over.

This book was meant, is meant, to capture them at their height, to explain how they got there, in their own words and in the words of those who were with them at the time. What they did together was unique. By some mysterious alchemy, their different talents and personalities intermingled, overlapped, overran, so that the result was a mixture that was so much finer and stronger and more original than the sum of their parts. What they produced as Beatles, during that relatively short span together, is what I am still happy to remember them by and for which I give thanks. The Beatles are now long dead. Long may they live.

HUNTER DAVIES
London, 1985

APPENDIX A

Discography of Beatles' original records

all compositions by Lennon and McCartney unless otherwise stated

Germany 1961

As the backing group for singer Tony Sheridan they recorded eight numbers. Only one was an original composition, an instrumental number called 'Cry For A Shadow', written by Lennon and Harrison. On one other, 'Ain't She Sweet', John Lennon was the lead singer. On the other six they were simply the backing group: 'My Bonnie', 'The Saints', 'Sweet Georgia Brown', 'Take Out Some Insurance On Me, Baby', 'Why', 'Nobody's Child'.

Single playing records by The Beatles issued by Parlophone Records in England

Year	Month	Title
1962	*Oct*	Love Me Do/PS I Love You
1963	*Jan*	Please Please Me/Ask Me Why
	Apr	From Me To You/Thank You Girl
	Aug	She Loves You/I'll Get You
	Nov	I Want To Hold Your Hand/This Boy
1964	*Mar*	Can't Buy Me Love/You Can't Do That
	Jul	A Hard Day's Night/Things We Said Today
	Nov	I Feel Fine/She's A Woman
1965	*Apr*	Ticket To Ride/Yes It Is
	Jul	Help!/I'm Down
	Dec	Day Tripper/We Can Work It Out
1966	*Jun*	Paperback Writer/Rain
	Aug	Yellow Submarine/Eleanor Rigby
1967	*Jan*	Penny Lane/Strawberry Fields Forever
	Jul	All You Need Is Love/Baby, You're a Rich Man
	Nov	Hello, Goodbye/I Am The Walrus
1968	*Mar*	Lady Madonna/The Inner Light (Harrison)

Single playing records issued by Apple Records

Year	Month	Title
1968	*Aug*	Hey Jude/Revolution
1969	*Apr*	Get Back/Don't Let Me Down
	May	The Ballad of John and Yoko/Old Brown Shoe (Harrison)
	Oct	Something (Harrison)/Come Together
1970	*Mar*	Let It Be/You Know My Name

Long playing records issued by Parlophone, England

Year	Month	Title and track listing	
1963	*May*	***PLEASE PLEASE ME***	
		I Saw Her Standing There	*Songs not composed by the Beatles:*
		Misery	Anna
		Ask Me Why	Chains
		Please Please Me	Boys
		Love Me Do	Baby It's You
		PS I Love You	A Taste of Honey
		Do You Want To Know A Secret	Twist and Shout
		There's A Place	
	Dec	***WITH THE BEATLES***	
		It Won't Be Long	*Songs not composed by the Beatles:*
		All I've Got To Do	Till There Was You
		All My Loving	Please Mister Postman
		Don't Bother Me (Harrison)	Roll Over Beethoven
		Little Child	You Really Got A Hold On Me
		Hold Me Tight	Devil In Her Heart
		I Wanna Be Your Man	Money
		Not A Second Time	

Long playing records issued by Parlophone, England, continued

Year	Month	Title and track listing	
1964	*Jul*	***A HARD DAY'S NIGHT***	
		A Hard Day's Night	Can't Buy Me Love
		I Should Have Known Better	Any Time At All
		If I Fell	I'll Cry Instead
		I'm Happy Just To Dance With You	Things We Said
			When I Get Home
		And I Love Her	You Can't Do That
		Tell Me Why	I'll Be Back
	Dec	***BEATLES FOR SALE***	
		No Reply	*Songs not composed by the Beatles:*
		I'm A Loser	Rock And Roll Music
		Baby's In Black	Honey Don't
		I'll Follow The Sun	Mr Moonlight
		Eight Days A Week	Kansas City
		Every Little Thing	Words Of Love
		I Don't Want To Spoil The Party	Everybody's Trying To Be My Baby
		What You're Doing	
1965	*Aug*	***HELP!***	
		Help!	You Like Me Too Much (Harrison)
		The Night Before	
		You've Got To Hide Your Love Away	Tell Me What You See
			I've Just Seen A Face
		I Need You (Harrison)	Yesterday
		Another Girl	
		You're Going To Lose That Girl	*Songs not composed by the Beatles:*
		Ticket To Ride	Act Naturally
		It's Only Love	Dizzy Miss Lizzy
	Dec	***RUBBER SOUL***	
		Drive My Car	Girl
		Norwegian Wood	I'm Looking Through You
		You Won't See Me	In My Life
		Nowhere Man	Wait
		Think For Yourself (Harrison)	If I Needed Someone (Harrison)
		The Word	
		Michelle	Run For Your Life
		What Goes On (Lennon, McCartney and Starkey)	

Year	Month	Title and track listing	
1966	*Sep*	*REVOLVER*	
		Taxman (Harrison)	Good Day Sunshine
		Eleanor Rigby	And Your Bird Can Sing
		I'm Only Sleeping	For No One
		Love You To (Harrison)	Dr Robert
		Here, There And Everywhere	I Want To Tell You (Harrison)
		Yellow Submarine	Got To Get You Into My Life
		She Said She Said	Tomorrow Never Knows
1967	*Jun*	*SERGEANT PEPPER'S LONELY HEARTS CLUB BAND*	
		Sergeant Pepper's Lonely Hearts Club Band	Being For The Benefit Of Mr Kite
		With A Little Help From My Friends	Within You, Without You (Harrison)
		Lucy In The Sky With Diamonds	When I'm Sixty-Four
		Getting Better	Lovely Rita
		Fixing A Hole	Good Morning, Good Morning
		She's Leaving Home	A Day In The Life

Long playing records issued by Apple Records

Year	Month	Title and track listing	
1968	*Nov*	*THE BEATLES (DOUBLE ALBUM)*	
		Back In The USSR	I Will
		Dear Prudence	Julia
		Glass Onion	Birthday
		Ob-la-di Ob-la-da	Yer Blues
		Wild Honey Pie	Mother Nature's Son
		The Continuing Story of Bungalow Bill	Everybody's Got Something To Hide Except Me And My Monkey
		While My Guitar Gently Weeps	Sexy Sadie
		Happiness Is A Warm Gun	Helter Skelter
		Martha My Dear	Long Long Long
		I'm So Tired	Revolution 1
		Blackbird	Honey Pie
		Piggies	Savoy Truffle
		Rocky Raccoon	Cry Baby Cry
		Don't Pass Me By	Revolution 9
		Why Don't We Do It In The Road	Good Night

Long playing records issued by Apple Records, continued

Year	Month	Title and track listing	
1969	*Jan*	***YELLOW SUBMARINE***	
		Yellow Submarine	Sea Of Time
		Only A Northern Song	Sea Of Holes
		All Together Now	Sea Of Monsters
		Hey Bulldog	March Of The Meanies
		It's All Too Much	Pepperland Laid Waste
		All You Need Is Love	Yellow Submarine In
		Pepperland	Pepperland
	Oct	***ABBEY ROAD***	
		Come Together	Sun King
		Something (Harrison)	Mean Mr Mustard
		Maxwell's Silver Hammer	Polythene Pam
		Oh! Darling	She Came in Through the
		Octopus's Garden	Bathroom Window
		I Want You (She's So Heavy)	Golden Slumbers
		Here Comes the Sun (Harrison)	Carry That Weight
		Because	The End
		You Never Give Me Your Money	
1970	*May*	***LET IT BE***	
		Two of Us	One After 909
		I Dig a Pony	The Long and Winding Road
		Across the Universe	For You Blue (Harrison)
		I Me Mine (Harrison)	Get Back (version two)
		Dig It (Lennon, McCartney,	
		Harrison, Starkey)	
		Let It Be (version two)	
		Maggie Mae (arr. Lennon,	
		McCartney, Harrison, Starkey)	
		I've Got a Feeling	

Extended Players

Year	Month	Title and track listing	
1967	*Dec*	*MAGICAL MYSTERY TOUR* (Two EPs) Magical Mystery Tour Your Mother Should Know I Am The Walrus	Fool On The Hill Flying (Lennon, McCartney, Harrison, Starkey) Blue Jay Way (Harrison)

NOTE: There were 12 other extended players, but only one contains a song ('I Call Your Name' on the EP *Long Tall Sally*), not already on an LP or single.

Lennon and McCartney songs recorded by other artists:

Up to April 1968 there had been over 1,000 different recordings of Lennon-McCartney songs made by other singers, groups, orchestras or bands. The most popular was 'Yesterday', which had been recorded by 119 different artists, ranging from Pat Boone, Johnny Mathis and Connie Francis to Kenneth McKellar, the Big Ben Banjo Band and the Band of the Irish Guards.

The Top Ten in Popularity with other Artists

Title	No. of Different Recordings
Yesterday	119
Michelle	80
A Hard Day's Night	57
Can't Buy Me Love	52
I Want To Hold Your Hand	46
All My Loving	43
And I Love Her	42
She Loves You	39
Help!	32
Please Please Me	28

APPENDIX B

Beatles places to visit: 2002

Liverpool

Beatles Story, Albert Dock, Liverpool.
Tel: 0151 709 1963
Beatle exhibition and museum centre,
which re-creates the Beatle lives. Lots of
memorabilia. Lots of stuff to buy.

Cavern City Tours, 10 Mathew Street,
Liverpool, L2 6RE. Tel: 0151 236 9091
For tours, events and the annual Beatles Week.

20 Forthlin Road, Liverpool
Paul's old home, now owned by the
National Trust and open to the public.

Mendips, 251 Menlove Ave, Liverpool.
John's old home. Also now in National
Trust hands.
For information, telephone 0151 708 8574.

Further information on Beatle guides,
Beatle conventions, Beatle maps and tours,
and a list of shops selling Beatle stuff in
Liverpool, which tend to open and close
frequently, can be obtained from: Tourist
Information Centre, Tel: 0151 709 3285.

London

Abbey Road Recording Studios, 3 Abbey
Road, London NW8.
First place in London for all Beatle people
to gape at, though not open to the public.
This was where the Fab Four recorded
almost all their records, from 'Love Me Do'
in 1962 to 'Abbey Road' in 1969. The
famous zebra crossing, if you want to be
photographed walking over it, is at the
corner of Abbey Road and Grove End Road.

London Beatles Store, 231 Baker Street,
London NW1. Tel: 0207 935 4464
Souvenirs, tourist tat, but also information
on Beatles events nationally.

7 Cavendish Avenue, London NW8.
Just a few streets away. Paul's London
home, which he bought in 1966. Still owns
it, though he lives elsewhere, on the south
coast, at an address I dare not reveal.
Hundreds of fans used to sleep outside
here, hoping for a glimpse.

3 Savile Row, London W1.
HQ of the utterly incredible, utterly daft
Apple Corps, though nothing to do with
them now. 'Let it Be' was recorded on its
roof on 30 January 1969, the Beatles' last
performance in front of an audience.

94 Baker Street, London W1.
Home of the ill-fated Apple Boutique from
1967 to 1968, when the Beatles decided to
give away all the clothes. Oh, those were
the days. You can still see the psychedelic
paintings on the outside walls.

Soho Square, London W1.
Your best chance of spotting Paul today.
This is the HQ of MPL, Paul's business
organization.

British Library, Euston Rd, London
NW1, 0207 412 7332.
Collection of original, handwritten Beatles'
lyrics, on show beside stuff by Beethoven,
Shakespeare and Handel etc, in the Treasures
Gallery. Generously donated to the nation by
a very kind person.

APPENDIX C

Beatles memorabilia
– and their approximate prices in 2002

Everything Beatles-related has a value, so throw nothing out. If you think you have something of unusual interest, then any London auction house would value it for you, or sell it. John Lennon's psychedelic Rolls Royce was sold at auction by Sotheby's in June 1985 for £1,768,000 – still a record.

Original song manuscripts: Written in their own fair hands – £50,000–£150,000

Letters: Written by them. Depending on content, and preferably if they are pre-1963 – £10,000–£50,000

Instruments: A John Lennon guitar has been sold at auction for £16,000, but this was rather unusual. For an ordinary guitar, which you can prove was held in Beatle hands – £10,000

John Lennon drawings – £1,000–£5,000

Unpublished photographs: Preferably pre-1963, and with the copyright – £1,000–£5,000

Autographs: By the four of them together – £700–£1,000
By the four of them, but signed on something Beatly, such as a programme, record sleeve, or even a menu – £1,500. (The highest price paid for their autographs was £2,000, for a signed *Sergeant Pepper* cover.)

Posters: For Beatles concerts, appearances. Pre-1963 – £2,000

Tickets: For any Beatle performance – £100 plus

Books: The Beatles – the authorized biography by Hunter Davies, Heinemann, 1968, or McGraw Hill, 1968. Must be first edition with the cover – £50
In His Own Write by John Lennon, Cape, 1964; Simon and Schuster, 1964. Must be first edition – £30
A Spaniard in the Works by John Lennon, Cape, 1965; Simon and Schuster, 1965. First edition – £30

Beatles Monthly: The fan club magazine, which ran from August 1963 to December 1969.
Issues 1–5 – £20 each
Other issues – £5 each
Complete set of 77 issues – £500

Beatles merchandise: Millions and millions of Beatle items were produced in the 1960s – wigs, stockings, tea trays, shirts, wallpaper, buttons, jigsaws, coat hangers, mugs, combs, pencils, etc. Several factories have tooled up to bring them out again, so make sure you have genuine 1960s rubbish. Daftest price known so far was £300 for a plastic toy guitar. Any 60s Beatles merchandise – £10 plus

NB As a *seller*, a dealer is going to give you a lot less than the above prices, and an auction house will take a percentage.

APPENDIX D
Beatles books

I estimate there must be 1,000 Beatles books now out there – with more appearing all the time. Now you have *this* book, there is really no need for any other, of course, but here's a small collection, chosen for various reasons, which should interest those Beatle fans trying to start their own Beatle library.

1 *The True Story of the Beatles* by Billy Shepherd, Beat Publications, 1964.
This was the first Beatles book to appear, yet it's still quite cheap, if you can find it. Little more than an extended fan club magazine, badly written and with awful drawings, in large print aimed at small minds, but now wonderful to read. Ah, such innocence.

2 *Love Me Do* by Michael Braun, Penguin Books, 1964.
First good bit of writing about the Beatles, done by an American journalist; rather limited, as it's mainly slice of life stuff, picked up on tour, but fascinating.

3 *A Cellarful of Noise* by Brian Epstein, Souvenir Press, 1964; Doubleday, 1964.
Brian's life story, in fact written by Derek Taylor, and not very well written at that, but this was how Brian wanted to present himself to the world, back in 1964.

4 *A Twist of Lennon* by Cynthia Lennon, Star Books, 1978.
An early confessional book, by someone who was there, but pleasant and harmless, compared to the flamed-up scandals that have come out since by people who were hardly there at all.

5 *Lennon Remembered* by Jann Wenner, Rolling Stone interviews, 1971. Published in UK 1972, Talmy Franklin.
This was the first, and best, of John shooting his mouth off. Some good stuff on the background to his songs.

6 *With the Beatles* by Dezo Hoffmann, Omnibus, 1982.
If you want a picture book, and there have been scores of them, this is about the most professional. Dezo claims to have taken more pix of them than any other photographer. (Personally, my favourite Beatle snaps are the ones taken by Michael McCartney in 1961–3.)

7 *John Winston Lennon* (1940–66) and *John Ono Lennon* (1966–80) by Ray Coleman, Sidgwick and Jackson, 1984.
Two volumes; very thorough, if a bit dry.

8 *Paul McCartney – Many Years From Now* by Barry Miles, Secker and Warburg, 1997.
Written with Paul's help, so that's a plus. There's a little too much self-justifying about Paul's contributions, but it does give an interesting insight into his relationship with and feelings about John, even after all these years. Very good on the background to Linda and how she came into Paul's life.

9 *The Complete Beatles Chronicle* by Mark Lewisohn, Chancellor Press, 1996.
Lewisohn is one of today's living, walking, breathing Beatles brains, who seems to know everything and have forgotten nothing. Gives the gen on almost every day of the Beatles' lives from 1957 to 1970. Invaluable.

10 *The Beatles Anthology*, Cassell & Co., 2000
A massive book, in size and content, with the Beatles' story from the mouths of the Beatles themselves, told in the way they want to present it – so there are not too many warts. The words and stories are mostly well known, and well loved, by Beatles fans, having appeared elsewhere, but a great many of the illustrations are new or have rarely been seen before. A fascinating and beautifully produced publication, which no fan should be without.

...and finally...

The Beatles Book
A monthly magazine, which restarted in October 1982, on the lines of the old *Beatles Monthly* fan mag, ceased publication in 2003, alas. But all Beatles fans should look out for old copies, especially the first 77 issues which ran from 1963-1969. Also check out the recently formed British Beatles Fan Club which has a quarterly magazine. For information go to www.britishbeatlesfanclub.co.uk

PICTURE CREDITS AND ACKNOWLEDGEMENTS

The author would like to thank Paul, Ringo, Yoko Ono, Olivia Harrison and George Martin for allowing him to continue to use their copyright material.

The publisher would like to thank the following individuals and photographic libraries for permission to reproduce their material. Every care has been taken to trace the present copyright holders. However, if we have omitted anyone, we apologise and shall, if informed, make corrections in any future edition.

Camera Press: 173; Jane Bown/ 188, 227; Bruce McBroom/ 379; Peter Mitchell/ 294; Terence Spencer/ 214, 220; David Steen/ 158; Bob Whitaker/ 6, 252, 257, 260; **Hunter Davies Collection:** 13, 20, 28, 31, 36, 48, 56, 59, 60, 68, 71, 72, 75, 76, 87, 90, 118, 126, 134, 138, 150, 152, 153, 186, 187, 190, 192, 201, 202, 211, 232, 239, 247, 258, 280, 284, 374; **Evening Standard:** 15; **George Harrison's Estate:** 355; **Bill Harry (Mersey Beat):** 176, 183; **Frank Herrmann:** jacket back flap; **Hulton Getty:** 10, 41, 79, 100, 103, 123, 124, 146, 199, 204, 206, 217, 224, 228, 242, 244, 248, 250, 269, 296, 302, 333, 364, 370, 380, 383, 386, 395; **Liverpool Echo:** 88; **Magnum Photos:** David Hurn/ 352; **George Martin Collection:** 180; **Paul McCartney:** 109, 376; **MPL Communications:** Richard Haughton/ 16; **Peter Nash:** 115; **Sean O'Mahony (Beat Publications):** 27; **Yoko Ono:** 45, 156, 279, 312, 319; **Stanley Parkes:** 55; **Private Collection:** 234; **Redferns:** Glenn A. Baker Archive/ 112; K&K and Astrid Kirchherr/ 52, 94, 106, 128, 130, 133; K&K and Ulf Kruger HG/ 185; David Redfern/ 196, 276, 322, 358; Max Scheler/ 32, 282, 292; S&G Agency/ 168; Jurgen Vollmer/ 82, 120, 148; **Rex Features:** 163, 265, 270, 272, 306, 319, 342; **Charles Roberts:** 66; **Ringo Starr:** 326, 336, 346, 366; **Topham Picture Point:** 171